The Origins
of Christendom
in the West

The Origins of Christendom in the West

Edited by
ALAN KREIDER

T&T CLARK
EDINBURGH & NEW YORK

T&T CLARK LTD

A Continuum imprint

59 George Street   370 Lexington Avenue
Edinburgh EH2 2LQ   New York 10017–6503
Scotland   USA

www.tandtclark.co.uk   www.continuumbooks.com

First published 2001

ISBN 0 567 08776 X

British Library Cataloguing-in-Publication Data
A catalogue record for this book is available from the British Library

Typeset by Waverley Typesetters, Galashiels
Printed and bound in Great Britain by MPG Books Ltd, Bodmin, Cornwall

Contents

vi

Introduction

ALAN KREIDER

When fifteen scholars from eight countries gathered in the Maison Nicolas Barré, Paris, in September 1996 to discuss the origins of Christendom, there was a sense of adventure. The participants met as a result of the intuition of the Missiology of Western Culture's History Group that Christendom might be a useful lens through which to gain a missiological perspective on the history of Christianity in the West.[1] But we didn't know each other, or what might happen when we gathered around a big table. As it turned out we were delighted. Over a period of three days we had long discussions, in cafés as well as around the table, which were both stimulating and profitable. The proof of the profitability is this book.

We met without any clear agreement as to what Christendom was. In part this was because we were a multilingual gathering.

---

[1] The Missiology of Western Culture Project (1992–7) was an ecumenical attempt to mobilize the thinking of leading scholars about the interplay of the Christian churches and message with the culture of the contemporary West. Subsidized by generous grants, notably from the Pew Charitable Trust, the project sponsored study groups in seven areas (the arts, ecclesiology, epistemology, social structures and systems, history, the individual, and health and healing), each of which groups organized its own study conferences and colloquia. The groups shared their findings with each other in September 1997 in a major international consultation at the Bon Secours Center, Marriottsville, Maryland, USA. Their learnings are gradually appearing in print. The first fruits of these are, from the Epistemology Group, J. Andrew Kirk and Kevin J. Vanhoozer, *To Stake a Claim: Mission and the Western Crisis of Knowledge* (Maryknoll: Orbis Books, 1999); also the current volume, which is the initial offering of the History Group, whose members were Dr Neal Blough, Paris; Prof. Hugh McLeod, Birmingham; Prof. Werner Ustorf, Birmingham; and Dr Alan Kreider, Oxford.

Many languages, such as French, make no distinction between such nouns as *Chrétienté* and *Christianisme*. In the Anglophone world, on the other hand, Christianity and Christendom are, or can be, different things. Christendom as a term is widely used; but, perhaps because people assume that its meaning is self-evident, very few scholars bother to define it. To some, such as Christian moral philosopher Oliver O'Donovan, Christendom is an idea of 'a professedly Christian secular political order'.[2] To an historian like John van Engen, on the other hand, Christendom is a society, an all-embracing Christian society which, 'rooted in practice and profession and given shape by liturgical, ecclesiastical, and creedal structures, included every person in medieval Europe except the Jews'.[3] In our brief to the participants, the History Group didn't attempt a full-orbed definition of Christendom. Instead, we simply indicated two elements of a definition: in contrast to Christianity, whose message and embodiment can take many forms, Christendom is a civilization in which (a) Christianity is the dominant religion and in which (b) this dominance has been backed up by social or legal compulsions.[4] We could have added to this definition, making it more detailed and more precise, but it was enough to provide general guidance and to get the discussion going. Not that that was difficult: Christendom, we discovered, is something that people can get exercised about.

Our colloquium was designed to elicit strong views. We in the History Group had been informed by the work of scholars, especially social historians of religion, who had queried the extent to which Medieval Christendom had been deeply Christianized.[5] We also had been influenced by writers in the

[2] Oliver O'Donovan, *The Desire of the Nations: Rediscovering the Roots of Political Theology* (Cambridge: Cambridge University Press, 1996), 195.

[3] John van Engen, 'The Christian Middle Ages as an Historiographical Problem', *American Historical Review* 91 (1986), 546.

[4] These are characteristics mentioned by Judith Herrin, *The Formation of Christendom* (Princeton: Princeton University Press, 1987), 8, 479.

[5] For samples of this, in the UK, L. G. D. Baker, 'The Shadow of the Christian Symbol', in G. J. Cuming, ed., *The Mission of the Church and the Propagation of the Faith* (Studies in Church History, 6) (Cambridge: Cambridge University Press, 1970); in the USA, James C. Russell, *The Germanization of Early Medieval Christianity: A Sociohistorical Approach to Religious Transformation* (New York:

Radical Reformation tradition; this had often had a rough time under Christendom and its modern adherents tend to be suspicious of the Christendom tradition.[6] Finally, we were intrigued by the reflections of a group of remarkable French Catholics. These people, worker priests during World War II ministering in areas of very low religious observance, viewed France, not as a Christian land but as a 'land of mission'. And they, to our fascination, were backed up by scholars who sensed that in modern Europe patristic studies would be especially useful. Appeals to Medieval models, or to coercion in the name of Christ, were inappropriate; in contrast, learning from early Christian models, for example in the area of conversion, might point the way forward for Christian witness.[7] Influenced by these three sources, we offered the following hypothesis for discussion: the coercion, control and domination that were part of the Christendom model of church and mission carry within themselves the seeds of the modern repudiation of Christianity in Europe.

So where did Christendom come from? The scholars who assembled in Paris – and whose writings are the substance of this book – are an ideal group to study Christendom's origins. Several things are special about them. For one thing, they come from a wide variety of backgrounds. They represent the intellectual traditions of eight countries, as well as many ecclesial traditions (or none). Second, they are distinguished scholars who have made significant contributions in their own areas of specialization. But because they represent a wide variety of disciplines (including

---

Oxford University Press, 1994); in France, Jean Delumeau, *Catholicism Between Luther and Voltaire: A New View of the Counter-Reformation* (London: Burns & Oates, 1977).

  [6] For samples of this literature, see John H. Yoder, 'The Constantinian Sources of Western Social Ethics', in his *The Priestly Kingdom: Social Ethics as Gospel* (Notre Dame: University of Notre Dame Press, 1984), 135–50; Stanley Hauerwas, *After Christendom* (Nashville: Abingdon Press, 1991).

  [7] Henri Godin and Yvan Daniel, *La France pays de mission?* (Paris: Cerf, 1943); edited, translated and incorporated in Maisie Ward, *France Pagan? The Mission of Abbé Godin* (London: Sheed & Ward, 1949), 65–191. For illuminating comment on the intellectual currents in French Catholicism in the 1940s, see Josef Blank, foreword to his translation of Gustave Bardy's classic *La Conversion au Christianisme durant les premiers siècles* (Paris: Aubier, 1949), in *Menschen Werden Christen* (Freiburg: Herder, 1988), 5–9.

ancient history, theology, missiology, liturgical studies) and historical periods, many of them had heard of the other scholars but had never met them. As one of them responded when accepting our invitation to take part, 'I'd love to meet these people!' Third, the scholars, although writing in their own areas of specialization, were encouraged to think across a broad sweep of time. We were concerned to discuss the origins of Christendom; and we recognized that to do so we would need to find scholars who would be willing to take risks: the risk of spanning the centuries; and the risk of asking big questions. Was the Christendom vision implicit in the Christian movement from the outset? Were there discernible changes as the church grew? What was the significance of the events following the conversion of the Emperor Constantine in the fourth century? Was it a 'fall', a 'turning', or a slight irregularity in a substantially straight line?

What was especially valuable in the scholars' work was their willingness to collaborate in the colloquium's attempt to think missiologically. Missiology is not a word that historians – even church historians – use very much; it is the scientific study of Christian mission, and specifically of the interplay between the gospel and culture. Under Christendom, mission has been located 'out there', in 'foreign parts', in El Salvador or Benin; so Westerners have used missiology primarily as a means of studying the Christian movement in non-Western societies. But things are changing. Was the Abbé Godin right when he stated fifty years ago that France was a *pays de mission*? Is this a helpful way to think about other European countries as well? If so, then the interplay of Christianity and culture in the West must also be subject to missiological investigation. And this changes the questions we ask when we do our studies. We may study the history of liturgy or of ecclesiastical institutions, but no longer solely for their own sake. We ask, rather, what does our study of these areas have to say about Christianity's impact upon culture and the culture's impact upon Christianity? How have changes in dogma, or worship, or the sociology of the church, or the ministry of women reflected and affected Christianity's relationship to society, and its capacity to communicate to those who have not accepted the Christian message? Thus, in the West as elsewhere in the world, the new discipline of 'missiology' offers fresh possibilities for the way that we study church history. A pioneering German series begun twenty years ago has said it succinctly: *Kirchengeschichte als Missionsgeschichte*.[8]

The papers in this volume are the products of this approach. They are clustered under four general headings. Three papers, in the section entitled 'Aspects of Conversion', dealt with the processes by which Western Europe was Christianized. One of these, which I wrote, studied conversion – as a word and as a phenomenon – as it developed across five centuries. My paper charted continuities in liturgical practice, while at the same time tracing changes in conversion's social significance – from voluntarily becoming counter-cultural (a many-faceted social change which incorporated the new believer into a community of deviants) to compulsorily becoming like everybody else (socialization of the new believers into society's norms, at times with only superficial change). Such an approach, which ranges widely across centuries and countries, needed to be complemented by a second paper which looked in detail at the complexities of the Christianization of a specific area. Rita Lizzi Testa of Perugia did this admirably as she presented her findings about the Christianization of the cities and valleys of northern Italy. She noted that in northern Italy the Christianization process was slow to begin, but then took place quite quickly – within three generations – in the late fourth and early fifth centuries. She monitored the changes as Christianization proceeded apace: Christian churches moved from being alternative communities to being equivalent with the civil population; bishops became communal leaders; and episcopal preaching (e.g. on the subject of wealth) altered its emphases as Christianity became the religion of the local élites. A final paper on the process of conversion, from Ramsay MacMullen of Yale, reflects his immensely detailed researches in the Western sources for the fourth to eighth centuries. His perspective is a severe one. During this period, he is convinced, Christianization proceeded unevenly; furthermore, it was largely unwilling. It did not manage to wean converts to Christianity away from their devotion to pagan

---

[8] Heinzgünter Frohnes and Uwe W. Knorr, eds, *Kirchengeschichte als Missionsgeschichte*, I: *Die Alte Kirche* (Munich: Chr. Kaiser, 1974); Knut Schäferdiek, ed., *Kirchengeschichte als Missionsgeschichte*, IIa: *Die Kirche des früheren Mittelalters* (Munich: Chr. Kaiser, 1978). The series unfortunately ended with these two volumes.

practices, and to a considerable extent it involved the paganization of Christian practices.

As the colloquium proceeded, differences of emphasis became apparent. This was especially evident in the four papers under the heading of 'Change and Continuity'. Wolfgang Wischmeyer of Vienna argued, on the basis of an impressive mastery of archaeological and epigraphic evidence, that little changed: Christianity prior to Constantine had already adjusted so fundamentally to the values of ancient élites that it was able to recruit them in considerable numbers to the church, both as members and as leaders. The Irish monk Eoin de Bhaldraithe's paper, on the other hand, discerned considerable changes in attitudes to wealth, war and the place of celibate people in the church. He argued that in Christendom it was the monastic movement that carried on, in enclosed communities, the values that had characterized the earlier church. The paper of Christine Trevett of Cardiff decisively countered any sense that all changes came as a result of Constantine. She pointed out that the prophetic dimension, although very evident in Christian communities in the second and early third centuries, by the mid-third century had generally been suppressed. Anne Jensen of Graz pointed out a similar struggle on the part of women to participate in the growing church. Her paper introduced us to specific women who demonstrate that, despite growing restrictions (and the suppression of evidence), women played significant roles in the thought and mission of the church.

The three papers which treated 'Liturgy and Christian Formation' also dealt with continuity and change. Everett Ferguson, of Abilene, Texas, traced the content of pre-baptismal catechesis from Justin to Augustine; his paper noted some fascinating developments, especially a shift in the catechists' preoccupation from lifestyle to doctrine. The liturgical scholar Paul Bradshaw of Notre Dame concentrated on the fourth century, when the church was growing rapidly. His paper subtly described the efforts of the churchmen of the time to respond to swollen congregations at a time of great concern for the maintenance of orthodoxy. He noted that these efforts were often counter-productive, clericalizing the worship and distancing the laity while limiting liturgical freedom and variety. One of the most significant liturgical changes, according to David Wright of Edinburgh, came in the area of baptism. Wright's paper traces the development of Augustine's baptismal thinking, and argues that his final view – that infant baptism is normative – was both innovative and formative of the pastoral life and ecclesiology of Christendom.

The colloquium dealt more with Christian practice than with theology; but two final papers addressed questions of 'Theology and Inculturation'. Archbishop Rowan Williams of Wales provided a rationale for the church's growing preoccupation with heresy. It was, his paper contends, a means of curbing the disruptive elements inherent in Christianity by providing the balance of a coherent symbolic universe, thereby enabling the growth of continuous communities under episcopal authority. Missiologist Antonie Wessels of Amsterdam, on the other hand, dealt with grass-roots theology. His paper noted the struggle between tendencies in the expanding Christian movement to repudiate and to incorporate beliefs and practices of the 'pagan' religions that were officially being superceded. His catalogue of pre-Christian practices that have been incorporated into the life-cycles of Christendom is an impressive one.

At the end of our papers, our rapporteur, church historian Kate Cooper of Manchester, surveyed what we had done. She pointed out that in our sessions it had become clear that in the early Christian centuries allegiance and belonging had taken on distinctive shapes, which after the reign of Constantine began to change both conceptually and institutionally. Cooper noted, on the other hand, the substantial gaps that we continue to have in our knowledge, not least the extent to which the ordinary Christians listened to the ideologues, preachers and writers. And she invited us to continue to study – to investigate further the role of the laity, the function of patronage, Christian attitudes to violence, and martyrdom. In conclusion, she presented several caveats: we must never minimize the diversity in early Christianity, and we must beware an approach which, after the pattern of Eusebius's *Ecclesiastical History*, sees a pristine early period and compromised later period.

These papers – and Kate Cooper's concluding comments – provided an ample diet for discussion and reflection, and it would have been difficult to incorporate more. There are, however, three topics which I believe should have been on the agenda and were not. In all three cases, we tried. We missed the insights that Horst Rzepkowski hoped to be able to bring us about the visual, iconographic dimensions of early Christianity. Our deliberations also suffered through the inability of Boniface Ramsey to be present to talk about the changing attitudes and practices of the church in the area of wealth.[9] Perhaps the greatest lack of all was our failure to persist in our search for a scholar who would have represented a Jewish perspective on our studies. There can be few more tell-tale indicators of Christendom's approach to power than its persecution of the Jews.

Our papers led to lively discussion about the early church, and our colloquium remained content to deal with missiology historically. But of course, when the participants went home, stimulated and happy, we had to face everyday concerns in the contemporary West. For some of us participants, as well as for many readers of this book, missiology raises questions about the church in its mission today. Our hope, in the History Group, is that the papers given at our colloquium can establish a conversation between Christianity's early experiences and our own times.

This can certainly happen in non-Western settings, as a couple of examples from my recent conversations will indicate. For example, a friend of mine who has been involved in Protestant evangelization in Borneo reports that conversions to Christianity are taking place at an astonishing rate. People there are asking whether, as in the New Testament, baptism should be immediate, or whether, as in Christianity's early centuries, methodical catechism leading to life-transforming conversion might be essential if the converts are in any meaningful sense to become Christians. On a recent trip to Japan I encountered other questions. The problem there is not one of a plethora of conversions. Quite the opposite: Christian churches in Japan have a long and often painful experience; despite sacrificial witness by countless believers the churches in Japan still number only one half of 1 per cent of the national population, and the number is not growing. Meanwhile, across the Japan sea, in Korea the churches have experienced

[9] Samples of the insight they would have brought are found in: Horst Rzepkowski SVD, 'Das Papsttum als ein Modell frühchristlicher Anpassung', in Theo Sundermeier, ed., *Die Begegnung mit den Anderen: Plädoyers für eine interkulturelle Hermeneutik* (Gütersloh: Gerd Mohn, 1991), 69–93; Boniface Ramsey OP, 'Christian Attitudes to Poverty and Wealth', in Ian Hazlett, ed., *Early Christianity: Origins and Evolution to AD 600 in Honour of W. H. C. Frend* (London: SPCK, 1991), 256–66.

astonishing growth; they could count the President of the republic as one of their members; and, according to a recent estimate, almost 30 per cent of the populace adheres to Christianity. What, the Japanese reflected, are they doing wrong at a time when their rivals and neighbours are being so successful? A Japanese pastor told me that he knew Christians who were praying for the conversion to Christianity of crown princess Michiko, who had been educated in a Catholic school; she was married to crown prince Naruhito; and if the Emperor could be converted . . .

Examples of the missiological relevance of the ancient church also surround us in the West. Do we seek revival, and, if so, of what? Or a reChristianization of the West? Do we advocate Christian programmes that involve the use of state power to achieve spiritual ends? To what extent should we 'inculturate' the Christian message into the contemporary youth culture, or the culture of middle classes? In what ways does the gospel challenge these cultures? Do we seek to rehabilitate Christendom, or do we greet its dissolution as Christians in the West become a 'diaspora' people?[10] For the participants in the project who care about such questions, the papers in this volume cannot provide answers; but the evidence from the early Christianization of Europe which they present can provoke us to think in new ways about the missiological challenges of our time.

A final comparison from fifty years ago indicates differing lessons that Western Christians might draw from the early church. In 1948 the venerable Anglican church historian, L. E. Elliott-Binns, published *The Beginnings of Western Christendom*. In his introduction he recommended that Western readers pay careful attention to the struggles of the early Christians, 'for their experiences are being lived out afresh in the younger churches' in China and India.[11] The early church, he maintained, can help us understand the global church. The following year the Cambridge

---

[10] For contrasting approaches, from eminent Anglican and Roman Catholic moral theologians, see O'Donovan, *The Desire of the Nations*, and Norbert Greinacher, 'Ist die Kirche noch zu retten? Die Bedeutung von Religion und der Sitz im Leben der institutionalisierten Kirchen in der säkularisierten Gesellschaft von heute', in Wolfgang Erk, ed., *Radius Almanach 1997/98* (Stuttgart: Radius Verlag, 1997), 87–126.

[11] L. E. Elliott-Binns, *The Beginnings of Western Christendom*, Lutterworth Library 29 (London: Lutterworth Press, 1948), 11.

historian and Methodist lay preacher Herbert Butterfield published *Christianity and History*. Butterfield also found the early church to be worth attending to: 'We are back for the first time in something like the earliest centuries of Christianity', he contended, 'and those early centuries afford some relevant clues to the kind of attitude to adopt'.[12] The early church is important for Western Christians, Butterfield believed, not just so we can understand the younger churches; the early church can help us Western Christians understand ourselves – now. The essays in this volume, I believe, indicate that both Elliott-Binns and Butterfield were right. But the latter was a missiologist of Western culture.

[12] Herbert Butterfield, *Christianity and History* (New York: Charles Scribner's Sons, 1949), 135.

PART ONE

Aspects of Conversion

Chapter 1

Changing Patterns of Conversion in the West

ALAN KREIDER

Christendom was the product of millions of conversions. In the early centuries, becoming a Christian entailed a many-faceted change which involved a rupture with conventional values: the converts' beliefs, belonging and behaviour were all expected to change. To foster this change, the church developed a process of catechesis and ritual (described in the *Apostolic Tradition*) which culminated in the cathartic experience of baptism. Justin Martyr and Cyprian both testify to the life-encompassing dimensions of conversion – effecting changed beliefs as well as a transformation of attitudes to enemies, acquisitiveness and status symbols. The conversion of the Emperor Constantine took place at the end of his life when he submitted to the church's prescribed process of catechism and baptism, resulting in a sense of belonging, a powerful experience and a change of behaviour. Under the Christian emperors the masses were converted by many means including inducement and compulsion; and conversion came to mean accepting the conventional religion and values of a Christian society. The Roman aristocrat Volusian is an example of coerced conversion, without a change of behaviour, to the Empire's only legal religion. Augustine urged people to be converted and baptized, while hoping for behavioural change; a century later Caesarius urged Christians who were already baptized to be converted. In Christendom, in which there was religious uniformity because non-Christians had been excluded, conversion continued to be a theme for Christian people.

In 542 Caesarius died; for forty years he had been Bishop of Arles.[1] Caesarius, as we shall see, was not content with the state of Christianity in Gaul. But in the longer perspective the development of Christianity in the five centuries since the life of Jesus of Nazareth had been remarkable. From its earliest beginnings as a cell in Jerusalem, the Christian movement had grown to be a global and society-dominating church. Its impact upon the cultures in which it spread was far-reaching. And it was not only cultures which were 'Christianized'. For Christianity spread by means of literally millions of conversions, by which individuals and groups came to adhere to the new faith. The ancient words for conversion – *epistrophe*, *metanoia* and *conversio* – all connoted change. But we might well ask: for those who became Christians, what changed? Belief changed, to be sure; we shall also observe that behaviour could be transformed; furthermore, at the same time a new sense of belonging could be created – and these changes were often associated with intense religious experience.[2] But we shall also note that, as Christianization ensued across five centuries, the pattern of change itself changed; the configuration of belief, belonging and behaviour, accompanied by experience, shifted. So the conversions which were so important to Caesarius – and which were to be typical of the Western civilization called Christendom – were different from those which were familiar to a second-century figure such as Justin of Rome.

Justin: transforming belief, belonging and behaviour

Let us begin with Justin. The story of his conversion is a familiar one.[3] At around AD 130 Justin left his hometown of Flavia Neapolis

[1] For a book-length statement of this chapter's argument, see Alan Kreider, *The Change of Conversion and the Origin of Christendom*, Christian Mission and Modern Culture (Harrisburg: Trinity Press International, 1999).

[2] These dimensions of conversion – a change of belief, behaviour and belonging, accompanied by experience – are my own construct. They are indebted to Eugene V. Gallagher, *Expectation and Experience: Explaining Religious Conversion*, Ventures in Religion 1 (Atlanta: Scholars Press, 1990), 120, who discerned in Justin's conversion 'the cosmic, moral, and social dimensions of Christian conversion'; also, for the alliteration, to Grace Davie, *Religion in Britain since 1945: Believing without Belonging* (Oxford: Blackwell, 1994).

[3] For a discussion of the historicity of the two accounts of Justin's conversion (*Dialogue with Trypho* 2–8; 2 *Apol.* 12) see Oscar Skarsaune, 'The Conversion of Justin Martyr', *Studia Theologica* (Oslo) 30 (1976), 53–73.

on a peripatetic search for philosophic truth. After encountering – and trying out – various philosophical systems, in Ephesus Justin encountered an old man with whom, in rather forward fashion, he began a lengthy conversation. The consequences of this conversation were far-reaching. The old man enabled Justin to see things anew: the Hebrew prophets he now saw as pointing to the Christ whose 'words possess terrible power in themselves and . . . [afford] the sweetest rest to those who make a diligent practice of them'. Christ's philosophy alone, he discovered, is 'safe and profitable'. For Justin, conversion involved a change of belief. And this new belief was confirmed by a new experience: according to Justin, 'a flame was kindled in my soul'.[4]

We don't know how Justin pursued his new convictions. When we next encounter him, he was in Rome functioning as a 'pneumatic teacher'[5] to students who came to his home. How had Justin been taught? From his first *Apology* we know how important his learning had been to him: repeatedly he used the phrases 'we have learned' and 'we have been taught'.[6] And now, in his maturity, Justin was functioning as a transmitter of the teaching of the churches in Rome, passing on what he had received and no doubt adding his distinctive slant to the material. From what he said about his own teaching we may, I believe, infer something about his own struggles in conversion.

According to his *Apology*, Justin imparted to his students Christian beliefs. He taught about God's character, about the worship and imitation which God desired, and about God's work through the prophets which prepared the way for 'our Teacher . . . who is the Son and Apostle of God the Father and Master of all, that is, Jesus Christ'.[7] Justin's catechesis then turned from belief to behaviour, and to the struggle that his hearers would have in living out the teachings of Jesus: their encounter with demonic forces who 'struggle to have you as their slaves'. Justin saw the task of the Christian leaders as 'attacking' the demons (in exorcisms?); the task of the would-be Christians, for their part, would

---

[4] Justin, *Dialogue*, 2–8.
[5] Ulrich Neymeyr, *Die christlichen Lehrer im zweiten Jahrhundert: Ihre Lehrtätigkeit, ihr Selbstverständnis und ihre Geschichte*, Supplements to *Vigiliae Christianae* 4 (Leiden: Brill, 1989), 33.
[6] Justin, 1 *Apology*, 10–13.
[7] Ibid., 12.

be to renounce the demons' thrall which kept people in unfreedom and thereby prevented their behaviour from changing to reflect the way of Christ. Justin listed four areas of behaviour in which there would be struggle with demonic power: sexual adventure, the magic arts, acquisitive materialism and xenophobic violence. 'We formerly rejoiced in fornication, . . . employed magical arts, . . . loved more than anything else ways of acquiring wealth and possessions, . . . hated and murdered one another and would not show hospitality to those not of the same tribe . . .'. The result of the struggle was *conversion* – a profound change of belief, behaviour and belonging. Justin knew that he, in the Christian community of renunciation and new possibilities, was among people who now 'embrace self-control alone', who now 'have dedicated ourselves to the good and unbegotten God', who now bring what they have 'into a common treasury and share with everyone who is in need', who now 'eat with others, pray for our enemies, and attempt to persuade those who hate us unjustly . . .'. In this community, whose members had renounced the demonic forces which subjugate and enchain, they could put into practice the 'good counsels of Christ' whose 'word was the power of God' and whose implications Justin proceeded to detail lovingly.[8]

For Justin conversion was a complex and multi-dimensional process of change. Those who chose to proceed to baptism were not only those who were 'persuaded and believe that the things we teach and say are true': they were also those who could 'promise to live accordingly'. Transformed behaviour was indispensable, for those not living as Christ taught 'should know that they are not really Christians'.[9] Belief and the will to a transformed behaviour were not enough, however, for it was in the rite of baptism that the liberation actually occurred. Justin was reticent about describing the ritual, but his understanding of its effects is clear. Through immersion in the baptismal waters, the

---

[8] 1 *Apology*, 14 (trans. Everett Ferguson, *Early Christians Speak*, rev. edn [Abilene: Abilene Christian University Press, 1981], 195–6; E. R. Hardy, in C. C. Richardson, ed., *Early Christian Fathers*, Library of Christian Classics 1 [New York: Macmillan, 1970], 249–50); for Justin's discussion of the applications of Jesus' teaching, see ibid., 15–17. See Wayne A. Meeks, *The Origins of Christian Morality: The First Two Centuries* (New Haven: Yale University Press, 1993), 34–5.

[9] Justin, 1 *Apology*, 15.

baptizands experienced rebirth, washing and illumination which made them God's children 'of free choice and knowledge'. Baptism also incorporated them as brothers and sisters in their new locus of belonging, the Christian family; after their immersion the baptizands were led to the assembly 'to those who are called brothers' for the unifying actions of prayer, the kiss, and the eucharist.[10] Conversion in second-century Rome, as Justin described it, involved a change of belief but much more: it also transformed behaviour and gave a new sense of belonging in a context of profound religious experience.

Cyprian: liberation from the addictions of privilege

A century after Justin, Cyprian wrote an account of his own conversion in which many of the same elements are evident. Cyprian was a successful Carthaginian rhetorician at the peak of his prowess. But Cyprian was dissatisfied with his lifestyle, possibly because he had met Christians whose lives seemed freer, less encumbered. In a remarkable passage in his *Ad Donatum* (3–4) he wrote about the components of a patrician lifestyle that he had come to despise but which nevertheless were 'radically engrained' within him.[11] Luxurious food: 'When does he learn thrift who has been used to liberal banquets and sumptuous feasts?' Elaborate clothing: how can one who has been used to 'glittering in gold and purple' become content with 'ordinary and simple clothing'? Civic power and influence with fawning retainers: how can one give up 'the charm of the fasces and of civic honours'?[12]

Cyprian felt himself to be addicted to his lifestyle. Despairing of change, he at times would 'indulge my sins as if they were

[10] Ibid., 61, 65–6.

[11] Translated in Ante-Nicene Fathers (ANF) 5, 275–80. Maurice Wiles has challenged the authenticity of this account, for he 'does not sense the personal anguish of soul' which he finds in what he evidently views as the exemplary conversion story, that of Augustine ('The Theological Legacy of St Cyprian', *Journal of Ecclesiastical History* 14 [1963], 140–1). With Elisabeth Fink-Dendorfer, I find it hard, in *Ad Donatum*, 3–4, not to detect ample indication of 'deeply felt spiritual strife' (*Conversio: Motive und Motivierung zur Bekehrung in der Alten Kirche*, Regensburger Studien zur Theologie 33 [Frankfurt-am-Main: Verlag Peter Lang, 1986], 40).

[12] Food, dress and retinue were among the classic components of the Roman aristocrat's 'appearance of power' (Ramsay MacMullen, *Corruption and the Decline of Rome* [New Haven: Yale University Press, 1988], 60–4).

actually parts of me . . .'. Cyprian's question was not whether he could believe what the Christians believed; it was rather whether he could live as they taught – and as many of them apparently lived. Was it possible for him to change? 'How . . . is such a conversion (*conversio*) possible, that there should be a sudden and rapid divestment of all which, either innate in us has hardened in the corruption of our material nature, or acquired by us has become inveterate by long accustomed use?' The answer lay in an empowering experience mediated through ritual. Cyprian did not tell us about the baptismal rite, but he was eloquent about its effects in his life. 'The help of the water of new birth' washed away the stains of his former sins; a light from above was 'infused into my reconciled heart'; and the Holy Spirit breathed from heaven restored him and made him a new man. The result of immersion in water and affusion of Spirit was a detectable 'clarification of feelings',[13] and it transformed his behaviour: 'in a wondrous manner, doubtful things at once began to assure themselves to me . . . [W]hat before had seemed difficult began to suggest a means of accomplishment, what had been thought impossible, to be capable of being achieved'.

Cyprian claimed that by this experience he had been liberated from his compulsions, and that this liberation expressed itself in transformed behaviour in a new community. According to his biographer Pontius, Cyprian gave his property away 'for the relief of the indigence of the poor'.[14] His early writings give expression to his new understandings. Part III of his *Ad Quirinum* is a collection of 120 maxims 'bearing upon the religious teaching of our school'.[15] Very possibly intended for the catechetical work of the Christian community in Carthage, each maxim was buttressed with a brace of biblical texts. They outline a powerful vision for a community of distinctive behaviour. Four headings will give the flavour of the 120: 'That charity and brotherly affection are to be religiously and steadfastly practiced'; 'That evil is not to be returned

---

[13] Fink-Dendorfer, *Conversio*, 43.

[14] Pontius, *Vita Cypriani*, 2 (ANF 5, 267–74).

[15] For a discussion of *Ad Quirinum* (ANF 5, 507–57), see Hugo Koch, *Arbeiten zur Kirchengeschichte* IV, *Cyprianische Untersuchungen* (Bonn: A. Marcus & E. Weber, 1926), 183ff. For its function in the Christian community in Carthage, see Antonio Quacquarelli, 'Note retoriche sui *Testimoni* di Cipriano', *Vetera Christianorum* 8 (1971), 204.

for evil'; 'That it is of small account to be baptized and to receive the eucharist, unless one profit by it both in deed and works'; 'That the believer ought not to live like the Gentiles' (c.3, 23, 26, 34). The Christian community did not fully live out these maxims, but Cyprian tirelessly worked to give them reality, especially in the area of wealth that he had found so addictive.[16] As presbyter and then bishop, Cyprian worked to make the Christians a distinctive presence in Carthage. Their response to the epidemic of 252, in which Christians stayed in the city to nurse their pagan neighbours, is an indication that he was not totally unsuccessful.[17]

The *Apostolic Tradition*: the ritual process of conversion

The initiatory rituals about which Justin and Cyprian were so reticent were more fully described in the *Apostolic Tradition*, which opens to us the conversion process as experienced by many ordinary Christians in the third century.[18] According to chapters 15 and 16 of this church order, the initiatory procedures for a

[16] Cyprian, *De Eleemosynis et Operibus*; *De Lapsis*, 5–6. The first and much the longest chapter of *Ad Quirinum* III advocates 'good works and mercy' which express themselves in economic redistribution.

[17] Pontius, *Vita Cypriani*, 9; Rodney Stark, 'Epidemics, Networks, and the Rise of Christianity', *Semeia* 56 (1992), 159–75.

[18] For editions, see Gregory Dix, ed., *The Treatise on the Apostolic Tradition of St Hippolytus of Rome*, rev. Henry Chadwick (London: SPCK, 1968); Bernard Botte, ed., *La Tradition apostolique de Saint Hippolyte: Essai de reconstitution*, 5th edn (Münster: Aschendorff, 1989). I have used the English version of G. J. Cuming, *Hippolytus: A Text for Students*, Grove Liturgical Study 8, rev. edn (Bramcote: Grove Books, 1987). This document, so precious in the information it provides, is at the moment a scholarly football; theories concerning its authorship and place and date of writing are being kicked back and forth. For recent interpretations, with varying views on location and date, see Thomas M. Finn, 'Ritual Process and the Survival of Early Christianity', *Journal of Ritual Studies* 3 (1989), 69; Marcel Metzger, 'Nouvelles perspectives pour la prétendue Tradition Apostolique', *Ecclesia Orans* 5 (1988), 241–59; idem, 'Enquêtes autour de la prétendue 'Tradition Apostolique'', *Ecclesia Orans* 9 (1992), 7–36; Paul F. Bradshaw, *The Search for the Origins of Christian Worship: Sources and Methods for the Study of Early Liturgy* (London: SPCK, 1992), 89–92; Allen Brent, *Hippolytus and the Roman Church in the Third Century: Communities in Tension Before the Emergence of a Monarch Bishop*, Supplements to *Vigiliae Christianae* 31 (Leiden: Brill, 1995). The results of this are fascinating but not yet conclusive. One thing is sure: the traditional view – which ascribes authorship of a single document as 'reconstituted' by scholars to Hippolytus of Rome – is no longer

potential convert began with the arrival of the would-be Christian, together with sponsors, at one of the church's early morning catechetical sessions. The catechists did not, as we might expect, welcome the potential convert with open arms. Instead, they grilled him (assuming that the candidate was a man) with questions about his motives for applying for instruction. His sponsors had to vouch for his probity and to state their conviction that he was 'capable of hearing the word'. If the candidate passed this test, other questions followed: whether he was a slave or freeman; concerning his marital state; and concerning his craft or profession. The catechists wanted to avoid scandal. Furthermore, they were committed to rejecting the application of someone in one of the professions declared off-limits by the Christian community – brothel-keepers, charioteers and gladiators, keepers of idols, soldiers who took life, magistrates of a city who wore the purple, prostitutes; these people's socialization and day-to-day activities prevented them from being able to *hear* the word.

Those who passed this scrutiny were admitted as catechumens. Every morning they gathered along with some of the faithful to receive instruction, which the *Apostolic Tradition* does not specify but which probably gave basic teaching about the narratives and behaviour of the Christian community.[19] But the conventions of the catechetical process emphasized that the candidates did *not* belong to the community. Chapter 18 makes it clear that they

---

tenable. But, although no other interpretation has yet arisen to command general assent, a hypothesis has recently been advanced that I find plausible. Paul Bradshaw has argued that, although the *Apostolic Tradition* was written by many hands over many years in several places, there is a substantial Roman core to the initiation material of the document into which later North African materials may have been interpolated. Paul F. Bradshaw, 'Redating the Apostolic Tradition: Some Preliminary Steps', in Nathan Mitchell and John F. Baldovin, eds, *Rule of Prayer, Rule of Faith: Essays in Honor of Aidan Kavenagh*, OSB (Collegeville: Liturgical Press, 1996), 3–31. See also Maxwell E. Johnson, 'The Post-chrismational Structure of *Apostolic Tradition* 21, the Witness of Ambrose of Milan, and a Tentative Hypothesis Regarding the Current Reform of Confirmation in the Roman Rite', *Worship* 70 (1996), 21–3. Controverted though its origins are, the *Apostolic Tradition* is thus still admissible, I believe, as evidence in our search for changing patterns of conversion in the West.

[19] Alan Kreider, *Worship and Evangelism in Pre-Christendom*, Alcuin/GROW Joint Liturgical Studies 32 (Cambridge: Grove Books, 1995), 21–5.

were to 'pray by themselves, separated from the faithful'; further-more, unlike the faithful they were not to exchange the kiss of peace, for 'their kiss is not yet holy'. But they were to watch the faithful, who were to give good example to them (*c.*41); and the faithful for their part were to monitor their progress in the behaviour that was being inculcated by the teacher and that was characteristic of the Christian community. This process could last for an extended period of time: one MS tradition of the *Apostolic Tradition* speaks of a three-year catechumenate, while in Spain the Canons of Elvira extended this trial period to five years. But the documents are clear: the point was not length of teaching (which could be shortened); it was attitude and especially behaviour – the candidates' conduct (*mores*) or deeds (*opera*).[20] The candidates must be resocialized according to the teaching and traditions of the Christian community; they must gain new reflexes, new habits, new folkways. If after a time it seemed that the candidates' behaviour had developed appropriately, they would be scrutinized again:

> Have they lived good lives when they were catechumens? Have they honoured the widows? Have they visited the sick? Have they done every kind of good work?

If those who had sponsored and accompanied the catechumens could vouch that they were *behaving* like Christians, then they were admitted to a final period of catechism prior to their baptism so that they would *believe* like Christians. 'Let them hear the gospel' (*c.*20).

In the final weeks before their baptism in the Easter vigil, the catechumens not only were instructed in Christian belief. Further, they also submitted to a regimen of repeated exorcisms to ensure that they were 'good' and 'pure', free from all alien spirits (*c.*20). These exorcisms culminated on the Saturday night prior to baptism, when all candidates whom the bishop had approved for baptism appeared for a final exorcism and exsufflation – the bishop breathing into their faces. After a whole night in prayer, at cockcrow the baptisms proceeded (*c.*21). The candidates, tired, hungry from fasting and no doubt emotionally drained, were

---

[20] *Apostolic Tradition*, 17; *Canons of Elvira*, 11; Jean-Michel Hanssens, *La Liturgie d'Hippolyte: documents et Études* (Rome: Libreria Editrice dell' Università Gregoriana, 1970), 104–5.

disrobed. Naked, having renounced Satan and all his works and been anointed by the oil of exorcism, they assented to Christian belief and were immersed three times in water. After they had been re-robed, the bishop anointed their heads with the oil of thanks-giving, signed them with the cross, and gave them a kiss symbolizing that they now belonged in the Christian family. The new Christians joined the assembly, where for the first time they prayed *with* the people, exchanged the 'kiss of peace', and took part in the eucharist. With this 'ritual homecoming'[21] the long and torturous journey of conversion had ended, and the new believers had encountered all three of its dimensions: they had been taught to behave like Christians; they were instructed in Christian belief; and they had attained belonging in the Christian family. How about the experiential dimension of their conversion? The *Apostolic Tradition* is not explicit about this, but the exorcistic and baptismal rituals of the Easter vigil seem to have been designed to produce catharsis.[22] Baptizands as different as Cyprian and the Emperor Constantine testified to the affective power of the experience.[23]

The attractions of Christianity: lifestyle and spiritual power

So far we have examined three samples of early Christianity – two conversion stories and a church order. All of them have demon-strated that conversion was central to the life and recruitment of the Christian communities. We have seen that conversion had three dimensions, belief, behaviour and belonging; and common to them all was the reality of change. *Epistrophe, metanoia, conversio* – all of these words connoted turning and change.[24] This was more than intellectual change; for the early Christian writers it was life-encompassing. For Cyprian, *conversio* entailed a transformation of inner disposition and outer custom.[25] For Tertullian it involved

[21] Finn, 'Ritual Process', 78.

[22] Ibid., 77; Margaret R. Miles, *Carnal Knowing: Female Nakedness and Religious Meaning in the Christian West* (Boston: Beacon Press, 1989), 24.

[23] Cyprian, *Ad Donatum*, 4; Eusebius, *Life of Constantine* (VC), 4.53: 'Now I feel assured that I am accounted worthy of immortality, and am made a partaker of Divine light.'

[24] On *epistrophe*, see Paul Aubin, *Le problème de la 'conversion'*, Théologie Historique 1 (Paris: Beauchesne, 1963).

[25] Cyprian, *Ad Donatum*, 3.

a *bouleversement* of understandings and life commitments.[26] Thus conversion was bound to challenge more than a person's mental ruts or philosophical categories; it was bound to be more than a *Glaubenswechsel* or a 'reorientation of the soul of an individual'.[27] Indeed the change in belief was often quite secondary to the change in behaviour. As we look at the events, often recorded by an élite to be sure, but involving ordinary people, we discover a familiar pattern. People were first attracted to the Christians, not by their ideas, but by their distinctive behaviour and/or by the mysterious spiritual powers that seemed to be among them. Only later, when it was clear that they could share in this lifestyle, were they deemed ready to be taught the doctrines of the community; and only later still could they in any meaningful sense be viewed as 'converted'.

Early Christian writers often commented that people were drawn to inquire about the faith by observing Christian behaviour. The apologists made a lot of this, in both East and West.[28] Minucius Felix contended that that 'beauty of life . . . encourages strangers to join the ranks'.[29] And this was important, for, as Cyprian stated with great economy, a transformed lifestyle was central to Christianity: 'the Kingdom of God consists . . . in the faith of the cross and in virtue of behaviour'.[30]

But just as frequently the early writers recorded the role of spiritual power in attracting people to the churches. Some writers referred to healings, visions and dreams: for example, the author of the *Passion of Perpetua* reported that her visions were 'a witness to the unbeliever and a blessing to the faithful'.[31] Far more often the writers pointed to the role of exorcism in conversion, so much so that Professor MacMullen has referred to exorcism as 'the chief

---

[26] Tertullian, *Adv Marc*, 5.13; *De Carne Christi*, 4.41.

[27] Kurt Aland, *Über den Glaubenswechsel in der Geschichte des Christentums* (Berlin: Töpelmann, 1961); Arthur Darby Nock, *Conversion* (Oxford: Clarendon Press, 1933), 7.

[28] On Origen, see Marcel Borret's comments in the introductory volume to his edition of *Contra Celsum*, Sources Chrétiennes 227 [henceforth *SCh*.] (Paris: Cerf, 1976), 209; John Clark Smith, 'Conversion in Origen', *Scottish Journal of Theology* 32 (1979), 219.

[29] Minucius Felix, *Octavius*, 31.7.

[30] Cyprian, *Ad Quirinum*, 3.69.

[31] *Passio Perpetuae*, 1 (Herbert Musurillo, ed., *The Acts of the Christian Martyrs* [Oxford: Clarendon Press, 1972], 107).

instrument of conversion'.[32] Exorcisms apparently took place at many times and in many aspects of the church's life; and, according to Tertullian, the 'multitudes' were aware of this.[33] On occasion they seem to have been staged in places open to the public: there are records of a few 'power contests' between Christian exorcists and their pagan and Jewish rivals, but most of these must have been very small-scale events.[34] More generally exorcisms took place in private, especially in response to people seeking help for troubled friends and relatives. According to Irenaeus, the people who had been exorcized were changed in both belief and belonging: 'frequently [they] both believe [in Christ] and join themselves to the church'.[35] Above all, as we have seen, exorcisms formed a central part of the initiatory regimen of the churches. And we must not forget that, as the accounts of Justin and Cyprian demonstrate, Christians had experiences of God's power in moments of illumination, or in the baptismal waters, in ways which were not expressly exorcistic or 'charismatic'.

A journey of multi-dimensional change

But none of these experiences, given the understandings of the time, by themselves constituted conversion.[36] Pagan husbands,

---

[32] Ramsay MacMullen, *Christianizing the Roman Empire (AD 100–400)* (New Haven: Yale University Press, 1984), 27. Cf. Everett Ferguson, *Demonology of the Early Christian World*, Symposium Series 12 (New York: Edwin Mellen Press, 1984), 129.

[33] Tertullian, *Ad Scap.*, 2.

[34] Justin, 2 *Apol.*, 6; *Dialogue*, 85. Cf. *Acta Petri*, 23–8, and, from the late fourth century, Gregory of Nyssa, *Life of St Gregory Thaumaturgus*, with discussion in MacMullen, *Christianizing*, 59f.

[35] Irenaeus, *Adv. Haer.*, 2.32.4; Minucius Felix, *Oct*, 27.5. Cf. Origen, *Hom. on Samuel*, 1.10.

[36] Cf. Ramsay MacMullen, 'Two Types of Conversion to Early Christianity', *Vigiliae Christianae* 37 (1983), 184, who defines conversion as 'that experience by which non-believers first became convinced that the Christian God was almighty, and that they must please Him'. I am reluctant to define conversion in terms of experience, for the early Christians, as I read them, saw conversion in terms of multi-dimensional change effected through a catechetical and ritual process. Experience, to be sure, could be vital in the conversion process, either as the source of a person's initial interest in the faith, or midway through the process in a confirmation of the Christian God's presence and power, or at the climax of the process in the baptismal rite that seems to have been designed to effect a

as in Tertullian's Carthage, could be astonished and irritated by the remarkable behaviour of their Christian wives: visiting the 'brothers' in the squalid huts (*tuguriae*) which lined the slum-like suburbs;[37] sharing with them 'from her food, from her cup'; providing hospitality for a 'pilgrim brother' from some other part of the translocal Christian family; exchanging the 'kiss' with the brothers. Conversion was the process by which one became the sort of person who belonged to that kind of community. When women were converted, husbands knew that they had been changed for the better; they also could sense, Tertullian reported, and be terrified by, the 'mighty works' (*magnalia*) and proofs of divine action which took place in the Christian communities. But it didn't convert the husbands to see these things; it only led them, if they wished to respond, to be 'candidates for God'.[38]

Conversion required something deeper. It required the 'candidates' – those who had been impressed by the Christians' exorcisms or question-posing lives – to submit themselves to a journey of multi-dimensional change. The catechetical programmes that emerge from the beginning of the third century were developed to superintend this change and to ensure that it was genuine. In the fullness of time, this journey would culminate in baptism as the candidates died to their old selves and were reborn. Then and then only would the process of conversion be complete. Through this process the new Christians had been resocialized into a voluntary community which was in tension with the dominant social matrix.[39] Through their conversion the recruits to this community – the new Christians – had left an old world of conventionally accepted beliefs and behaviour-patterns for a new

---

spiritual combat – and an experience – which for the baptizand him/herself would be unforgettable. There does not appear to have been a uniformity of experience amongst Christianity's recruits, and no doubt some new Christians experienced less of the 'almightiness' of God than others.

[37] Georg Schöllgen, *Ecclesia sordida? Zur Frage der sozialen Schichtung frühchristlicher Gemeinden am Beispiel Karthagos zur Zeit Tertullians* (Münster: Aschendorff, 1984), 152.

[38] Tertullian, *Ad Uxorem*, 2.4, 5, 7.

[39] Meeks, *Origins of Christian Morality*, 26. On p. 162 Meeks speaks of 'the resocialisation or "conversion" process'.

world. This was a world of immense scope: as Cyprian's disciple and biographer Pontius put it, 'to the Christians, the whole of their world is one home'.[40] But their world was also one of liminality and insecurity; its members called themselves 'resident aliens' (paroikoi).[41] Their faith was stigmatized as a superstitio; as its adherents they were viewed as people of 'madness' and 'insanity'.[42] Because they had committed themselves to a translocal peoplehood and an allegiance higher than the Emperor, they were viewed as awkward people whose very existence posed an implicit threat to the existing order. They were thus vulnerable to occasional outbreaks of persecution. All of these implications of conversion the early Christians accepted as consequences of their free choice. 'At our first birth,' Justin commented, 'we were born of necessity without our knowledge'; but in baptism the Christians had been reborn through their 'free choice and knowledge . . .'.[43] Their conversion was a free response to convincing persuasion; it was 'an assertion of true liberty'.[44] As such it was incompatible with force or compulsion, for the God whom the Christians worshipped did not work 'by violent means . . . but by means of persuasion'.[45]

[40] Pontius, Vita Cypriani, 11.

[41] The use of this term, which first appears in Christian use in 1 Peter 2:11, has been carefully studied by Pierre de Labriolle, 'Paroecia', Bulletin du Cange (Archivum Latinitatis Medii Aevi) 3 (1927), 196–9. He commented (198): 'The idea of the heterogeneity of the Christians from their pagan neighbours and the society where they live is one of those which one finds most frequently in the texts.' For other samples, see 1 Clement, preface; Polycarp, Phil., preface; 2 Clement, 5.1; Eusebius, HE, 5.1.3; Epistle to Diognetus, 5.5; Pontius, Vita Cypriani, 11. As J. H. Elliott has demonstrated, the word paroikos could have legal and social as well as theological significance for the early Christians (A Home for the Homeless [London: SCM Press, 1981], 48).

[42] Justin, 1 Apology, 13; Acts of the Scillitan Martyrs; Acts of Marcellus, 4; Tertullian, Apology, 23.

[43] Justin, 1 Apology, 61.

[44] Minucius Felix, Oct., 38.1.

[45] Irenaeus, Adv. Haer., 5.1.1; Diognetus, 7.4; Tertullian, Ad Scap., 2; Apology, 28.1, 39.5; Lactantius, Div. Inst., 5.19.9–24; 5.20.7–10. See also Cyprian, in a non-apologetic context (Ad Quirinum, 3.52), who stated that it was one of the Christian community's principles that 'The liberty of believing or not believing is placed in free choice'. Cf. Peter Garnsey, 'Religious Toleration in Classical Antiquity', in W. J. Shiels, ed., Persecution and Toleration, Studies in Church History 21 (Oxford: Blackwell, 1984), 25.

Constantine's conversion

In the early fourth century Christianity, having experienced a period of persecution which in some places was harrowing, found a new impetus for conversion – the conversion of the Emperor. In October 312, on the night before a decisive battle, the Emperor-claimant Constantine had a dream in which he was directed to paint 'the heavenly sign' on his soldiers' shields. The following day, under the 'cypher of Christ', they crushed the troops of his rival Maxentius.[46] Inspired by what he took to be a vindication of religious experience by historical event, Constantine then summoned 'those who were acquainted with the mysteries of [God's] doctrines' to inquire what the vision might mean and to find out more about the Christian God. These people apparently instructed Constantine briefly in Christian matters; but, as Pierre Batiffol argued as early as 1913, he seems not to have become a catechumen.[47] Constantine to be sure admitted Christian priests to his entourage. But instead of asking them formally to catechize him, Constantine decided 'to devote himself to the reading of the inspired writings' on his own.[48]

Eminent scholars have persisted in referring to the events of 312 as the 'conversion' of Constantine.[49] To be sure, Constantine

[46] Lactantius, *Mort. Pers.*, 44.4–6. Cf. the more elaborate, and much later, account of Eusebius, *VC*, 1.29–31 (Nicene and Post-Nicene Fathers [NPNF], 2nd ser. 1, 481–559). For comment on the dream/vision accounts, see Ramsay MacMullen, *Constantine* (London: Croom Helm, 1969), 72–8.

[47] Pierre Batiffol, 'Les Étapes de la conversion de Constantin', *Bulletin d'ancienne littérature et d'archéologie chrétienne* 3 (1913), 264. F. J. Dölger, 'Die Taufe Konstantins und ihre Probleme', in idem, *Konstantin der Grosse und seine Zeit* (Freiburg im Breisgau: Herder'sche Verlagshandlung, 1913), 439, unconvincingly in my view, saw Constantine as a 'hearer'.

[48] Eusebius, *VC*, 1.32. I have based the rest of my account on this text, aware of its limitations and yet confident that it is 'inherently plausible' (T. D. Barnes, 'Panegyric, History and Hagiography in Eusebius' Life of Constantine', in Rowan Williams, ed., *The Making of Orthodoxy: Essays in Honour of Henry Chadwick* (Cambridge: Cambridge University Press, 1989), 91–123, esp. 114–15. See also Friedhelm Winkelmann, 'Zur Geschichte des Authentitätsproblems der Vita Constantini', *Klio* 40 (1962), 187–243; Robin Lane Fox, *Pagans and Christians* (San Francisco: Harper & Row, 1986), 627.

[49] T. D. Barnes, 'The Conversion of Constantine', *Classical Views* n.s. 4 (1985), 371–91; Henry Chadwick, 'Conversion in Constantine the Great', in Derek Baker, ed., *Religious Motivation: Biographical and Sociological Problems for the Church Historian*, Studies in Church History 15 (Oxford: Blackwell, 1978), 1–13.

proceeded in the Edict of Milan to give Christianity a position of privileged equality with other religions. He adopted 'the victorious trophy, the salutary symbol' as his insignia for battle.[50] In numerous acts, especially after his victory over Licinius in 324, Constantine acted to promote the welfare of Christianity as he understood it; his acts of patronage and privilege, coupled with a selective despoiling of pagan shrines, are well known. From at least 314 he addressed Christian bishops as 'beloved brothers',[51] and he presided at a great ecumenical council to determine orthodox doctrine. But a careful reading of Eusebius's *Life of Constantine* raises the possibility that Constantine until the very end of his life never quite felt that he belonged in the Christian community. Indications of this are his activities, according to Eusebius, on Sundays and Easter. On Sundays he would not be at a eucharist with other Christians; instead, he would 'seclude himself daily at a stated hour in the innermost chambers of his palace ... in solitary converse with his God'. On Easter he did not celebrate the feast by joining with the throngs of the faithful in the vigil; instead he ordered immense wax tapers to be lighted throughout the city.[52] His *Oration to the Assembly of Saints*, which may date from Good Friday 325,[53] reinforces this impression. Constantine contrasted himself as an outsider to his audience of saints and initiates: 'We ... have received no aid from human instruction; nay, whatever graces of character are esteemed of good report ... are entirely the gift of God.'[54] Constantine seems defensive. Even though uncatechized, even though unbaptized, even though an outsider, 'surely all men know that the holy service in which these hands have been employed has originated in pure and genuine faith towards God'.[55]

It is not fully clear why Constantine didn't want to become a Christian by ordinary means. Why did he resist catechism

---

[50] VC, 1.37.

[51] Constantine to Catholic Bishops at Arles, 314, in P. R. Coleman-Norton, ed., *Roman State and Christian Church: A Collection of Legal Documents to AD 535* (London: SPCK, 1966), I, 59–61.

[52] VC, 4.22. Cf. the Pentecost of 337 following his baptism, of which Eusebius (VC, 4.64) remarked that 'the Emperor was admitted to all these rites'.

[53] Lane Fox, *Pagans and Christians*, 643.

[54] *Oration*, 11 (NPNF, 2nd ser. 1, 568).

[55] Ibid., 26.

and baptism? It is possible, but improbable, that Constantine wanted to play it both ways and remain amphibiously pagan as well as Christian; his progression towards Christian adherence seems erratic but genuine. Nevertheless Constantine (according to Eusebius) had *amphibolia* – he was hesitant, of two minds.[56] Consider what it would have meant for an emperor to become a catechumen. It would have meant, according to well-established tradition, a scrutiny of his lifestyle; hardly a non-violent soul, Constantine may have heard, perhaps from the churchmen themselves, that the Christians required a person who 'has the power of the sword, or is a magistrate of a city who wears the purple', to cease or be rejected.[57] For reasons of imperial responsibility Constantine may not have wanted to be baptized. Furthermore, Constantine as a catechumen would have to submit his independent theological judgement (so evident in his *Oration to the Assembly*) to the instruction of others. And he may have been a bit afraid of the mysterious elements of Christian initiation. Many Christian communities were becoming reticent about discussing the rite and meaning of baptism before outsiders; but Constantine may have heard rumours about the exorcisms: did he want some cleric to hiss imprecatory words in his face? The threefold baptismal immersions were more than symbolically life-threatening; was it responsible for an emperor to submit to them? And the whole ritual was designed to be levelling – to treat patrician and plebeian alike.[58] Furthermore, there was the Christian prohibition of

[56] Eusebius, *VC*, 4.62; Dölger, 'Die Taufe Konstantins', 426.

[57] *AT* 16 (see especially the Arabic text of the scrutiny of would-be catechumens: 'On [someone wearing] luxurious purple clothes . . . let him go out' (Hanssens, *La Liturgie d'Hippolyte*, 100–1). On Christian repudiation of the purple, see Tertullian, *De Idololatria*, 18; Minucius Felix, *Oct.*, 31.6; Cyprian, *Ad Don.*, 3; Meyer Reinhold, *History of Purple as a Status Symbol in Late Antiquity*, Collection Latomus 116 (Brussels: Latomus, 1970). On the mistrust of the magistracy, see the early fourth-century Canons of Elvira, 56: 'A magistrate is ordered to keep away from the church during the one year of his term as *duumvir.*'

[58] Cf. John Chrysostom, writing half a century after Constantine's initiation, on exorcism (*Baptismal Instructions*, 2.13; Paul W. Harkins, ed., Ancient Christian Writers [ACW] 31 [Westminster: The Newman Press, 1963]): '[T]his rite does away with all difference and distinction of rank. Even if a man happens to enjoy worldly honour, if he happens to glitter with wealth, if he boasts of high lineage or the glory which is his in this world, he stands side by side with the beggar . . . See what profit these words and these awesome and wonderful invocations bring with them.'

post-baptismal sin, and Constantine may simply have wanted to avoid depriving himself, as emperor, of recourse to actions that many Christian communities persisted in viewing as sinful. There were good reasons for Constantine to resist baptism.

Nevertheless, when facing death, Constantine demonstrated that he believed in the God of the Christians. Although he held out as long as possible, as he claimed so he could imitate Christ by being baptized in the Jordan,[59] Constantine had only got as far as Bithynia when he realized that his health was dangerously uncertain. So he decided to seek purification 'from any errors which he might ever have committed . . . by the power of the secret words and the saving washing'.[60] Constantine confessed his sins, and then 'for the first time' received the imposition of hands and prayer. Thereby, as Edward Yarnold has recently argued, Constantine became a catechumen.[61] Shortly thereafter Constantine expressed the desire to 'be numbered henceforth among the flock of the people of God', so that he could 'share within the congregation in the prayers alongside all the others . . .'. The Emperor wanted to belong to the Christian community. In addition, Constantine promised to change his behaviour: 'I shall now impose upon myself rules of life which are worthy of God.' Having made this promise, he underwent the initiatory procedures 'in the usual manner'. He received 'all the necessary injunctions' (about behaviour as well as belief?). He was baptized, and was 'reborn'. Whereupon, Eusebius reports, thirty years after the experience of his momentous dream, Constantine had a second experience. Its power evidently surprised him:

---

[59] This was not the only way in which Constantine pursued an *imitatio Christi*. As Rudolf Leeb has demonstrated, Constantine modestly adopted the device of the victorious Christ treading on the serpent for his imperial iconography; thereby, on his new palace in Constantinople, he and his sons were depicted as carrying on Christ's work of subduing evil (Eusebius, *VC*, 3.3). 'Inasmuch as Constantine overcomes the evil in the world, he is the fulfiller of the will of the Christ God, who therefore helps him' (*Konstantin und Christus: Die Verchristlichung der imperialen Repräsentation unter Konstantin den Grossen als Spiegel seiner Kirchenpolitik und seines Selbstverständnisses als christlicher Kaiser*, Arbeiten zur Kirchengeschichte 58 [Berlin: Walter de Gruyter, 1992], 49–52).

[60] This account is based on Eusebius, *VC*, 4.61–2. I use the translation of E. J. Yarnold, 'The Baptism of Constantine', *Studia Patristica* 26 (1993), 95–6.

[61] Yarnold, 'The Baptism of Constantine', 98.

[Constantine] rejoiced in the spirit, was renewed and filled with divine light, delighting in his soul through the excess of faith, and astonished at the clear manifestation of the divine power.

At long last Constantine belonged. And in the few days remaining to him, according to Eusebius, he behaved differently, 'having resolved never to come in contact with purple again'. '*Now,*' he exulted shortly before he died, 'in truth I know myself to be blessed.'[62]

Converting the masses by carrot and stick

Constantine's career was so significant, and his subsequent reputation so great, that he has never ceased to be the subject of controversy. Some recent historians, such as Ramsay MacMullen, have emphasized the watershed which Constantine represented; others, such as Henry Chadwick, have seen Constantine's conversion 'as one of those many revolutions that in retrospect ... seem like mild ripples on the water making relatively little difference to what was already happening'.[63] I accept that the period of toleration following the end of the persecution under Valerian freed the church to acculturate in new ways; that the appeal of Christians to the Emperor in 270 against a bishop represented their heightened sense of safety and social respectability; and that some – possibly many – Christian communities, such as that in Abthungi in North Africa had by the early fourth century

---

[62] These eleventh-hour changes in Constantine's behaviour did not have a lasting effect on the imperial behaviour. After Constantine's death imperial conventions quickly reasserted themselves. Soldiers lifted his corpse, laid it in a golden casket which they swathed in purple cloth; after embalming the body, courtiers displayed it in the imperial palace 'arrayed in the symbols of sovereignty, the diadem and the purple robe' (Eusebius, *VC,* 4.66). And throughout the fourth and fifth centuries, as Christian emperors succeeded each other, there was a 'standardisation of the use of purple in the imperial insignia'. In the same period, purple was also gradually adopted as a distinctive attire for the upper clergy (Reinhold, *History of Purple*, 62, 68, 73).

[63] Ramsay MacMullen, *Christianizing,* 102; Henry Chadwick, 'The Church of the Third Century in the West', in A. King and M. Henig, eds, *Roman West in the Third Century* (British Archaeological Reports, 1981), 6. See also Wolfgang Wischmeyer, *Von Golgatha zum Ponte Molle: Studien zur Sozialgeschichte der Kirche im dritten Jahrhundert*, Forschungen zur Kirchen- und Dogmengeschichte, 49 (Göttingen: Vandenhoeck & Ruprecht, 1992), 129.

come to coexist comfortably and tolerantly with their pagan neighbours.[64] I find it also possible that, by the late third century, the church in the West had reached a ceiling to its voluntary growth which it was finding it difficult to exceed.[65] Had nothing changed, possibly Christianity and paganism could have lived side-by-side in an Empire that would have continued to be pluralist.[66]

But things did change, and Constantine's life-work provided the impetus for it, not least by bringing to conversion what Michele Salzman has called the 'carrot and the stick'.[67] The stick first. Constantine's conversion and the events emanating from it changed the legal impetus for conversion in the Roman Empire. From 313 Catholic Christianity moved from its status in the Edict of Milan – favoured equality amongst various religious options – to its position in 392 of being the sole legal public cult, infractions of whose monopoly were punishable by swingeing penalties.[68] Conversion was not compulsory until Justinian's edict of 529, but prior to this a variety of laws had brought the reality of compulsion to bear on those who resisted Christianity's advance.[69] Second, the carrot. One of these inducements, benefits for the churches, is symbolized by Constantine's grant in 320 to clergymen of immunity from onerous public duties. The stated reason is significant – 'that the churches' assemblies may be

[64] R. A. Markus, *Christianity in the Roman World* (London: Thames & Hudson, 1974), 70–86; T. D. Barnes, 'The Constantinian Settlement', in Harold W. Attridge and Gohei Hato, eds, *Eusebius, Christianity and Judaism*, Studia Post-Biblica 42 (Leiden: Brill, 1992), 635; Claude Lepelley, 'Chrétiens et païens au temps de la persécution de Dioclétien: le cas d'Abthungi', *Studia Patristica* 15 (1984), 226–32.

[65] W. H. C. Frend, 'A Note on the Influence of Greek Immigrants on the Spread of Christianity in the West', in Alfred Stuiber and Alfred Hermann, eds, *Mullus: Festschrift Theodor Klauser* (Münster: Aschendorff, 1964), 128.

[66] R. M. Price, 'Pluralism and Religious Tolerance in the Empire of the Fourth Century', *Studia Patristica* 24 (1993), 184–8.

[67] Michele Renee Salzman, 'The Evidence for the Conversion of the Roman Empire to Christianity in Book 16 of the *Theodosian Code*', *Historia* 42 (1993), 378. Other historians have used parallel terms: 'inducement and compulsion' (Herbert Butterfield); 'flattery and battery' (Ramsay MacMullen); 'direkter Zwang und indirekte Nötigung' (Hans-Dietrich Kahl).

[68] Eusebius, *HE*, 10.5.1–14; *Codex Theodosianus* [*CT*], 16.10.12.

[69] *Codex Iustinianus* [*CI*], 1.11.10.

crowded with a vast concourse of people'.[70] Another carrot was enrichment: Constantine and his successors gave with largesse to the churches what they had confiscated from pagan temples. Still another carrot was the prospect of jobs: Christianity became known as the Emperor's religion, and many careerists duly converted.[71] Within a century, the imperial upper classes – even the males, who had so stolidly resisted conversion – were within the Christian fold, bringing into play new forms of coercion upon their adherents and underlings.[72] Enveloping these inducements was the kudos of respectability. As early as 341 an imperial edict began a new verbal convention by stigmatizing pagan worship as a *superstitio*;[73] and by 380 the orthodox authorities were soon flinging at the adherents of 'heretical' Christian groups (and by 408 at the pagans) the traditional epithets – so recently thrown at them – of madness and dementia.[74]

Working together, the carrot and stick had their predictable effect, and the Christian church grew rapidly. To some extent the traditional impetuses of recruitment still operated. The lifestyle of exemplary Christians was still attractive to some; and 'miracles' still took place – but primarily on the frontiers of missionary expansion, and, except in conjunction with relics, rarely in Christianity's emerging heartlands.[75] The new recruits seem not always to have

---

[70] *CT*, 16.2.10.

[71] Sozomen, *HE*, 2.5.

[72] Peter Brown, 'Aspects of the Christianisation of the Roman Aristocracy', in his *Religion and Society in the Age of Saint Augustine* (New York: Harper & Row, 1972), 161–82. For 'top-down' conversions, see Augustine, *Enarr. in Ps.*, 54.13; *CD*, 19.14 (A proprietor, out of love for God and neighbour, 'ought to endeavour to get his neighbour to love God . . . he ought to make this endeavour in behalf of his wife, his children, his household [and] all within his reach'); John Matthews, *Western Aristocracies and Imperial Court, A.D. 364–425* (Oxford: Clarendon Press, 1975), 155–6.

[73] *CT*, 16.10.2: Michele Renee Salzman, '"Superstitio" in the Codex Theodosianus and the Persecution of Pagans', *Vigiliae Christianae* 41 (1987), 172–88.

[74] *CT*, 16.1.2; *Constitutiones Sirmondianae* [CS], 12.

[75] On the rarity of miracles, see Ambrose, *De Sacramentis*, 2.15; Augustine, *Sermon*, 88.3. The miracles which Augustine lists in *City of God*, 22.8 are apologetic of decline ('even now miracles were wrought in the name of Christ'), and are largely in connection with relics. For a frontier miracle, see the ministry of Martin of Tours in the region of the Loir, recorded by Sulpicius Severus, *Dial*,

had impeccable motives: Eusebius clucked his tongue about 'the scandalous hypocrisy of those who crept into the church, and assumed the name and character of Christians', but that was an inevitable by-product of growth under these circumstances.[76] So much changed, not least (in view of the contributions of fourth-century Christians to the theological formulations of the church) the locus of theologizing: from the margins of society the theologians moved to its centre, including the imperial court. As the century progressed, the churches took on the trappings and iconography of the court, while many bishops graduated from the 'mean' attire, which had been observed soon after Constantine's accession, to the sartorial splendour which Ammianus Marcellinus described with distaste.[77]

Conforming to the norms of Christian society

The product of all this – the stick, the carrot and the church's size – was a fundamental shift in the social function of conversion. In the early centuries of the church, we have noted, conversion entailed a process of 'resocialization' which taught converts the skills and understanding necessary to live the deviant life of an alternative society; and this required of every candidate a 'change of life'. Now, after Constantine, the alternative society was becoming society itself; and conversion was enabling the now-deviant pagans to shape up, equipping them to conform to the

---

2.5. Martin had preached without great effect. But after he had participated in the raising of a woman's dead son, 'Then, truly, the whole multitude, raising a shout to heaven, acknowledged Christ as God, and finally began to rush in crowds to the knees of the blessed man, sincerely imploring him that he would make them Christians. Nor did he delay to do so. As they were in the middle of the plain, he made them all catechumens . . .'. Even on the frontiers of faith, under the pressure of large numbers attracted by a miracle, the catechumenate showed its resilience in the West. See also Sulpicius Severus, *Vita Martini*, 17 for a miracle which leads to entry into the catechumenate, baptism following 'not long after'.

[76] Eusebius, *VC*, 4.54.

[77] Johannes Quasten, 'Mysterium Tremendum: Eucharistische Frömmigkeitsauffassungen des vierten Jahrhunderts', in A. Mayr, J. Quasten and B. Neunheuser, eds, *Vom Christlichen Mysterium* (Düsseldorf: Patmos Verlag, 1951), 72; Johannes Quasten, *The Mass of the Roman Rite: Its Origins and Development (Missarum Solemnia)* (Westminster: Christian Classics, 1986), I, 39–40; Eusebius, *VC*, 1.41; Ammianus Marcellinus, *Res Gestae*, 27.3.14.

now normal norms of a Christian society.[78] As this happened, the processes of conversion changed.[79] Not completely, of course. The baptismal rituals retained the shape of their predecessors in the *Apostolic Tradition*; indeed, they became ever more elaborate and awe-inspiring.[80] But the procedures of pre-baptismal instruction altered markedly. The catechumenate, for example, had involved an intensive period of instruction in Christian belief and behaviour lasting for a long time – in some places up to three years. In the fourth century, the connection between the catechumenate and formal catechesis was severed. All those who, like the child Augustine, tasted the exorcized salt, were signed with the cross and received the laying on of hands were accounted among the catechumens, and thus able to attend the non-eucharistic parts of the Sunday services. They were not baptized, but people viewed them as 'Christians'; and although they were called 'catechumens' they were not being catechized, except insofar as they, if they attended the services, listened to the sermons. Many of them would remain unbaptized for their entire lives and be baptized, if at all, 'clinically' on their deathbeds, which the churchmen at the early fourth-century Synod of Neocaesarea disdained, as being the result 'not of a spontaneous decision, but of necessity'.[81] On the other hand, those who were serious about proceeding to baptism 'gave in their names', often at the beginning of Lent, and received some weeks of intensive instruction. Significantly, however, the subject matter that they were taught was shifting from earlier patterns. The teachings of Jesus which had been central to early catechesis had now, in Milan, been supplanted by stories of the Old Testament patriarchs and behavioural guidance from the

[78] Meeks, *Origins of Christian Morality*, 21–2, 162–3.

[79] For discussion of these, see Alan Kreider, 'Baptism, Catechism, and the Eclipse of Jesus' Teaching in Early Christianity', *Tyndale Bulletin* 47.2 (1996), 315–48.

[80] See Edward Yarnold, *The Awe-Inspiring Rites of Initiation: Baptismal Homilies of the Fourth Century* (Slough: St Paul Publications, 1971); Suzanne Poque, ed., *Augustin d'Hippone, Sermons pour la Pâque*, Sources Chrétiennes 116 (Paris: Cerf, 1966), ch. 1.

[81] The large numbers of these unbaptized 'Christians' led to a plethora of sermons appealing for 'conversion'. For examples, see Ambrose, *De Elia et ieiunio*; Augustine, *Sermons*, 19, 20, 40, 82, 87, 132. For the Synod of Neocaesarea (c.12), see Charles Joseph Hefele, *Histoire des Conciles*, 1 (Paris: Letouzey, 1907), 332–3.

proverbs;[82] and the stories and examples of Jesus, which were evidently useful to Arian apologists, had been supplanted by stories and examples of the saints.[83] Meanwhile, the formation of Christian conduct had come to be replaced by a concentration on the Lord's Prayer and the Creed.[84] And the liturgical scrutinies were now concerned to establish whether the baptismal candidates had been properly exorcized; they were no longer concerned to find out whether the candidates, like the catechumen Cyprian, had 'loved the poor'.[85]

Of course, the catechists still required *conversio* – a change of life. And conversion from the earliest days of the Christian church had always involved inculturation – the expression of the Christian faith and way of life in vocabulary, visual images, philosophical categories and customs which Christians negotiated with classical antiquity.[86] After Constantine's conversion the borrowing, which had previously been selective and self-critical, became more embracing. Christian catechists still warned against some aspects of the social conventions and culture of late antiquity, but not many. The only aspect of North African society about which Bishop Quodvultdeus of Carthage warned his hearers in the 430s

[82] Compare Justin, I *Apol.*, 14–17 and Cyprian, *Ad Quirinum*, 3 with Ambrose, *De Mysteriis*, 1.1; *De Abraham*; *De Ioseph*. According to Peter Brown, 'For the first time, the events of the Old Testament had become the true *gesta maiorum* of a large body of the Roman governing class' ('Saint Augustine's Attitude to Religious Coercion', in his *Religion and Society*, 274). In Hippo, Augustine introduced another Old Testament plumbline – the Decalogue – into Christian catechesis (Gregory J. Lombardo, ed., *Augustine, On Faith and Works*, Ancient Christian Writers 48 [New York: Newman Press, 1988], 85n.).

[83] Robert L. Wilken has observed that many orthodox Christians in the fourth century, in part owing to their conflict with the Arians, ceased to appeal to Jesus as an exemplar: the saints 'filled the space left vacant by the departure of the Master' (*Remembering the Christian Past* [Grand Rapids: Eerdmans, 1995], 126–7, 133).

[84] Augustine, *Sermons*, 56–59, 212–13; Quodvultdeus, *Sermones de symbolo ad catechumenos*, 1–3.

[85] Thomas M. Finn, 'It Happened One Saturday Night: Ritual and Conversion in Augustine's North Africa', *Journal of the American Academy of Religion* 58/4 (1990), 602; Pontius, *Vita Cypriani*, 6.

[86] Anton Wessels, *Europe: Was it Ever Really Christian? The Interaction between Gospel and Culture* (London: SCM Press, 1994), ch. 2; Horst Rzepkowski, 'Das Papsttum als ein Modell frühchristlicher Anpassung', in Theo Sundermeier, ed., *Die Begegnung mit dem Anderen: Plädoyers für eine interkulturelle Hermeneutik* (Gütersloh: Gerd Mohn, 1991), 69–93.

was the untoward goings-on in the hippodrome.[87] The other side of this is obvious: the Christians had now come to be more receptive of the values and mores of the host culture. In Gaul there occurred what Professor Fontaine has called a *conversion continuée*, a 'sense of exchange and of symbiosis, far more than alternative or confrontation' as Christianity spread into the countryside and inculturated into the cultures of the latifundiaries and even, more gradually, of the peasantry.[88] In Rome throughout the fourth century the aristocracy progressively became adherents of a 'respectable Christianity' which to a remarkable extent managed to preserve the values of the élite culture of the capital.[89] The intellectual paganism of the urban élites was suppressed, but the bucolic paganism of the soil and agricultural year proved to be hardy – and assimilable to local expressions of acculturated Christianity.[90] In such a setting of rapid Christian expansion by favour and fiat, accommodation was only to be expected. Whatever its earlier values, Christianity's advance did little to hinder the rise – so widespread in late antiquity – of socio-economic differentiation and judicial barbarity. The one area, according to Professor MacMullen, in which Christianity made a significant impact on society was in its sexual mores.[91]

[87] Quodvultdeus, *Sermones de symbolo ad catechumenos*, 1.2; 2.1.4. For the 'fatal passion for the circus' (Augustine, *Confessions*, 6.7) in Christian North Africa, see Claude Lepelley, *Les Cités de l'Afrique Romaine au Bas-Empire*, II (Paris: Études Augustiniennes, 1981), 44–7; Henry Chadwick, 'Augustine and Almachius', in Louis Holtz and Jean-Claude Fredouille, eds, *De Tertullien aux Mozarabes* (FS Fontaine) I (Paris: Études Augustiniennes, 1992), 299–303.

[88] Jacques Fontaine, 'Valeurs antiques et valeurs chrétiennes dans la spiritualité des grands propriétaires terriens à la fin du IVe siècle occidental', in *Epektasis: Mélanges patristiques offerts au Cardinal Jean Daniélou* (Paris: Beauchesne, 1972), 573, 580; idem, 'L'apport de l'archéologie française a l'histoire de la christianisation des Gaules', in Noël Duval, *et al.*, eds, *Naissance des Arts Chrétiens: Atlas des monuments paléochrétiens de la France* (Paris: Imprimerie Nationale, 1991), 16, 25.

[89] Peter Brown, 'Aspects of the Christianisation of the Roman Aristocracy', in his *Religion and Society*, 164, 168, 178.

[90] Lepelley, *Les Cités*, 361, 361n.; Pierre Chuvin, *A Chronicle of the Last Pagans* (Cambridge: Harvard University Press, 1990), 129.

[91] Ramsay MacMullen, 'What Difference did Christianity Make?' *Historia*, 35 (1986), 322–43; idem, 'Judicial Savagery in the Roman Empire', in his *Changes in the Roman Empire: Essays in the Ordinary* (Princeton: Princeton University Press, 1990), 209, 214.

Volusian: a pagan aristocrat joins the Christian mainstream

An interesting example of conversion in this period is the experience of Rufius Antonius Agrypinus Volusianus (Volusian).[92] Volusian was a member of the illustrious Caeonii family, in which a growing number – including the elder and younger Melanias – were Christians. But Volusian, like others of the family's men, resisted conversion despite the best efforts of the women to influence them for the faith. When Volusian in 411–12 was sent to Africa as proconsul, the elder Melania wrote to a circle of prominent Christians in Carthage urging them to befriend him. So the tribune Marcellinus and others saw him daily, and from Hippo, Augustine corresponded with him with seriousness and respect.[93] From the Carthage group came a clear picture of Volusian's hesitations about Christianity, which probably were typical of Roman aristocrats of his circle. Volusian found the beliefs of Christianity to be problematic; the incarnation and miracles were hard to comprehend. More seriously for a Roman aristocrat, Volusian was convinced that the behaviour taught by Christianity, for example that believers should not return evil for evil, was 'not adaptable to the customs of the state'.[94] Augustine replied to Volusian directly in letters to him and indirectly at greater length through Marcellinus, addressing Volusian's theological and practical concerns. Volusian, Augustine asserted, would have to submit to Christian beliefs if he wanted to become a Christian. But no one would challenge him, unlike Cyprian a century and a half earlier, to change the behaviour characteristic of Roman patricians. The teachings of Jesus which were problematic for Volusian, according to Augustine, referred to the 'interior dispositions of the heart' rather than to Christian public morality;

---

[92] For Volusian's genealogy and career, see André Chastagnol, 'Le Sénateur Volusien et la conversion d'une famille de l'aristocratie romaine au bas-empire', *Revue des études anciennes* 58 (1956), 241–53; idem, *Les fastes de la Préfecture de Rome au Bas-Empire*, Études Prosopographiques 2 (Paris: Nouvelles Éditions Latines, 1962), 276–79; Elizabeth A. Clark, ed., *The Life of Melania the Younger*, Studies in Women and Religion 14 (Lewiston: Edwin Mellen Press, 1984), 129–33.

[93] Marcellinus to Augustine (Augustine, *Ep.* 136); Volusian to Augustine (Augustine, *Ep.* 135); Augustine to Volusian (*Epp.* 132, 137).

[94] Augustine, *Epp.* 135–6.

the behaviour of Christian rulers would be governed by 'a sort of kindly harshness' in the interest of the welfare of others. It was kindness that obliged the good to wage war to restrain licentious behaviour; and the Christian gospel sanctioned this in John the Baptist's instructions to the soldiers: as Augustine pointed out, John did not tell them to throw down their weapons, but rather to avoid gratuitous violence and to be content with their wages (Lk 3:14). Volusian had heard rumours that the Christian faith was inimical to public order. On the contrary, Augustine asserted, Christianity made for 'the greatest safety of the state'. For someone as 'distinguished and excellent' as Volusian, conversion would not require a fundamental change in aristocratic behaviour.[95]

Even so, Volusian resisted conversion. We next meet him twenty-three years later, in 436. In that year, according to our source, Gerontius's Life of Melania the Younger, the ageing Volusian – still a pagan – was sent as an ambassador of the Roman court to Constantinople. His assignment: to help arrange the marriage of the Western emperor Valentinian III to the Eastern princess Eudoxia. From her monastic community near Jerusalem, Volusian's niece, the younger Melania, heard of his journey eastwards, so she hurried to Constantinople to see her uncle and to try yet again to convert him.[96] They had an emotional reunion, in which Melania immediately came to the point: she begged her uncle to 'approach the bath of immortality' to gain 'eternal goods' and avoid 'eternal fire'. Making oblique reference to imperial legislation of 408 and 416,[97] she threatened to report him to the Emperor as a civil servant who was obdurate in his paganism. Volusian found this painful. He was ready, he said, to wash away the stain of his unspecified 'many errors'; but he begged Melania not to take from him 'the gift of self-determination' which God had given him. If he came to baptism as a result of the Emperor's command, he would be

---

[95] Augustine, Epp. 137–8. Cf. Rita Lizzi's observation based on northern Italy: 'In order to encourage the conversion of the wealthier citizens, the bishops modulated their preaching, dealing in an appropriate fashion with the topics of wealth and alms-giving' ('Ambrose's Contemporaries and the Christianisation of Northern Italy', Journal of Roman Studies 80 [1990], 167).

[96] The best source for this is Gerontius, The Life of Melania the Younger, 51–5 (trans. E. A. Clark, see n. 92 above).

[97] CT, 16.5.42; 16.19.21.

capitulating to force and would 'lose the reward of my free decision'. So Melania backed off, and tried to secure Volusian's willing conversion. At her behest, the persuasive patriarch Proclus came to talk to Volusian about his salvation; at some unspecified time he was made a catechumen; and when his health took a turn for the worse, a few hours before his death Volusian was baptized. Persistence, persuasion, changing social convention, the threat of force and impending death had finally conquered him. And what about Volusian's baptismal experience, which had been so important to Cyprian and Constantine? Perhaps it is no accident that Gerontius says nothing about it. Nevertheless, Melania rejoiced, for the entire family of the Caeionii was Christian. A century earlier, in Constantine's baptism, the church had required the Emperor to change his lifestyle; in Volusian's baptism – whether in Augustine's correspondence or Melania's manoeuvrings – there is no hint that conversion required a respectable aristocrat to change, whether in his attentiveness to the needs of the poor, in his attitude to violence, or apparently in the opulence or colour of his dress. It is hardly surprising that in Rome the result was 'a respectable, aristocratic Christianity'.[98]

Augustine: urging the masses to conversion

Augustine, of course, is the most famous convert of early Christianity.[99] From his own experience he knew that conversion involved a change of life. Although in the second decade of the fifth century he was under pressure from a circle of biblically-literate lay people to baptize first and only then to teach about

[98] Brown, 'Aspects of the Christianisation', 177. For the Christian conviction that conversion might require Christians to leave governmental service, see Gregory of Nazianzus, Or. 40.19; also Council of Arles (314), c.7, which stipulated that governors who were Christians and involved in administration should be 'watched over by the bishop of the place, and that, if they happen to commit acts contrary to the [ecclesiastical] discipline, then only should they be excluded from communion'.

[99] For Augustine's use of the language of conversion, and a survey of the literature upon Augustine's own conversion, see Goulven Madec, 'Conversio', in Cornelius Meyer, ed., Augustinus-Lexikon I (Basel: Schwabe, 1986–94), 1282–94. Interestingly in his preaching Augustine does not seem to have presented his own conversion as normative, which was left for later generations to do.

Christian lifestyle, Augustine as Bishop of Hippo (395–430) showed no signs of being tempted by change-free conversion.[100] Instead throughout his pastoral life he tirelessly urged people to come to receive forgiveness and to 'change your manner of life for the better' (*Sermon* [henceforth S] 29.6).[101] But this was easier urged than realized. By the early fifth century North African society was dominated by Catholic Christians, but people were recalcitrant, either holding back from the rites of Christian conversion, or, once they had been baptized, behaving as if they had not been.

No one had done more than Augustine to bring about the Catholic dominance. In the years after his own Christian conversion Augustine, in the classical Christian tradition, had doubted that compulsion brought true change. This was true, he reflected, of the way he had studied the Latin language: 'I learnt Latin without the threat of punishment from anyone forcing me to learn it. My own heart constrained me . . . This experience sufficiently illuminates the truth that free curiosity has greater power to stimulate learning than rigorous coercion.'[102] Augustine sensed that this was true about religion as well.[103] But in conflict with the Donatists his imperious paternalism got the better of his earlier convictions. Not only, he had come to believe, was it right to collaborate with the state to coerce the recalcitrant sectaries into the church; it was also right to seek measures to put pressures on the pagans. In this Augustine saw himself as a surgeon, who 'cuts to heal'.[104] But Augustine sensed that compulsion did not produce behaviour-changing conversion, and he struggled with this.

---

[100] Augustine, *Faith and Works, passim*. On this see Kreider, 'Baptism, Catechism, and the Eclipse of Jesus' Teaching', 341–3.

[101] For Augustine's Sermons, I have used the translation of Edmund Hill (New York: New City Press, 1990–).

[102] Augustine, *Confessions*, 1.14.23.

[103] Augustine, *Retractions*, 2.31; G. G. Willis, *Saint Augustine and the Donatist Controversy* (London: SPCK, 1950), 127–9.

[104] Augustine, *Enarr. in Ps.*, 34/2.13. Legally there was not yet a compulsion for pagans to join the church, simply a denial of their right to worship. And yet, see Augustine, *Enarr. in Ps.*, 88, which reflects what must have been the case in many localities: 'For long Christians did not dare answer a pagan; now, thank God, it is a crime to remain a pagan.'

Augustine sought a solution in the well-established tradition of the Christian ritual processes of catechesis and baptism.[105] It was not easy, to be sure, to get pagans to express enough interest in Christianity to apply for admission to the catechumenate. He was aware that Christians gave the pagans ample excuse to remain unconverted. Pagans would look at the Christians and sniff derisively, 'Look at these Christians!'[106] Nevertheless, the carrot and the stick operated in Hippo as elsewhere. Pagans would apply to become catechumens, Augustine recognized, 'in the hope of deriving some benefit from men whom he thinks he could not otherwise please, or to escape some injury at the hands of men whose displeasure or enmity he dreads'.[107] In his instruction to catechists for these initial encounters with enquirers (*De Catechizandis Rudibus*), Augustine advised the catechists to build upon these motives, even if they were 'counterfeit'. Having thus established rapport, they were to deliver to the long-suffering candidates – who might well be apathetic – a sixty-minute narration of salvation history from creation to judgement day, culminating in exhortations to good behaviour.[108] If candidates assented to this they received the salt and signing with the cross, thereby entering an open-ended period as catechumens.[109] They could now call themselves 'Christians' and attend the prayers and sermons in the churches.

The catechumens were not, of course, yet converted. So each year, as Easter approached, Augustine applied rhetorical pressure to get them to enter the final stage of preparation for baptism. In his sermons Augustine pleaded with the catechumens and threatened them. They were adept, he knew, in temporizing, so he warned them, 'This is the thing that kills many people, when they say, "Tomorrow, tomorrow" . . .'. Wielding one of his most useful texts (Ecclus. 5:7) which warned that 'suddenly the Lord's wrath

---

[105] For illuminating insight into the catechetical vision and activities of Augustine, see William Harmless, *Augustine and the Catechumenate* (Collegeville: Liturgical Press, 1995).

[106] Augustine, *Sermons*, 5.8; 179.4; 228.2. 'When someone is pressing [a pagan] to believe, he will answer, "Do you want me to be like that so-and-so and the other one?"' (*Sermon*, 15.6).

[107] Augustine, *De Catechizandis Rudibus*, 5.9.

[108] Ibid., 13.18, 16.25–25.49.

[109] Ibid., 26.50.

will be upon you' bringing judgement and death, Augustine warned the catechumens not to delay in being converted. 'In terror I aim to terrify. Be afraid with me in order to rejoice with me' (S40.5).

Those who were moved by this 'entered their names' and became *competentes* – 'people seeking together' – who would share with one another the 'ritual process of conversion' (S216.1).[110] A scrutiny of the candidates' lives and professions ensued. As Augustine pointed out, 'The church has always held the old and strict practice of not admitting' some people; 'prostitutes, actors, or any disreputable person' (and especially adulterers) had to leave their jobs or cease their untoward behaviour.[111] Augustine did not indicate, perhaps because he did not know, that the church had dropped its old and strict practice, recorded in the *Apostolic Tradition* 16, of refusing to admit soldiers who killed, or governors who wore the purple. One gets the feeling that Augustine's criteria were more difficult for the *humiliores* of Hippo to meet than for aristocrats like Volusian. For those who withstood the scrutiny of professions there was an intensive period of pre-Easter preparation. There were sermons but, because of the press of candidates, there could be no personal guidance: 'We clergy instruct you with sermons; it is up to you to make progress in your conduct' (S216.1). The candidates were instructed about lifestyle, how to avoid the detestable sins of 'drunkenness, avarice [and] calumny', and 'how one must live who wishes to be joined to the body of Christ'.[112] The catechists taught them the meaning of the Creed and the Lord's Prayer, which the candidates were to memorize and make a part of their daily disciplines. All of this was accompanied by strong spiritual medicine – fasting, abstinence and exorcism.

In the Easter vigil the ritual process came to a climax. An awesome final scrutiny determined, not whether the candidates had been good to the poor, but whether they were free of demonic possession.[113] Those who withstood these exorcisms were, at long last, immersed in what Augustine called 'the bath of amnesty' (S223.1). The immensely impressive process had come to its goal. The candidates were now reborn, enlightened, dead to the powers

---

110 Finn, 'It Happened One Saturday Night', 590.
111 Augustine, *Faith and Works*, 18.33.
112 Ibid., 9.14; 18.33.
113 Finn, 'It Happened One Saturday Night', 603, 610.

of darkness, and reclad in Christ, ready to 'tread in their Master's footsteps' (S37.16). Finally they were converted.

But were they? Augustine thought of the early days of the church, recorded in Acts 2, when people were 'thoroughly and perfectly' converted (S77.4). Even in his day, he knew some people who sought to follow Christ, to pray for their enemies, and to distribute their goods to the needy. To their behaviour – which is what Justin and Cyprian had viewed as the product of conversion – the response of many baptized people was incredulous: 'Why are you acting crazy? You're going to extremes; aren't other people Christians?' (S88.12–13). Augustine knew that the ritual shock of the Easter vigil didn't work for everyone: there were many people who 'even after baptism ... want to do the same things as they used to do before' (S14.4).[114] The unrepentant – the hairy, the lame, the lukewarm – continued as members of the visible church; but even the converted – the smooth, strong and earnest – would struggle; they were still convalescing, like the mugged man whom the Good Samaritan had helped, in the inn of the church (SS4.14; 5.8; 88.12–13). The church was thus capacious and healing, but it was not a place to challenge the values of society. Rich and poor would coexist within it, not attempting to alter the social balances, for from a spiritual vantage point wealth was as great a burden as poverty (S164.9). Almsgiving, on the other hand, which alleviated poverty but didn't seek to alter society, was beneficial to the Christian; it was helpful in getting one's prayers heard and in 'getting God to help you change your manner of life for the better' (S29.6).

Caesarius: preaching post-baptismal conversion

From Augustine's North Africa we move northwards to Gaul, where for forty years Caesarius was Bishop of Arles (502–42). Born into a wealthy Gallo-Roman family, Caesarius wanted to renew the church in Gaul in keeping with the traditions of Mediterranean Christianity from which he thought it had deviated.[115] In

[114] G. P. Jeanes, 'How Successful was Baptism in the Fourth Century AD?' *Studia Patristica* 20 (1989), 380.

[115] Robert A. Markus, 'From Caesarius to Boniface: Christianity and Paganism in Gaul', in Jacques Fontaine and J. N. Hillgarth, eds, *The Seventh Century: Change and Continuity* (London: Warburg Institute, 1992), 154.

his almost 250 sermons, which articulated his pastoral concerns, Caesarius paid tribute to Augustine not least by borrowing heavily from his sermons. Like Augustine Caesarius was concerned to promote 'conversion to a better life'; but there are intriguing differences – not least because Caesarius was responding to conditions almost a century later than his illustrious predecessor.

Caesarius's sermons convey the impression that it was normal – at least in the towns of Gaul – to be Christian. There are reports of 'many miracles' in the ministry of Caesarius; and these demonstrations of divine power served to establish Christianity's credibility in the eyes of local people.[116] But Caesarius appealed to human power as well, to landlords who could dissuade their peasants from worshipping at field shrines: 'Chastize those whom you know to be [guilty]; ... beat them if you have the power; if they are not improved by this, cut off their hair too. And if they still persevere, bind them in iron shackles, so that those whom the grace of Christ does not hold, a chain may hold' (S53.2).[117]

Despite these pressures, there were still unbaptized people in Arles. Some of these were pagans and Jews; a few were 'heretics'. Caesarius encouraged his hearers to pay careful attention to his sermons so they could explain the mysteries of Christianity to the outsiders. He also warned them to guard their behaviour, so they would not discourage a non-Catholic from 'being converted to God'. Who knows? God might desire that the pagan 'will deserve to hold the first place among the saints' (S180.1).[118] But with another category of the unbaptized – the 'Christians', probably long-term catechumens, who deferred baptism until old age – Caesarius was impatient. Warning them of the many ways in which they could be 'snatched out of life' unexpectedly, he pressed them to present themselves for baptism (SS70.2; 129.5; 200.4–5).

In early sixth-century Arles the traditional rites of initiation were still operating, but with changes. Candidates for baptism were to submit their names, but only 'ten days or at least a week'

[116] *Vita Caesarii*, 1.48; William E. Klingshirn, *Caesarius of Arles: The Making of a Christian Community in Late Antique Gaul* (Cambridge: Cambridge University Press, 1994), 166.

[117] For Caesarius's Sermons, see the translation of Wilfrid Parsons (1953).

[118] Caesarius's interest seems to have been less in converting the pagans or Jews than in differentiating the Christians from them (SS96, 104, 107, 163); see Klingshirn, *Caesarius*, 179.

before Easter; the *competentes* were thus still a part of church life, but the time of their catechizing had been whittled down dramatically – from the *Apostolic Tradition*'s three years to the Lenten period in Augustine's Africa to ten days in Caesarius's Gaul (SS225.6; 200.2). Caesarius urged the *competentes* during these few days to examine their consciences; if they had committed serious sins, or if they continued to cherish poisonous attitudes, they were to ask God's mercy. But there does not appear to have been special catechesis during this period; the catechetical work in Arles was done by Caesarius in his Sunday sermons (S200.3–5).[119] The abbreviation of these initiatory rites resulted from the arrival of a new group which outnumbered the traditional category of initiates: the children, often very young, whose names would be given in at the same time as the adults, made their approach. In baptism there would thus be 'infants, whether they are old men or young' (S129.5). For both the very young and adults, the rites of exorcism and baptism would be appropriate; but it was hard to catechize the young, and it was apparently thought to be unnecessary or impracticable to catechize the adult *competentes*. So the initiatory rites of previous centuries were still intact, and Caesarius presented baptism with utmost seriousness – a renuncia-tion of 'the Devil's pomps', rebirth in Christ, and significantly a 'pact with the Lord'; but baptism as most people experienced it could not have seemed 'awe-inspiring'. Nor could it have had its erstwhile moral weight. Caesarius made it clear whose job it was to instruct the newly baptized – the sponsors. They were themselves to remember the Creed and the Lord's Prayer and to teach them to their godchildren. 'I do not know with what boldness a man says he is a Christian,' Caesarius expostulated, 'if he refuses to learn a few lines of the Creed and the Lord's Prayer' (S13.2). In another sermon, Caesarius urged the sponsors to admonish and rebuke the 'sons of the sacred fount' so that they should manifest Christian behaviour: 'cling to justice, guard chastity, preserve virginity until marriage ... avoid magicians, eagerly and often attend church services, condemn verbosity, recall the discordant to harmony' (S204.3). But Caesarius could also appeal to those

[119] Henry G. J. Beck, *The Pastoral Care of Souls in South-East France during the Sixth Century*, Analecta Gregoriana 51 (Rome: Pontifical Gregorian University, 1950), 174.

who had been baptized as infants. Recalling the 'pact' which they had made with the Lord through their sponsors, Caesarius urged them to live in active renunciation of the devil and fidelity to Christ (S12.3).[120]

Despite godparental admonitions and his own catechetical sermons, the behaviour of the Christians of Arles troubled Caesarius. Their lifestyles continued to be unchanged. They had received the sacrament of baptism but they had not improved their behaviour. Some of them were even playing 'the mad game of draughts which is opposed to the soul' (S116.2–3). In church services they at times misbehaved scandalously. Some came to the services only to bolt the building immediately after the gospel reading (and before the sermon and Mass); in order to forestall this, Caesarius 'often' locked the people in so that they might 'rejoice . . . at their chastizement and spiritual progress'.[121] This didn't mean that the people, among whom were 'usually a goodly number of clerics', would behave or listen; to Caesarius's consternation they spent the time 'in calumnies or in idle chatter' (S74.3). But worse than the people's behaviour in and out of church was their predilection for paganism. They not only refused to destroy countryside shrines; they attacked those who did attempt to demolish them (S53.1). When they pointed out that the tried-and-

---

[120] Cf. the later sixth-century sermon of Martin of Braga, *De correctione rusticorum*, 15–16 (trans. J. N. Hillgarth, *Christianity and Paganism, 350–750: The Conversion of Western Europe* [Philadelphia: University of Pennsylvania Press, 1969], 62–4):

. . . [C]onsider the nature of the pact which you made with God in this baptism. For as each of you gave your name at the font, for example, Peter or John or any name, you were then questioned by the priest: 'What is your name?' You replied, if you were old enough, or at least the one who made the profession of faith for you and who lifted you up from the font, and said, for example: 'His name is John'. And the priest asked: 'John, do you renounce the devil and his messengers, his worship and idols, his theft and fraud, his fornication and drunkenness, and all his evil works?' And you replied: 'I do renounce them'. After this renunciation of the devil, you were again asked by the priest: 'Do you believe in God the Father Almighty?' You replied: 'I do believe'. . . . Lo, such is the guarantee and confession of yours that God holds against you! How is it possible that some of you who have renounced the devil . . . turn again to worship the devil? To light candles besides rocks and besides trees and beside fountains and at crossroads, what is this but worship of the devil? Lo, you . . . have broken the pact which you made with God.
[121] *Vita Caesarii*, 1.27.

true folk customs seemed to work, and that magicians could heal snakebite and that 'impious remedies' were therapeutically effective, Caesarius was unimpressed; these customary rites and remedies were literally soul-destroying. When they engaged in such pagan practices, people 'immediately lose the sacrament of baptism ... [and] repent of their conversion to God' (S54.1).

The remedy which Caesarius never tired of advocating for misbehaviour and recidivism was conversion. Conversion, as Caesarius presented it to his people, was in many ways similar to the conversion that Augustine had urged a century earlier in Hippo. It involved renouncing the world, emptying one's self, and being filled by God (S173.3). Further, it involved a serious commitment to transform one's behaviour. In Arles, as in Hippo, despite their preachers' expostulations, people persisted in deferring conversion, year after year. In both cities, the preachers responded by thundering the same text (Ecclus. 5:7) at their flocks. They pleaded with them not to delay their conversion, for 'suddenly the Lord's wrath will come upon you'.[122] But there was one striking difference between Augustine and Caesarius; whereas Augustine had appealed to as yet unbaptized catechumens to be converted, Caesarius urged conversion upon baptized Christians, even upon clerics.[123] Conversion was an appropriate message for erring people of all sorts and conditions: 'both men and women, religious and lay, young and old, boys and girls' (S64.4). Of course, the term *conversio* was now coming to have a special meaning for monks and nuns; in his monastic writings, Caesarius used it to refer to an entry into religious life.[124] So Caesarius could not have been surprised when a denizen of Arles protested, 'I am young and married; how can I cut my hair or assume the religious habit?' The point, Caesarius retorted, was not the person's habit but his habits, which were evil. A person must die to sin, change his behaviour, do good and noble works, give alms and thereby experience a 'true conversion'. Clothes alone wouldn't do the trick;

[122] Caesarius, *Sermons*, 18; 56.3; 60.4; 61.4; 66.3; 79.6; 180.5; 184.7; 209.1.

[123] Caesarius, in a rush to construct a sermon to appeal for the conversion of the already baptized, could draw heavily from a sermon which Augustine had given to secure the conversion of the not yet baptized. Cf. Caesarius, *Sermons*, 18 with Augustine, *Sermon* 82.

[124] Caesarius, *Statuta sanctarum virginum*, 4, 58; *Regula*, 1.

a cleric without good works was as much under God's judgement as an unrepentant layman (S56.3).

To all who would listen, Caesarius presented an exalted vision of the converted life. Of course Christians should be reverent and attentive in church; to be sure they should avoid participating in anything tainted with paganism; naturally all believers were to memorize the Lord's Prayer and Creed. But Caesarius's primary concern was that Christians should 'observe the precepts of Christ' (S209.3). To be sure, a genuine conversion was effected by almsgiving and prayers, 'but most of all by wholehearted love of our enemies' (S61.4). It is clear that Caesarius's hearers in the rough-and-ready society of sixth-century Gaul found this hard to comprehend. 'He could do it, but I cannot', his hearers told him; 'I am a man, He is God'. And Christ gave orders that were too harsh and impossible to do (S35.2). Caesarius was unmoved. Christ's teachings were difficult, he conceded, but God enabled Christians to obey them. And in urging his disciples to love their enemies, Christ 'did not give us a counsel but a command'; for Caesarius enemy-love was a 'precept', not a counsel like observing virginity, refraining from wine and meat, and selling one's goods and giving to the poor (S37.4). The results of obedience to this precept were manifest: it built peace in the church, was an antidote to war and hatred, and differentiated Christians from 'the pagans and the animals' (SS160b; 37.5). Indeed, loving the enemy was an instrument of conversion; there was 'no medicine so salutary and efficacious for the wounds of all sin' as this (S37.1).

Constructing a community religion: syncretism

In this, as in many ways, Caesarius advocated a vision that was too ambitious to be realized in sixth-century Gaul. The vision of radical conversion to the way of Jesus, including enemy-loving, was difficult to achieve in Justin's Rome, despite the careful catechizing of voluntary inquirers in a setting of relative intimacy. It was no doubt even more difficult in Cyprian's Carthage, with larger-scale and no doubt more impersonal catechesis. But in Caesarius's Arles it was far beyond the reach of most believers. The church had grown vastly stronger numerically and institutionally than in the days of Justin or Cyprian. But it had grown too fast for the measured rhythms of conversion to take place;

resocialization and rehabituation, through imitation and catechesis as well as rite, took time. Of course, the 'awe-inspiring rites', although somewhat attenuated, were still structurally intact; but when everybody experienced them, generally as infants, they inspired more ennui than awe. Furthermore, the church had grown by means – the carrot and the stick, to say nothing of 'binding people in iron shackles' – that were not conducive to a radical conversion of life. So Caesarius's people were right. They – especially those locked in the church while Caesarius hectored them – could not follow the precepts of Christ, which were beyond them.

They probably did not want to. They were more concerned to negotiate their own accommodation with traditional Gallic behaviour patterns, and with traditional Gallic beliefs. Bishops would come and go, but the local ways of coping with the dangers and mysteries of life would be durable. When seventh-century missionary Bishop Eligius preached in a primarily pagan village near Noyon, denouncing 'diabolical games' and 'other superstitions', the local leaders interrupted him:

> Roman that you are, although you are always bothering us, you will never uproot our customs, but we will go on with our rites as we always have done, and we will go on doing so always and forever. There will never exist the man who will be able to stop us holding our time-honoured and most dear games.[125]

These pagans would nevertheless be Christians. As William Klingshirn has pointed out, the people's choice was not whether they would be Christians; it was rather what sort of Christians they would be. And their answer was a 'community religion they designed for themselves'.[126]

This, of course, raises questions about inculturation. Recent students of missiology have recognized that the Christian message must be inserted into a cultural framework, and that this inevitably entails the 'interior assimilation of cultural elements'. If the assimilation is done thoughtlessly or too quickly, the result is

---

[125] Cited by Paul Fouracre, 'The Work of Audoenus of Rouen and Eligius of Noyon in Extending Episcopal Influence from the Town to the Country in Seventh-Century Neustria', in Derek Baker, ed., *The Church in Town and Countryside*, Studies in Church History 16 (Oxford: Blackwell, 1979), 82.

[126] Klingshirn, *Caesarius*, 243.

'syncretism' – a bad thing; if it is done properly, the result is 'a truly critical symbiosis' – a good thing.[127] For the latter to happen, there needs to be a 'second stage' which Hans-Dietrich Kahl has called *innerkirchliche Nacharbeit* (intra-ecclesial follow-up work) of catechism and life formation.[128] In the Europe of the sixth to the eighth centuries this second stage never materialized. In Merovingian Gaul there was virtually no catechesis; the councils of the period were tediously interested in church property and episcopal rights, but they showed no interest in encouraging the priests to teach the people.[129] Nor is there record of a 'formal, ecclesiastical post-baptismal catechesis for children'.[130] In Carolingian times, to be sure, some churchmen who were interested in instructing converts produced some new catechetical writings; but by earlier Christian standards these were rudimentary. They were largely based upon the *narratio* in Augustine's *De Catechizandis Rudibus*.[131] But Augustine had not designed this to be a catechism, but to be a first taster in Christianity for people who might someday enrol for serious baptismal preparation. And most early-medieval Christians never encountered materials as developed as these. Most church leaders were content if the people learned the Lord's Prayer and the Creed.[132] The result was inevitable. In the absence of systematic and committed

[127] Anscar J. Chupungco, *Liturgies of the Future* (New York: Paulist Press, 1989), 29; Aylward Shorter, *Toward a Theology of Inculturation* (London: Geoffrey Chapman, 1988), 11–12.

[128] Ary Roest Collins, 'What Is So New About Inculturation?' in idem, *Inculturation: Working Papers on Living Faith and Cultures* 5 (Rome: Pontifical Gregorian University, 1984), 13, cited by Russell, *Germanization*, 101n.; Hans-Dietrich Kahl, 'Die ersten Jahrhunderte des missiongeschichtlichen Mittelalters', in Knut Schäferdiek, ed., *Kirchengeschichte als Missionsgeschichte*, IIa, *Die Kirche des früheren Mittelalters* (Munich: Chr. Kaiser, 1978), 49.

[129] C. E. Stancliffe, 'From Town to Country: The Christianisation of the Touraine, 370–600', in Baker, *The Church in Town and Countryside*, 59.

[130] M. E. Jegen, 'Catechesis II (Medieval and Modern)', in *New Catholic Encyclopedia* 3 (New York: McGraw-Hill, 1967), 209.

[131] Jean-Pierre Belche, 'Die Bekehrung zum Christentum nach Augustins Büchlein de Catechizandis Rudibus', *Augustiniana* 27 (1977), 26–64; A. Etchegaray Cruz, 'Le rôle du *De Catechizandis rudibus* du Saint Augustin dans la catéchèse missionaire dès 710 jusqu'à 847', *Studia Patristica* 11 (1972), 316–21; Ursmar Engelmann, *Der heilige Pirmin und sein Missionsbüchlein* (Konstanz: Jan Thorbecke Verlag, 1959); Alcuin, *Epp.*, 107, 110.

[132] Jegen, 'Catechesis II', 209.

teaching, the host cultures exercised a tremendous power over the Christianity of the West.

Clermont: religious uniformity through persecution

Two points remain to be noted. First, the leaders of the Christianized West were not content for their culture to be orthodoxly Christian in prevailing belief and 'noise' – late antiquity's equivalent of the control of the television station.[133] They also wanted absolute uniformity; all the people of the West must adhere to the dominant faith. Edicts such as Justinian's of 529 loomed in the background, but the actual repression of non-Christian religions was exercised by bishops collaborating with local élites.[134] This led to a wide disparity in practice from one area to another. In general it seems that churchmen and regional lords were less worried by paganism (they could reach a certain accommodation with that) than by the impenetrable integrity of the faith and communities of Judaism. A cluster of events in Gaul in 576 will crystallize the issues for us and show the direction in which things were going.

Clermont, a city in the Auvergne, had for centuries had a large number of Jewish residents.[135] And every year on Good Friday its bishop, Avitus, had prayed for their conversion. On Good Friday 576 his prayers were answered: a Jewish man asked to be baptized on Easter. Did he receive a crash catechetical course on Holy Saturday? We do not know. What we do know is that at Easter, while processing through the streets with the other white-robed baptizands, the convert received unction from on high: a Jew who was unamused by his conversion poured rancid oil on his head. The Christians of Clermont were infuriated, and wanted to stone the pourer. With difficulty Bishop Avitus restrained them.

---

[133] For the useful concept of 'noise' see MacMullen, *Christianizing*, 84.

[134] Klingshirn, *Caesarius*, 238.

[135] My account is based on Gregory of Tours, *History of the Franks,* 5.11, with elaborations based on Venantius Fortunatus, *Carmen*, 5.5. For comment, see Marc Reydellet, 'La conversion des Juifs de Clermont en 576', in Holtz and Fredouille, *De Tertullien aux Mozarabes*, I, 371–9; Bernhard Blumenkranz, *Juifs et Chrétiens dans le monde occidental, 430–1096* (Paris: Mouton, 1960), 140–1; Walter Goffart, 'The Conversions of Avitus of Clermont, and Similar Passages in Gregory of Tours', in J. Neusner and E. S. Frerichs, eds, *'To See Ourselves as Others See Us': Christians, Jews, 'Others' in Late Antiquity* (Chico: Scholars Press, 1985), 473–97.

For over five weeks anti-Jewish hostility smouldered. Finally, on Ascension Day it burst into flame, and the crowd got the action they wanted. While taking part in an episcopally-led procession, they broke loose, rushed to the synagogue and razed it to the ground. Avitus could have responded to this by censuring his violent flock. Instead, he sent a threatening message to the Jews. 'I do not use force nor do I compel you to confess the Son of God. I merely preach to you ... If you are prepared to believe what I believe, then become one flock, with me as your shepherd. If not, then leave this place.' The Jewish leaders huddled in a house, besieged by an armed mob of Christians. After three days of anguished argument, Jewish spokesmen emerged to give a majority report. Confessing their belief that 'Jesus Christ is the Son of the living God' who was promised by the prophets, they applied for baptism. A mass baptism duly happened with great solemnity a week later on Pentecost, and Clermont's Christians welcomed more than 500 white-robed new members into their community. There was, of course, also the minority of Jews who, faced by a choice between their faith and Clermont, chose to be true to Judaism; these, with what pain we can imagine, made their way south to the still-hospitable city of Marseilles. Clermont, however, was as full of joy – so says Gregory of Tours – as 'Jerusalem when the Holy Spirit descended on the Apostles'. The intolerable anomaly – 'The people of Clermont ... was not one in trust (*fides*) though the city remained one' – had been overcome. What Avitus had desired had come to pass; in Clermont – as in Western Christendom generally – there was a unity between belief and belonging.[136]

Conversion when everyone is a Christian

Second, even in Christendom, even in a society in which there was no room for dissenters, conversion continued to be important in the religious vocabulary and experience of the people; but

---

[136] Venantius Fortunatus, *Carmen*, 5.5.17. This is not the place to give the history of enforced conversion, whether of the Jews, who as members of a trans-local family were often given the option of moving on, or of the *pagani* – the people of the place – who had nowhere else to go. For an account of the mass and individual conversions of Jews to Christianity, see Amnon Linder, 'Christlich-Jüdische Konfrontation im kirchlichen Frühmittelalter', in Schäferdiek, *Kirchengeschichte als Missionsgeschichte*, IIa, 414–39.

its meaning had changed. Where everyone was a Christian, conversion no longer had its earlier sense of a change in belief, for the Christian civilization's theology was, at least ostensibly, uniformly orthodox. Nor did conversion have its prior meaning of a change in belonging, for the Christian civilization's populace had all (except in those places where a Jewish minority was tolerated) been baptized into the church as infants.[137]

Nevertheless, conversion continued to be a reality in the Christian civilization of the West. As we have seen in Caesarius, *conversio* was a useful word to describe an inner repentance, most likely many years after baptism, which led to a change of behaviour (good works, the giving of alms) and which secured God's forgiveness. The sixth-century Gallic councils, so uninterested in catechesis, were perhaps for that reason greatly interested in conversion. The fourth Council of Arles (524), for example, ordered that no one was to be ordained to the priesthood or diaconate without having demonstrated the fruits of *conversio* for an entire year (*c.*2). The fifth Council of Orleans (549) made a similar stipulation for a bishop; no one was to be elevated to the episcopacy 'without there having preceded a year of *conversio*, so that during that year he may be instructed more fully, by learned and tried men, in the discipline and spiritual rules' (*c.*9). At least the bishops were to be catechized! But the documents also pointed forward to a use of *conversio* that by Carolingian times had come to be dominant and that had a fascinating twist. For it entailed, in a civilization in which everyone was Christian, a change involving belonging as well as behaviour: the entrance into the religious life.[138] Monastic profession entailed a new identity and a new

---

[137] The baptism of infants can be documented at least from the mid-second century, and in some Christian communities it was reasonably widely practised. But for centuries it remained extraordinary, much less widely practised than adult baptism. In the West, the baptism of adults became more rare in the course of the sixth century and disappeared altogether by the time of Gregory II (715–30). See David F. Wright, 'The Origins of Infant Baptism – Child Believers' Baptism?' *Scottish Journal of Theology* 40 (1987), 1–23; Beck, *Pastoral Care of Souls in South-East France*, 164; Thomas M. Finn, *Early Christian Baptism and the Catechumenate: Italy, North Africa and Egypt*, Message of the Fathers of the Church, 6 (Collegeville: Liturgical Press, 1992), 91–2.

[138] Second Council of Tours (567), *c.*16. Christine Mohrmann, *Études sur le latin des Chrétiens*, II, *Latin Chrétien et médiéval* (Rome: Edizioni di Storia et letteratura, 1961), 341–4.

primary community; marked as it was by vows and an impressive ritual, it was often described as a second baptism.[139] In this sense, there continued in the West to be an inner drive, on the part of many Christians, to experience something that they called conversion. As John Van Engen has commented, '[M]edieval folk themselves recognized real distance between the mass of baptized Christians and the "converted", between the "simple faithful" and the "religious", between those whose souls had and had not been "won".'[140]

Conclusion

From Justin whose conversion led to martyrdom to the monks whose conversions were their martyrdoms, we have travelled far. In our journey we have watched and listened as people have experienced and advocated conversion in its various forms. Our destination has been 'Christendom', the Christian civilization which for a millennium was regnant in the West. Christendom is controversial. About it, scholars, both historians and theologians, have strong and differing views. A Roman Catholic historian has recently asserted that Christendom was a culture which Christianity transformed into a 'radically Christian' civilization; another Roman Catholic scholar, by contrast, has seen medieval Christendom in the West as a Germanic culture which transformed Christianity into a 'worldly, heroic, magico-religious, folk-centred' faith.[141] The debate will go on. As it does, perhaps scholars will begin to reflect more deeply on the salient characteristics of Christendom.[142] One of these will no doubt have to do with belief – the dominance of Christian theology and ideology. Another will have to do with belonging – an equivalence of civil and religious populations. Yet another will have to do with behaviour – a general sense of the behaviour that is acceptable, and unacceptable, for both ordinary

[139] Edward E. Malone, 'Martyrdom and Monastic Profession as a Second Baptism', in A. Mayr, J. Quasten and B. Neunheuser, eds, *Vom Christlichen Mysterium: Gesammelte Arbeiten Zum Gedächtnis von Odo Casel OSB* (Dusseldorf: Patmos Verlag, 1951), 128–9.

[140] John Van Engen, 'The Christian Middle Ages as an Historiographical Problem', *American Historical Review* 91 (1986), 547.

[141] Markus, 'Caesarius to Boniface', 168; Russell, *Germanization*, 189.

[142] See Kreider, *Change of Conversion*, ch. 8.

and 'perfect' Christians. Inevitably Christendom will be associated with power – a symbiosis of religious and state authorities, and the ultimate sanction of force. But whatever the characteristics of Christendom turn out to be, I believe that they will – at least in part – be a product of the patterns of conversion which brought Christendom to birth.

Chapter 2

Christianization and Conversion in Northern Italy

RITA LIZZI TESTA

Christianity probably began to emerge in northern Italy in the third century. There is little surviving evidence of missionaries; the evidence largely reflects the development of episcopal centres, which were based in commercially and strategically important cities. In the fourth century, Christianity spread at first hesitantly and unevenly. The period of Constantius I to Valentinian I in mid-century was a turning point; and the final two decades marked the triumph of Christianization in the cities, although the peasants, whose lords were exhorted to impose Christianity upon them, remained superficially Christianized. The move of the imperial court to Milan assisted in the Christianization process. More important still was the role of bishops, whose role was transformed in the fourth century. No longer mere leaders of substantial urban minorities (Zeno of Verona), they had become heads of Christian cities whose religious and civic populaces were identical (Maximus of Turin). A dominant figure in the Christianization of northern Italy was Ambrose of Milan, unbendingly anti-Arian, organizationally skilful, and sensitive in fostering a new generation of episcopal talent. The bishops' sermons changed throughout the fourth century from urging the faithful not to be avaricious like the pagans, to urging the Christian upper classes to be charitable without threatening their fundamental values.

I. THE SPREAD OF CHRISTIANITY IN NORTHERN ITALY: A LATE PROCESS

Although as the fifth century progresses the sources for the history of the Italian peninsula become increasingly scarce, available data allows us to assume that from the early decades of the century the integration between civic body and Christian community was already complete in almost the whole of the northern part of the peninsula. It is possible, in this period, to identify the tangible effects of a civilization in which Christianity had become the dominant religion. The most obvious indication is in the central position occupied by the bishop within the city. As the recognized head of the whole community, and not merely of a group made up in various ways of Christians, the bishop exercised an effective power of control over the citizens. Since he knew as much about the private lives of the faithful as about their public image, he, better than any magistrate, could intervene to direct their civic choices and their moral behaviour.

The example of Turin, for which we have the sermons of Maximus, bishop of the city from 398 until around 420, is sufficient evidence from which to generalize about the whole region which we are studying.[1] In times of civic breakdown, when the disintegration of society must have reached very high levels under the pressure of resisting frequent barbarian incursions, Maximus developed to the full the vocation implicit in his role as bishop in order to make himself 'leader' of the community, able to inspire Christians to fulfil their religious duties and especially their civic responsibilities. Strict laws accompanied the consolidation of Christianity, and the nature of the episcopal office took on legally significant overtones. In a comparison with bees, priests *aculeum legis exercent*, with great ambiguity about the double moral and juridical value of the term.[2] Maximus also expressed the specific

---

[1] Maximus was certainly Bishop of Turin at the time when a Synod of bishops of northern Italy and Gaul was organized: see *Sermones*, 21 and 71 (*CCSL*, 23, ed. Almut Mutzenbecher, Turnhout: Brepols, 1962). The date of this Council has been the subject of long controversy (for which see Rita Lizzi, *Vescovi e strutture ecclesiastiche nella città tardoantica: L'Italia Annonaria nel IV–V secolo d.C.* (Como: Edizioni New Press, 1989), pp. 209–10, n. 195 with bibliography), but September 398 now seems the most likely date. The determination of the length of time Maximus was bishop is based on Gennadius of Marseilles (*Vir. ill.*, 41), who places his death 'in the reign of Onorius and Theodosius II' (408–23). From internal evidence gleaned from Maximus's sermons, however, it appears that he was still alive after 412 (the year of the eclipse of the moon of which he speaks in *Sermones*, 30–1).

[2] Maximus of Turin, *Sermones*, 92.52–4; 93.32–5 and 94.1–43, where he explains the use of the metaphor; 89.7–10 for the comparison with bees.

role of the priest by comparing it to the *speculator* of Israel. Like a sentry, the priest was the person responsible for the salvation of his city. In fact, since the physical protection of the city walls depended to a large extent on the moral strength of its inhabitants, the bishop exercised a kind of *tuitio populorum*, able to guarantee the removal of *supervenentia mala*.[3] This double function, which the bishop felt obliged to carry out in order to protect both ethical and legislative norms, is reflected in a kind of semantic slippage, evident in a number of terms present in Maximus's sermons. In the words he used, *iustitia* coincided with the religious observance of fasting and prayer, while *pietas* was identified with love for a *dulcis mater*, which is not the church as in Chromatius, but one's fatherland.[4]

It is clear that the fifth-century bishop, while retaining his position as a figure primarily outside the formal institutions of the State, was in fact endowed with certain real public functions, so that, in times when the State was at its weakest, he was ready to take over the role of the city's functionaries and magistrates, while at the same time keeping alive in the *civitas* the ideological continuation of the Roman idea.

In northern Italy, in the area north of the Arno and the Esino which corresponds to the administrative district of the imperial vicariate, these were some of the immediate results of an impressive process of penetration, legitimization and growth of city-based Christianity, which appears to have been achieved in the space of a century and a half. In fact, the chronological limits within which our sources allow us to operate run from the middle of the third century to the beginning of the fifth. They begin with the earliest indications of nuclei of Christians appearing in various cities with their bishops already in place and end with the late evidence of the

[3] Maximus, *Sermo*, 92 *extr*. For its authenticity, see Mutzenbecher, 'Bestimmung der echten Sermones des Maximus Taurinensis', *Sacris Erudiri* 12 (1961), 264.

[4] Maximus of Turin, *Sermones*, 82.25–7; 27–31; 29–50; Chromatius of Aquileia, *Sermones*, 33.5 (*SCh.*, 164, ed. Joseph Lemarié, Paris: Cerf, 1971), 178; cf. Lellia Cracco Ruggini, 'Per la storia di una città "periferica"', *Studia et Documenta Historiae et Iuris* 60 (1994) (Rome: Apollinaris, 1996), 32, n. 43. The image of city as mother, unknown amongst ecclesiastical writers, can be found in other contemporary authors: cf. Claudianus, *Cons. Stil.*, 3.175; Rutilius Claudius Namatianus, *De Reditu suo*, 2.60.

sermons of Maximus of Turin, all of which demonstrate a real evolution in understanding accompanying the conversion of the area to Christianity and its effects.

The early stages of conversion

There is very little to say about the origins of Christianity in this area, given the infrequent and uncertain evidence which we have. Late local traditions attribute to the bishoprics of various cities an apostolic foundation, but these are substantially without credibility.[5] The oldest epigraphic and archaeological documentation dates from the era of Constantine and relates to the northeastern area, which evidence indicates was the first centre of the expansion of Christianity as it followed the principal routes of land and river traffic. This view is supported by the surviving evidence of those who were delegates to the Councils of Arles (314) and Serdica (c.343). Around the middle of the third century, it seems that the community of Aquileia was already well organized under Hermagoras, while Theodorus (responsible between 308–19 for the construction of a double hall basilica, paved with stupendous mosaics which have partially survived) was the fourth or fifth bishop of the city and in that capacity was a delegate to the Council of Arles.[6] Apollinaris, the first Bishop of Ravenna, can reasonably

---

[5] Cracco Ruggini, 'Storia totale di una piccola città: Vicenza romana', in *Storia di Vicenza, I, Il territorio – La preistoria – L'età romana* (Vicenza: Neri Pozza Editore, 1987) 283–4; eadem, 'La cristianizzazione nelle città dell'Italia settentrionale (IV–VI secolo)', in Werner Eck and Hartmut Galsterer, eds, *Die Stadt in Oberitalien und in den nordwestlichen Provinzen des Römischen Reiches*, Kölner Forschungen 4 (Mainz: Verlag Philipp von Zabern, 1991), 235–49, particularly 236, nn. 3–4.

[6] On the claimed ordination of the local notable Hermagoras by the Apostle Peter in Rome, see Francesco Lanzoni, *Le diocesi d'Italia dalle origini al principio del secolo VII (an. 604)* (Faenza: Studi e Testi 35, 1927) 2, 876ff.; Sergio Tavano, *Aquileia cristiana* (Udine: Antichità Alto Adriatiche 3, 1972), 12–13 [henceforth *AAAD*]; Silvio Tramontin, 'Origini cristiane', in *Storia della cultura veneta dalle origini al Trecento* (Vicenza: Neri Pozza Editore, 1976) I, 102–23. On the attribution to Bishop Theodorus (whom an inscription credits with building the south hall) of the whole complex (two parallel halls for worship joined by a transverse hall), see Giovanni Brusin-Paolo Lino Zovatto, *Monumenti paleocristiani di Aquileia e Grado* (Udine: Deputazione di Storia patria per il Friuli, 1957), 18, 65. On the architectural and historical function of this type of double basilica, which marks the limit of the historical development of the *domus*

be placed in the same period, if it is true that one of the signatories at the Council of Serdica, Severus, was the twelfth bishop of that church.[7] Equally, the Lucillus who was a signatory to the same synod was sixth in the list of bishops of Verona, allowing us to deduce that in that city too the Christian group must have been organized around its first bishop, Euprepius, towards the middle of the third century.[8] Slightly later, that is from early in the reign of Constantine, are the claims for the foundation of the churches in Brescia and Padua (Clatheus was bishop of the former, Prosdocimus of the second), whose tradition of Christian worship has its roots between the fifth and sixth centuries.[9]

---

ecclesiae, preceding the diffusion of the Constantine basilica, see Guglielmo De Angelis D'Ossat, 'I due poli dell'architettura paleocristiana nell'Alto Adriatico: Aquileia e Ravenna', *AAAd* 13 (1978), 329–97; Mario Mirabella Roberti, 'Architettura tardoantica fra Aquileia e l'Occidente', *AAAd* 19 (1981), 213–24; Pasquale Testini, 'Basilica, *Domus Ecclesiae* e Aule Teodoriane di Aquileia', *AAAd* 22 (1982), 369–98.

[7] Lanzoni, *Le diocesi*, 2, 737ff. On the place and date of the Council of Serdica (Autumn 343?) see Leslie W. Barnard, 'The Council of Serdica – two questions reconsidered', in *Ancient Bulgaria. Papers presented to the International Symposium on the Ancient History and Archaeology of Bulgaria, University of Nottingham 1981* (Nottingham: Dept. of Classical and Archaeological Studies, 1983) 2, 215–32. Peter Chrysologus, Bishop of Ravenna in the second quarter of the fifth century, has left a short homily on Apollinaris: *Sermones*, 128, *PL*, 52.552–5. In the seventh century, when the Byzantine Emperor Constans II granted Ravenna autocephaly in regard to Rome (666), the Church of Ravenna also began to boast of its apostolic origins, claiming its first bishop, Apollinaris, was an Antiochene, a disciple of Peter, consecrated by the Apostle. Cf. *Passio Apollinaris ep. Ravenn (Bibliotheca Hagiographica Latina* 623); Lanzoni, *Le diocesi*, II, 749–53.

[8] Lanzoni, *Le diocesi*, 919; the oldest part of the Verona catalogue is without doubt genuine. According to the list, Zeno (for whom see later) is the eighth.

[9] For Brescia, the evidence of an acrostic hymn ascribed to Gaudentius (certainly pre-ninth century) is that Filastrius (who was certainly alive in the Ambrosian period) was the seventh bishop of the city. The fifth bishop of the city, Ursicinus, took part in the Council of Serdica. Although Maria Pia Billanovich ('San Prosdocimo *metropolitanus multarum civitatum*: Acquisizioni e problemi delle ricerche storiche', *Arch. Veneto* 120 [1989], 133–47) argues that Prosdocimus was not the first bishop of Padua at the time of the persecutions, but was almost certainly a predecessor of Crispinus, signatory of Serdica and mentioned around 350 by Athanasius of Alexandria in connection with the support he had been promised during his exile in the West (in 345) by Lucillus of Verona, Crispinus of Padua and Fortunatianus of Aquileia: Athanasius, *Apologia ad Constantium*, 3,

In the central area of the Po valley, the Bishop of Milan (Miroclis) who participated in the Council of Arles was apparently the sixth bishop of that city, which would make the foundation of that see contemporaneous with those of Aquileia and Ravenna. However, information indicating that the first Bishop of Milan was a disciple of Peter or that the area was evangelized by Barnabas is certainly false. For Milan, too, the origin of a properly organized church, with its own bishop (Anathelon or Anatolius or Anatalon), is to be dated in the middle of the third century.[10]

There is as yet no support for the hypothesis that the northwest area received Christianity equally early from Gaul, where already in the second century there were active Christian communities in Lyons and Vienne and where in the third century episcopal sees appear to have multiplied along the Rhone from Lyons to Marseilles.[11] The earliest dated Christian inscription of the region in fact is from 362, discovered near Finale Ligure on the Tyrrhenian coast, while another which was found in the Po area of Liguria is from about forty years later. Definite information about the first bishops of a number of important bishoprics in the northwest area comes, as we shall see, from the second half of the fourth century.[12]

SCh., 56. 91; Lanzoni, Le diocesi, 2.911; Charles Pietri, 'Une aristocratie provinciale et la mission chrétienne: l'exemple de la Venetia', AAAd 22 (1982), 124 = in Christiana Respublica. Éléments d'une enquête sur le cristianisme antique (Rome: CÉFR 234, 1997), II, 901–49 [henceforth ChR].

[10] Cracco Ruggini, 'Nascita e morte di una capitale', in Studi in memoria di Santo Mazzarino, Quaderni Catanesi di cultura classica e medievale 2 (1990), 12.

[11] Franco Bolgiani, 'La penetrazione del cristianesimo in Piemonte', in V Congresso Nazionale di Archeologia Cristiana (Torino-Aosta, 22–23 settembre 1979) (Rome: Viella, 1982) 1, 37–61; Charles Pietri, 'Remarques sur la topographie chrétienne des cités de la Gaule entre Loire et Rhin (dès origines au VIIᵉ siècle)', Revue d'histoire de l'èglise de France 62 (1975), 189–204 = ChR, I, 447–62.

[12] Giovanni Mennella, 'La più antica testimonianza epigrafica sul cristianesimo in Liguria', Rivista Ingauna e Intemelia n.s. 36–7 (1981–2), 1–8; Giovanni Mennella-Giovanni Coccoluto, 'Liguria Reliqua Trans et Cis Appenninum', in Inscriptiones Christianae Italiae septimo saeculo antiquiores. Regio IX (Bari: Edipuglia, 1995), nos 34 and 4. The Revello stele, until recently dated to 341 and considered important proof of the relatively early penetration of Christianity into outlying areas of Piedmont, would appear to date from 489: Giovanella Cresci Marrone, 'Per la datazione dell'iscrizione paleocristiana di Revello', Rivista di archeologia cristiana 59 (1983), 313–20.

This picture of the first episcopal foundations does not in itself solve the problem of Christian origins in northern Italy. It reflects the process of the organization into a church of local groups of citizens and is not to be confused with the very different process of evangelization, for which, however, we have no direct evidence. On the basis of data relating to the placing and chronology of the first episcopal sees, we can assume that the spread of Christianity through the whole of this area began late, during the second century, and that the direction it followed was partly from the East and partly from Rome itself, which was the only centre in northern Italy of this period which had its own well-organized church. The analogy with what seems to have happened in the south of Italy confirms the hypothesis: it was only in the third century that Christianity began to show itself in a diffuse fashion in various parts of the peninsula, as the communities which already existed here and there began to organize themselves internally to take account of worship practice and the carrying out of the liturgical *officia*.[13] However, it does not necessarily follow that the Christian communities which appear to be the earliest to register the presence of a bishop are those where the new faith first spread. Some of those where Christianity had developed earliest could have continued to be headed by simple presbyterial colleges. Others of more recent Christianization could have been the first to accept the idea of having a single head. So this problem is linked to the problem of the emergence of the centrality of the bishop amongst ecclesiastical communities, a phenomenon which dates from a period in which it is difficult to establish what was going on and which in any case varies from area to area.[14]

[13] Giorgio Otranto, 'Dalla *civitas* alla diocesi nella Puglia tardoantica', *Invigilata Lucernis*, 11 (1989), 411–41; idem, *Italia Meridionale e Puglia paleocristiana* (Bari: Edipuglia, 1991), 3–95.

[14] It is well known that the hegemony of the bishop within the Christian community (i.e. the ascendancy of the so-called monarchical episcopate) can be identified fairly early in the second century. When Ignatius of Antioch (*c.*100–30) in his epistles first presented three distinct orders of clergy, a superior spiritual supremacy was already attributed to the bishop: in the analogy between heavenly and earthly hierarchies, the bishop was placed in a line of authority which proceeded from God and Christ, in so far as he was the unifying centre and supreme reference point of his own church (Ign., *Magn.* 4 and 6, 1; *Eph.* 3, 2; *Tr.* 3, 1: cf. William R. Schoedel, *Ignatius of Antioch: A Commentary on the Letters*

The consolidation of ecclesiastical institutions

In general, however, we can only really perceive the Christianization of the northern area, whether in the apparently earlier Christianized eastern parts or in the centre-west where conversion appears to have taken place more slowly, when we interpret the different aspects of evangelization through the more concrete evidence of the consolidation of ecclesiastical institutions. From the picture which we have of the principal dioceses known from the middle of the fourth century it is possible to understand the pattern followed by Christianity in the process of becoming a church. Various factors had influenced this process. Cities which were of greater political or economic importance or of strategic value as road junctions also grew in importance as Christian centres. There were also other factors – the presence of military units, frequent visits by the Emperor or his representatives on journeys – as well as more strictly religious considerations, such as the position adopted by the local Christian group in relation to doctrinal conflicts, once certain areas had begun to define themselves as Nicene or pro-Arian. All these factors had a strong influence on the institutional development of city churches, and between the third and fourth centuries they determined that a greater number of bishoprics would be concentrated in some areas rather than others. In fact, at the Council of Serdica the bishops indicated that it was criteria of a clearly non-religious nature which would determine the creation of new episcopal sees. The sixth decree of the Council, which ratified the practice which had hitherto been followed and to which it allowed no exceptions,

---

of Ignatius of Antioch (Philadelphia: Fortress Press, 1985), 22ff. Around the same time however, in the Pastoral Epistles (attributed to Paul, but dating from the period of Trajan), there does not yet seem to be any distinction between bishops and presbyters and, as in the most ancient Christian cells, the ministry appears to be genuinely collegiate: see 1 Timothy 3:1–7; 8–13; 5:17–19; Titus 1:5–14. The idea that these texts also presuppose the formation of the monarchical episcopate is now outdated: Wayne A. Meeks, *The First Urban Christians* (New Haven: Yale University Press, 1983), 111–39, esp. 134–46; idem, 'Il cristianesimo', in *Storia di Roma* II, 3 (Turin: Einaudi, 1992), 311. In fact, the episcopal role gains importance progressively through three centuries, following the stages of growth and expansion of Christianity through increasingly wider levels of urban existence.

forbade the foundation of bishoprics 'in every village or town of little importance so that the name and authority of the bishop are not brought into disrepute'.[15] This ban was confirmed at the end of the fourth century by the Council of Laodicea.[16]

For the church in the first half of the fourth century, it was clear that what would increase overall the expansion of the new creed would not be the uncontrolled multiplication of sees; it would rather be the planned ecclesiastical organization of groups which already existed in the more important towns. It is not surprising, therefore, to find that from the time of Constantius, when Christianity in northern Italy became a phenomenon which can be defined in terms of the stability of its episcopal sees, it was henceforth dominated by a few communities, each of which was well-organized around a saint bishop who was celebrated for his ability to establish the faith in his own city and its surrounding area. This phase, however, was followed by one which was very different. If we examine globally the period under consideration (from the middle of the fourth to about the middle of the fifth century), the process of Christianization is marked by a strong sense of a turning point, coinciding with the Valentinian dynasty (364–87). In fact, during those years northern Italy took on a new and exceptional strategic and military importance, starting from its eastern-central area. The city of Milan, which had already under Valentinian I become a stable point of reference, from which to face barbarian pressure on the Rhine and the Danube, in 381 welcomed Gratian and his court, which had permanently moved there from Trier.[17] At the same time, in 374 the see of

---

[15] Decree 6, in Carl Joseph Hefele-H. Leclercq, *Histoire des conciles d'après les documents originaux* (Paris: Letouzey et Ané, 1907 = Hildesheim, Georg Olm, 1973) I/2, 737ff.

[16] Decree 57, in Hefele-Leclercq, *Histoire des conciles* I/2, 989ff.

[17] On Valentinian I's choice of Milan, according to an acceptable interpretation of Ammianus 26.5.4 (*diviso palatio ut potiori placuerat, Valentinianus Mediolanum, Costantinopolim Valens discessit*), see Marta Sordi, 'Come Milano divenne capitale', *L'impero romano-cristiano. Problemi politici, religiosi, culturali* (Rome: Nuova Coletti Editore, 1991), 33–45. On the development of northern Italy, in relation to the transformation of Rome and Milan into two complementary centres of gravity for the political, economic, religious and cultural life of the period, see Lellia Ruggini, *Economia e società nell' 'Italia Annonaria': Rapporti fra agricoltura e commercio dal IV al VI secolo d.C.* (Milan: A. Giuffré Editore 1961 = Bari: Edipuglia, 1995); Cracco Ruggini, 'Nascita e morte di

Milan, which had hitherto been led by the Arian Auxentius, a Cappadocian who had never learnt Latin, now passed into the hands of Ambrose, *ex consularis Aemiliae et Liguriae*. Even if we cannot see the choice of the new prelate of Milan as the result of a detailed plan developed by Sextus Petronius Probus, it is clear that the two phenomena are very closely connected.[18] It would be impossible to comprehend how wide-ranging was the area in which Ambrose sought to be active (in spite of his exceptional personality), without also taking into account the central position which Milan occupied in the same period. The moment of greatest political importance of the city and of greatest expansion by the church in Milan coincided, while Christianity was increasingly stabilized in the whole of northern Italy and enjoyed a period of growth rapid enough to usher in a new phase of its history.

II. FROM CONSTANTIUS I THROUGH VALENTINIAN I: THE SIGNS OF STABILIZATION

The first *plebes*, the first bishop saints

Whatever the directions followed by evangelization, some centres in northern Italy with a more dynamic political administration show evidence, in the period between 340 and 360, of a clearly defined ecclesiastical organization and a strong and prestigious lay Christian presence. Sources for Aquileia in the north-east, Vercelli in the west, in the centre Milan and, at a slightly later stage, Verona and Brescia offer evidence of cities which pioneered in the process of establishing the new faith. In the first instance, the indications outlined by the Council of Serdica (although issued

---

una capitale', 5–51. The permanent transfer of the capital from Trier to Milan, already carried out by the time Gratian arrived in the spring of 381, is implicit in the continuity between coins minted in Trier and those minted in Milan: Michael F. Hendy, 'Aspects of Coin Production and Fiscal Administration in the Late Roman and Early Byzantine Period', *The Numismatic Chronicle* 7, 12 (1972), 127.

[18] The most recent and well-balanced reconstruction of the religious and political context within which this election took place is that of Neil B. McLynn, *Ambrose of Milan: Church and Court in a Christian Capital* (Berkeley: University of California Press, 1994), 44–52.

in relation to local contexts very different from those of northern Italy) seem to have been followed faithfully in the organization of these first dioceses. Almost all of the sees referred to were already in existence before the middle of the fourth century. The only new one, Vercelli, matched exactly the criteria of wealth and military and strategic importance laid down by the Council.[19] It is also likely that this particular method of church organization in the area was affected by the problem of recruiting personnel. We should not forget that when Constantius II conferred wide tax immunities on the senior clergy, he declared explicitly that he was doing it in the hope of 'ensuring the participation of many people in holy orders'.[20]

So, in the course of twenty years, with the exception of Vercelli, there is no evidence for any other episcopal foundations. On the contrary, we have the impression that in this period there developed a kind of local entrenchment of Christianity, through a reorganization of structures which already existed. Such structures were

[19] The strategic importance of the city was due to its position on the roads which linked Milan with Gaul and the *limes* on the Rhine. For the importance achieved by Vercelli in the second half of the fourth century, see the judgement of Jerome (*civitas . . . olim potens*), though he did describe it around 374 as *raro habitatore semiruta* (Jerome, *Ep.*, I, 3). On the possibility that it was Vercelli's changing character as a result of its position as a military garrison town, which was corrupting its civic, catholic and orthodox side (since most of the troops were barbarian Arians), see Cracco Ruggini and Giorgio Cracco, 'Changing Fortunes of the Italian City from Late Antiquity to the Early Middle Ages', *Rivista di filologia ed istruzione classica* 105 (1977), 448–75.

[20] *Codex Theodosianus* (henceforth CT), 16.2.10 (*Ut ecclesiarum coetus populorum ingentium frequentetur, clericis ac iuvenibus praebeatur immunitas*), dated 26 May 353. Theodor Mommsen had already pointed out that on that date Constantius was not in Constantinople and therefore he preferred to see it as a reference to Constantine in 320 (*CT editio*, p. 838). However, the correction by Otto Seeck is more likely, in *Regesten der Kaiser und Päpste für die Jahre 311 bis 476 n. Chr.* (Stuttgart: Metzler, 1919), 194, which attributes the arrangement to 346, keeping to the place of issue and the consulate of Constantius in the *subscriptio*, but assuming that there was an error between VI and IIII in the indication of the consulate number. With this constitution, Constantius guaranteed the clerics immunity from *munera civilia et sordida*, from the *lustralis collatio* and from the land tax (*a censibus etiam iubemus perseverare immunes*). This attitude of complete support is confirmed by CT, 16.2.14, dated by its *subscriptio* to 6 December 357, but which, in accordance with Seeck (*Regesten*, 203), has to be moved to 356, the year of the ninth consulate of Constantius and the second of Julian.

intended to deal with the cultural requirements of a greater number of Christian groups, which were geographically very distant from each other. Each of this small number of bishoprics was, in fact, at the centre of wide stretches of territory which included many *plebes Christianorum*. In spite of the differences in their ages, from this point of view Vercelli and Aquileia offer significant parallels. The only explicit evidence for the existence and exercise of metropolitan jurisdiction in Aquileia are two letters of Pope Leo the Great in 442.[21] From these, it appears that the church in Aquileia was at the head of some twenty suffragan bishoprics in Italy and ten or so north of the Alps.[22] However, it is very likely that its geographical limits reflect the spread of the area of influence already achieved by that see around the middle of the fourth century. At that time, as well as the *plebes* spread across the province of *Venetia et Histria* (incorporating *regio X* of which the city had been the capital), Aquileia had acquired the spiritual leadership of Christians in Rhaetia Secunda (the easternmost of the two Rhaetias), Noricum, Pannonia Prima and Savia. On the other side of northern Italy, and more or less in the same period, Vercelli too was rapidly becoming a focal point for the groups of Christians in a large number of small centres spread throughout the westernmost part of *regio XI*, as well as in part of the *IX* and across the Alps in the zone which bordered the area of Narbonne. From around 350, Eusebius, the first bishop of the city, writing from exile[23] (a consequence of his refusal to accept the pro-Arian decrees of the Milanese Council of 355 under Constantius II), counted among his own flock not only the citizens of Vercelli but also the *plebes Christianorum* of Novaria, Eporedia and Dertona. According to some variants in the manuscript tradition of his letters, Augusta Pretoria, Industria and Agaminae ad Palatium[24]

---

[21] Leo, *Epp.*, 1–2, in *PL*, 54, 593–8.

[22] Tavano, *Aquileia cristiana*, 30–2; Gian Carlo Menis, 'Le giurisdizioni metropolitiche di Aquileia e di Milano nell'antichità', *AAAd* 4 (1973), 271–94.

[23] Eusebius was a Sardinian from a well-to-do family who had travelled widely and had received the rank of *lector* in Rome, before being elected by popular acclaim in the Piedmont town, according to Jerome, *De viris ill.*, 96.

[24] Eusebius of Vercelli, *Ep.*, 2, 1–4 CCSL IX (ed. Vincentius Bulhart, Turnhout: Brepols, 1957), 104. According to the edition of G. S. Ferrero, Bishop of Vercelli from 1559 to 1610, the list of *plebes* which Eusebius addressed was longer: . . . *Dilectissimus: fratribus at satis desideratissimis presbyteris, diaconibus et omni*

were also among Eusebius's spiritual correspondents. In the period following his exile, his jurisdiction appears to have widened even more. In the *Vita beati Marcellini confessoris* (apparently reliable on this detail, though completely legendary in others), Eusebius is remembered for having ordained, alongside his colleague from Valentia, the first Bishop of Ebredunum. The city was at the end of the road which ran from Augusta Taurinorum along the Val di Susa, through the Alps, finishing at the borders of the territory of Narbonne.[25] It has been assumed that the limits of the territorial jurisdiction of the two sees were in the area between the Hautes Alpes and the Basses Alpes, in the territory of Ebredunum.[26]

It is not improbable that the moment of widest spread of the zones of influence of Vercelli and Aquileia coincided with the episcopate of the Arian Auxentius in Milan (355–74). In a reversal of their previous subjection to Milan, the Christian groups of the neighbouring sees seem to have taken advantage of the effective lack of authority of this Greek-speaking bishop, who, in the twenty years of his episcopate, had remained an extraneous figure within the local Christian community. In this context, the development of relations between Milan and Brescia is significant, since the Brescia community is supposed to have been originally under the direction of the Milanese bishop, Anatolius. Under Auxentius, however, Filastrius of Brescia is recorded as having functioned as spiritual director not only to the people of his own see, but also of the Nicene group in Milan.[27] The areas of influence of the individual bishoprics were redefined therefore in this period in relation to the doctrinal make-up of the relative majority groups. Those where the Nicene faith was more strongly established became stronger because of the support of Liberius, around whom the anti-Arian resistance gathered. It could well have been that

---

clero, sed et sanctis in fide consistentibus plebibus. *Vercellen, Novarien, Hipporegien* (variant of *Eporedia*), *Augustanis, Industrien et Agaminis ad Palatium nec non etiam Derton* . . . However, it is not clear in which codices Ferrero could have found these variants: cf. Bolgiani, *La penetrazione*, 42, n. 11.

[25] *Vita beati Marcellini (Acta SS, Aprilis)*, II, 750–3; *Bibl. Hagiogr. Latina* II, 776.

[26] Fedele Savio, *Gli antichi vescovi dalle origini al 1300 descritti per regioni: Il Piemonte* (Turin: Bocca, 1898), 5; Bolgiani, *La penetrazione*, 45, n. 17.

[27] Gaudentius of Brescia, *Tractatus*, 21, *PL*, 20, 999.

Liberius instigated the decision to establish Vercelli as an episcopal see by sending a *lector* of the Roman Church to that city. In fact, only a few years after his ordination, it was to Eusebius that the Pope turned, calling on his skill to strengthen the links between the Christian groups bound together in their struggle against the Arian attack unleashed by the Emperor, instead of turning, for example, to Dionysius of Milan who was also destined to be driven into exile together with Eusebius and Luciferus of Cagliari.[28]

The way in which this doctrinal dispute was resolved, i.e. the fact that from the reign of Theodosius I onwards the church supported by the Emperor coincided with the church recognized in the Nicene formula, has placed a large question mark over the reliability of our documentation. It is not chance that the communities whose development and consolidation between about 350 and 380 we can best follow are also those in which the orthodox group predominated. We know next to nothing about the see of Rimini, which, however, must have achieved a certain importance, for Constantius II chose it as the location for a Council. Nothing has been preserved about its bishop, who, at the time of the council, must have been pro-Arian.[29] The same is true of the Christian community of Parma (*colonia Iulia Augusta Parmensis*). The almost total silence about the origins of this centre is probably due to the Arian character of its dominant Christianity, as may be deduced from the decree of Gratian and Valentinian II issued to the vicar Aquilinus ordering the expulsion of Bishop Urbanus from the city. The latter had been denounced as a heretic by the bishops of the Council of Rome in 378. Although he was expelled on that occasion, Urbanus had probably already been deposed at the time of the Synod of Rome in 372 which had been called to take action against Auxentius of Milan. Both of these bishops, however, had managed to hold on to their bishoprics, relying on the policy of toleration decreed by Valentinian I. Urbanus' episcopate, however, went back to a period before the Council of Rimini, since Hilary of Poitiers mentions an Urbanus among the bishops

---

[28] Liberius, *Epp.*, 1–4, CCSL IX, 121–4. The expansion of the sphere of influence of Aquileia can also be attributed to the action of Liberius, according to Cracco Ruggini, 'Storia totale', 286, n. 328.

[29] It is thought that it was Rimini's first bishop, St Gaudentius, widely celebrated in hagiographic legends in Romagna: Lanzoni, *Le diocesi*, 707.

who prevaricated in 359.[30] To understand the importance of this factor on the quantity and quality of our sources, we only need to observe that information on Milan is almost totally absent for the years 355–74. Yet the religious influence of the see of Milan up to the episcopate of Dionysius must have been equal, if not superior, to the influence of Aquileia.[31]

The best documented sees in this period then are those led by strong anti-Arian bishops. It is possible to draw a picture of these through the image, tinged with sanctity, handed down by their successors. In the years in which the Nicene faith triumphed, an attempt was in fact made to concentrate popular devotion around the figure of these bishops. In a letter to the clergy and people of Vercelli, Ambrose spoke of Eusebius as a *confessor* and dedicated various paragraphs to his activity as evangelizer of the area. These passages may well reflect the content of the sermons delivered on the occasion of the liturgical commemoration of Eusebius.[32] Eusebius' reputation for sanctity grew rapidly. In Vercelli, in the acrostic of a late epigraph written in his honour, he is defined as *martur*, which demonstrates the spread of the belief that he did in fact suffer martyrdom at the hands of the Arians.[33] Anniversary celebrations for Eusebius were held at Turin during the episcopate of Maximus. Although the two sermons *de sancto Eusebio* are considered spurious, Gennadius nevertheless showed his knowledge of two sermons composed by Maximus in his honour.[34] The cult of Eusebius also spread fairly rapidly across the Alps. Gregory of Tours in fact records that his mother had gathered a number of the saint's relics in the oratory of their house.[35] In addition, Ambrose himself gave the title of *martyr* to

---

[30] *Collectio Avellana*, 54–6; Lanzoni, *Le diocesi*, 807.

[31] Menis, 'Le giurisdizioni metropolitiche', 281ff.

[32] Ambrose, *Epp.*, 63, 2, 59, 65 (*PL*, 16, 1189–90; 1204–5; 1206–7).

[33] This epigraph perhaps ought to be included in the group of *carmina flavianea* which can be dated to the middle of the sixth century: see Luigi Bruzza, *Iscrizioni antiche vercellesi* (Rome: Suggiani Santini, 1874 = phot. reprint Vercelli, 1973), 296–301; Sergio Roda, *Iscrizioni latine di Vercelli* (Turin: Vincenzo Bona, 1985), 116–21.

[34] For the inauthenticity of the two sermons, see Mutzenbecher, 'Bestimmung', 225–7; Gennadius, however (*De viris ill.*, 40, *PL*, 58, 1082), attributes the two to Maximus.

[35] Gregory of Tours, *Liber de gloria confes.*, III, *PL*, 71, 831–2.

Dionysius of Milan who had died in exile.[36] It is not certain whether
he brought the remains of his Nicene predecessor to Milan,
since the information is given only in the Gallic martyrology of
Floro, written sometime before 837. Such a hypothesis, however,
is made less unlikely if we see it as analogous to what happened
in the same period in Constantinople. There in 381 Theodosius,
for a specifically anti-Arian purpose, ordered the body of Paul,
the Nicene bishop of the capital who had died in exile, to be
brought back to the city.[37] It also seems to have been Ambrose
who fixed 8 February as the *dies natalis* of Dionysius and who
encouraged the devotion around a tomb (possibly a cenotaph)
which grew into an oratory. This still existed in the fifth century
near the Eastern Gate, which in fact took its name, *Armenia*, from
Dionysius.[38]

In Brescia, as well, at the same period, the commemorative
liturgy in honour of Filastrius was increasingly used, probably
because of Milanese influences. Like Eusebius, Filastrius had been
a bishop staunch in the struggle for orthodoxy against heresy and
in fact the one to whom the Nicene group in the city owed its first
concrete establishment.[39] The sermon given by Gaudentius shows

[36] Ambrose, *Ep.*, 63, 68–70 (*PL*, 16, 1208); *Ep.*, 21a (*Sermo contra
Auxentium*), *PL*, 16, 1212.
[37] Sozomen, *HE*, VII, 10, 4; Socrates, *HE*, V, 9; Gilbert Dagron,
Constantinopoli (Turin: Einaudi, 1991), 467.
[38] There is reason to doubt that the body of the Bishop Dionysius of Milan,
who had died in Cappadocia, was sent back by Basil to Ambrose: see Jean-
Charles Picard, *Le souvenir des évêques: Sépultures, listes épiscopales et culte
des évêques: en Italie du Nord dès origines au Xe siècle* (Rome: Bibliothèque des
Écoles Françaises d'Athènes et de Rome 268, 1988), 609–13ff. The *Martirologio
Geronimiano* says that Dionysius died at Riditio in Armenia, a place which Picard,
however, would identify with the *Municipium Riditarum* on the Dalmatian coast
near Sebenico. On this whole question, see Cracco Ruggini, 'Nascita e morte di
una capitale', 33, n. 46.
[39] According to Gaudentius's character sketch of Filastrius, the struggle against
pagans, Jews and especially against the Arian *perfidia* had been carried on by the
Bishop with a faith so strong that he had suffered a scourging because of it
(Gaudentius, *Tractatus*, 21, 6); his love for the true faith had also made him
leader of the flock of neighbouring Milan, where he fought against the Arian
Auxentius (7); by his efforts *Brixia rudis quondam sed cupida doctrinae* was
transformed into fertile ground (8); his life was made outstanding by his
exemplary continence and by his long nights spent in studying the holy Scriptures
(5).

how these annually repeated funeral orations created a model of sanctity, and thereby favoured the early development of a devotion to the city's bishop in the same way as they encouraged a devotion to the relics of martyrs. The tribute of civic devotion which grew up around a bishop's body – and particularly the attribution to it of a kind of life *post mortem* which encouraged the belief that he was still the community's true *pater* – ensured that people also believed that the functions of guardian and dispenser of charity which had characterized his life continued after his death.[40] The genesis of the medieval cult of the patron bishop is rooted in this conceptual change. The prerequisites for this had already been established in the Ambrosian era, in a period when it appeared important to take advantage of the attachment which individual communities had to figures of the recent past, so that in the collective memory they could fulfil the role of symbol-figures of the new Nicene direction of the imperial church.

The church, its ministers and ascetics

The image, which was developed towards the end of the fourth century, is of orthodox bishops of a number of important northern Italian bishoprics who were bastions of the battle against heresy in the forty-year period between the reign of Constantius II and that of Theodosius I. Although this picture is somewhat exaggerated, it does reflect undeniable historical facts. For us they represent several elements of the direction taken by Christianity in this phase. The doctrinal steadfastness in rejecting the Arian heresy is certainly the most striking aspect. In this, Eusebius was exemplary. Even after his return from exile, during the reign of Valentinian I, he continued to maintain close links with Rome with the intention of liberating those northern Italian sees which were still in the

---

[40] Gaudentius of Brescia, *Tractatus*, 21, 14 (the anniversary of Filastrius has been celebrated for fourteen years); 1 (tribute is still paid to him as if he were still alive); 4 (he is dead and his tomb is in the city, but his life is in Christ); 15 (through his intercession, requested benefits can be obtained). For the interpretation of *Tractatus* 21 as an example of the early spread of the cult of Filastrius in Brescia, see Lizzi, 'Tra i classici e la Bibbia: l'otium come forma di santità episcopale', in G. Barone, M. Caffiero, F. Scorza Barcellona, eds, *Modelli di santità e modelli di comportamento: contrasti, intersezioni, complementarietà* (Turin: Rosenberg & Sellier, 1994), 43–64.

hands of heterodox bishops.[41] In Aquileia, Fortunatianus (342–68?) had been less steadfast; in 359 he had preferred to avoid exile by subscribing to the formula which the Emperor proposed.[42] However, this must have been an uncommon moment of weakness which did not damage the substantial orthodoxy of his actions. After having given shelter to Athanasius who had been exiled from Alexandria after 339, Fortunatianus managed to keep the Christian group free from Arian influences. This fact is important, particularly if we consider the numerous contacts and cultural exchanges (in an archaeological sense as well) between Aquileia and Illyrian circles.[43] The vulgarization of the Gospels, upon which Fortunatianus rewrote 'in a shorter and simpler way' (*brevi sermone et rustico*), would seem to indicate the care which he gave to instructing the *rustici*. This group of rustics included not only the population of the countryside around the cities but also the uneducated peoples of the Arian regions in Rhaetia, Noricum and Pannonia, which were already by this time under the spiritual guidance of Aquileia.[44] There is a parallel to this literary activity in the work of Eusebius, to whom is attributed the *Codex Vercellensis*, which contains the oldest Latin text of the Gospels. In this case, too, the intent must have been the Christianization of the *plebes*. Their 'boorishness' (*rusticitas*)

---

[41] Manlio Simonetti, *La crisi ariana nel IV secolo* (Rome: Inst. Patristicum Augustinianum, 1975), 380.

[42] For this action Fortunatianus was severely criticized by Jerome (*De vir. ill.*, 97): *et in hoc habetur detestabilis, quod Liberium, Romanae urbis episcopum, pro fide ad exsilium pergentem, primus sollicitavit et fregit et ad subscriptionem haereseos compulit.* However, we still have the evidence of the high esteem in which Liberius (before his exile) held the Bishop of Aquileia: Liberius, *Ep.*, 3.2.1 (*CCSL* IX, 123) to Eusebius in 353.

[43] Athanasius, who stayed in Aquileia on several occasions, celebrated Easter there in 345 amongst the faithful packed into the large church called *Theonae*, which was still under construction, since the church which was normally used did not have enough room for the crowd: Athanasius, *Apol. in Constantium imperatorem* (AD 356), 15, *PG*, 25, 613. For Aquileia's cultural contacts with Noricum and Rhaetia, which are demonstrated by the strong architectural similarities in the forms of early Christian archaeology, see Lizzi, *Vescovi*, 140, n. 5.

[44] Here I follow the hypothesis of Cracco Ruggini, 'Aquileia e Concordia: il duplice volto di una società urbana nel V secolo d. C.', *AAAd* 29 (1987), 76, 86ff.

was to some extent a consequence of their social heterogeneity, made up as they were for the most part of travellers, Arians, pagans, or at any rate people who had not been baptized. Around Vercelli, as around Aquileia, these country people were the object of the missionary efforts of those bishops who can be earliest identified historically.[45] At a slightly later date, Filastrius of Brescia also wrote treatises against pagans, Jews and heretics, of which only his *Diversarum hereseon liber* remains.[46]

From these scattered pieces of evidence, it is clear that the extension of conversion and Christianization to ever-increasing and more devout urban crowds implies a capillary action by the religious organization in the region. In order to increase the number of sees, of course, the church needed ever more religious personnel. As we shall see, the question was solved in different ways in the Ambrosian period. In the earlier period, however, the bases for that solution were already being established. In fact, the first ascetic vocations date from the years 350–70 and are apparently connected with the conflicts provoked in the Western church by the strong pressures stemming from Constantius II's anti-Nicene stance.[47] They also appear closely linked to the problem of church recruitment. The links between the choice of a religious life, conducted in solitude and virginal purity, and the anti-Arian group are evident. In northern Italy, the creation of a first nucleus of ascetic clerics is attributed to the initiative of Eusebius of Vercelli, who had combined in his own person two separate virtues: 'the continence of the monk and the way of life of the priest' (*monasterii continentia et disciplina Ecclesiae*).[48] If, as Ambrose claims, it

[45] Philip Levine, 'Historical Evidence for Calligraphic Activity in Vercelli from St Eusebius to Atto', *Speculum* 30 (1955), 461–81. An ancient manuscript claims Eusebius as the author also of the *De Trinitate*, a collection of seven pamphlets, elsewhere ascribed to Athanasius or Vigilius of Tapsus: Ercole Crovella, *S. Eusebio di Vercelli. Saggio di biografia critica* (Vercelli: SETE, 1961); idem, *La chiesa eusebiana. Dalle origini alla fine del sec. VIII* (Vercelli: Quaderni dell'Ist. di Belle Arti di Vercelli 10, 1968), 80–135.

[46] It is Gaudentius who tells us of the notable literary activity of his teacher and predecessor: *Tractatus*, 21. His anti-heretical composition is edited in *CCSL*, IX, 217–324.

[47] Lizzi, 'Ascetismo e monachesimo nell'Italia tardoantica', in *Los origines historicos del monacato. IV Seminario sobre El Monacato (Aguilar de Campoo, agosto 1990), Codex Aquilarensis* 5 (1991), 56.

[48] Ambrose, *Ep.*, 63, 66.

was the ascetic life which prepared Eusebius for exile, then the Eusebian ascetic group (with its characteristic mix of monastic and clerical elements) could date to a period before 355.[49] Limenius and Honoratus, who accompanied the bishop into exile and succeeded him in the see, were part of the group, as was Gaudentius of Eporedia, elected Bishop of Novaria in the years following 380. It is possible that Maximus, the future Bishop of Turin, also received formation in the same group. The oriental character which pseudo-Maximus attributed to the Vercelli community, rather than deriving from Eusebius's experiences during his journeys in exile from Antioch to Alexandria via Cappadocia, could have come from the promptings he received in the years he spent in Rome, where Athanasius appears to have sown fruitful ascetic seed.[50] The Alexandrian bishop, persecuted by the Emperor, had withdrawn to spend six years with the monks of the desert (356–62). For him as for many others of the Nicene group, ascetic retreat must have represented a way to avoid persecution and violence without giving in to imperial compromises.

It is precisely in this climate that Sulpicius Severus places the foundation of the first Martinian monastery in the city of Milan. Forced to leave Poitiers, rather than go towards Gaul, where the accusations levelled against Hilary had left the field to the Arian group of Saturninus of Arles, Martin 'founded a sort of monastery for himself in Milan'. Yet even there, *ibi quoque*, stresses Sulpicius, he was followed by the persecution of Auxentius, *auctor et princeps Arrianorum*, which drove him to take refuge in an even more inaccessible place, the island of Gallinara.[51] This reference to what happened to Hilary allows us to date this episode on Martin's life to a period shortly after the Council of Béziers (356), in answer to which Hilary had written a long letter of recapitulation to Constantius, who had then sent him a reply sentencing him to

---

[49] Ambrose, *Ep.*, 63, 67.

[50] As well as Ambrose, there are also some sermons of uncertain date and unknown author, published under Maximus's name, which talk of Eusebius's initiative. The one included in Mutzenbecher's edition (*CCSL* XXIII, 24–6) seems chronologically close to the *Ep.* 63 of Ambrose. For the Athanasian influence on the first ascetic vocations amongst Roman noblewomen, see Jerome, *Ep.*, 127.5.

[51] Sulpicius Severus, *Vita Martini* 6, 4–7, 1; cf. Jacques Fontaine, *Commentaire à la Vie de saint Martin*, SCh., 134 (Paris: Cerf, 1968), 582–99.

exile.[52] Our sources on the nature of the *monasterium* in Milan are very unforthcoming. If we take into account the meaning which the term would have had in that period (indicating a group of hermits, rather than a monastic building in the strict sense), we could only conclude that Martin's was a small cell in the immediate vicinity of Milan where he lived alone for some while or together with a companion (perhaps the same one who followed him into exile on Gallinara). In this sense, it seems impossible to assume that we can identify the place inhabited by Martin with the *monasterium* at Milan which existed at the time of Ambrose outside the walls of the city, which Augustine talks about in his *Confessions*.[53] However, we cannot exclude the possibility that the two centres represented a continuous settlement, especially if we consider the fact that Ambrose seems to have inherited and developed in both a real and a symbolic sense the same power of resistance to heresy, which Martin's primitive asceticism had already exemplified.

The same importance is evident also in the group which had grown in Aquileia, another city in which the Athanasian accounts of the life and deeds of the monks of the Egyptian desert appear to have exercised a great influence. The monastic group, which had come into being under Fortunatianus, or more likely under his successor Valerian (368?–88), had counted amongst its members Jerome and Rufinus in 370–3. Like the Vercelli community, this one too, had members who were ready to fight against the inroads made by the Arians, even into nearby Illyria. Amongst these was Chromatius, certainly at this time *presbyter* and later successor to Valerian in the see of Aquileia; his brother Eusebius, perhaps the future Bishop of Concordia; Jovinian; Eliodorus (future Bishop of Altinum); Julian (whom a critical variant in the *Historia Ecclesiastica* of Rufinus allows us to identify with the similarly named Bishop of Parenzo);[54] Bonosus; Niceas; Criysocomas; Florentinus; and Nepotianus.[55] On a par with the cleric monks of

---

[52] Simonetti, *La crisi ariana*, 222.

[53] Augustine, *Confessions*, VIII, 6.15.3.

[54] Rufinus, *HE*, 2, 27–8 (*GCS*, 1033–4, with the correction to the text suggested by Theodor Mommsen).

[55] Jerome, *Ep.*, 52, 5, p. 180, 11, for the conscious distinction between the simple *clericus* and the *clericus monachus* with which he designated Nepotianus. Jerome, *Ep.*, 7, 6, pp. 30–1: Jerome praised Chromatius, Eusebius and Jovinus

Vercelli, the members of what Jerome defined as 'a multitude of the blessed' (*quasi chorus beatorum*) were men well along the road of a church career, active in the performance of prestigious *officia* within the community such as helping the poor, the sick and the needy, or instructing and baptizing catechumens.[56] The total of these elements – asceticism, struggle against heresy, being part of the hierarchy – was joined in both communities to an intense activity of study and exegesis of sacred texts. All of these components would later be praised by Ambrose, who developed in Milan a clerical ascetic group linked to the church and from which was required the spiritual perfection which for years characterized the Nicene Christianity of northern Italy. When the creed to which this group adhered became that of the official church and the group's members succeeded in filling the highest ranks in the church hierarchy, the monastic movement which had developed within it remained closely linked to the upper echelons of the church. In this context it is easy to understand why the early monastic movement in the West, particularly in northern Italy, had a character which was so particularly dependent on church control.

At the same time, in almost all the bishoprics we have so far examined, there developed the first forms of female asceticism. At Vercelli, alongside the group of cleric-monks, it seems that a kind of female convent also arose. An anonymous writer reported that Eusebius 'introduced the pattern of the sacred female virginity and of the strong monastic life for men'; during his exile, he wrote to the *sanctae sorores* in Vercelli as well as to the *fratres*.[57] Some inscriptions known through the manuscript tradition (as well as through one piece of epigraphic evidence) confirm that in a later period there was a community of *virgines* in the city linked

---

for having added to the personal glory of their faith in Christ the merit of having driven from Aquileia the *virus* of the Arian dogma, perhaps a reference to the compromise position taken by Fortunatianus.

[56] Jerome, *Chronicon ad a.* 374, *PL*, 27.697. Rufinus was baptized at Aquileia by Chromatius: Rufinus, *Apol. contra Hier.* I, 4, *CCSL*, 20, 39.

[57] Pseudo-Maximus, *Sermo*, 7.2.33–5, of uncertain date and attribution. Eusebius, *Ep.*, 2.11.1 of 356; cf. 2.8.1 where there seems to be implicit a comparison with the state of persecution, in the place of exile where Eusebius then was, of the *puellae sanctimoniales* who were imprisoned equally with the *viri* who helped them.

spiritually to their bishop.[58] In Aquileia, too, the sisters of Chromatius, Jerome along with other pious young women shared the religious choices of their brothers, leading a consecrated life of prayer, meditation and virginity. This life was similar to that of the sister of Damasus and Ambrose's sister Marcellina, who received the veil from Pope Liberius at a time which must therefore have fallen within the period of his papacy (354–60), who were living in the same period in Rome. Such examples recall similar experiences in the East of Macrina and Basil and other families whose various members all decided to dedicate themselves to the religious life.[59] The link with a male figure, who belonged to some level of holy orders within the church, differentiated the female asceticism which we are now examining from the asceticism which aristocratic women in Rome were developing at the same time, although the two had many things in common.[60] Almost in accordance with a developing pattern, Albina and Marcella gathered round the virgin Asella in the same way as Marcellina in Rome lived with her widowed mother and with another virgin, whose name we do not know, but whose sister Candida was living in Carthage, at a very advanced age, at the time Paulinus was writing the *Vita Ambrosii*.[61] Candida's sister was not the only virgin to join Marcellina. Indicia, the Veronese virgin whose hardships at the time of Bishop Syagrius are related in two of Ambrose's letters, spent many years in Rome in the house of Marcellina, after having been consecrated by Bishop Zeno of Verona at the beginning of his episcopate.[62]

---

[58] Bruzza, *Iscrizioni vercellesi*, 309–13; 316–18, nn. cxxxii–cxxxiii; CIL V, 6741; cf. Roda, *Iscrizioni latine*, 130–1.

[59] Susanna Elm, *Virgins of God: The Making of Asceticism in Late Antiquity* (Oxford: Clarendon Press, 1994), 78–105.

[60] Common features were domestic retreat in the city, in a separate wing of the *domus*, or in suburban *villulae*; the organization into small groups made up of household members; the practice together of virginity; abstinence from food; study and prayer: see Lizzi, 'Ascetismo e monachesimo', 55–8.

[61] Paulinus, *Vita Ambrosii*, 4. The two young women remained together even after the death of Marcellina's mother, as Paulinus mentions in his account of a visit by Ambrose to the capital *post annos aliquot ordinationis suae* (ibid., 9).

[62] Ambrose, *Epp.*, 5–6, PL, 16.891–904, particularly 21.898. The respect and affection which Marcellina had for Indicia impelled her to intervene vigorously in her defence when Indicia, after having returned to her father's house in Verona, was the victim of slanderous gossip and accusations. On the probable economic

Zeno of Verona: preaching to a minority Christian community

The information that in Verona, too, virgins received the *velatio* and that a kind of female monastery had been organized there like the ones recorded at Aquileia and Vercelli, allows us to broaden our discussion to include the form which Christianity assumed in this northern Italian bishopric. For us, it is essentially dominated by the figure of Zeno, the first bishop before Ambrose from whom there is a surviving collection of homilies.[63] In fact, the dates of Zeno's episcopate are uncertain, but it must have started at least fifteen years before that of Ambrose, and continued during the time that the literary and spiritual authority of the Milan prelate was gaining ground.[64] For example, it has been established that the contemporary sermons of Ambrose have an influence on some of Zeno's sermons.[65] Others can be dated with some accuracy by referring to historical events of the time which the bishop mentions. In general, these sermons provide precious evidence of the characteristics of Christianity in the towns, in the pivotal period (between the age of Constantius–Valentinian and that of Theodosius) which we have already identified as a significant turning-point in the process of the Christianization of the area.

---

motives which had impelled the virgin's brother-in-law to bribe false accusers in order to take possession of her share of the family inheritance, see Lizzi, 'Una società esortata all'ascetismo: misure legislative e motivazioni economiche', *Studi Storici* 1, 30 (1989), 129–53, particularly 142. Ambr., *Ep.*, 5.897 makes specific reference to the female monastery of Verona.

[63] Various of Zeno's sermons, strongly Cyprianic in tone and showing Novatianist influences, have been collected in a critical edition (*CCSL*, 22, ed. Bengt Löfstedt, Turnhout: Brepols, 1971). They were unknown to Jerome and Gennadius.

[64] The period of Zeno's episcopate was traditionally fixed between 362 and 380 (Migne, *PL*, 11.81). A. Bigelmair (*Zeno von Verona*, Münster: Aschendorff, 1904), 51 cut the chronology to nine years, calculating its length on the basis of the number of his Easter sermons. Löfstedt's new critical edition has undermined Bigelmair's arguments. Many elements in the sermons in fact suggest that Migne's dates are more likely.

[65] Zeno's *De continentia* seems to be set in the context of the first two Ambrosian treatises on virginity: Yves-Marie Duval, 'L'originalité du *De Virginibus* dans le mouvement ascétique occidental: Ambroise, Cyprien, Athanase', in idem, ed., *Ambroise de Milan: XVIᵉ Centenaire de son élection épiscopale* (Paris: Études Augustiniennes, 1974), 9–66.

On its own, the fact that Zeno almost certainly came from Africa is a very important prosopographic element which, at this period, appears common to the upper ranks of the churches of almost the whole of northern Italy. In the main, the holders of these high offices come from elsewhere. Fortunatianus too was African, Eusebius was from Sardinia, Limenius was a Greek, Auxentius a Cappadocian, Filastrius was not from Brescia, and Ambrose himself, in 374, came from Rome. This foreignness, however, did not hinder Zeno in his promotion of Christianization, although it was far from extending to the entire city of Verona. Some of Zeno's sermons refer specifically to the continuation of pagan worship and to the joint presence, without necessarily too much conflict, of exponents of the two faiths. Traditional sacrifices were practised in city temples, the official pagan calendar was still observed, the *parentalia* were celebrated, and soothsayers were normally consulted.[66] On the other hand, Christian buildings for worship still seem to have been very few and could in no way compare with the beauty and size of the pagan ones; mixed marriages between Christian women and pagan men were frequent.[67] In general, especially in moral treatises, Bishop Zeno underlined the contrast between the 'illicit behaviour' (*illiciti mores*) of those who still clung to the ancient ways of worship and the sanctity of a small group of neophytes.

It is evident that the bishop was still operating in a city which was only partially Christian. The situation was still the same towards the end of his episcopate, when a few sermons, datable to the period around 378–9, indicate that the situation had remained essentially unchanged. The similarity between the final section of Zeno's *Tractatus* 14 and some passages of Ambrose's *De officiis* which relate to the ransoming of soldiers who had been captured at Adrianople, allows us to consider the possibility that that text was written at a period not long after the serious defeat suffered in Thrace by the Roman army. The consequences of those dramatic events were widely felt in north-eastern Italy. The mass arrival of populations fleeing from devastated territories and the danger of a barbarian invasion through the Alpine passes triggered some

---

[66] Zeno, *Tractatus* II, 7.14–16, 174–5; I, 25, 11, 75, 95; I, 25, 11, 75, 90–4; 95–6.

[67] Zeno, *Tractatus* II, 6.168.9–12; 7.11, 174; 119–21.

typical reactions, especially the hiding of accumulated wealth.[68] In particular, hoards of money, often found throughout the Po valley region, testify to hurried burials in the face of imminent danger.[69] Zeno, in fact, appears to refer to this practice when he described the care with which the better-off citizens tried to hide in the ground 'the gold and silver which with so much effort were taken from the ground', or elsewhere, when he alluded to the hiding places of precious stones and jewels.[70] In such a difficult situation, Zeno distinguishes between the behaviour of those to whom the sermon was addressed and the behaviour which his words condemned: 'we have composed this sermon not to avaricious people but about avaricious people . . . and these words are not directed to you, brothers, whose generosity is known to all the provinces'.[71] In fact, the Christian group had distinguished itself by its generosity in paying ransom for all those who had been captured. They had welcomed the fugitives, and applied to foreign people the same charity which they normally exercised on a daily basis towards the local poor and indigent.[72]

The contrast evident between one part of the population and the rest seems a clear sign of the position held by Zeno, head of a still limited group of faithful. A very different tone was adopted by those bishops who in similar situations addressed themselves to cities in which, although Christianity appeared to be an established fact, there remained the permanent real problem of conversion, that is of that radical change of life which full

---

[68] Many Illyrian refugees reached Veneto and Emilian territory where they were employed as day labourers: Cracco Ruggini, *Economia e società*, 62–3; eadem, 'Uomini senza terra e terra senza uomini nell'Italia antica', *Quaderni di Sociologia Rurale* 3 (1963), 33.

[69] Most of the hoards of money discovered in the area date from the third century (e.g. the Venéra hoard from near Verona), but there are still some from the fourth century, alongside finds of money in burial settings, both of which can be linked to military presences and war activity: Cracco Ruggini, 'Milano nella circolazione monetaria del tardo impero: esigenze politiche e risposte socio-economiche', in *La zecca di Milano: Atti del Conv. Int. di studio (Milano 9–14 May 1983)* (Milan: Società Numismatica Italiana, 1984), 49.

[70] Zeno, *Tractatus* I, 14.3.57.25–33; cf. 5.58.41–6.

[71] Zeno, *Tractatus* I, 5.3.38.18–28; 7.39.50–63; 18.41.132–8: *non ad avaros, sed de avaris sermonem fecimus . . . sed haec non ad vos, fratres, quorum largitas provinciis omnibus nota est.*

[72] Zeno, *Tractatus* I, 14, 8, 59, 74–7.

acceptance of the Christian way of life ought to involve. In these cases, the same description of different immoral forms of acquiring wealth lost its stereotypical character, still evident in many of Zeno's sermons, and changed into an open denunciation of the profiteering on the back of other people's misfortunes perpetrated in times of war.[73] Amongst the characteristics of sermon production, this greater concreteness with reference to city life represented the first tangible reflection of the different position of the bishop as head, not just of one part, but of the whole community. This is also shown by the other collections of sermons preserved in northern Italy in the period following the 380s.

III. RELIGIOUS DYNAMICS IN THE LAST TWO DECADES OF THE FOURTH CENTURY

Accelerating ecclesiastical activity

After the end of the reign of Valentinian I, religious life in northern Italy seems to show a kind of acceleration. Although it is difficult to establish the size of the increase in the number of converts or how it took place, and although the picture derived from the extant sermon collections does not support the idea of a totally Christianized region, it is however beyond doubt that the process of institutional consolidation of the church enjoyed a phase of great increase. It is characterized by two very important factors. During the episcopate of Ambrose, and to a large measure due to his initiative, many new sees were established through successive divisions of the few, very extensive dioceses on which our reconstruction of the Christian *facies* in the preceding period is based. Furthermore, Nicene bishops were elected in almost every city of the imperial vicariate. In parallel with the methods of recruitment

[73] See, e.g., Maximus of Turin, *Sermo.*, 18, 61–70. Many of the stereotypes and abstractions which characterize Zeno's sermons are probably due to the way in which the collection was put together. The collection was compiled a long time after the death of the bishop by an editor who attempted to classify texts of every nature and size, including also Hilary of Poitiers or Rufinus's translations of Basil which had come to form part of the literary legacy of the bishop. See Vittore Boccardi, 'Quantum spiritaliter intellegi datur. L'esegesi di Zenone di Verona', *Augustinianum* 23 (1983), 445 ff. The liturgical use which appears to have been made of Zeno's sermons may explain the brevity and similarity of many of them.

of the imperial bureaucracy, which appeared of major importance for regional administration through the active presence of the court at Milan, these bishops were almost all of local extraction.[74]

For the most part, the new bishops belonged to families which were consecrated to religious service and almost all came from the type of monastic community discussed earlier. Sabinus, one of those Milanese deacons who, by disassociating themselves from the heretical trends imposed by Auxentius, had discovered in Filastrius their point of reference, became Bishop of Placentia (modern Piacenza). His election is traditionally fixed at the time of his return from the East, where in 374/5 he had carried out a series of prestigious missions to keep alive Western contacts with Nicene circles.[75] At almost the same time, Bassianus was elected bishop. He is described by Paulinus as being present together with Honoratus of Novaria as Ambrose was breathing his last.[76] His bishopric, Laus Pompeia (modern Lodi), was very close to Placentia, demonstrating that now the era of large dioceses of vast territorial spread had gone and a completely new and different policy of church territorial organization had begun.

[74] A first attempt to analyse the careers and history of the higher echelons of the church in northern Italy can be found in Pietri, 'Aristocratie et société cléricale dans l'Italie chrétienne au temps d'Odoacre et de Théodoric', *Mélanges de l'École Française de Rome* 93 (1981), 417–65 = ChR, II, 1007–57; idem, 'Une aristocratie provinciale'. For the reflections on the sociology of the clergy in parallel with that of the local lay élites, see Cracco Ruggini, 'La cristianizzazione', 247; eadem, 'La fisionomia sociale del clero e il consolidarsi delle istituzioni ecclesiastiche nel Norditalia (IV–VI secolo)', in *Morfologie sociali e culturali in Europa fra tarda Antichità e elto Medioevo* (3–9 apr. 1997) (Spoleto: CISM XLV, 1998), 851–901.

[75] It is not clear whether Placentia had a bishop before Sabinus: Lanzoni, *Le diocesi*, 815. Sabinus, who was a signatory to the Council of Aquileia and is remembered in Gregory the Great's *Dialogi* (III, 10) as a saint and miracle worker, is almost certainly the same Sabinus who exchanged letters with Ambrose. In 372, as *diaconus* he had signed the Rome Synod organized against Auxentius and was then given the task of taking to Athanasius the letter from the Rome Council. He also took an authenticated copy of the letter to Basil of Cesarea, and in return received letters for a number of bishops in Italy and Gaul: Marcel Richard, 'Saint Basile et la mission du diacre Sabinus', *Analecta Bollandiana* 67 (1949), 178–202.

[76] Paulinus, *Vita Ambrosii*, 47. The start of Bassianus's episcopate predates the Council of Aquileia, since he was one of the signatories, but it would not appear to have started much earlier: Alessandro Caretta, 'Le origini della primitiva comunità cristiana di Laus Pompeia', in AA.VV., *San Bassiano vescovo di Lodi: Studi nel XVI centenario della ordinazione episcopale 374–1974* (Lodi: Curia Vescovile, 1974), 43–70.

Between 381–6, Como too had its first bishop. On the anniversary of his episcopal ordination, Felix received a note of good wishes from Ambrose, which contained an invitation for him to come to Lodi to take part in the consecration of the *basilica Apostolorum*, as well as some hints on how to solve various problems in his diocese.[77] Ambrose sent similar letters to Constantius of Claterna and Vigilius of Tridentum, who had been raised to the episcopate between 379 and 385–8, both of them moving in the sphere of influence of the Bishop of Milan.[78] Ambrose intervened in two other cities of northern Italy as well. Towards 396/7, he ensured a favourable successor to Filastrius at Brixia, threatening Gaudentius, who was then in the East, with universal excommunication if he refused to be elected in that city.[79] Around 388 Chromatius too, had risen to the episcopate of Aquileia, after a long period as deacon and presbyter alongside the Nicene Valerianus. At almost the same time, his brother Eusebius was appointed to Concordia, the Istrian Iulianus to Parenzo, and Eliodorus to Altinum.[80] In spite of the almost total lack of biographical information on these two young city bishops, from the tome of Ambrose's letters (and sometimes from their own writings) it is evident that they were members of the recently-formed local Christian community and exponents of those lower middle classes to whom Christianity offered an outstanding opportunity for cultural improvement, as well as a secure career in the ranks of a rapidly expanding hierarchy.[81]

[77] F. Lanzoni, *Le diocesi*, 575–8; Savio, *Gli antichi vescovi*, 276. Ambrose, *Ep.* 4 is a short note of good wishes, which demonstrates the close relations which linked the new bishops to Ambrose and to each other. The church in Lodi founded by Bassianus is probably to be found under the present Romanesque building in Lodi Vecchio: Caretta, 'La dedicazione della basilica XX Apostolorum di Laus Pompeia', in *San Bassiano Vescovo di Lodi* (Lodi: Curia Vescovile), 63–70; Antonio Frova, 'Rapporto preliminare su saggi di scavo a Lodi Vecchio', *Archivio Storico Lodigiano* (1955), 16–29; idem, 'Scavi a Lodi Vecchio', *Archivio Storico Lodigiano* (1958), 70–6.

[78] Ambrose, *Ep.* 2 to Constantius and *Ep.* 13 to Vigilius.

[79] On the process of choice, see Gaudentius of Brescia, *Tractatus*, 16, PL, 20, 956; cf. Lizzi, *Vescovi*, 97–109.

[80] For the election of Chromatius, see Joseph Lemarié, ed., *Chromace d'Aquilée. Sermons* I, SCh., 154 (Paris: Cerf, 1969), 46. For the supposed Istrian origin of Julian and the identification of the bishops of Concordia and Altinum, see Cracco Ruggini, 'Storia totale', 284–5.

[81] Lizzi, *Vescovi*, 17, n. 5.

Amongst the signatories to the Council of Aquileia in 381 appears a certain Exuperius, identified with the first Bishop of Dertona (modern Tortona). The city, whose *christiana plebs* had once moved in the orbit of Vercelli, was probably the first of those recalled in the *inscriptio* of the letter of Eusebius to establish itself as an autonomous see. Its political importance in fact increased together with the redimensioning of other neighbouring centres, which were becoming more marginalized in respect to the traffic which now centred on Postumia.[82] Its fortunate geographical position, together with the continuity of its settlement and the extent of territory it controlled had contributed to the rapid increase of Christian penetration, allowing its early organization as a bishopric. The establishment of the diocese, which must have been before 381, can probably be dated to the period around 370–80, and is part of a pattern of development of other dioceses in these years throughout northern Italy. It was only at the end of the fourth century, however, slightly later than Dertona, that the remaining *plebes* under the direction of Vercelli each became autonomous dioceses. Immediately after the death of Ambrose, and following a fortunate prediction by him, Novaria was entrusted to Gaudentius, the deacon from Eporedia whom a *Life* of the eighth century claims to have been a pupil and companion in exile of Eusebius.[83] Maximus too, who was elevated to the see of Augusta Taurinorum (Turin) in this same period, seems to have belonged to the same group.[84] The Bishop of Turin, who organized the Council in the city in 398 and who was the author of a large part of the sermon collection preserved under his name, was certainly a different person from the Bishop of Turin of the same name who was signatory to the provincial synod held in Milan in 451.[85] It is, however, very difficult to establish exactly the date when Eustasius became Bishop of Augusta Praetoria (Aosta) and Eulogius of

[82] Nearby Libarna, for example, had already begun to decrease in population in the course of the fourth century and all that survived was a modest population near the Roman settlement: Giovanni Mennella, 'Introduzione', in *Regio IX. Dertona. Libarna. Forum Iulii Iriensium. Inscriptiones Christianae Italiae* 7 (Bari: Edipuglia, 1990), XIff.

[83] Lanzoni, *Le diocesi*, 1032ff.

[84] The author of *Sermo.*, 7.2.24 describes himself as 'disciple of Eusebius' in the collection handed down under the name of Maximus, but Mutzenbecher ('Bestimmung', 225–7) has expressed serious reservations about its authenticity.

[85] Lizzi, *Vescovi*, 189.

Eporedia (Ivrea). Together they sent to the Council the priests Gratus and Floreius (tradition has it that they were too old and infirm to attend themselves). There was a Eustatius, however, who signed the Milan synod of 390 and a bishop of the same name appears in the *De laude sanctorum* (396) of Victricius of Rouen. No matter how doubtful it may appear, we cannot entirely rule out an identification between these individuals.[86]

Augusta Praetoria and Eporedia, therefore, could date from the same time as Augusta Taurinorum, springing up as episcopal centres towards the end of the fourth century. The analogy with what had happened around 380–90 in the centre-east of northern Italy, when small towns which had formerly depended on Milan or Aquileia became independent dioceses, could suggest that the process (though taking place ten to twenty years later) of the institutionalization of the church went through the same stages, leading to the almost simultaneous development of several neighbouring bishoprics in the same area. The chronological order of their foundations was probably influenced by non-religious factors, such as the position and the wealth of the town. In this sense, after Tortona, Turin must have been the first, if only because of its position as a meeting point for the roads in the Po valley, and equally as point of departure for important roads into Gaul. The other two towns must have followed shortly afterwards. Both Ivrea, whose production of epigraphs throughout the period of the empire is of very high quality, and Aosta (whose palaeochristian sacred buildings make up one of the best preserved groups of the entire Alpine region) enjoyed a position of considerable strategic importance along the Great St Bernard Road, and emphasized their importance in a period in which there was an enormous increase in the movement through the Alpine passes of armies, goods and foodstuffs.[87]

[86] Lanzoni, *Le diocesi*, 1052ff.; Victricius, *De laude sanctorum*, PL, 20, 444; doubts about the identification of these three men called Eustasius were previously expressed by Savio, *Gli antichi vescovi*, 71. For the Christianization of Ivrea, see now Rita Lizzi Testa and Lellia Cracco Ruggini, 'Dalla evangelizzazione alla diocesi', in *Storia delle Chiesa di Ivrea dalle origini al XV secolo* (Rome: Viella, 1998), 5–74.

[87] For Ivrea's inscriptions, see Giuseppe Corradi, *Inscriptiones Italiae* IX, II, *Eporedia* (Rome: La libreria dello Stato, 1931), and the recent contributions on the local epigraphy Antonella Piacentini, 'Epigraphica Eporediensia: iscrizioni inedite e riedite di Ivrea e del suo territorio', *Bollettino Storico Bibliografico Subalpino* 84 (1986), 437–64.

Ambrose and the bishops of the imperial vicariate: a *concertatio inter amicos*

The rapid multiplication of dioceses which took place in the last two decades of the fourth century does not necessarily reflect an equally large increase in the number of converts (since there is a large number of variants to be taken into consideration). However, there was a certain relationship between the expansion of the new faith and its hierarchical structure. Christianization was spreading. Its progressive steps were the result of the groundwork laid in previous years by its diligent missionary activity, in the sense of its anti-heresy campaigns, which had been undertaken in the most prestigious bishoprics. The development of Christianity could now count on the immediate availability of church personnel who had sharpened their skills in the ascetic-clerical communities which had flourished around the principal churches of northern Italy. It was above all Ambrose who gave effect to this potential. In the first place, in spite of a period of progressive weakening of Arian and other internal and external forces which might have challenged the establishment of the orthodox Christian faith, Ambrose was able to keep alive the spirit of a church which, according to its own way of thinking, must have considered itself permanently in a missionary state, that is, committed to growth in a constantly hostile environment. Its ministers and its *plebes* had to show perfection and ethical excellence, an inner strength and a mode of behaviour which was powerful enough to fight off the enemy always in ambush.[88] The interventions of the Milanese bishop in the fight against Arianism are well known: he organized Councils such as the one in Aquileia and, for the same purpose, he ensured that in newly-created sees, or in those which already existed, only people of proven orthodoxy were appointed.[89] Similarly, Ambrose was always ready to intervene to block any resurgence of official paganism or imperial choices which seemed

---

[88] A large part of the programme of evangelization started by Ambrose appears to have been inspired by an essentially defensive strategy: *De officiis* I, 14–18; cf. I, 20: *haec sunt arma iusti, ut cedendo vincat.*

[89] Lizzi, 'Ambrose's contemporaries and the Christianization of northern Italy', *Journal of Roman Studies* 80 (1990), 157–61.

to favour any religious groupings which were not orthodoxly Christian.[90]

The fact that Ambrose's background was in a lay culture which was clearly aristocratic and that his administrative abilities had been developed in his years in imperial service all contributed to making his episcopate a unique experience: it was exemplary in demonstrating the ways of administering a huge diocese. However, he never missed an opportunity to learn lessons from other colleagues in doctrinal matters, in which, at least at the beginning, he must have been somewhat inexperienced. This is shown by the correspondence he conducted with various bishops and churchmen who, having come from the religious orders, could boast of a deeper and more 'technical' religious culture than his. From his correspondence with Sabinus and Simplicianus, one can observe that both of them collaborated in developing the religious formation of the Milanese prelate. Ambrose sent outlines of his books to Sabinus, as well as paraphrases of sermons he preached on the occasion of public debates organized to repudiate the views of individual heretics who were attempting to gain the upper hand over his community. He also questioned Sabinus about the correct interpretation of certain biblical passages and sent him works he was writing for approval before putting them into circulation.[91] Simplicianus, whom Ambrosius wanted as his successor in spite of his advanced age, had taken on the role, from the beginning, of a kind of spiritual director, encouraging Ambrose in brief works of exegesis.[92] All the letters Ambrose sent him are spiritual dissertations or allegorical interpretations of biblical events.[93]

---

[90] On the episode of the battle with Symmachus and the Roman senate, see McLynn, *Ambrose*, 151–2, 166–70, 264, 302, 312–13, 344–5; for the question of Callinicum, see ibid., 298–300, 307.

[91] Ambrose, *Epp.*, 45, 46, 48; cf. Lizzi, *Vescovi*, 36–41.

[92] McLynn, *Ambrose*, 54, suggests that Simplicianus had prepared Ambrose for baptism or that he had in person baptized Ambrose: cf. Augustine, *Confessiones* 8.2.3.

[93] Ambrose, *Epp.*, 37, 38, 65, 67. Simplicianus's fame as an interpreter of the Scriptures, which around 350 had inspired the spectacular conversion of the rhetor Marius Victorinus in Rome, was well-known also to Augustine, who consulted him in Milan when he was close to conversion and who continued to correspond with him from Africa, sending him copies of his writings: cf. Augustine, *Confessiones*, 8.1.1; 3.4; 5.19; *Retractiones*, 2.1; *Ep.*, 37.

Although only one letter remains of those which Ambrose sent to Chromatius in Aquileia, it is likely that Ambrose availed himself widely of the doctrinal preparation of this priest who had filled a succession of ecclesiastical career posts before being appointed bishop.[94] Ambrose certainly consulted him on the occasion of the Council of Aquileia. Thanks to Chromatius' intervention, the discussion at Aquileia hinged decisively on the christological question, which was central to the conflict between the Arians and the Nicenes. Later, it was also Chromatius who at Palladius's request raised suitable points of jurisdictional practice to allow the intervention of *auditores* and *exceptores* in the Council.[95] Naturally, the few bishops whom Ambrose had wanted at Aquileia were all his trusted friends. Sabinus was there and Eusebius of Bononia, who earned from Palladius the ironical nickname of Ambrose's *adsessor*.[96] Both seem to have played a not insignificant part in supporting Ambrose's programme in his see of stimulating female conversions to asceticism. In fact, groups of young women from Placentia and Bononia flocked to Milan, hoping to be consecrated by the new bishop of that city.[97]

Once he had gained prestige and *auctoritas*, Ambrose worked actively to create throughout northern Italy an ecclesiastical front which was as homogeneous and united as possible in the direction in which he wished Christianity to go. Many of the letters which he wrote to younger colleagues have a similar direction and purpose. In almost all of them, after an initial reference to their recent consecration and an organic definition of the office of priesthood, the main part of the letter comprises a kind of set of ethical rules intended to determine the social behaviour of the

[94] It is well known that the ninety-two letters of Ambrose which have reached us are only a part of the letters he wrote, probably only a section of those he intended to publish during his lifetime. Of his correspondence with Chromatius we only have *Ep.* 50, which Ambrose presented as the first in a series (*Ep.* 50.16).

[95] Cracco Ruggini, 'Il vescovo Cromazio e gli ebrei di Aquileia', *AAAd* XII (1977), 359–61.

[96] Palladius, *Apol.*, 117 (Roger Gryson, ed., *Scolies Ariennes sur le Concile d'Aquilée, SCh.*, 267, Paris: Cerf, 1980), 343 r.

[97] This is the most likely interpretation of Ambrose, *De virginitate*, I, 57: cf. Lizzi, 'Una società esortata all'ascetismo', 137. On the identity of Eusebius as addressee of *Epp.*, 54–5 of Ambrose, see McLynn, *Ambrose*, 66, nn. 46–7.

communities. This is not simply a standard or conventional procedure, since it refers in detail to specific problems which the individual bishops were called on to solve.[98] For instance, when Ambrose wrote to Constantius, Bishop of Claterna, he called on him to intervene in order to sort out the relationships between the great landowners of his city in order to limit their attempts to expand their land holdings.[99] He addressed himself directly to them so that they would be aware of the condition of the 'workers' (*operarii*), of the 'farm labourers' (*mercenarii*), and of the 'slaves' (*servi*), all of whom they were refusing to recompense adequately.[100] Ambrose's emphasis was not so much on general themes of the desire for wealth, as on specific situations which affected the relationships between *domini* and between them and their *servi*. In his letter to Vigilius of Tridentum, however, Ambrose reminded him to put particular emphasis on themes of *hospitalitas* in the specific sense of a 'tax on landowners' (*munus hospitalitatis*). Since this imposed on citizens the heavy burden of accommodating military establishments in their landed estates (*praedia*), it must have been particularly burdensome for cities such as Tridentum which had once more – after the collapse of the *limes* of Rhaetia – become frontier posts.[101]

To the people and the clergy of Thessalonica, who were called on to choose a successor to Acolius, Ambrose sent a funeral eulogy of the late bishop which was intended to serve as a management model which any future bishop should follow.[102] In a city such as Thessalonica which Acolius had turned into a Nicene stronghold in the middle of Arian territory, it was essential to ensure the choice of a bishop who would guarantee to continue the policy of his predecessor. A subsequent letter in which Ambrose congratulated Anysius, disciple and deacon of Acolius's church, shows the extent to which his advice had been followed.[103] We can interpret in a similar context his letter to the people and clergy of Vercelli. Here, Ambrose recollected the work carried out in the

---

[98] Lizzi, 'Codicilli imperiali e *insignia episcopalis*: un'affinità significativa', *Rendiconti Instituto Lombardo* 122 (1988), 3–13.

[99] Ambrose, *Ep.*, 2.30.

[100] Ambrose, *Ep.*, 2, 12, 31.

[101] Ambrose, *Ep.*, 19; Lizzi, *Vescovi*, 51–2.

[102] Ambrose, *Ep.*, 15.

[103] Ambrose, *Ep.*, 16.

city by its first bishop, Eusebius, leading not only to a suggestion as to Limenius' successor, but also to ensuring that the new
bishop would pursue a religious policy committed to the Eusebius–
Ambrose line.[104] In such cases, when Ambrose was dealing with
the difficulties which Christianization in the towns could expect
to have to face, he normally addressed himself to particular groups
from whom he might expect more vocations to the priesthood to
come. In a letter to Felix of Como shortly after his appointment
to the bishop's throne he wrote, 'The harvest of Christ is great,
but the workers are few, and it is hard to find those who can help.
It is true, but great is the Lord who will send workers for his
harvest. Certainly, there are many among the decurions of Comum
(*in illo ordine Comensium*) who have begun to believe in your
government . . .'.[105] Ambrose was clearly referring to the order of
city decurions, a group which already at the end of the fourth
century in small towns like Como must have developed a clearly
defined character. In order to build the urban structure of the church
it was essential that the members of such classes should adhere to
Christianity. It was from them in particular that the new ministers
of Christianity would come in ever-increasing numbers.

IV. PROMOTING THE CHRISTIAN COMMUNITY
IN THE CITIES

Gaudentius of Brescia: interpreting scripture for the urban upper classes

A critical approach to the problem of conversion requires that
we give adequate attention not only to the results of the process
(in what ways and how rapidly it developed), but also to the
means by which it was carried out. From this point of view,
northern Italy offers the historian a privileged situation, comparable to the situation in Cappadocia under Basil and the two
Gregories or in the Syria of John Chrysostom or Theodoret of
Cyrus. Fortunately, we have the sermons of a number of bishops,
linked to the figure of Ambrose, who were active at the end of
the fourth century in cities whose religious lives appear to have

[104] Ambrose, *Ep.*, 63.
[105] Ambrose, *Ep.*, 4, 7.

maintained a considerable vitality. We can study these texts to understand the spirit and mentality which inspired them and the kind of Christianity they advocated in relation to the prevalent religious situation in their bishoprics. The literature which has been preserved is anything but stereotypical. The homilies, epistles and sermons of the northern Italian bishops allow the practical problems of the local Christian communities to filter through the exegesis of the Gospels or the commentary on the holy Scriptures. The primary intention of this preaching seems to have been to spread the faith to wider and wider areas of the *civitas* (with an almost total disregard for the countryside), with a special concern to convert the well-to-do classes.

In this sense, the homily production of Gaudentius of Brixia offers a model example of the process of Christianization. The fact that it was an *honoratus* who was encouraged to produce in written form the sermons he had given during Easter week for the instruction of neophytes, is in itself an indication of the preferential relationship which the bishop had established with the upper classes of citizens.[106] In the preface, Gaudentius stated the spiritual motives which induced him to respond to the request of Benivolus.[107] Moreover, the way in which the bishop presented Benivolus to his readers makes quite clear what the effects might be when groups from the ruling classes adhered to Christianity: 'In the same way as you are the most worthy leader of the *honorati* of our city so too you are of the people of God.'[108] The pre-eminence of Benivolus was not of a merely spiritual order, but was based also on a real political excellence. Benivolus in fact had been appointed to several positions in the service of the court and was an exponent of those emerging local classes to whom the moving of the capital to northern Italy had recently offered new career opportunities in the imperial bureaucracy. The structural balance of the period appears to suggest a close connection between spiritual advancement and political eminence, in such a way that

---

[106] The collection consists today of eighteen *Tractatus*, a letter to Benivolus which acts as preface to the first fifteen, and another two letters on problems of exegesis. All are almost certainly authentic, including number 16 on his ordination and 17 on the dedication of the *basilica Apostolorum*.

[107] *Praefatio*, 830–1.

[108] Gaudentius of Brescia, *Praefatio*, 2.

one justified the other and vice-versa. Benivolus was 'spiritual leader of the people of God' (*Caput Dominicae plebis*) because in his position as *magister memoriae* at the court of Milan he had preferred to resign his post rather than subscribe to a law against the Nicenes proposed by the Empress Giustina, while he was first among those who had public offices (*caput honoratorum*) insofar as he combined an outstanding public life with unshakeable Christian principles.[109] It is clear that the bishop tended to attribute to the faithful a spiritual superiority which was proportionate to their level in society, which must have considerably eased the spread of the Christian message among the upper classes of the city.

Amongst these citizens, the bishop had achieved a significant central position as the only person qualified to interpret the Scriptures. No one who wanted 'to examine the innermost meanings of the Word', no matter how high his level of secular education, could bypass the bishop. Two letters which are preserved in the collection together with the group of sermons are evidence of the lively circulation of epistles inspired by Ambrose which took place within Christian groups in northern Italy. The addressees of the two letters are unknown, but at least one of them, 'learned in secular culture' (*mundanae sapientiae litteris eruditus*), must have been a lay member of the Brescia community, whom Gaudentius's influence had won over to the reading and close examination of the sacred texts.[110] Serminius is in fact usually presented as the person whom the bishop addressed, drawing upon his outstanding cultural knowledge to clarify passages in the Gospels which were particularly difficult to explain.[111] Encouraged by educated members of the community, the bishop had become a mediator of knowledge for them too; at least this is how he chose to present himself.

The formal tone of his collection confirms this interpretation. While the stylistic sophistication may well be the result of the literary reworking, a high doctrinal and cultural level must have

---

[109] Ibid., 5–6. The event, which can be dated to 385, is recorded also by Rufinus, *HE*, II, 16 and Sozomen, *HE*, VII, 13.5. The law in question was issued by the Praetorian prefect Eusignius (*CT*, 16.1.4).
[110] Gaudentius of Brescia, *Tractatus*, 18.971.
[111] Gaudentius of Brescia, *Tractatus*, 18.972.

been present in the original oral preaching. The taste for connections, parallels, and symmetry of thought and expression is reflected in the structure of individual sermons, in each of which Origen's scheme of *historia, mysterium, mores* is carefully reflected. The boldness of some of the allegorical interpretations goes back to the oldest Alexandrine tradition. In educated Christian circles, who were willing inheritors of Origen's teachings, the literal aspect of the texts seemed to be the symbol of a deeper meaning which needed a suitable interpreter. The deeper the exploration of the sense of the scriptures, the more exalted appeared the level of holiness of the person explaining them. Apparently to lead his contemporaries to a deeper understanding of the extracts, Gaudentius introduced into his commentaries etymological explanations of words from Hebrew or Greek. However, alongside his frequent claim to have checked the readings concerned in the original language in the manuscripts, this sounds to the modern reader like Gaudentius was somewhat ostentatious in his demonstration of his learning and of the 'scientific' nature of his interpretative method.[112] His *Tractatus* are good examples of how the process of assimilating Graeco-Roman rhetorical culture by the higher ranks of the church was frequently determined by, or closely linked to, the progression of Christianization among the upper classes of the city.

The method Gaudentius used in dealing with the theme of alms, which maintained an even balance between the justification of wealth and an exhortation to use it wisely, is another indicator of the bishop's intention to avoid alienating the sympathies of the political and economic power groups, to whom the church could offer new ideal recognition.[113] Gaudentius addressed numerous vigorous appeals to the rich, evoking emotional scenes of the oppression of the poor, in line with that Stoic–Cynic literature which for centuries had dealt with problems related to poverty, to the benefits of a moderate life and other similar situations.[114] However, in the places where his attack on the lack of charity in the attitude of the *domini* was strongest, Gaudentius was careful

---

[112] Gaudentius of Brescia, *Tractatus*, 8.892; 11.922; 12.930; 12.931; 13.935.

[113] Gaudentius of Brescia, *Praefatio* 835: *non malitiose sed providenter te fecit Deus divitem, ut per opera misericordiae invenires peccatorum tuorum vulneribus medicinam.*

[114] Gaudentius of Brescia, *Tractatus*, 13.942.

to soften his tone. In the exegesis of the parable of the unjust steward (*vilicus iniquitatis*), he was eager to condemn the wicked *procurator* who, with reprehensible generosity, had wasted his master's substance by commuting all the peasants' debts.[115]

Chromatius of Aquileia: encouraging the enthusiasm of the town-dwellers for ecclesiastical projects

Exhorting people to almsgiving, together with reprimanding them for the negligence with which they carried it out, could be described as a leitmotiv of episcopal preaching in the fourth and fifth centuries. It developed along the lines of a series of *topoi* so that when the bishops presented the spiritually positive results guaranteed by charitable activity, they established a deep connection between such action, fasting and prayer, using these virtually as interchangeable terms in relation to the remission of sins. However, even in the stereotypes of sermons organized around this theme, minor differences in the way in which it is presented reflect significant variations in the relationship between bishop and faithful. Chromatius, for example, always tackled the theme very gravely and with no particular bias.[116] He invited the citizens to recreate the spirit of the primitive apostolic communities by pooling all their goods. Elsewhere he exhorted them to free themselves from avarice and greed for earthly things. If, however, we compare this with a similar sermon by Maximus, we can see how marginal such a problem was for the Bishop of Aquileia.[117] The difference in tone between the two sermons is only partly explained by the different level of development of Christianization amongst the upper classes of the two cities; more important was the unequal social and economic situation of the faithful to whom the bishops were addressing their preaching. Maximus's audience was made up of groups of landowners reduced to dire straits by heavy tax demands.[118] Chromatius, on the other hand, seems to

---

[115] Ibid., 18.974.
[116] Chromatius of Aquileia, *Sermones* I, 7.118–30; III, 1.9–11; 2.25–6; V, 5.74–9; XXXI, 4.116–39.
[117] Maximus of Turin, *Sermo.*, 71.
[118] Cf. the lively responses of the faithful to the bishop's invitation to give generously to the poor: *tributa sunt gravia, fiscalia explicare non possumus* (*Sermo.*, 71.3.44–51).

have been addressing people who were accustomed to the *negotiationes* characteristic of a town with a flourishing economy; they therefore were more inclined to spend a part of their fortune on charitable actions, with the by-product of acquiring prestige and authority within their community. The close comparison which Maximus developed between the beneficial effects of alms-giving and the devastating effects caused by taxation allows us to see the latent tension between the requirements of a church still in the organizational phase and the demands of a state presented as oppressive and in fact damaging to the well-being of its citizens.[119] However, the significance of the operation carried out by the Bishop of Turin is quite clear; he was convinced that he would obtain a satisfactory response from the faithful by presenting their offerings in such a way as to emphasize the notion of voluntary contribution (as opposed to the compulsory nature of tax demands), to which townspeople were traditionally accustomed.

Maximus's sermon shows clearly how able the church was to turn the traditional attitudes of the town-dwellers to its own advantage; but their response to the programmes of the Bishop of Aquileia demonstrates how successful such a tradition was. Because Chromatius skipped over the problem of alms in his sermons, it does not mean that the bishop did not encourage the faithful to give. Rather, it means that he was able to fit himself into an already well-tried tradition of the Aquileia bishopric. The level of voluntary donations of the most economically active classes was demonstrated by the construction in the city of splendid places of worship, some going back to the beginning of the fourth century.[120] Chromatius began the construction of a series of buildings, some in Aquileia, others in neighbouring centres (such as Concordia and Grado), gaining for himself the description of 'the Bezalel of our time', which Rufinus used to link him to the biblical builder of the tabernacle.[121] At least three churches in Aquileia can be dated to the period between the end of the fourth century and the beginning of the fifth (the basilica of Fondo Tullio alla Benigna,

---

[119] Maximus of Turin, *Sermo.*, 71, 51–6, 298–9.
[120] On the buildings which can be attributed to Theodore, Fortunatianus and Valerian see Lizzi, *Vescovi*, 139–45.
[121] Rufinus, *Praef. in Orig. Rom.*, 26.

S. Giovanni and the Basilica of Monastero).[122] Even if we allow that only the initial phase of many of these monuments is attributable to the bishop, the building programme which he undertook is still impressive. In the extent and richness of decoration, there is no comparison between this programme and that of any other bishop in the north Italian cities who managed at the most to build a single basilica or one or more oratories dedicated to some local martyr. This is what happened in Lodi, a few years after the election of Bassianus, so too in Como, Brescia and Turin.[123] Only in Milan, where in two decades Ambrose completed at least four basilicas (the *basilica Nova*, the *basilica Apostolorum*, later S. Nazaro, the *basilica Ambrosiana*, today S. Ambrogio, and probably the *basilica Virginum*, or S. Simpliciano) could the building projects rival those of Aquileia.[124]

The outstanding number of mosaic dedications gathered in the buildings attributable to the period of Chromatius shows how enthusiastically the citizens welcomed his initiatives. The donations, which are remarkably uniform in their size, reflect the homogeneous social origins of the donors, who belonged to that middle class which seems to have been, more than any other, sensitive to the bishop's exhortations. The tone of his sermons confirms this impression. His homilies, which are usually straightforward and simple in style, are rich in metaphors drawn from everyday life, particularly from the reality of trade from which come, for instance, images relating to the technicalities of lending money at interest, which must have been well known to members of his congregation.[125] Although we cannot deduce anything definite about Chromatius's attitude to *feneratio*, which other fathers denounced as immoral, we can, however, note the examples that the bishop used to refer to a type of lending, investment lending, which was particularly widespread among the merchant classes of *negotiatores*. It was probably among these that the

---

[122] Giovanni Brusin-Zovatto, *Monumenti romani e cristiani di Iulia Concordia* (Pordenone: Il Noncello, 1960), 143, 239, 271, 301; Luisa Bertacchi, 'Un decennio di scavi e scoperte d'interesse paleocristiano a Aquileia', *AAAd* 6, (1974), 63–91.

[123] Lizzi, *Vescovi*, 57.136–7; 205–9.

[124] Lizzi, *Vescovi*, 159–60, n. 75; McLynn, *Ambrose*, 226–36.

[125] Chromatius of Aquileia, *Sermones* XLI, 1, 5–6; IV, 3, 41–52 (on lending at interest).

bishop's sermons had the greatest effect, while his building programme helped to increase the development of those groups of medium and small artisans whose productive enterprise is variously documented in Aquileia in the first half of the fifth century. It is not especially easy to establish the level of Christianization amongst the upper classes. Apart from the Parecorius Apollinaris epigraph, according to which the *consularis Venetiae* contributed to the building of the *basilica Apostolorum*, we have very few other elements on which to base our conclusions.[126] However, Parecorius's dedication is sufficient to show that while Chromatius was capable of appreciating and stimulating the collection of modest donations, he was also able to see the importance of keeping good relations with the local élite.

All the evidence of Christianity which we gain from Aquileia shows the progressive spread of the church's social and economic importance. Chromatius's great enterprise of constructing sacred buildings had made the bishop a reference point for different groups of citizens, from the artisan workers to the local magistrates, even to the senior imperial officials who lived in the city. Its fortunate geographical position, which preserved it from the devastating effects of the frequent destructive barbarian raids of the period and ensured that it maintained excellent facilities for trade, had also encouraged the early spread of Christianity. In the fifth century, the predominance of the Christian faith in city life was visibly expressed in the numerous sacred buildings which had gradually transformed its old appearance and had completely changed the focal points of the city.

Maximus of Turin: leading a Christianized city, delegating the aggressive Christianization of the countryside

Maximus's sermons reflect a relationship between bishop and community which was much less homogeneous and more confrontational than that of Chromatius. This confirms how, within the same region and at about the same time, local situations cannot be reduced to discussions of a more general nature. There is very

---

[126] *CIL* V, 1582; on the identification of the church which had the co-operation of the *consularis*, see Lizzi, *Vescovi*, 144, n. 16.

little that is new in Maximus's doctrinal preparation, although he appears to have had a direct and personal link with the faithful, whose still contradictory spiritual demands he attempted to direct towards Christianity. His sermons only rarely took their inspiration from the interpretation of passages from the Scriptures. More frequently they developed as commentaries, with reference to the sacred texts, on events which had recently taken place, or on examples of collective behaviour which had caused the bishop some concern. So in the case of types of profiteering which had taken place during barbarian attacks, the bishop denounced publicly, and with a harshness which is surprising in a sermon, those who 'had allowed avarice to turn them into wolves and followed the trail of the robbers, consuming in their greed what the rapacity of the robbers had spared'.[127] He was equally blunt on another occasion, when an eclipse of the moon had caused a kind of collective panic throughout the population, driving many people to forget their Christian faith and to turn again to their forefathers' practices of exorcism.[128] It is in fact in this characteristic of close connection with current events that we can identify one of the most original elements of Maximus's work. It also demonstrates the degree of control which the bishop felt obliged to exercise on the faithful. As formal head of the whole city, he could attempt to choose the leisure activities of the population and organize their time according to rhythms laid down by the church. The liturgical cycle by now contained a number of important feasts which were occasions when the Scriptures were read and commented on.[129] By monitoring the participation of the citizens in such ceremonies, Maximus measured their constancy and commitment to their faith. With equal severity, he rebuked the members of the clergy and others of the faithful if they were less than assiduous in their worship.[130] The life of the city was by now clearly

[127] Maximus of Turin, *Sermo.*, 18, 49–70; 65–6: . . . *intellegis te praedae magis esse socium non venditionis emptorem!*

[128] Idem, *Sermo.*, 30.22–5.

[129] For Advent and Christmas see *Sermones*, 60; 61a; 61b; 61c; 62; 97; 99. For Epiphany, *Sermones*, 13a; 13b; 64; 65; 100; 101. For Lent, *Sermones* 35; 36; 50; 50a; 51; 52; 66–71; 111. For Easter, *Sermones*, 29, 37; 38; 53–5. For Pentecost, *Sermones*, 40; 44; 56.

[130] Maximus of Turin, *Sermo.*, 32, 38–50; for the *increpationes* addressed to members of the clergy, *Sermones*, 26.73–98; 27, 29, 108–10; 79, 27–33.

marked by a succession of sacred moments which all were obliged to respect.

We have already seen how the bishop, in his concern to enliven the faith of the citizens, exhorted them to distribute alms, by pointing out the advantages a Christian could gain from good works. Generosity towards one's brothers in faith gained forgiveness of the most grievous crimes, freeing one from guilt and 'persuading' God to be merciful to someone he would otherwise have punished.[131] Like a second baptism, almsgiving was even more effective, because it was repeatable.[132] In his attempts to persuade citizens to carry out charitable works, Maximus went so far as to admit that they had an expiatory and penitential nature, introducing in this way an important new aspect into Christian spirituality in northern Italy. Up till now, baptism had been central, endowed as a sacrament with the distinctive value of irrevocability in the conversion of an individual. Its ritual signified entry into a group which was intended to be characterized by norms of excellence and perfection. But Maximus, it is clear, reflected an idea of a church which was developing and changing from the way Ambrose had conceived it. Moral tolerance for converts, associated with an incredible intransigence towards religious minorities, was the price which the new institution paid for its speedy expansion.

Maximus's preaching also introduced significant variants into the definition of the principal functions which the bishop felt called to exercise. In particular there were changes in the hierarchy of values which, following Ambrose's lead, bishops like Gaudentius and Chromatius had shared. For Maximus, the *officium docendi* was no longer the most important task of a bishop, but was subordinated to the practical management of the church's wealth. The first duty of the priest was now the same as that carried out by the upper classes of citizens: to give away wealth in alms.[133] The conditions which up to this point had ensured that the teachings of Ambrose were an essential part of the exercise of the

---

[131] Idem, *Sermo.*, 61.23–32.
[132] Idem, *Sermo.*, 22a.67–9.
[133] Maximus of Turin, *Sermo.*, 27.3–6; cf. Chromatius, *Sermo.*, IV, 3.41–52, who underlines the religious importance of the *negotium*, in which the currency of trade was the word of God.

priesthood were clearly changed. The preaching of the Gospels had been of outstanding importance in the life of the church, so that it had become a function of the increase in the bishop's sphere of influence in the city. The intellectual power of his sermons had been a weapon against heretics and Jews. With their formal rigour, homilies could attract and win over even the most educated pagans. However, once the process of Christianization was an established fact, the bishop developed the potential of other functions (such as looking after and distributing wealth), while more and more frequently invoking the law against religious minorities.

The way that Maximus decided to solve the problem of the survival of pagan beliefs in the Turin countryside is symptomatic. In comparison with the city, in which the bishop was aware of only isolated examples of superstition,[134] the countryside, according to Maximus, was a hotbed of idolatry. In the countryside, ancient fertility rites were continued and soothsaying and sacrificial practices were perpetuated which in their bloodthirsty nature recalled the most atrocious gladiatorial spectacles; the diabolical force unleashed by such actions had the power to infect every product of the countryside.[135] This also fell heavily on the *conscientia* of the *possessores* to whom ideally was entrusted the Christianization of their own colonies.[136] According to Maximus, however, the consequences of the *possessores* passively accepting or even conniving in what went on were not of a merely ethical nature. The terminology which the bishop used and his open appeal to imperial legislation show that he intended to make use of the support of the State to impose specific legal obligations on the *domini*. An edict issued in 392 prescribed for the conniving lord (the *dominus conivens*) a fine equal to that imposed on the person carrying out the sacrifice.[137] Any person who did not intervene to prevent the celebration of pagan rites on his land was in fact made guilty of connivance (*coniventia*).[138] To ensure that the law was respected, the Emperor counted on the surveillance of *iudices*,

---

[134] On the occasion of lunar eclipses and at Christmastide when even the most devout Christians celebrated the start of the new year in pagan fashion after having solemnized the sacred rites in church (*Sermo.*, 61c, 64–75).

[135] Maximus of Turin, *Sermo.*, 91.23–8, and *Sermo.*, 107 onwards.

[136] Idem, *Sermo.*, 108.7–8.

[137] CT XVI.10.12.

[138] Maximus of Turin, *Sermo.*, 106.13–18.

defensores and *curiales singularium urbium.* Many property holders in Turin had to take on such positions, when they were encouraged by the bishop to exercise proper coercive powers.[139] The aggressive approach which Maximus demanded from the faithful in order to tear the farmers away from the 'error of the pagans' is completely different from the cautious attitude which Ambrose suggested to his priests. The discrepancy can be explained, however, if we consider the different social backgrounds of the groups which still practised paganism. Conversion was imposed on the peasants of the Turin countryside, as it was on those in Gaul, without any half measures. The new attitude of Christians also reflected the degree of legitimization which the ecclesiastical institution had achieved, supported as it was by imperial legislation which for twenty years between the late fourth century and the early fifth century incessantly listed new privileges and confirmed the old ones.

The martyrs of the Val di Non: an example of semi-urban Christianization

The approach of Maximus, who willingly delegated the Christianization of the country areas to the *domini*, confirms an important aspect of the path followed by Christianization in this period: it was prevalently urban in character.[140] One gains the distinct impression of a pronounced lack of interest in evangelizing the countryside, which was not dispelled by the incident in 397 in which three men whom Vigilius of Tridentum had sent into the Val di Non were martyred. The event is usually interpreted as evidence of the missionary desire of a church which was trying to expand in rural areas in which ancient pagan worship still survived.[141] Interpreting this event has been problematic because

---

[139] Idem, *Sermo.*, 106.24-5, 417.

[140] In the same way, Gaudentius when referring on at least one occasion to paganism in the countryside around Brixia held the *domini* responsible for its continued presence: *Tractatus*, 13.940.

[141] Many of the divinities whom the peoples of the Alpine regions still worshipped, such as Mars, Hercules, Silvanus, Saturn and even Victory, although redefined in relation to the Roman pantheon, still kept attributes and functions which were by nature Celtic. The more recent worship of Mithras, however, was connected to the massive military presence: see Cecil Bennet Pascal, *The Cults of Cisalpine Gaul*, Collection Latomus 75 (Brussels: Latomus, 1964), *infra.*

93

of an incorrect reading of the two letters sent to Simplicianus of Milan and to John Chrysostom to inform them about what had happened and to accompany the gift of the relics of the three martyrs.[142] These are explicitly hagiographic texts, written to promote the canonization of the clerics who had perished in the struggle against the pagan people of the area. Because this is their intention, the two letters confer on the area an exaggeratedly rustic nature, emphasizing the narrowness (*angustiae*) of a place which in itself nourished acts of perfidy. However, evidence from other sources, particularly inscriptions, demonstrates the high level of Romanization of Anaunia.[143] The inhabitants of the rich and flourishing villages which stud the region (which had never been accorded the *status* of proper *civitates*) had enjoyed Roman citizenship from the time of Claudius.[144] It is also clear from Vigilius's text that the church was already well established in these large semi-urban communities. The three clerics had specific hierarchical functions and they regularly held acts of worship in a small sacred building.[145] The bloody outcome of the clash, marked by the repressive intervention of the Empire, did, however, have positive results for the triumph of Christendom.[146] The killing of the three clerics (who were only a few of those who perished in similar clashes and who were only transformed into martyrs for the faith by the clever ecclesiastical policy of Vigilius and Simplicianus) apparently completed the work of Christianization of the valley. This is clear from the satisfaction expressed at the end of Vigilius's letter to Chrysostom: 'But the Church grew more prolific after the injury, more lasting from the death, happier from

---

[142] Vigilius, *Epp.*, I–II in *Acta Sanctorum Mai* VII, 41–5 = PL, 13.549–58. The traditional interpretation, according to the view supported and reaffirmed by local scholars and antiquarians from the nineteenth century onwards, is reassumed in Igino Rogger, 'Sisinno, Martirio, Alessandro', *Bibliotheca Sanctorum* XI (Rome: 1969), 1251–3.

[143] Lizzi, *Vescovi*, 70–80.

[144] On the *Tabula Clesiana* and its identification of the Anauni as one of the *populi adtributi* to the *municipium* of Tridentum, see Umberto Laffi, '*Adtributio*' e '*Contributio*': *Problemi del sistema politico amministrativo dello Stato romano* (Pisa: Studi di lettere, storia e filos. della Scuola Normale Superiore di Pisa, 1966).

[145] For the importance of these elements, see Lizzi, *Vescovi*, 59–96.

[146] From Augustine we learn that the culprits, who were caught and sentenced to death, were saved only through the bishop's intercession with the Emperor: Aug., *Ep.*, 139.

the affliction . . . These are the centuplicated incomes of the Passion [of Christ and of the three martyrs]'.

It is pointless to question the sincerity of so many conversions. In other situations, in other periods, episodes of bloody struggle very frequently led to phenomena of mass conversions. The strength of ties binding members of restricted rural communities which did not allow any differences in behaviour could condition people much more effectively than any slow and patient work of missionary activity.[147] The clash which took place in the Val di Non acted in the same way. In the place of the small church which had previously existed, a bigger basilica was built. In a place which was holy by tradition, popular piety could be nourished by the worship of the new saints, worship which was in many ways very close to that offered to the ancient divinities.[148]

---

[147] Ewa Wipszycka, 'La christianisation de l'Egypte aux IVe–VIe siècles: aspects sociaux et ethniques', *Aegyptus* 68 (1988), 117–65 = eadem, *Études sur le christianisme dans l'Egypte de l'Antiquité tardive* (Rome: Institutum Patristicum Augustinianum, 1996), 63–105.

[148] The positioning of churches and oratories is an important aspect of the way in which the process of evangelization subsumed part of the folklore culture into the culture of the church: Jacques Le Goff, 'Cultura ecclesiastica e tradizioni folkloriche nella civiltà merovingia', in *Agiografia altomedievale* (Bologna: Il Mulino, 1976), 215–26.

Chapter 3

Christianity Shaped through its Mission

RAMSAY MacMULLEN

Christianity spread rapidly in the West between the fourth and eighth centuries. This growth was largely unwilling. It took place not by evangelistic sermons, but by wonderful acts which demonstrated divine power. Further, the growth resulted from preachers pressurizing wealthy élites to secure the conversion – by threat or force – of their underlings. In this they were backed up by rulers with their laws and armed forces. The conversion which these methods elicited was incomplete. Pre-Christian religious observances associated with trees and springs, or with festivals such as the Kalends and the Lupercalia, persisted in Christendom despite the opposition of church leaders. So also did rituals at tombs, out of which grew the cult of the sanctified dead, who brought various benefits to the people. As a result, the Christianity which developed was changed – to a significant degree it was paganized – as it appropriated attitudes and practices which hitherto had been associated with paganism.

Three points that make a sort of chain of explanation appear in the record of conversion over the fourth to eighth centuries in the West: first, that conversion was largely unwilling; second, that it was incomplete; third, that it introduced into the church, as a condition of further success, some significant degree of paganization.

Unwilling conversion

I begin with the year of the Edict of Toleration, AD 313. The church then constituted perhaps as much as a tenth – let us call

97

them 6 million – within the population of the Mediterranean world, though considerably less than this proportion in the Western areas. A scholarly consensus is forming around the figure 50 per cent or 30 million in the church at the turn of the next century. Why should there be only 6 million converts in the first 250 or 260 years, but 25 million more over the next seventy-five? What accounts for the huge acceleration of church growth?

As a result of the edict, the surroundings of the church underwent a sharp change. They became, not neutral, not at times actively hostile, but rather officially nourishing through several important agencies and processes. Immediately, the preventive of fear was removed from conversion; imperial favour added great prestige; privileges and wealth were showered on church leaders. To explain the acceleration in the rate of church growth, various historians have chosen now one, now another among these changes to be specially emphasized. No preference can be justified in conventional terms of proof; each may be urged according to what someone supposes is common sense, or probability, without anything probative underlying it. On the face of it, however, some admixture of material benefit must be allowed, along with a now unafraid desire, to explain the rising tide of conversion.

In addition, in trying to judge motive, we find some guidance in the measures to increase growth chosen by church leaders themselves. They were, after all, on the scene and able to judge what worked, and certainly very eager.

We notice, in the first place, that they did not go around preaching. Modern observers of the ancient world raised on the New Testament have the greatest difficulty in confronting this fact. They recall Paul's career, they think of him with his companions on endless travels and before endless numbers of tiny, generally inhospitable audiences, and they suppose this must have been the only way church growth could be achieved. Once the life and spell of this one man were spent, however, almost nothing of the sort can be again discovered until the sixth century, and then principally beyond the confines of the ancient world, in Ireland or Germany or Scandinavia.

Beyond the question, whether preaching to pagans constituted a church routine of any significance, its effectiveness in changing people's minds is rarely indicated; and that fact seems equally strange to modern observers. It should have been within the powers of eloquence simply to talk people into belief. Was the job so difficult? But instead, what is ordinarily attested in conversion-scenes are responses to demonstrations of superhuman power: perceived as miracles, in turn they were perceived as proofs of genuine divinity attaching to whatever deity was invoked and credited. Of this sort of evidence, and for the period I have chosen to discuss, I point out elsewhere what I have been able to find.[1] To sum it up briefly: the forms of wonderful act most familiar in pre-Constantinian conversions, namely, through exorcism, first, and other healings of mind or body, and less often through other miscellaneous acts in contradiction of natural laws – these forms are still to be found after Constantine as well. Examples are well known in the campaigns of Martin and in the powers of his relics from his tomb; likewise, in the powers of other saints and relics. St Amandus raised a dead man to life. The miracle, we are told, 'was spread abroad, far and wide, whereupon, immediately, the natives of the region flocked to him to be made Christians'. It is plain that there was an interest in such accounts because the crowds at saints'-day festivals were large and were addressed in the very most admired and most effective style that the ranks of the leadership were able to supply. Those who listened, however, were of course Christians; they were already in the church; and what was said to them can't be called preaching in any evangelical sense, whatever favourable notoriety it might generate by their retelling, in turn, when they were at home. There was no effort by the church to make a routine of this.

Conversion by threats of the élites

What is more easily documented is the church's encouraging of the wealthy to do the job themselves. Despite what is often thought to have been the case – that everyone who was Christian attended services every Sunday and festal day, thus to hear the sermons we now have before us in their Benedictine edition or whatever modern form – in fact, attendance was largely limited to what we would call the upper-middle class and aristocracy. While the evidence for this is more abundant in Eastern settings, still, in north Africa through Augustine and through Caesarius in France we can see

[1] R. MacMullen, *Christianity and Paganism in the 4th to 8th Century* (New Haven: Yale University Press, 1997), ch. 1, hereafter cited as *Christianity*.

who was addressed from the pulpit: almost though not quite exclusively rich males, owners of slaves and fields and money to spend on expensive possessions. Only in the small churches of country districts where no such upper crust really existed does the tone change, as in northern Italy, for example; yet still it is suited to the best class the district can afford.[2]

To this audience, a bishop would make the plea that they should speak on his behalf to the unconverted who were on their land. This is insisted on again and again in sermons and in the canons of councils in Africa, Spain, France and Italy from the later fourth century into the sixth.[3] But words wouldn't be enough, that much was clear; so the landowners were told also to threaten. First in the series of fifth-century measures of this sort is imperial legislation aimed at the reform, not of pagans, but of schismatics, who, if they belonged to the higher classes, must be corrected by heavy fines, and 'peasants, *coloni*, by frequent flogging, unless their masters themselves should prefer to be held liable to the aforesaid fines'.[4] It is safe to say that the procedure was not of Honorius' invention, but recommended to him by ecclesiastical advisers. The method appealed later to Caesarius in the early years of the sixth century, adjuring the landlords who stand before him to destroy on their lands all altars and sacred trees – the latter being in France from time immemorial among the commonest of cult-objects. 'Chastize those persons whom you know to be guilty,' Caesarius tells them; 'warn them very harshly, berate them very severely, and if they are not improved by this, cut off their hair, too. If they still persevere, bind them in iron shackles.' He reverts to the problem and its solution more than once: 'Berate them severely, flog them even with your whips,' he says again.[5] A century later,

---

[2] Ibid., 10, 167–8.

[3] For the command that landowners browbeat their slaves, servants, peasants and dependents, to convert them, see *Conc. Illiberr.* can. 41 (Mansi 2.288), or Maximus of Turin, *Serm.* 101 (*PL* 57.733f.) = 107.1f. Mutzenbecher (*CCSL* 23.420f.), directing inspection of dependants' huts; *Serm.* 102, the same charge to landlords; *Conc. Arelat.* a. 452 can. 23 (Mansi 7.881); Caesarius of Arles, *Serm.* 53.223f. and 54.229; and *Conc. Bracar.* a. 571 frg. 22 (Mansi 9.844).

[4] *Codex Theodosianus* (henceforth *CT*) 16.5.52 (412).

[5] In W. E. Klingshirn, *Caesarius of Arles: The Making of a Christian Community in Late Antique Gaul* (Cambridge: Cambridge University Press, 1994), 239; *Vita Caesarii* 54.5, 53.2 and 13.5.

Pope Gregory has the same recommendations to make to his bishops in Sardinia, where apparently the population was hardly touched by Christianity: 'If they are slaves, chastize them with blows of the lash and tortures, but if freemen, they deserve a term in the lock-up' (of the sort that big estates ordinarily had in readiness). Through correspondence he brought to bear a convenient Duke with his troops, and went on to complain to the empress.[6] It may be easily guessed what sort of mission the Duke was expected to bring to bear. Sicily's unbelievers received the Pope's attention, too, through both his bishops and the civil governor; likewise the tree-worshipping Christians of Spain, directed to the attention of the Count Maurus, while, among the Franks, Queen Brunigild was asked to police her Christian subjects, given as they were to the worship of trees and idols or demons – this, in 597. King Childebert later joined in, with decrees forcing landowners who did not persecute heathenism on their estates to give sureties for their more proper behaviour. With rising exasperation, the bishops assembled at Toledo in 681, quoting Deuteronomy to set the tone (17:2ff., that idolaters are to be stoned to death), and directing everyone found in the worship of sacred stones, springs, or trees to be beheaded by the civil authorities, unless, of course, their lords undertake to flog and manacle them and prevent any repetitions of their acts of worship. Heathen offerings could be confiscated by the local church and any person of high status who got in the way should be fined a great sum of gold (three pounds), while slaves were to receive a hundred lashes. So said King Egica a decade later, drawing in the civil authorities to the campaign; similarly, Dagobert threatening physical compulsion against anyone who refused baptism.[7] Next perhaps to be mentioned, the Council of Estinnes in 744 directed the collection of fines of 15

---

[6] Gregory the Great, *Registrum* 4.23, 5.38, 8.4 (*CCSL* 140.521), 8.19 (539) and 9.205 (764); also *Ep.* 4.23 and 25, 3.59 (207), and 9.204, in I. Rochow, 'Zu einigen oppositionellen religiösen Strömungen', *Byzanz im 7. Jahrhundert: Untersuchungen zur Herausbildung des Feudalismus* (Berlin: Akademie-Verlag, 1978), 251f., 253.

[7] Childebert I, *Praeceptum* (*MGH Legum* 2, 1, p. 2); *Conc. Tolet.* XII a. 681 can. 11; *Conc. Tolet.* XVI a. 693 can. 2 (*PL* 84.537 = *MGH Legum* 1,1.481f.); *Vita Amandi* 13 (*MGH SRM* 5.437).

solidi for any act of idolatry.[8] So it went up into the reign of Charlemagne, a champion in due course thought worthy of sanctification: he too decreed fines for heathen practices, if one had the money, but otherwise, perpetrators were to be made slaves and given to the church.[9]

Pressure from rulers and laws

During the course of these 300 or 400 years, as a steady companion in their efforts, bishops had the emperors and, at times quite as important, empresses as well. The fact appears in certain isolated incidents, it may be suspected behind others, and it is made explicit, of course, in legislation. Most relevant laws are gathered in the tenth chapter of the sixteenth book of the Theodosian Code. Those directed at unlicensed acts of worship confront Jews, Manichaeans, and dozens of declared heresies in addition to pagans, in the East more obviously than in the West. Within only the series in the West, Constantius marks the beginning in the 340s. His successors pursue the persecution for as long as there are any regions still under their rule: in Africa in 407 (§20, repeated as the twelfth Sirmondian), still in 425, imposing exile; and in Italy, continuing the penalties of compulsory enrolment in financially onerous civic duties for everybody not of the orthodox faith.[10] Perhaps evidence might be drawn into the West from the East, where the effect of such laws shows in the fear that attended hold-out paganism. But such evidence is slight, occasional, anecdotal and from a different region. How close to impossible it is, to penetrate to people's inner thoughts and motives, generally, in our observing of the past and most particularly in trying to understand conversion!

---

[8] A. Dierkens, 'Les survivances du paganisme (en Neustrie mérovingienne)', in P. Périn and L.-C. Feffer, eds, *La Neustrie: Les pays au Nord de la Loire, de Dagobert à Charles le Chauve (VIIe–IXe siècles)* (Rouen: Musées et Monuments départmentaux de Seine-Maritime, 1985), 16.

[9] *MGH Legum* 2, 1.69 §21, in D. Harmening, *Superstitio: Überlieferungs – und theoriegeschichtliche Untersuchungen zur kirklich-theologische Aberglaubensliteratur des Mittelalters* (Berlin: E. Schmidt, 1979), 57, for cult-acts addressed to springs, groves, or trees, a 60-solidus fine, or condemnation to slavery in the church. On the prevalence of tree-cult, see *Christianity*, ch. 2 n. 112.

[10] *CT* 16.5.63; 12.1.157 a. 398.

Secular authority could provide men at arms. That was just what the bishops wanted, and in his time, the Pope wanted, too. It especially needs emphasis because of its effectiveness, quite limited, yet least so against those pagans who had most to lose: the wealthy and prominent. They were subject to action in the courts, therefore to delation, therefore to painful loss of money; but their neighbours would not readily confront them without some backing. Just how well or how often legal threats influenced conduct, no one can assert nor even guess in any manner to be substantiated with cases in point; yet there is the indirect testimony of Augustine. He says his enemies of another faith 'hide and flee in fear of the laws'; and it was in the belief that the laws worked that he and other bishops had joined in appeals to the throne for helpful legislation.[11] They obtained the mission of two imperial officials in 399 to destroy temples and idols throughout the province; they were sent three other agents in 408, backed up by the emperors' insistence that 'proprietors, *domini*, of the landholdings shall be compelled to destroy altars and temples' on their estates; and in 421 they rejoiced to see the procurator in charge of imperial estates instructed to carry out the persecution across the huge area, and a corresponding agricultural population, subject to his authority.[12]

With this population we return to the role of the rich. The masses were largely beyond the reach of government, porous as was its structure and limited its presence. But you could certainly get at them through their lords and masters. An imperial procurator must be an important ally in the cause of conversion. Concerning another person of local distinction, 'that nobleman', says Augustine, 'that nobleman, if he were only Christian, not a pagan would be left. Men often say, "Not a pagan would be left if *he* were a Christian!"'[13] A century later, Salvian explains how 'the great rich houses shape the city's crowd ... Slaves are all like their masters'.

---

[11] F. Dolbeau, 'Nouveaux sermons de saint Augustin pour la conversion des païens et des donatistes', *Revue des études augustiniennes* 37 (1991), 48, of about a. 404 referring to legislation of 399, and pp. 40f. and 55.

[12] *CT* 16.10.16; *Conc. Afr.* a. 401, Mansi 3.766 = C. Munier pp. 196 §58 and 205 §84, with *CT* 16.10.19.1 = *Sirm.* 12 a. 408, quoted, and including also imperial estates; and *Prosopography of the Later Roman Empire*, 2.1192, s.v. 'Ursus'.

[13] R. MacMullen, *Christianizing the Roman Empire (AD 100–400)* (New Haven: Yale University Press, 1984), 65, with notes 16f.

Augustine's and Salvian's remarks reflect the realities of life, or what may be called the structure of power in ancient society. They were hardly changed since Paul's day, when whole households might be converted from the top down.

Within the cities of France or Italy in the fourth to seventh centuries, the amount and ambition of ecclesiastical building demonstrate the advance of Christianity. Yet it lost ground in Spain.[14] In north Africa, we have not only the same sort of archaeological evidence but, in addition, Augustine's testimony for his own day. He indicates the prevalence of unconverted private piety in rural residences and certain urban centres almost totally pagan, though others, the reverse. There is also valuable epigraphic information recently presented and put in context by C. R. Galvao-Sobrinho. What he collects to show the more conscious and self-affirming spirit of the Christian population in the face of death, through the custom of epitaphs, also shows peaks in numbers for selected Western cities and areas only after 525; and, as the total population certainly did not increase, the lower numbers pre-525 must suggest proportions of the converted among the total of residents. By that interpretation, Christians would constitute a tenth of the population in the fifth century.[15]

Protests against coerced conversion

Where information is so sparse and problematical for so compli- cated a thing as religious loyalties, perhaps no rough estimates are rough enough; but for my purposes I need only demonstrate that conversion was really difficult, an unpopular thing, much against the grain. That much seems to me clearly established. It follows

[14] S. McKenna, *Paganism and Pagan Survivals in Spain up to the Fall of the Visigothic Kingdom* (Washington, DC: Catholic University of America, 1938), 115f.

[15] Augustine, *Serm.* 62.18, 'statues abundantly to be seen in the gardens of private villas'; C. R. Galvao-Sobrinho, 'Funerary epigraphy and the spread of Christianity in the West', *Athenaeum* 83 (1995), 463ff., where only the curve of the graph for Rome and for Belgica reach their highest point earlier than 525, while Spain, the Vienne region in eastern France, and four African cities do so post-525. The estimate of a tenth of the African urban population I draw from Fig. 3, not supposing it is truly accurate.

that there might be protest. The bishops in 658 demanded that 'trees sacred to *daemones*', as Christians called non-Christian deities, 'and which the people, the *vulgus* hold so reverend that they dare cut neither branch nor twig, be hewn down to the roots and burnt up'. I notice the piety of the believers, freely acknowledged by the persecutors. St Eligius had thundered, Cut them down.[16] Very good; but when St Martin had tried it, much earlier, the pagans had refused him permission; those to the south in Arles in Caesarius' day, when such a thing was done, wouldn't take the remains home as firewood. Caesarius was amazed.[17] Only a zealot could be. The obstinate heathens had, after all, lived their lives individually and as a people for as long as memory could reach, under the benevolent protection of beings they knew as gods, often tested, whether or not some ignorant bigot (with various sorts of secular Powers behind him) chose to call them *daemones*.

Worshippers brought together for a festival in the square before the church were lectured by the bishop from the steps, in angry and insulting phrases, provoking a forthright answer (as his biographer tells us): 'No matter how often you rebuke us, Romans, you will never succeed in tearing out our customs. We will rather perform our rites as heretofore, and always and forever gather for them; nor will there be a man ever to prohibit our ancient and dearest festivals.'[18] This, in the 640s. The spokesman for the crowd deluded them: the violent overthrow of idols, cutting down of sacred trees, and burning of shrines by the odd visitor among them from time to time, steadily reduced the ranks or at least the visible presence of non-Christians. The archaeological evidence, in the form of the minutely fanatical breaking to pieces of holy images and architectural members of shrines, confirms and amplifies the hagiographical. For this, there is as much evidence as one could

---

[16] In Harmening, *Superstitio*, 61, the Synod Nannetense a. *c.*658 can. 20 (Mansi 18.167 = K. J. Hefele, *A History of the Councils of the Church* 5 [Edinburgh, 1895], 478); Eligius in a model sermon, cf. Audeonius, *Vita Elig.* 2.15, *MGH SRM* 4.707.

[17] Sulpicius Severus, *Vita S. Mart.* (*CSEL* 1.122); Caesarius, *Serm.* 54.5, in Klingshirn, *Caesarius*, 213.

[18] E. Vacandard, 'L'idolâtrie en Gaule au VIᵉ et au VIIᵉ siècles', *Revue des questions historiques* 65 (1899), 447, notices the quoted passage, Audeonius, *Vita Eligii* 2.19 (*PL* 87.554A = *Vita*, 2.20, *MGH SRM* 4.712).

wish – unless one could wish for less. The violence of Christian hatred is too clear.[19]

The first point I wished to defend, that conversion was largely unwilling, now can be seen for what it is – strictly speaking, an inference, no more. It is not proven. Only a large number of before-and-after interviews would do the job to our modern taste. In default of such proof, however, we do have circumstantial evidence good enough, I would say, to take before a jury. It consists of much physical force amply documented and not to be explained except by resistance; also, occasional episodes of such physical resistance supported by spoken protest; and, in the background, the fact that a majority of a settled population has never in history, I believe, abandoned its settled religion except in the face of superior secular force. Given that the inequality of force between Christians and non-Christians was significant but not overwhelming, we would expect, then, just what we find, as confirmation of my view: we find some rapid and easy conversions, of which many a religion has boasted before and since, but a greater success, only after many centuries of persecution.

Incomplete conversion

Next, the case for incomplete conversion. Here the evidence is far more clear, but requires a preliminary explanation. There is, to certain minds, a thing called a 'good Christian', who alone is in fact 'a Christian' at all. Around both titles shines an aureole of perfection accredited by some certain authority: that of the approving observers, or someone else they also approve. To the extent the aureole is dim or quite indiscernible, the title 'Christian' is to be denied. Therefore the incomplete convert is no convert at all; there is no such thing as a half-Christian.

Were we all Dukes of Alva or Conrads of Marburg, were we all Savonarolas, we could agree on this without more debate; but

---

[19] Smashing of idols, most famously by Martin but also, e.g. in Noricum, cf. Eugippius, *Vita S. Severini* in P. Régerat, *Vie de Saint Séverin*, *SCh.* 374 (Paris: Cerf, 1991), 105, or near Oust in France, *Vita Walarici* 22, in L. Musset, 'De saint Victrice à saint Ouen: la christianisation de la province de Rouen d'après l'hagiographie', *Revue d'histoire de l'église de France* 62 (1976), 141–52; arson by St Gall, in Gregory of Tours, *Vitae patrum* 6.2 (*PL* 71.1031). On the material evidence of shrine- and idol-destruction, see my *Christianity*, 51, 66–7, 188, 199.

historians are a generally weak-willed lot. They generally make an effort not to choose up sides, so as to omit no one from their sympathy. Thus, if someone is baptized, if he says he's a Christian, they are inclined, as I am inclined, to allow his claim to membership in the term. As to a more precise definition of the church's boundaries, as about the boundaries of citizenship in any state, in any association, or any corporation, let the lawyers argue it out in court. Their wrangling can only concern quite peripheral considerations.

Regarding conversion in the western provinces of the Empire and the successor kingdoms, it must be recalled that nine-tenths of what we think we know is to be learnt from sermons and conciliar decrees directed at ordinary accepted congregations, among whom, however, we discover much about religious life that the bishops describe in detail, only for the purpose of correcting it. The misguided are, for instance, part of Martin of Braga's flock. In the 570s he points out how wrong his people are to worship trees, stones and springs, as they do; to worship the old gods in other forms and places; to cling to the cult of the dead at their tomb-side with memorial banqueting; or to go wild with precatory partying and noisy song and dance on the opening days of the new year. These acts he knew and said were religious, or rather sacrilegious, yet pervasive. Again they draw rebuke from the French bishops assembled in 658.[20] They were ineradicable. Similarly Salvian in the 440s deplores the continued worship of the great goddess of Carthage, Caelestis, by Christians simultaneously with the worship of Jesus. He singles out for reproach the local élite, whose position gave them some immunity from persecution. An echo sounds in Augustine's mention of a leader in the Attis-celebrations in Hippo, the very priest of that cult, clad in his sacral costume, a Christian! He rebukes his audience, too, for appealing to Juno or Minerva or, as he says with airy irritation,

---

[20] In Martin's *Capitula ex orientalium patrum synodis* 69, *prandia ad defunctorum sepulchra*, and §73, tree worship by the baptized, also celebration of Kalends and Vulcanalia, libations to household gods, and much else, as also in Martin of Braga, *De corr. rust.* 16, and general condemnation of worshipping pagan gods, *daemonia*, ibid. §1 and 3, and worship of stones, §7, with context in C. W. Barlow, *Martini episcopi Bracarensis opera omnia* (New Haven: Yale University Press, 1950), 140, 184, and 198f.; and tree- and spring-cult among Christians still in *c.*658, cf. above, n. 16.

'demons and idols and who knows what Powers', *potestates*.[21] St Amandus two centuries later in northern France discovered tree worship among the baptized; Zeno, Caesarius, and Pope Gregory complain of Christians who are worshippers simultaneously of the old gods.[22] With his episcopal associates in councils, one of these three, Caesarius, in fact returns to the problem again and again. In their exasperation the bishops almost shout at their churches. Finally: Agobard in the ninth century, speaking of the Lyon area, reports that 'in these regions nearly everyone, noble or lowly, city-folk or rustics, young or old, believe hailstorms and thunder lie within the control of man', called *tempestarii*, whose incantations they seek out.[23]

Enough of these instances and attestations. More would risk adventuring into times too late and different; and for the moment it seems best not to approach too close to the dividing line between magic and religion (where lies another distracting dispute over definitions). The principal conclusion to which the texts of the preceding paragraph all point is the distance between a strict definition of right conduct in one's religion, taught by the bishops, and a looser definition easily discoverable among the laity.

Looseness sometimes extended to outright challenge. One of his own people protests to Augustine, 'Of course I visit idols, and I consult inspired men and soothsayers, but I do not leave the church of God. I am a Catholic'.[24] The speaker sounds devout; he needs religion and expresses his need in his actions, but, his bishop might have said, he expresses too much – too much, in too many directions, in total confusion. Again, there might be confusion and challenge of another sort, heard from the noble Agila. He declares to no less a Christian personage than Gregory of Tours, 'As we put it in common parlance, if, on your way between the

---

[21] Salvian, *De gub. dei* 8.2f. (*PL* 53.154f.); Augustine, *In Ioann. evang. tract.* 7.6 (*PL* 35.1440); *Enarr. in ps.* 26.2.19, 34.1.7, and 62.7 (*PL* 36.209, 526f., and 752).

[22] *Vita Amandi* 13 (*MGH SRM* 5.436f.); Zeno, *Tract.* 21 *de Ps.*, 2 (*PL* 11.460B), Caesarius, *Serm.* 53.1 (*CCSL*, 103.233), and Gregory the Great, *Registrum*, 8.4 (*MGH Ep.* 2.7).

[23] Agobard, *Liber contra insulsam vulgi opinionem* 1 (*PL* 104.147).

[24] Augustine, *Enarr. in ps.* 88.14 (*CCSL*, 39.1244), in C. E. Stancliffe, *St Martin and his Hagiographer: History and Miracle in Sulpicius Severus* (Oxford: Clarendon Press, 1983), 213.

pagan altar and God's church, you bow to each, there's no harm done'.[25] Between the two kinds of confusion, the one of indiscriminate need, the other of no need at all, it is often impossible to distinguish. Let me instance Ausonius who calls himself a Christian and has a chapel, a *sacrarium* in his villa; yet he also has a statue of Liber Pantheus in his villa; and the tone of his verse seems too frivolous, at points indeed too close to obscene, to be Christian.[26] Which type of religious nature does he represent? There has long been scholarly argument over the question, as over other figures well known and interesting, because literary. Both types in different ways may give us (in quotation marks, to show dubiety) 'incomplete' membership in any religious body.

Both may be seen particularly in two settings: in festivals, and, of much more historical significance, at the tomb's side.

Festivals: the Kalends and the Lupercalia

First, among the rituals of the Kalends on 1–3 January, the Lupercalia, the Spurcalia, Brumalia, and imperial cult, all attested as vigorous into the sixth century and beyond and all invested with religious feelings and traditions, as their critics emphatically declare, I pause on the first alone: the Kalends. They constituted an irrepressible tradition throughout the western provinces, as indeed in most of the eastern as well.

Like so much about ancient religion in late antiquity and the medieval period, they are known to us through their detailed denunciation by the bishops.[27] Worshippers believed that this point of the year served as prognostic of all the rest. Good spirits and happiness at the commencement would guarantee the same throughout all that followed. So for a term of three days the exchange of presents among friends and neighbours, feasting, drinking, singing, dancing, jokes and capers of all sorts were in order; the doors of one's house decorated with laurel, prayers

[25] Gregory of Tours, *Hist. Franc.* 5.43 (*MGH SRM*[2] 1, 1, 1.249), in F. Graus, *Volk, Herrscher und Heiliger im Reich der Merowinger: Studien zur Hagiographie der Merowingerzeit* (Prague: Nakladatelstvi Ceskoslovenske Akademie ved, 1965), 169.

[26] R. P. H. Green, 'The Christianity of Ausonius', *Studia patristica* 28 (1993), 40f., 45.

[27] *Christianity*, 36–9, 179–80.

offered to the Penates, constraints relaxed between master and slave, old and young; then celebrations and parades in public places, with fancy costumes, cross-dressing, and wearing especially of heads or masks of heifers and stags (the latter at least identifiable in Celtic lands with the god Cernunnos, but other and better-known deities were represented); finally, after all-night partying, a third day of shows, horse races and civic ceremonies.

Except in the privacy of the home, the Kalends in this late period involved no sacrifices of any sort and were identified with no single particular cult. For this reason it was possible both for the baptized but anxious, and for the baptized but little-caring, to participate in what they saw either as extra insurance in exchange for their extra piety, or what they saw as meaningless. In either state of mind, there they were to be seen at the edge of the New Year, making a most un-Christian hullabaloo in the very streets, costumed like pagan gods, and (some of them) happily drunk. The council assembled at Tours (can. 22) was not the only one to use the word 'worship', *colere*, of these rites. They all were shocking, even the exchange of gifts suspect, to the pastoral eye. To give Christians something better to do, ecclesiastical authorities drew attention to other reasons for celebration at this particular season of the year. The alternative inserted into the ecclesiastical calendar never caught on – never, to become our own New Year's day celebration and its variants in Scotland or Switzerland. Rather, Kalends celebration in the old style continued and in some way to this day continues irrepressibly.

Tomb-side rituals

As to tomb-side rituals, though these were not peculiarly western, they may be outlined in that context alone. They brought families together in a pattern of days after a decease, and then annually on the birthday of the individual, but also annually on 22 February for a time of more general recall and loving celebration under the Roman title of the Caristia. The third Arles council spoke of 'sacrifices' for the dead (can. 5, *sacrificare*); that of Tours, of 'offerings to the dead' (can. 22), and, afterwards, to other beings as well. The Caristia was seen as religious, that is, sacrilegious. To this festival, too, the church offered an alternative, commemorative of St Peter's throne; but it had very limited success.

There were elements about tomb-side cult too nearly essential to human nature, too nicely attuned to the changeless necessities of the race, to be easily displaced. Celebration began with the belief that the invisible essence of each personality survives the death of the flesh, and lingers in and about the remains. In this essence the capacity for fleshly enjoyment was thought to persist, along with other aspects of material vitality (for example, in the capacity to move about or to be distressed within the tomb). Family gatherings of respectful, affectionate character but with singing, good food and drink, toasts and happy remembrances brought pleasure to the dead as to the pious living. It was right and proper to invite close friends to the scene. So, in sum, memorial cult took the form of evening feasts in cemeteries, often extended through the night. To accommodate them, not only were sloping benches sometimes built, on which to place cushions for diners to lie on, but the top of the tomb itself might be more cheaply cut on a slant for the same purpose; not only might there be an adjoining stone or brick serving-table and perhaps an exedra for it, but the tomb-top might have cups and receptacles of various shapes carved in it to receive foods. To carry wine to the deceased, who was hailed as the host of the party, a lead or terracotta tube might run down from the surface to the interior, ending at or near the mouth of the deceased. In all these respects, the cult of the dead was perpetuated apparently among most Western pagans and, from the later second century, most Christians as well. So far as it is possible to estimate participation in these, or most of these, points of ritual, I would suppose them to have been known and accepted in virtually every Christian community from the second to the sixth century, and actually to have been practised by a third or more of Christian families within the same period. Members of the two faiths of course met in and used the same cemeteries, at least for a long time.[28]

The evidence for all this is largely archaeological – regarding the Christian portion alone, some of it very well known, deriving as it does from excavations under St Peter's and other great churches in Rome. Long known, also, are certain illustrations of the cult from north African sites, and more recent work in Sardinia

[28] Ibid., 63–4, 105–14, 198, 217–22.

by A. M. Giuntella adds much to the dossier.[29] The whole picture is in fact panoramic, taking in Jugoslavia, Morocco, Spain, Sicily and southern Italy, not to mention sites in Germany and France. The non-Christian matrix within which identical burial customs may be traced is naturally still larger and more widely attested.

The identity of practices was not lost on the church leadership, which, beginning with Ambrose, therefore tried to forbid them as pagan. They persisted nevertheless for many centuries, up to the edge of living memory. In the face of their official condemnation, evidently Christian ideas about life after death, and emotional needs arising out of those and related ideas, found satisfaction only through traditional rituals, which thus persisted within the church for an uncertain time, but certainly for many generations after the first prohibitions.

The cult of the sanctified dead

In the third century the cult of the sanctified dead began to distinguish itself from that of the unsanctified, but without abandoning these various customs and accommodations. Again, some of the most familiar evidence is to be found in Rome under St Peter's and other basilicas. The martyrs are invited to the parties held in their ghostly presence; a special chair is set there for them; they are toasted and hailed and comforted, served with wine, and of course also asked for benign attentions in general, to be vouchsafed to the petitioner and his kin. With or after their meal, they are surrounded with song and dance. The latter, dancing, is still attested on saints' days into our own century in southern France and other western as well as eastern European localities.[30] The faithful around St Felix, as Paulinus of Nola describes them, brought all sorts of offerings, not only animals for the feasting, which bishops emphasized were gifts to the poor, but offerings of coin or precious metal or such cheaper little gifts as they could afford – lamps, for example – in return for help in life's difficulties.

---

[29] A. M. Giuntella, *Mensae e rite funerari in Sardegna: la testimonianza di Cornus*, Mediterraneo tardoantico e medioevale. Scavi e ricerche 1 (Tarentum: Scorpione, 1985).
[30] *Christianity*, 105–6, 110–11, 216–17, 219.

St Felix of Nola could, for instance, help to locate their strayed animals. Or, like Eastern gods we know of, whose personal dignity, so to speak, required them to respond to insult in their very *temenos*, and who were thus invoked to oversee oath-taking in their presence, so St Felix could be invoked to decide between two persons each swearing he had told the truth. That was the suggestion of Augustine.[31] The same suggestion was to be heard again a thousand times in centuries to come. Above all, St Felix could heal. Exactly of the sort to be seen in pagan temples, on the walls of his shrine versified inscriptions and carved or modelled representations of body parts declared how and where he had exerted his powers to relieve suffering. Such Christian votive objects are widely attested to: a foot, a pair of eyes, a hand. One such was discovered beneath St Peter's, a gift to him of the sixth or seventh century.[32] At the same time that such plastic testimonials were being dedicated in thanks at martyria, bishops were condemning their display! – so, for example, the Council of Auxerre.[33] The practice was too notoriously pagan; yet it was simultaneously Christian.

To St Peter's tomb, to the tomb of St Stephen in Augustine's day, to St Martin's and hundreds or rather thousands of other martyria, visitors flocked, most of them from the close vicinity (they do not answer to our sense of 'pilgrims') but some from afar, looking for the power to bear children, or walk, or see; looking for a straight back or a sane mind. They might simply pray and make an offering, exactly as pagans did; they might take away a curative decoction of dust or weeds from near the tomb, exactly as is attested of pagans; or they might ask for advice as from any human physician, or any pagan deity or oracle; and it would be made known to them in a dream for which they stayed the night, or sometimes weeks or months, at the shrine. As so-called incubation, this usage is well known from pagan traditions, not only of Asclepius-shrines in the East but of other deities in

---

[31] Augustine, *Ep.* 78.3.

[32] M. Guarducci, *La tomba di San Pietro* (Milan: Rusconi, 1989), 35, a gold votive representation of two eyes, signed with a cross.

[33] Paulinus, *Carm.* 21.369; *Conc. Autessiodurense* a. 578 (Mansi 9.912) can. 3, cf. E. J. Jonkers, 'Die Konzile und einige Formen alten Volksglaubens im fünften und sechsten Jahrhundert', *Vigiliae Christianae* 22 (1968), 52; in the *Indiculus* §29, *de ligneis pedibus*, etc. in Dierkens, 'Survivances', 22.

Roman France. Everything in the healing procedures by the saints was indeed faithfully traditional. The worshippers knew nothing else.[34]

Paganization

Without leaving the safe ground of procedures for the more problematic grounds of thought and belief accompanying them, certainly the cult of saints represents 'a significant degree of paganization'. That was how my third *probandum* was worded at the outset. In particular, significance may be emphasized. Saints-cult constituted the principal point of growth within Christianity from the fifth century on at least into Carolingian times. Through its requirements, the ecclesiastical calendar was radically changed; for its celebration, much building and re-building, much artistic and literary activity was inspired; and with it came a sort of reshaping of the superhuman world as it was conceived by Christians, in which not only God and his angels confronted Satan and *his*, but a new legion of superhuman beings was discovered in the sanctified deceased.

They were of a convenient and accessible size and proximity. Such characteristics no one attributed to God, any more than to Zeus or Jupiter; no one brought the agony of a toothache or bewilderment over a deranged child to the throne of such more-than-mighty beings. Instead, as Augustine explains, there are 'those misguided men who count God as necessary for eternal life, for that life of the soul, but think these [lesser pagan] Powers must be worshipped by us on account of temporal matters'. 'There are those who say God is good, great, the top, beyond our perception, incorruptible, who will give us eternal life and that incorruptibility which he has promised in the resurrection, while temporal matters and matters of this world belong to *daemones*' [lowlier Powers].[35] Holding to such beliefs, or error (as Augustine in many passages insists), new Christians could only feel defenceless in the face of

---

[34] On the thousands of martyr-shrines, see D. Nineham, *Christianity Medieval and Modern: A Study in Religious Change* (London: SCM Press, 1993), 83 (1300+ in eighth-century France alone); on other points, see *Christianity*, 54–6, 127, 130, 190–1, 229.

[35] Ibid., 120–1, 225.

their problems – problems of exactly the sort, of course, which the traditional deities had solved. Without these latter, conversion involved intolerable loss. Out of sheer human necessity, though out of Eastern roots that were demonstrably pagan, first, the church's heroes as superhuman and then the operation of their beneficent powers from the tomb, were welcomed among the most central Christian perceptions and beliefs; and so the intolerable was made tolerable.

About one aspect of this welcome, Augustine speaks revealingly. His strictures one day had provoked much grumbling from his congregation: hadn't the people, before, who raised no objections, been Christians? This challenge Augustine confronted on the morrow with carefully chosen words.

> That it might not seem as if we wished to put down our forebears, who had either tolerated or did not dare to forbid such excesses of an unthinking people, I explained by what necessity this bad custom seemed to have arisen in the church. For, when peace came after so many and such violent persecutions [i.e. post-313], crowds of pagans wishing to become Christians were prevented from doing this because of their habit of celebrating the feast days of their idols with banquets and carousing; and, since it was not easy for them to abstain from these dangerous but ancient pleasures, our ancestors thought it would be good to make a concession for the time being to their weakness and permit them, instead of the feasts they had renounced, to celebrate other feasts in honour of the holy martyrs, not with the same sacrilege but with the same elaborateness, *luxus*.[36]

Between Augustine, Ambrose, Paulinus, and their like, who never had to cook a meal for themselves let alone worry if it would be forthcoming at all, and who were thus free for decades on end to think about their faith and tease out its implications and definitions – between such ecclesiastical leaders and their followers must lie some separating distance in the refinement of their

---

[36] Augustine, *Ep.* 29.8f., on the feast of St Leontius, a former bishop, translation based on Johannes Quasten, *Music and Worship in Pagan and Christian Antiquity*, trans. Boniface Ramsay (Washington: National Association of Pastoral Musicians, 1983), 172, a passage in which Augustine decries the *imperita multitudo*, cf. *De moribus eccl. cath.* 1.34.75 (PL 32.1342), the *turbae imperitorum*.

theology.[37] Quite inevitably. The gap could be illustrated by a great many passages of the fifth and later centuries; its meaning has been discussed many times, circling around terms like *vulgus*, superstition, folklore, élite and primitive, the lettered and unlettered.

Without reviving such discussion, however, it seems safe to say, in explanation of my term 'paganization', first, that the very great majority of the population both within and without the church, defined as baptized, counted as illiterate, primitive, the *vulgus*. They lived on the countryside, which explains much. As a majority, they cannot be ignored by the historian of Christendom. They *were* Christendom (without here meaning to exclude other habits of mind and ritual that the likes of Ambrose or Boniface might have preferred) .

Appropriating pagan attitudes and practices

And second: Augustine and others of the ecclesiastical élite adopt a tone of distance when they speak of practices among their congregations obviously pagan in origins and pagan, too, in present character. If these cannot be effectively excluded, the bishops would have liked at least to keep them at arm's length. But it couldn't be done. So central a concept as *do ut des*, pay up to divine power and get what you want by propitiation – that piece of non-aristocratic or lowbrow pagan belief which the church aristocracy insisted could not exist in Christianity – nevertheless did exist. Testimonies to it in words, deeds, and material objects centring in martyr-cult are too many to deny. Belief in the presence of the dead alive still in their tombs entered the churches conceptually from old Roman sources, surviving in tales of martyrs' miracles, martyr-cult, and saints'-day festivals. So did a large number of practices also survive, implying ideas about superhuman power: the apotropaic use of bells, for example, in moments of address to the divine. I point to an antecedent in the imperial cult of second-century Spain.[38] The use of bells, however, may not have been

---

[37] *Exempli gratia*: Paulinus' tone is caught by F. van der Meer, *Augustine the Bishop: The Life and Works of a Father of the Church*, trans. B. Battershaw and G. R. Lamb (London and New York: Sheed & Ward, 1961), 512ff.; Augustine, *Epp.* 22(23).3 (*PL* 33.91) and Ambrose, *De Helia*, 62 (*PL* 14.719).

[38] *Inscr. Lat. Selectae*, ed. H. Dessau, no. 8622.

native to the West; and if a canvass of pagan elements in art, architecture, symbolism, gesture, liturgy, music, or ceremonial were to include what originated in the eastern provinces, it would be enormously enlarged. Respecting, then, the western boundaries, I end with two rites at church entrances: one that Paulinus and other western sources mention, the rite of kissing the doorway, and the other at St Peter's, where the faithful of the fifth century mounted the steps to the top and there, before entering to worship, turned about toward the rising sun and bowed to it. Both practices were pagan.[39]

Christian attacks on the more easily policed acts and physical objects of forbidden faith certainly did away with much of the past, but much less than was intended by the ecclesiastical authorities; and in their engagement with the enemy their own edifice of beliefs and rituals suffered invasions at more than a few points. In the interests of historical accuracy it is good to acknowledge and measure such points. Beyond measurement, they raise the question to be answered at other moments and in other regions of hostile engagement between faiths – the question, what parts of each did the other least regard? Or it might be rephrased: at what parts was each faith ready, if really necessary, to compromise and accommodate without yielding anything of its essence? Does an answer not require some recognition of the characteristic structure of each religious system and, in the course of persecution and mission, historical consequences traceable to structural differences?

[39] Leo I, *Sermo* 27 (*PL* 54.218f.) quoted by F. J. Dölger, *Sol Salutis: Gebet und Gesang im christlichen Altertum*, 2nd edn (Münster: Aschendorff, 1925), 3; E. Lucius, *Les origines du culte des saints dans l'Église chrétienne*, translated (from the German of 1904) by E. Jeanmaire (Paris: Fisbacher, 1908), 387 n. 3.

PART TWO

Change and Continuity in the Christianization of Europe

Chapter 4

The Sociology of Pre-Constantine Christianity: Approach from the Visible

WOLFGANG WISCHMEYER

The most reliable evidence for early Christianity is not the writings of the church fathers; it is evidence which was visible in the early centuries and which still remains: architecture, epigraphy, papyri. This evidence reveals growing churches of great diversity. Some of their members travelled widely, and confessed their faith in public inscriptions. Records of the church in Cirta (North Africa) show that congregations could have considerable material resources with which their leaders could engage in trade as well as poor relief. The church's teaching about God led to a relativization of the *saeculum* and, in an age of anxiety, to a bridging of the gulf between earth and heaven which was reassuring and attractive. In this the martyrs pointed the way. The church's bishops, who were increasingly drawn from the urban upper classes, appropriated the martyr tradition in giving public expression to Christianity. The church, led by the bishops, emerged well before Constantine as an authoritative and credible organization within Roman society, which acculturated as it expanded.

The Egyptian city of Oxyrhynchus, source of 158 papyri concerning Christianity and Judaism from the second to the seventh century, according to the *Historia monachorum* (5.1f.) had 10,000 monks and 20,000 nuns among its inhabitants in around AD 400. We can therefore estimate an actual population at that time of around 15,000 to 20,000.[1] According to one papyrus (POxy 1357), in the years AD 535–6 there were approximately forty-seven churches and twenty-one monasteries in the city; and of these, twelve churches can be traced back to the beginning of the fifth century, although we are unable to locate a single church today. However – and this is what is surprising – two Christian churches were so publicly known by the end of the third century (POxy 53 v I 10 and III 19) that they appear in an at least semi-official list of city guardians, and the city administration and the general public alike were fully aware of their existence.

The two listed churches were both close to city gates at the northern and southern ends of the main street, the north church on the west side near to the *Kaisereion* (which was also converted into a church in AD 406) and the south church close to the gymnasium. Neither building can be located by archaeologists – a fate shared with most of the city's well-known sacred buildings and all of its public ones. Yet we do know that both lay at the extreme edges of the city, though this in no way implies a low social standing.

At the end of the third century, however, the two churches are also interesting in another respect – in the city they stand in contrast to a single synagogue (POxy 1205, of AD 291) and twelve temples. So the Christians were most certainly a minority, but they were a minority that stood out and mattered in the city's public life. The two churches are among the city's notable structures for the further reason that they can be found at each end of the main street (*Plataia*) running from north to south. Although most traffic must have entered the city by the harbour on the Bahr Jussuf, taking the southern thoroughfare, overland travellers entered the city from the north and the south.

Travellers and religion

However noticeable or unnoticeable the churches were, travellers of that time had an understanding of how closely related religion

[1] See J. Krüger, *Oxyrhynchos in der Kaiserzeit* (Frankfurt: Peter Lang, 1990) 69f. disputing I. F. Fichman, 'Die Bevölkerungszahl von Oxyrhynchos in byzantinischer Zeit', *Archiv für Papyrusforschung* 21 (1971), 111–20. For POxy 43, see also R. Lane Fox, *Pagans and Christians* (London: Viking, 1986), 589f; W. Wischmeyer, *Von Golgatha zum Ponte Molle: Studien zur Sozialgeschichte der Kirche im 3. Jahrhundert* (Göttingen: Vandenhoeck & Ruprecht, 1992), 8f.

and travelling are, and people loved to thematize this connection. On this topic, let us turn our attention to two second-century travellers. Firstly, there is a certain Nearchos, whose letter to a Heliodorus we have in another surviving papyrus.[2] Aswan and the First Cataract on the Nile, the very source of the Nile, Libya, even the Siwa oasis – he sought out all these spots and then described them to his friend. And like many other travellers he named a form of cultural tourism as his driving force, tourism 'to see the works of art made by human hand'. But that is not all. A religious motif came into play: not only for himself, but also for his friends: he left behind a *proskynema* (a memorial inscription) at every shrine he visited, an everlasting and visible act of reverence in the form of name inscriptions. To him, the most important of his visits was to the oasis, 'where Ammon prophesies for all people and proclaims harmony'.[3] The 'not entirely uneducated Greek',[4] who certainly lived in Egypt, reveals to us here a religious socialization, similar to that found in the sayings of Sasnos (second or third century): 'Worship the divine, offer sacrifice to all gods, make a pilgrimage to every shrine and leave behind a *proskynema*, hold in especially high esteem the gods of the fathers and worship Isis and Serapis, the greatest of the gods, the redeemers, the good, the well-pleasing, the benefactors' (Wilcken, no. 116).

This form of religiosity perhaps had more to do with civil religion than with what is conventionally considered popular religion. The worship of, and assistance from, in particular, the ancestral gods (*patrioi theoi*) was crucial to this religiosity: 'For our *patrioi theoi* [ancestral gods] always help us and give us health and well-being' (POxy 935, Wilcken, no. 119). The *patrioi theoi* served as a lingua franca for religiously-inclined people, reflecting Roman military inscriptions from Philae (Dessau 8995) to the

---

[2] PLondon, 3.854; L. Mitteis and Ulrich Wilcken, *Grundzüge und Chrestomathie der Papyruskunde* (Berlin: B. G. Teubner, 1912), no. 117.
[3] G. Geraci, 'Ricerche sul proskynema', *Aegyptus* 51 (1971), 3–211; on the oracle active there into the Justinian period, see G. Wagner, 'Les Oasis d'Egypte', *Institut Français d'archéologie orientale*, B 100 (1987), 331; on Christian use of *proskynema*, see H. C. Youtie, *Zeitschrift für Papyrologie und Epigraphik* 28 (1978), 265–8 (= *Scriptiunculae posteriores I* [Bonn, 1981], 451–4); *New Documents Illustrating Early Christianity* 3 (1983), 77f.; 4 (1987), 59–62.
[4] Wilcken, *Chrestomathie*, 147.

North Sea[5] (Dessau 9266) and at the same time stretching from the *penates* of the state into the realm of the home. Simultaneously, a connection was made here between the sphere of the state cult, on the one hand, and individual cult organizations on the other, the fundamental incompatibility of which had been established by Plato (*Leg.* 909f.) and many since him. However, what has been regarded in general religious feeling as something complementary subsequently led to the following opinion being given: 'It was through the household and the house church that Christianity and its otherworldly "assembly" first put down its roots, then grew to undermine the old civic values and the very shape of the pagan city.'[6]

It is from this area of Christianity that our second second-century traveller came. He is to be our witness for the connection between the topic of travel and the religious. The text to which we shall return comes from the place which a traveller of that time would normally cross when immediately approaching a city: a burial ground. The traveller did not first come across traces of Christianity on passing through the city, but before entering it. One of the oldest Christian monuments is the gravestone of a certain Abercius,[7] presumably from the end of the second century. The story of its discovery resembles a novel. The text of the gravestone did not even need to be discovered. It was already known through the legend of a Bishop Aberkios (22 October), perhaps composed at the end of the fourth century, which was passed down in Menologium Constantinopolitanum. At first scholars thought that the text of the inscription quoted in the *Vita*[8] could not be authentic. The astonishment was all the greater when W. M. Ramsay confirmed this text in 1882–3 by discovering two inscriptions near today's Koz-Hissar in Turkey, the Hierapolis of

---

[5] Hermann Dessau, *Inscriptiones Latinae Selectae* (Dublin: Weidmann, 1974), 3.2, nos 8995, 9266.

[6] Lane Fox, *Pagans*, 89. For *ta patria*, cf. also R. MacMullen, *Paganism in the Roman Empire* (New Haven: Yale University Press, 1981), 3f. Particularly important here is the emphasis of Christian apologists for proof of the age of the Bible and, in turn, the priority of eventual Christian ideas; cf. Tertullian *Ap.*, 19.1–4; Justin 2 *Ap.*, 13.4: E. P. Sanders, in *Jewish and Christian Self-Definition I* (London: SCM Press, 1980), ix.

[7] Cf. W. Wischmeyer, *Lexikon für Theologie und Kirche*, 3rd edn, 1 (1993), 46f. (Lit.).

[8] *PG*, 115, 1211–48.

Phrygian antiquity. Firstly, Ramsay found an inscription belonging to an Alexander, dated AD 216, now in the Istanbul Museum of Antiquity, and secondly he found two fragments of Abercius's original writing, now in the Vatican's Museo Pio Cristiano. These two fragments arrived in the Vatican in 1888 as a gift from two scholars – the Scot Ramsay and the Turk Abd-el-Hamed – to Leo XIII in commemoration of the golden jubilee of his priesthood. The dispute over the Christianity of the Abercius inscription, using primarily the arguments of the school of *Religionsgeschichte* (which is reminiscent of the argument that what cannot be may not be), is over. The dispute did, however, create a greater awareness of the fact that these monuments, as well as most other monuments of early Christianity, show us a Christianity with a cultural power which does not become visible in the high ranks of patristic theology. Instead, this cultural power lies in the strength of acculturation, and in this sense it is included in the concept of *Antike und Christentum*.[9]

Thanks to Ramsay's discovery we have in our possession fifteen of the twenty-two hexametric verses of the oldest Christian grave epigrams in epigraphic record, and we are able to complete the rest by literary tradition.[10] We can also see here the beginnings of Christian poetry. The metaphorical language which is specific to this genre, and which is strongly Homeric in character, is additionally accentuated in its echoes of language and imagery found in 5 Ezra, the *Shepherd* of Hermas, the *Gospel of Peter* and the *Martyrdom of Perpetua and Felicitas*. These were, then, echoes of contemporary old Christian literary works which belong either to the literature of martyrs or, in the biblical tradition, to the so-called Apocrypha. The topic of genre is relevant to the theme of travel.

We return to our point, the combination of travel and religion. Abercius told those who approached his home city of Hierapolis

---

[9] Cf. E. A. Judge, 'Antike und Christentum', *Aufstieg und Niedergang der römischen Welt* (henceforth *ANRW*) 2.23.1 (Berlin: Walter de Gruyter, 1979), 3–58; W. Wischmeyer, *Wörterbuch des Christentums* (Gütersloh: Gerd Mohn, 1988), 70–2; W. Wischmeyer, *Lexikon für Theologie und Gemeinde* I (Freiburg: Herder, 1992), 43–7.

[10] In addition to G. Pfohl and C. Pietri, *Reallexikon für Antike und Christentum* (henceforth *RAC*) 12 (1983), 467–590, cf. also regarding Jewish epitaphs P. W. van der Horst, *Ancient Jewish Epitaphs* (Kampen: Kok Pharos, 1991), and idem, 'Jewish Poetical Tomb Inscriptions', in idem and J. W. van Henten, eds, *Studies in Jewish Epigraphy* (Leiden: Brill, 1994), 129–47.

that there were Christians there, Christians who were at home in the entire *oikoumene* and who knew the Christian communities from Rome to the Euphrates, thus hyperbolically uniting East and West. Even Persia entered the frame with mention of Nisibis and the crossing of the Euphrates. On this monument (which is typical and not unostentatious for the local upper-class), Abercius sang the praises of belonging to this worldwide Christian *oikumene* and of participating in the eucharistic community. The burial stele is approximately 1.10 metres high, with a crowned cippus, like numerous others, and decorated exactly in keeping with these others: a wreath on the left side is preserved, perhaps a pitcher and/or a bowl was on the right side. The encounter with this conventional inscribed monument in the cemetery of the Phrygian city marks perhaps the earliest natural point of access to our question of the increasing visibility and the appearance of Christianity in the late imperial period: a drawing near to an ancient city of that time.

Christianity makes its appearance

But the following general question arises from this natural point of access: how did Christian churches in particular become visible, how did Christian communities make their appearance within the consciousness of their general surroundings, and when? This cluster of questions presents us with further questions which in turn invite very different answers, for the circumstances in one of the metropolises of the Empire such as Rome or Alexandria, Carthage or Antioch were different to those in Oxyrhynchos or in Hierapolis, in African garrisons or in Gallic country towns. Circumstances differed in times of persecution compared to times of relative peace in the church;[11] they also differed regarding the aspects of the church which were publicly visible. We must assume that the church's outdoor effect differed greatly depending on context, so that it had a very varied significance for the public. There are, in addition, two other important perspectives: how did the church see itself as an organization, and how was it seen from the outside, for example in terms of its hierarchical structure?

---

[11] Periods of persecution are directly connected to our problem of the perceptibility of the church. Cf. the range of explanations offered for persecution from *odium generis humani* to interest by the state in confiscating Christian property and wealth.

But then again, how does antiquity appear to us today? How does it appear in the preparation of a museum or an archaeological dig? In cases of the continuity or discontinuity of settlements, how do archaeologists consciously – or how does history unconsciously – make it appear? How does it appear in the imagination and skill of an interpreter of written sources, faced with an inscription or sitting in a library? Here and there, we are confronted with still lifes which must painstakingly be reanimated. It is with good reason that we speak of *'les villes mortes'* of Syria and of the 'seas of debris' in North Africa. Yet these were the result of epochal alternations of culture, economics and society that occurred over a long period; therefore an analysis of a third-century stratum of this debris can only be performed with extreme difficulty.

In this respect, a place like Dura-Europos is of exemplary significance for the third century. This Roman garrison town became a *municipium* in the first half of the third century under Caracalla, and was conquered and subsequently given up by the Sassanids soon after AD 256; a coin from this year provides the latest dated record of the town. Its short-lived blossoming brought about much new construction work and, to a certain extent, a 'decisive change in the pattern of the city's life'. Included in this urban facelift were the rebuilding of the synagogue and the simultaneous renovation of a private house into a 'Christian building' in AD 244–5.[12]

In seeing Oxyrhynchos, Hierapolis or Dura, we can avoid the danger not always seen in academic history, the danger of becoming a slave to the knock-on effect of metropolises, of applying the circumstances found in the large cities to the entire Roman Empire, and of writing Romanocentric history. At the same time, it would be unfair to say that the record of sources on pre-Constantine church history was too poor, for that would not give proper regard to the difficulties in dealing with such historical records. Of course, we would love to have additional sources, but every historian says that. Every historian is dissatisfied with 'how it might have been', as well as with the implications involved in

---

[12] Cf. C. H. Kraeling, *The Christian Building: The Excavations at Dura-Europos: Final report* 8.2 (New Haven: Dura-Europos Publications, 1967), 26–39; A. Perkins, *The Art of Dura-Europos* (Oxford: Clarendon Press, 1973), 25–32.

models of interpretive reconstruction, implications for the wide range of historical enquiry and its interdisciplinary co-operation, from the history of ideas and religion to the history of language and mentality. In comparison to the problems which historians of ancient history and religions face in studying Mani and Mithras, for example, Christian records are not bad.

In attempting to answer the question 'How does antiquity appear to us today?', a further aspect of these records comes into play, namely the continuity of Christianity. We must be conscious of the fact that Christian selection from the body of traditions presents a tempting inheritance. It introduces sharp contours to a grey area which is more strongly characterized by a diffuseness in which Christianity does not stand out as clearly as the statements of some church fathers presuppose. Or is it that the fathers' efforts were so very sharp and certain so that they can create these contours?

For many reasons it is correct to speak here of a grey area with reference to both early Christianity's appearance and its process of appearing. We have a Christian minority and as such, it found itself nevertheless in the midst of a tremendous process of growth and expansion in terms of its numerical strength, its geographical dissemination and its degree of acculturation into Graeco-Roman culture and into the political and administrative framework of the Roman Empire.

The question of the church's appearance from the end of the second century to the time of the tetrarchs must be posed in many different ways because there are many varied perspectives on them.[13] There are such different perspectives due to a lack of

---

[13] Thus in addition to the magisterial work by A. von Harnack, *Die Mission und Ausbreitung des Christentums in den ersten 3 Jahrhunderten*, 2 vols (Leipzig: [1902], 1924), today we have not only the supplementing work by H. Frohnes and U. W. Knorr, eds, *Kirchengeschichte als Missionsgeschichte* I: *Die Alte Kirche* (Munich: Chr. Kaiser, 1974), but also, year on year, the relevant archaeological and epigraphic new discoveries and revisions. For their presentation, cf. for example *New Documents Illustrating Early Christianity*, published since 1981 by the Ancient History Documentary Research Centre (Macquarie University, Sydney, Australia), and the bibliography in *Byzantinische Zeitschrift*. For the history of the early church in general: R. A. Markus, 'The Roman Empire in Early Christian History', *The Downside Review* 81 (1963), 340–53; idem, 'Church History and Early Church Historians', *Studies in Church History* 11

uniformity in outsiders' assessments of the phenomenon of Christianity, outsiders here being non-Christian contemporaries and among them, in turn, the Roman state (represented by the Emperor), which presented a particular viewpoint. But also within the church, the process of fixing and unifying local variants of Christianity and of their differing theological expressions and certainties on orthodoxy, as well as on their marginal groups, had not yet come to an end.[14] As an historiographic model of contemporary historiography, heresy and schism are an inheritance from that time. Differing self-perceptions led to differing perceptions in general which as such cannot be accepted without question.

In all its diversity, though, it is the visibility – indeed, the 'perceptibility' – of Christianity which is of greatest interest nowadays. We can clearly identify a range of possible reactions, which extends from mission via coexistence to persecution which presents a clear and quantitative increase beyond that of second-century evidence.[15] While the Christians constituted what was certainly the largest religious group in the Roman Empire at the beginning of the fourth century, they were still a minority, making up approximately 10 per cent of the population.

Christianity beyond the Empire

Outside the Empire – the only area in question here being present-day Iran – this minority was considerably smaller still. In the 'Syrian

---

(1975), 1–17; and for the entire field of ancient history: Averil Cameron, 'The Writing of History', in eadem, ed., *History as Text: The Writings of Ancient History* (London: Duckworth, 1989), 1–10; for the particular problem of literacy, eadem, 'Literacy in the Roman World', *Journal of Roman Studies,* Suppl. 3 (1991). As this paper is concerned with group behaviour and group identity, cf. R. C. Trexler, ed., *Persons in Groups: Social Behavior as Identity Formation in Medieval and Renaissance Europe* (Binghamton: Medieval and Renaissance Texts and Studies, 1985) and his introduction (3f.) in particular.

[14] On the theological position – associated with the term *Urchristentum* – on heresy and the theory of decadence, cf. W. Bauer, *Rechtgläubigkeit und Ketzerei im Ältesten Christentum,* 2nd edn (Tübingen: Mohr, 1964), and now S. Alkier, *Urchristentum* (Tübingen: Mohr, 1993), which traces the historiography of the theory of decline from Gottfried Arnold (1666–1714) to Ferdinand Christian Baur and the so-called Tübingen school.

[15] On the numerical problem of Christianization, cf. W. Wischmeyer, *Golgatha,* 165.

church within the Persian Empire, which went back at least as far as the second century',[16] the Syro-Mesopotamian border region was at first the main focus between the Parthians, then the Sassanids, and the Romans, and its centre was Edessa.[17] Our most important written source, the *Acts of Thomas*, written in the first half of the third century, covers the region from Mesopotamia to the 'India of the Parthian horizon' in novelistic fashion, without enabling us to make reconstructions today. This is supported by other sources such as the Bar Daisan (*Lib. reg.* 607 f. Nau), the chronicle of Seert in AD 260, and the Chronicle of Arbela in AD 225; and the lists of bishops in Nicaea in AD 325 mention a Bishop of Persia and India.[18] Any concrete evidence of this Persian–Syrian expansion as far as the mouth of the Indus is just as difficult to find as evidence of that older Egyptian mission to southern India, a mission connected with Bartholomew. In AD 296 or 297, the metropolitan David of Basra travelled to India, an act which must be seen in connection with the Sassanid policy of expansion around the Indian Ocean.[19] Around AD 300, the Thomas tradition begins to replace the older tradition in southern India as well, so that an east Syro-Persian community is to be found even on Socotra, the old base of the Egyptian route to India.[20] There was even mention in the *Acts of Thomas* of an Aksumite martyrdom of the Apostle.[21]

An important factor in the growth of the Persian church in the third century was the politico-military success of the early Sassanid Empire. It not only led to the disappearance of churches – as was

---

[16] A. Dihle, 'Antike und Orient', Suppl. Sitzungsbericht Heidelberg, Phil. Hist. Kl. II (1983 [1984]), 63 with literature.

[17] Along with E. Kirsten, *RAC* 4 (1959), 554f., cf. J. B. Segal, *Edessa: The Blessed City* (Oxford: Clarendon Press, 1970); J. Neusner, 'Conversion of Adiabene to Christianity', *Numen* 13 (1966), 144–50; H. J. W. Drijvers, 'Jews and Christians at Edessa', *Journal of Jewish Studies* 36 (1985), 88–102.

[18] A. Mingana, in *Bulletin of the John Rylands Library* (henceforth *BJRL*) 10 (1926), 495.

[19] Dihle, 'Antike und Orient', 73.

[20] Cosmas Indicopleustes, *Topographica Christiana* 3.65.6–13, SCh., 114 [Paris: Cerf, 1968], 503–5); cf. E. Sachau, 'Zur Ausbreitung des Christentums in Asien', *Abhandlung der Akademie der Wissenschaften,* Berlin Phil. Hist. Kl. (henceforth *AAW*), 1919, 1, 69f.; L. Brandi, 'Sokotra: Die ehemals christliche Insel', *Oriens Christianus* 57 (1973), 162–77; G. Fiaccadori, 'Teofilo Indiano', *Bibl. Felix Ravenna* 7 (1992), 14f.

[21] *Cod. Par. Gr.* 1613, cf. Fiaccadori, 'Teofilo', 79 to Harnack, *Mission*, 698.

the case in Dura – but also led large numbers of Christians to settle further east, thus into Persis: after Sapor's victory over Valerian in AD 260, Rev-Ardashir soon became the seat of a metropolitan. The linguistic and cultural division in the community is a feature of this church from the beginning: Greek and Syrian communities existed alongside one another.

Within the Persian sphere of influence there were also the communities of the Arabian peninsula. According to the Chronicle of Arabela, there was an attack on the diocese of Qatar[22] – the refuge of the anchorite Jonan on his way to India.[23] To what extent the pre-history of the fifth- or sixth-century church near Al Qusur (the ancient Ikaros) on Kuwait's offshore island of Faylakah can be traced back to the third century must remain open.[24]

Nevertheless there is increasing concrete evidence to support Hans Lietzmann's general statement that 'along with the native religions of the Syrians and Iranians, Judaism and Christianity spread further east in the beginning of the third century'.[25] This was not limited to Judaism, for which J. Neusner has provided a nice summary.[26]

Yet this eastward expansion of Christianity was clearly not only connected to politico-military factors, for trade routes also played a large part. Perhaps this in particular also led to the point at which 'the pre-Constantinian spread of Christianity beyond the borders of the Imperium Romanum' can only be discussed with regard to Iran, as well as Armenia[27] and Georgia.[28] This spread 'is astonishingly modest in view of the enormous expansion within the Empire and seems more coincidental than anything else'. H. C. Brennecke places his explanation of Christianity in society

---

[22] E. Sachau, *AAW*, 1915, 22.62.

[23] *Bibliotheca Hagiographica Orientalis* (Brussels: Soc. Bollandiani, 1910), n. 527f., cf. Fiaccadori', 'Teofilo', xx.

[24] Fiaccadori, 'Teofilo', xx with lit; B. Finster, 'Arabien in der Spätantike', *Archäologischer Anzeiger* (1966), 287–319.

[25] H. Lietzmann, *Geschichte der Alten Kirche*, 3rd edn, II (Berlin: Walter de Gruyter, 1961), 275.

[26] J. Neusner, 'The Jews East of the Euphrates', *ANRW* II.9.2 (1978), 46–69.

[27] G. Klinger, *RAC* I, 678–89; W. Hage, *Theologische Realenzyklopädie* (henceforth *TRE*) IV, 40–57.

[28] J. Aßfalg, *TRE* XII, 389–96.

THE ORIGINS OF CHRISTENDOM IN THE WEST

at the turn of the 'Constantinian era'[29] under the quote from Optatus of Milevis: 'The church is within the state, that is the Roman Empire.'[30]

The church as a trading-post

In comparison to the spread of Christianity beyond the imperial borders one can indeed speak of its 'enormous expansion' within the Empire. Here, too, there is a wealth of evidence – not least our Abercius himself – from which we have already become aware that trade played a relatively considerable role in the expansion of Christianity. This connection between the history of the Christian mission and that of trade is basically nothing new, but rather occurred generally in ancient – and particularly in Jewish – contexts. But because of its diaconal duties, the church retained to a certain extent the 'character of a trading-post' from the outset and this no doubt contributed more than a little to its public image. In conversions to Christianity[31] – be they on a highbrow or low-brow level, be they as a religion or a philosophy,[32] without there being a clear distinction – there came into play a further socio-historical dimension: namely the economic.

The church's participation in trade (as P. Armhurst 3a shows) explains what Cyprian was summarizing with the phrase 'looking after secular business' (*procuratio rerum saecularium*).[33] The Roman authorities' questionnaire-like enquiry forms regarding church assets, which were to ease their collection in the persecution under Diocletian (POxy 2673), included not only precious metals

[29] H. C. Brennecke, *Jahrbuch für biblische Theologie* 7 (1992), 209–39, 217.
[30] *Against the Donatists*, 3.3.
[31] For a new discussion of conversion and Christianization, cf. R. MacMullen, 'Conversion: A Historian's View', *The Second Century* 5 (1985/86), 67–81; subsequently W. Babcock, 'MacMullen and Conversion', *The Second Century* 5 (1985/86), 82–9 and R. A. Markus, *The End of Ancient Christianity* (Cambridge: Cambridge University Press, 1990), 1–17.
[32] Cf. F. C. R. Thee, *Julius Africanus and the Early Christian View of Magic* (Tübingen: Mohr, 1984).
[33] Cyprian, *De Lapsis*, 6; H.-J. Drexhage, 'Wirtschaft und Handel in den frühchristlichen Gemeinden', *Römische Quartalschrift* 76 (1981), 1–72; M. J. Hollerich, 'The Alexandrian Bishops and the Grain Trade', *Journal of the Economic and Social History of the Orient* 25 (1982), 187–207; W. Wischmeyer, 'Zur Sozialgeschichte der Kirche im 3. Jahrhundert', *Studia Patristica* 18.1 (1985), 99–103; W. Wischmeyer, *Golgatha*, 88.

such as gold and silver as well as cash, but also clothing, live-stock, slaves, houses and estates and income from donations and wills.[34] Due to the procedural necessities arising from the early Donatist controversy, we are in a position to take a good look at the circumstances in the 'house where the Christians met' in Numidian Cirta in AD 303.[35] Here we actually come across a warehouse in the rooms adjoining the bishop's church in this town which is known to have been the seat of a bishop since AD 256 (*Sent.* 87 *ep.* 8), in other words shortly after or at the time of the dissolution of the *Res Publica Quattuor Cirtensium*. And in the confiscation reports of AD 303, we find not only the liturgical vessels but also further church furnishings: 'two golden cups, six silver cups, six silver jugs, a silver casket, seven silver lamps and eleven bronze lamps with chains'.

This, however, as well as what we know about the clerics in Cirta, does not yet account for Paul Monceaux's assessment that: 'The community of Cirta is better known to us than any other community in the Christian world in the time of Diocletian.'[36] Among the clergy was Victor, acting as a reader (*lector*) assigned to the decurionate and hence to the *Honestas*, even though he was excused from the public offices. Victor came from a Roman military family of African origin and referred to himself as *professor romanarum litterarum, grammaticus latinus*; therefore, when questioned, he emphasized his *dignitas* which appeared to be recognized and respected by the Numidian governor, Domitius Zenophilus.[37] Claude Lepelley sets out the municipal context of the enquiry, a context which is particularly striking in a provincial capital like Cirta where the governor of Numidia lived. Lepelley emphasizes the significance of the municipal employees: 'the often essential role played in the shadow of the office-holders (*dignitaires*)

[34] Wischmeyer, *Golgatha*, 82.

[35] *Gesta apud Zenophilum*, ed. Ziwsa, CSEL, 26, 185–97; English trans. in Ramsay MacMullen and Eugene N. Lane, eds, *Paganism and Christianity, 100–425 C.E.: A Sourcebook* (Minneapolis: Fortress Press, 1992), 247–260; C. Lepelley, *Les cités de l'Afrique Romaine au Bas-Empire* 2 (Paris: Études Augustiniennes, 1981) 391–4; Wischmeyer, *Golgatha* 85f.

[36] P. Monceaux, *Histoire littéraire de l'Afrique chrétienne 3* (Paris: E. Leroux, 1920), 95.

[37] For further information on the career of Zenophilus, see *Prosopography of the Later Roman Empire* I, 993.

by the administrative personnel'.[38] He perhaps overemphasizes the difference between the town's office-holders and their staff, although a 'history of categories' perspective on the written reports can presuppose such differences. When questioned about the lectors, though, even the bishop could stress the following to the leader of the enquiry, Munatius Felix, who was no less than the 'high priest of the imperial cult of the province and advocate of the town': 'You know all of them.' Despite all the differences between the Numidian metropolis and the small rural town of Abthungi in the shadow of Carthage, similar relations 'on friendly terms'[39] between the Duumvir Alfius Caecilianus and Bishop Felix of Abthungi (reported in the *Gesta proconsularia quibus aplatus est Felix*) cannot be ruled out.[40]

However, in addition to church staff and furnishings, this best-known Christian community of the period of persecution also owned a library and a warehouse – a fact which is important in the context of this paper. Regarding the staff, we know, from the record, of the bishop, four presbyters, two deacons, four sub-deacons,[41] and at least six grave-diggers (fossors) as well as seven lectors (among them the *grammaticus* mentioned above), at least one of whom was married.[42] The position and function of the elder laypeople (*seniores laici*) of Cirta were not even described in

---

[38] Lepelley, *Les cités*, 2, 393.

[39] W. H. C. Frend, *The Donatist Church* (Oxford: Clarendon Press, 1952), 4.

[40] *CSEL*, 26, 199.

[41] The report refers to three of them as fossors. This is obviously a mistake in the report, for Marculius later stresses that he is a subdeacon like Catullinus. Both are arrested because they refuse to name the lectors, while the other two, who apparently must have accompanied the curator on his rounds through the town confiscating books from lectors, are not arrested, despite a similar refusal. The question as to whether Victorinus, who unexpectedly appears along with Silvanus and Carosus at the end of the report of AD 303, is also a subdeacon remains unanswered. In any case, the position of Silvanus – the future Donatist Bishop of Cirta – is once again described precisely by the *grammaticus*, Victor, in a further enquiry in AD 320: 'The most honourable governor Zenophilus said: "What about the function Silvanus had in the clergy then?" Victor answered: "When persecution started in the time of Bishop Paul, Silvanus had the degree of a subdeacon"'.

[42] And who, with regard to the handing over of books, is apparently of the opinion that he could not be considered one of the betrayers (*traditores*) if it were his wife who gave the books to the curator.

AD 303, and we hear of them only in connection with a letter from the notorious Purpurius of Limata, read out to Zenophilus in AD 320.[43]

Comparable statistics on the twenty-four member clergy of Cirta in AD 303 can be found only in the letter from the Roman Bishop Cornelius concerning Novatus, which recorded for the mid-third century church in Rome a clergy of at least 155 men who were entrusted with the special care of over 1,500 widows and other people in need.[44] We can only guess what kind of economic potential in Rome lay behind this, especially as there is no mention of fossors in this context.

Our record from Cirta in AD 303 does not only mention the actual church buildings and their furnishings, as already stated, but also the dining hall (*triclinium*)[45] and the library, normally the home of the thirty-three codices which were eventually confiscated and the four other volumes mentioned by the grammarian, Victor. However, at the time of the search, the bookshelves were empty.[46]

As a final point, we must also assume that there was a fourth room, the actual warehouse, although it was not specifically named in the report of AD 303. From our North African source, we also gain a clear picture of the 'trading-post character' of a church as claimed earlier. In the ecclesiastical centre of Cirta we find a store of clothing: 'eighty-two women's tunics, thirty-eight veils, sixteen men's tunics, thirteen pairs of men's shoes, forty-seven pairs of women's shoes and nineteen belts for farmers'. The large amount of women's clothing – sometimes more than five times as much as men's – stands out here and reminds us of the widows in Cornelius's statistics and the other needy people he mentioned. Yet we must not allow this – and the accusation made by a fellow bishop in connection with Silvanus of Cirta that the betrayer

---

[43] *Gesta apud Zenophilum*, 189; on this subject, see Brent D. Shaw, 'The Elders of Africa', in *Mélanges offerts en hommage au Révérend Père Etienne Gareau* (Cahiers des études anciennes 14 [1982], 207–26); A. Faivre, *Les Laïcs aux origines de l'église* (Paris: Centurion, 1984).

[44] Eusebius, *HE*, 6.43.11ff.

[45] There were four caskets and six jars here. We may as well count the little manuscript (*codex perminium maior*) which was confiscated here along with the library's remaining thirty-two codices.

[46] Regarding furnishings in addition to the empty *armaria*: 'a silver casket, a silver lamp, jars'.

(*traditor*) was also 'thief of the goods of the poor'[47] – to tempt us into thinking that the warehouse in the rooms adjoining the bishop's church was designated solely for the care of the poor. Later laws clearly show that it was considered completely normal for the clergy to be involved in trade until the mid-fourth century, when church legislation introduced a strict ban on clerical enterprise.[48] A recurrence of Cyprian's concern culminating in the choice of words at the Carthaginian Council under Gratus indicates the continuity in the clergy's trading activities.

As such, the warehouse belonging to the clergy also becomes visible as an economic factor in the town. A number of things must be considered here. Firstly, there is, of course, trade. Then there is the care for the dead, also a community concern to an extent which is difficult to establish, pointing not least of all at the position of the fossors belonging or related to the clergy.[49] Furthermore, we have the institution of the community cemeteries, especially if they were organized as generously and on as large a scale as the Roman catacombs which had developed as a genuine attraction in the crisis of the funeral societies (*collegia*) connected with the newly fashionable transition to inhumation burial. Lastly, we must bear in mind the charitable community centre provided by the church, administered by various specialized officers connected with and integrated into the clergy. All of this again raises the question: what did conversion to Christianity mean in this decisive phase of the central power's great persecutions of Christians throughout the Empire and of the contemporaneous growth of the church 'in geometric progression'?[50] What were the implications of emerging from the shadowy niche of concealment for those who came out, as well as for the public?[51]

[47] *Gesta apud Zenophilum*, 189.

[48] Council of Carthage 345/48 *c*.6 and 9.

[49] Cf. J. Guyon, 'La vente des tombes', *Mélanges de l'École Française de Rome, Antiquité* 86 (1974), 549–96; E. Conde Guerri, 'Los "fossores" de Roma paleocristiana', *Studi di antichità christiana* 33 (Città del Vaticano: Pontificio instituto di archeologia cristiana, 1979); in general: A. Faivre, *Naissance d'une hierarchie* (Paris: Beauchesne, 1977).

[50] Harnack, *Mission*, 899.

[51] Here, the socio-historically predetermined town–country contrast is to be related with the much less intensive, yet still present, Christianization of the countryside, to which there are very different approaches, such as banishment or the allocation of land to discharged soldiers (cf. Wischmeyer, *Golgatha*, 42–4).

The 'arbitrary God' and a distinctive lifestyle

For both groups, Christians and non-Christians, the implications of emergence were a matter of lifestyle – and the key words *community centre, economic factor* and *burial system* focus on different levels. This lifestyle is to be seen primarily from the perspective of the city and, beyond this, only secondarily from the perspective of the Empire. Lifestyle, here, was doubtless a shifting concept. It is therefore highly indicative that the question 'What does it mean to be a real Christian?'[52] first became a burning one around the end of the fourth century and then gained its sharpest contours with Augustine's reactions to his ascetic and Pelagian opponents. In the twilight of the term 'lifestyle', which Christians chose for themselves and which was seen by contemporaries as the lifestyle of Christians (one could also mention group consciousness and identity), we are not dealing with 'honouring the gods' (*religionem colere*) and 'observing the Roman traditions' (*ceremonias recognoscere*), as the expressions of the Valerian rescript of AD 257 handed down in the *Acta Cypriani* can be generalized in translation;[53] we are rather dealing with an accord:

In addition there is the factor of a geographically very different degree of Christianization, for example between Syria or North Africa on the one hand and northern Gaul and southern Italy on the other. The language barrier may also have played a role here, cf. 'Die Sprachen im Römischen Reich der Kaiserzeit', *Bonner Jahrbücher Beiheft* 40 (1980). In the context of trade and mission which we are stressing, multilingualism and knowledge of regional languages is to be taken into account, cf. the inscription of Julianus qui et Eutecnius from Syrian Laodicea, and of the famous merchant of Lyon, J. Pouilloux, *Journal des Savants* (1975), 58–75; M. Guarducci, *Epigrafa Greca* 4 (Rome: Instituto poligrafico delli Stato, 1978), 494f. and C. P. Jones, 'A Syrian in Lyon', *American Journal of Philology* 99 (1978), 336–53; C. P. Jones, 'L'inscription grècque de Saint Just', *Les martyrs de Lyon* (177), *Coll. Int. CNRS* 575 (Paris: Editions du CNRS, 1978), 119–27; Wischmeyer, *Jahrbuch für Antike und Christentum* (henceforth *JbAC*) 23 (1980), 36f.

[52] As in the anonymous Pelagian *Epistula ad adolescentem, PL Supplementum* 1, 1377 from the beginning of the fifth century.

[53] On these Acts, cf. Wischmeyer, 'Der Bischof im Prozess: Cyprian als episcopus, patronus, advocatus und martyr vor dem Prokonsul', in A. A. R. Bastiaensen, *et al.*, eds, *Fructus centesimus: Mélanges G.J.M. Bartelink*, Instrumenta Patristica 19 (Steenbrugge: in Abbatia S. Petri, 1989), 363–71; idem., 'Cyprianus episcopus 2. Der 2. Teil der *Acta Cypriani*, in G. J. M. Bartelink, et al., eds, *Euologia: Mélanges A.A.R. Bastiaensen*, Instrumenta Patristica 24

namely the connection between a community-oriented 'philosophical and intellectual life' (*bios philosophikos*) – regardless of
level – and a religion of redemption which repudiated promiscuous
religiosity and which claimed to be absolute. The well-known
God of this religion, an 'arbitrary God'[54] in the creation, led his
followers to a vehemence (unknown in antiquity) in their claim
that they had definite knowledge about the existential themes of
death and resurrection.[55]

The form of numinous behaviour accepted by society at that
time in an open, even public, form of sacrifice was not crucial.
Such sacrifice respected God's changeless aseity, unknown to man,
and signified the practice of a piety which, according to Pseudo-
plutarch, guaranteed that one did not 'plunge into a coarse and
hardened atheism in an effort to escape superstition and therefore
go beyond the *eusebeia* which lies between the two'.[56]

Integral to Christian faith was its orientation around a biblical
'guiding principle' (H. Dörrie), whether that faith be explained by
various lowbrow or highbrow methods. Such a guiding principle
was alien to the Graeco-Roman images of gods, characterized by
self-sufficiency, incomprehensiblity and unspeakablity. Genesis 1:1,
according to which God is the creator of heaven and earth, thereby
became the guiding principle of a monotheism which has constantly
remained alien to Greek images of God. This biblical monotheism
took its curious form in becoming a christological declaration
arising from Christ's life, and Christian theology then gradually
'draws conclusions in all directions'.[57] 'Non-Christian religiosity
was not rooted in a conception of God, which explains why, with
logical consistency, it did not give rise to a creed. Non-Christian

---

(Steenbrugge: in Abbatia S. Petri, 1991, 407–19; on persecution under Valerian:
K.-H. Schwarte, 'Die Christengesetze Valerians', in W. Eck, *Religion und
Gesellschaft in der römischen Kaiserzeit*, FS F. Vittinghoff (Cologne: Böhlau,
1989), 165–83.

[54] R. L. Wilken, *The Christians as the Romans Saw Them* (New Haven: Yale
University Press, 1984), 83; on *creatio ex nihilo*, cf. G. May, 'Die Entstehung der
Lehre von der Creatio ex nihilo', *Arbeiten zur Kirchengeschichte* 48 (1978),
especially 63ff.

[55] Wischmeyer, *Golgatha*, 158ff.

[56] Ps. Plutarch, *De superst.*, 161f. Cf. Wilken, 74f.

[57] H. Dörrie, 'Gottesvorstellung', *RAC XII* (1983), 81–154.

antiquity, when asked for a conception of God, did not have an answer ... Religiosity in antiquity was not manifested in a conception of God, but rather in a wealth of statements which produced evidence of vastly different images of the gods and the divine.'[58]

Death, resurrection and cemeteries

When the intellectual opponents of Christianity paid so much attention to the theme of death and resurrection, they came across an important point of Christian attraction as well as of Christian opinion. Under Bishop Marcellinus († AD 304), the deacon Severus bought and decorated a double room in Rome S. Callisto; in this room, he put up a grave inscription for his daughter Severa, which is now to be found in the Quasiversus. In this inscription, we read:[59]

> a two-room suite, with tombs and air shaft,
> by order of his Bishop Marcellinus
> the deacon Severus constructed a quiet resting place in peace
> for himself and his family.
> There the sweet limbs will be preserved in sleep
> for the Maker and Judge for a long time.
> Severa, sweet child to parents and servants,
> died a virgin on 25 January.
> The Lord let her be born in the flesh
> full of wisdom and skill,
> and her body is buried here in quiet and peace
> until it rises from here.
> The Lord by his Holy Spirit
> took her chaste, pure and ever inviolable soul
> and he will restore it again to spiritual glory.
> She lived nine years and eleven months and fifteen days.
> So was she taken from the world.[60]

The mixture of old and new stands out; the juxtaposition of themes is especially striking in the lack of skill – not to say the

---

[58] H. Dörrie, 'Gottesbegriff', *RAC* XI (1981).

[59] E. Diehl, *Inscriptiones latinae christianae veteres*, rev. edn (Dublin and Zürich, 1967–70), no. 3458. Cf. C. M. Kaufmann, *Handbuch der altchristlichen Epigraphik* (Freiburg: Herder, 1917), 129f.; A. Ferrua, 'Nuove Correzioni alla Silloge del Diehl', *Sussidi allo studio delle antichità christiana* 7 (1981), 113. The Transsene was reused and bears an older non-Christian grave inscription on the reverse side, *Corpus Inscriptionum Latinarum* 6, 27128.

[60] This translation owes much to Eoin de Bhaldraithe, OCist.

clumsiness – of the versification, which even fails linguistically. Here we are discussing a relatively lavish burial site of a deacon of the city of Rome,[61] in other words a member of the episcopal central authority, whose main task was charity work. In a traditional way, our deacon Severus stresses – not without playing associatively with his own and his daughter's name, and the verb *servare* – that he has erected the grave as *memoria*, that is to say, to honour the family, and that it equally serves (and here we find a new tone which transforms the traditional, euphemistic theme of sleep) to preserve for the creator and judge the sweet limbs, resting in sleep, for a long time. And so the old 'eternal house' (*domus aeterna*) became a 'quiet resting place in peace' (*mansio in pace quieta*).

Pax, here, is a timeless, eschatological category. It is naturally not to be understood conceptually as it was later by Augustine,[62] but rather, as the dual use here shows, in such a way as to allow the deceased to have a share in the glory of God already in the grave, which glory will be intensified hereafter in resurrection. It was the might of the Holy Spirit which took the deceased from this *saeculum*, thereby the grave became the sign of unavailable *pax*, the expression revealing the simultaneity of divine glory which offers creation and resurrection. The old idea of a 'commonwealth of gods and men'[63] finds a new opportunity of topicality which gives the clumsy inscription from the Roman clerics' cemetery its meaning.

The Christian community cemetery accommodated the general needs of the time according to a representative decorum, and thus became so important for the church's public image that it won people over to Christianity. The approach to death and its connection with this cemetery involves an answer to the riddle of

---

[61] No changes can have been made to the diaconal seven which was supported for the middle of the third century by Eusebius, *HE*, 6.43 and was oriented towards the New Testament; cf. Jerome, *Epp.*, 146.2; catalogue of the list of bishops of Rome up to Liberius' accession in 352 preserved in the Roman Calendar of 354 (M. R. Salzman, *On Roman Time* [Berkeley: University of California Press, 1990]); *Liber Pontificalis* (ed. Duchesne), 5; cf. Th. Klauser, *RAC* 3 (1957), 397–900.

[62] R. A. Markus, *Saeculum: History and Society in the Theology of St Augustine* (Cambridge: Cambridge University Press, 1970), 197; cf. E. Dinkler, *RAC* 8 (1972), 434–505 and especially 477–80.

[63] Cicero, *Leg.*, 1.23; fin. 3.64.

death and its unsettling challenge. The claim was made here to a certain knowledge that the world as we encounter it was only a limited part of human reality, the *saeculum* of our inscription, from which one would be taken in death without destroying individual existence. This did not happen – as the Stoics had argued – due to the laws of nature or reason, but rather because God the creator and judge wished it so.

In this way the deceased, saved by the miracle of God's absolute monarchy, could be saved by a God who, with his self-willed and active behaviour, has called every single human being to life and allows it to die and be resurrected. God, in an independent ceremony, will even crown the deceased with glory – in his time, God will supersede and exceed the deified and heroized deceased.[64]

Bridging the gap between earth and heaven

This theme was depicted in Christian cemeteries by images of the Jonah cycle, the most common pictorial theme in pre-Constantine art.[65] A transitory moment is translated: 'Life is a shipwreck', but in the resurrection of the body it finds 'a harbour and an everlasting place'.[66] This hope appeared in the metaphorical language of the time and became portrayable in accordance with the rules of pictorial art in late antiquity. The transitory moment entered the picture: hope for *pax* became a real picture, indeed a picture of reality like the fate of the biblical hero. In the Jonah cycle, not only did the deceased appear on the other side as a present reality; the other side itself also appeared, characterized by a universal happiness (*felicitas*) and *pax* through the appropriate unambiguous Roman pictorial formula 'on land and on water' (*terra marique*). In this way, present redemption acquired a representation, regardless of its transcendent character, through the addition of contemporary ideals of happiness, and nevertheless the biblical accent

---

[64] H. Wrede, *Consecratio in formam deorum* (Mainz: Verlag Philipp von Zabern, 1981), 170–5 for the increase in the heroizing trend in the gravestones of the third century.

[65] Cf. Wischmeyer, Akten 10 *Int. Kongreß CA* 1980 (1984) 2, 707–19; idem, *Vigiliae Christianae* 35 (1981), 253–87; idem, *Zeitschrift für Kirchengeschichte* 92 (1981), 161–79; idem, 'Der Tod des Jonas', in A. Franz, ed. *Streit am Tisch des Wortes: zur Deutung und Bedeutung des Alten Testaments und seine Verwendung in der Liturgie*, Pietas Liturgica 8 (St Ottilien, 1997), 183–217.

[66] Ambrose, *Ps.*, 12 (*CSEL*, 64, 355).

THE ORIGINS OF CHRISTENDOM IN THE WEST

and Christian credo Christianized both hope and the people of hope.

Identifying with the fate of the biblical hero appears as the actual message of the Jonah pictures, which made the Christian credo of hope visible and accessible to a non-Christian public. The biblical hero was interpreted and presented in the moment of transition, as a result of which the direct instant of salvation was depicted against the backdrop of the greatest danger. This depiction corresponded to the religious, social and cultural mentality of the third century, which is not unjustly referred to as an age of anxiety.[67]

Saving the endangered – and again the most common Jonah picture portrays this as calm[68] – is called peace. With reference to the large community and to its public image, the self-portrayal of the 'church of martyrs' corresponded to the Jonah picture both on an individual level and in the context of cemeteries, freed from isolation by the *ecclesia*. On the one hand, we would like to stress that a genuine, specific connection with the biblical theology of the cross was present.[69] On the other hand, under no circumstances should one revive the apologetic or romantic picture of a church of catacombs and martyrs which recent researchers have fortunately abandoned.[70] The legal formulation of a particular crime, whose many aspects referred to the community, enabled a

[67] E. R. Dodds, *Pagans and Christians in an Age of Anxiety* (Cambridge: Cambridge University Press, 1965).

[68] On the reduction of the Jonah scenes to Jonah at rest in third-century grave sculpture, cf. J. Engemann, 'Untersuchungen zur Sepulkralsymbolik', *JbAC Ergänzungsband* 2 (1973); idem, *Atti 9. Congr. Int. CA* (1975), *Studi di antichità christiana* 32, 1, 489f.; in contrast H. Sichtermann, 'Der Jonaszyklus', *Spätantike und frühes Christentum* (Frankfurt: Propyläen-Verlag, 1983), 241–8.

[69] For this the two parts of the Christian Bible are to be seen as a literary source and which determines the theology as well as the cult, liturgy and piety; cf. E. and E. Dinkler, *Reallexikon zur byzantinischen Kunst* (Stuttgart: Hiersemann, 1991), 1–219.

[70] Cf. in addition to W. H. C. Frend, *Martyrdom and Persecution in the Early Church* (Oxford: Blackwell, 1965), and idem, *The Rise of Christianity* (London: Darton, Longman & Todd, 1984), *passim*, especially J. Vogt and H. Last, *RAC* 2 (1954), 1159–228; J. Moreau, *Die Christenverfolgungen im römischen Reich* (Berlin: Töpelmann, 1961); J. Stoeßl, *TRE* 8 (1981), 23–62; Lane Fox, *Pagans and Christians*, 419–92. On the reasons for the persecutions of Christians in antiquity: F. Vittinghoff, 'Christianus sum: Das 'Verbrechen' von Außenseitern der römischen Gesellschaft', *Historia* 33 (1984), 331–57.

variety of rhetorical equivalents to the accusation of atheism.[71] The number of martyrs for this crime was small rather than large, but its significance was very great for the Christian mentality in terms of its solidarity in a non-Christian environment, a solidarity which was criminalized, or could at any moment be made an offence. This confrontation can be represented in the prototype of the confrontation between Jesus and Pontius Pilate. This prototype is of course oversimplified, but it nevertheless does contain all the social implications of the situation.

The church believed – and clarified for the public – that the death of martyrs offered all Christians the opportunity of a united self-identification, and therefore it offered them the opportunity of simultaneity with the celebrated martyr, a simultaneity similar to that in the cemeterial Jonah-motif, in the shameful, even fatal discipleship of the cross and at the same time in its heavenly glorification. Begun by the Scillitan martyr acts, the acclamation was a genre-specific element of the acts of martyrs which pointed to a liturgical practice which allowed the community to join in the acclamation during the reading of the Acts of martyrs.[72] Augustine's endorsement of this[73] was not an innovation but rather was in accordance with an old custom.

Thus the author of the *Acta Cypriani* added the *deo gratias* after the death sentence on the Carthaginian Bishop. He did so because he wanted to lead his listeners to a liturgical simultaneity with the martyr-bishop who answered the sentence in this way. Once again we are speaking of a transitory moment – in a liturgy which transcended present worship with the reading of the past martyrdom, leading into a heavenly liturgy and by this means

[71] G. E. M. de Sainte Croix, *Past and Present* 26 (1963), 33; cf. also R. MacMullen, *Enemies of the Roman Order*, 2nd edn (Cambridge: Harvard University Press, 1992), 156f. In this context we must take into account the early beginning, as J. J. O'Donnell observed, of the demise of paganism, cf. *Traditio* 35 (1979), 45–8, especially 65f.: 'Paganism – the worship of the false gods – was fast departing from the Roman scene; but paganism – a tolerant, even careless attitude toward worship in general – was a more tenacious institution'. For the Christian side: W. Daut, 'Die "halben Christen" unter den Konvertiten', *Zeitschrift für Missionswissenschaft und Religionswissenschaft* 55 (1977), 171–88.
[72] As in R. Reitzenstein, *Nachrichten von der Gesellschaft der Wissenschaften*, Göttingen, phil. hist. Klasse 1914 (1915), 89.
[73] Augustine, *Serm.* 30; cf. *Enarr. in ps.*, 104.

placing the active listener, but also the public, into the new state of the *pax* of *communio sanctorum*.[74]

For Christians, this liturgical simultaneity, which gave the community a share in the *pax*, meant 'being a member of the group that extended across the gulf which divided heaven and earth'.[75] This was also the assumption of the later martyr-cult, already laid down in pre-Constantine times, and offered the opportunity, if not to question, then certainly to bridge the sensation of the great caesura of the post-Constantine period. If the martyr-cult played a central role in the imperial church for ensuring the identity of the church of martyrs, then the chasm to be bridged in this 'annexation of the past' was perhaps not as wide as Robert A. Markus maintains.[76]

The public character of the church

Cyprian was also concerned with an *ecclesia in monte* (*Epp.*, 41) which understood the public character of the church in such a way that it established itself in the world and oriented itself towards the Capitoline, which in Carthage was the Byrsa, and towards the political and social situations represented there.[77] But *confessio* and *martyrium* were also the church's guarantees for this group, as will be shown later. Indeed, they have the quasi-automatic effect of a *restitutio in integrum* for the fallen church. In this way, the bearers of charisma, the martyrs, also exclusively occupied the *magisterium* and the *cura animarum*.[78] Cyprian no doubt saw this otherwise than as a bishop merely preserving his position of power.

In his Christian self-awareness, Cyprian was much more interested in objectifying the *pax* for the sake of its eschatological character. And he saw this only in a process of repentance which found a structured and accepted modus in the community of

[74] Cf. Wischmeyer, in Instrumenta Patristica 19 (1989), 363–71; idem, in Instrumenta Patristica 24 (1991), 407–19.

[75] Markus, *End of Ancient Christianity*, 22ff.

[76] The individual perception of the caesura is something different. Parts of the imperial church, especially in monasticism but also in the clergy and among the theologians, became more and more strongly sensitive, even scrupulous.

[77] Wischmeyer, *Studia Patristica* 21 (1987), 130–9.

[78] Wischmeyer, *Golgatha*, 183f.

bishops united under the image of the *cathedra Petri*. For Cyprian, Christianity's public image was connected to authority and credibility. The church conferences which he assembled were already a public event due to their very size: the position which he held, in comparison with, for example, the two governors, as portrayed in the *Acta Cypriani*, laid claim to be a public one, and his *translatio* to the place of execution became a public event.

But this did not remain limited to an individual level. Rather, it revealed to the public how the church had taken shape as a local church with a structured clergy, at the head of which was a quasi-monarchical episcopate with an episcopal central authority, with individuals responsible for church buildings, cemeteries and properties, with welfare services for the poor and with the clergy of presbyters responsible for spiritual welfare – just as found in larger or smaller synod assemblies for one or more provinces. Indeed, as the example of the Synod of Antioch in AD 268 shows,[79] such synods received imperial attention, and it was then the Emperor himself who proceeded to elevate an alien, namely Christian, theological college in the capital, Rome, to the level of a decision-making authority.

In addition, there was the episcopate's power of attraction for an élite mostly made up of members of the town councils but also of the *ordo equester*, so that the older patronal class of rich women and freedmen faded in importance. Without having any official administrative connection to the Roman episcopate, the Emperor found this episcopate so interesting that after one word from Cyprian, Decius was more interested in the choice of a Roman bishop than in the proclamation of an anti-emperor.

We must get used to bearing in mind this public image of the pre-Constantine church (as, incidentally, the apologists had already done with their leap from the school of philosophers to the genre of *legatio* originating in the political *polis*-tradition) as well as to emphasizing context and difference in religious forms in the imperial period. The various local Christian churches were not secret societies, despite claims to this effect in a spate of anti-Christian accusations, and it was only for parts of the Sunday liturgy that the oft-cited Christian *disciplina arcani* played a role. This role cannot have gone beyond the cultural mystery of classical

---

[79] Eusebius, *HE*, 7.21ff.

cults such as Eleusis, which were debated publicly in Rome under Augustus.[80] Even the secretive category of the crypto-Christians contained the appeal of the esoteric and of the romantic, but the problems which were to be clarified here can be explained more properly and more simply by a model of acculturation.

A Christian self-awareness aiming itself at the public may have been typical, as it reveals itself in the self-description 'Christians', even in images of the cross on gravestones. Here we are referring to the so-called 'Christians for Christians' inscriptions of Phrygia.[81] On these, dedicators described themselves and their deceased as Christians openly in public; indeed, they could even add a cross at a prominent point. In addition, objects which portrayed riches in daily life were very realistically shown, just as can be seen on non-Christian gravestones. The mutuality of this iconography and also of epigraphical formulae is so great that it allows no differentiation on the part of the Christian group. The Christians lived in harmony with their neighbours, 'sharing in Graeco-Roman culture, its sentiments, language, and art . . . Like their neighbours these Christians exult in their wealth and their culture. It is natural that they exult in their new religion too'.[82]

Relativizing the *saeculum*

Without being able to rule out a Montanist character to the inscriptions *a priori*, as W. M. Ramsay originally maintained,[83] Gibson's recent investigation also found no positive indication of such character.[84] Far more important are the early crosses on these Phrygian inscriptions, for example, crosses in wreaths, with clear connotations of Victoria, approximately fifty years after the Abercius inscription which had only an empty wreath. These are joined with items of daily life which are also portrayed. They do

[80] Suetonius, *Aug.*, 93.
[81] Cf. E. Gibson, *The 'Christians for Christians' Inscriptions of Phrygia* (Missoula: Scholars Press, 1978).
[82] Ibid., 143.
[83] W. M. Ramsay, *The Cities and Bishoprics of Phrygia* 1.2 (Oxford: Clarendon Press, 1897), 490f. and 536f., cf. W. M. Calder, *BJRL* 7 (1922/23), 309–54 and idem, *BJRL* 13 (1929), 254–71; idem, *Byzantion* 6 (1931), 421–5; idem, *Anatolian Studies* 5 (1955), 25–38.
[84] Cf. Wischmeyer, *JbAC* 23 (1980), 166–71.

not only have the character of a confession already pronounced in the Christian name, but they also add a clearly pronounced, eschatological accent which publicly finds expression in pre-Constantine times, and even visualizes what is suitable for the church of martyrs in the discipleship of the cross: not the radicalism of martyrdom, but rather the relativization of the *saeculum* through the creation and the gift of *pax* which transcended the structures of both the time and of political and social pacification.

It was part of the work of the third-century church to make this visible in as many areas as possible, not only in the solitary heights of a theology of Origen, but also in elementary contexts of life. Part of this was no doubt the attraction of the hierarchy, particularly of the bishops for members of the urban upper classes. This was the case not only for Cyprian in Carthage or for his colleagues in other large towns, but also for someone like M. Julius Eugenius in the small rural town of Laodicea in Asia Minor.[85]

Each century has to be receptive to this message and its forms, from which we find an echo in the quantitative rise in the number of the communities, and in the number of their members. We also find an echo in an innovative push in the direction of accommodation. This should not necessarily be dismissed: it was a constant effort to fill old skins with new wine, making the most of the fact that change could occur in the swirling development since the present was robbed of its claim to absolute right.

Christian love and philanthropy

One such change was the movement from the euergetism of antiquity[86] to a form of philanthropy which constantly updated the message as well as the new virtue of *agape*. *Agape* fundamentally questioned and relativized the absoluteness of prevailing conventions of the political and the social, of art and philosophy, without actually resolving them. Within this context of a new

---

[85] Cf. the contributions of H. Chadwick, P. Brown, R. M. Grant, R. MacMullen, and M. H. Shepherd, in E. C. Hobbs and W. Wuellner, eds, *The Role of the Christian Bishop in Ancient Society: Protocol of the 35th Colloquy 1979* (Berkeley: Center for Hermeneutical Studies in Hellenistic and Modern Culture, 1980); Wischmeyer, *Zeitschrift für die neutestamentliche Wissenschaft* 81 (1990), 225–46.

[86] P. Veyne, *Le pain et le cirque* (Paris: Seuil, 1976).

euergetism, there was also the work of Christian charity, which we have referred to several times, such as in the list of Bishop Cornelius and in the warehouse in Cirta. Though individual charity and alms were important, the officers concentrated in the diaconal central authority of the bishop came into the public eye ever more strongly and with increasing means. The officers had no need to create for themselves a group of followers in given social circumstances. Pre-modern society was to a large extent characterized by an elementary poverty: at the beginning of late antiquity, we have a society with an upper class which was disproportionately small – even minimal – in numbers, yet was favoured by the law in every respect; then we have the rest of the population, a wide lower-class base which to a large extent had no rights at all. Thus there were more than enough people who had to rely on charity. Indeed there were more people in this category than could be cared for by imperial and private donations (with all their problems for the poor: being dependent on chance and 'crumbs' from the tables of the rich), and even by the church's social welfare services within and without the church itself.

Meeting people's elementary needs in everyday life was certainly more important than the cemeterial work. This was particularly true in the case of the urban lower classes, but also in the cases of the deserving poor and of those deprived of their rights who, according to their status, ought to be placed in a higher category. The external effect of the church social welfare services cannot be pictured fully without also realizing that connected missionary aspirations were being fulfilled, and that such aspirations must always have been linked to charity. Perhaps the indirect mission was stronger, too: you do not bite the hand that feeds you.

Incidentally, in this the church was following in Jewish footsteps, and these Jewish charitable works could be extensive, e.g. the Jewish soup-kitchen relief around the third century in Aphrodisias.[87] The Jewish relief efforts certainly have to be seen as a means of gaining

---

[87] Cf. J. Reynolds and R. Tannenbaum, 'Jews and Godfearers at Aphrodisias', *Cambridge Philological Society Supplement* 12 (1987). H. Botermann's attempt to give it a later date is unconvincing in 'Griechisch-jüdische Epigraphik', *Zeitschrift für Papyrologie und Epigraphik* 98 (1993), 184–94. Cf. also P. W. van der Horst, 'Jews and Christians in Aphrodisias', in idem, *Essays on the Jewish World of Early Christianity* (Göttingen: Vandenhoeck & Ruprecht, 1990), 166–81.

sympathizers if not as an instrument of a Jewish mission. The church – unlike the Jews – was not hampered by a discussion of the mission's value which very quickly came to a negative conclusion. It also did not devalue the link between its charity and its mission, either, for the postulate of a genuine human love is an ethical appeal of Kantian persuasion, although its taking shape is something else.

As incidental as recorded facts for early Christianity are (can sources be otherwise?), we know that the so-called Christian human love itself caused offence even to Julian and was a thorn in his side. There is an indication (which cannot be overrated) of a change in mentality which must be linked to the Christian welfare services causally, and we come across it in epigraphic wordings: the transition from the 'friend of Caesar' (amicus Caesaris) to the 'friend of the poor' (amicus pauperum). This transition, in conjunction with another (from the 'brief light' [lux brevis] to the 'perpetual light' [lux perpetua]), curiously reveals the dimension of late antiquity.[88] We find these new epithets concentrated on the epitaphs of clergymen and especially of bishops.[89]

A church of the martyrs and the bourgeoisie

But if one can speak here of a new euergetism, especially with reference to the bishops (and the architecture necessary for the fast-growing church provided a rich field of activity which was also tied to the euergetism of antiquity), then this leads to one final observation. The third-century church was both the church of a new Christian bourgeoisie, and a church of martyrs. It was the integrating function of the bishops to keep this together: to maintain the unity of the church of confessors and martyrs and of the 'semi-Christians', those in large numbers from all spheres of society who now feel themselves connected to the church. The 'struggle and advance'[90] of Christianity in the third century not only led to debates between state and society on the one hand, and church on the other, but these debates were also echoed in the church itself in a long chain of struggles throughout the Empire, from the Montanists and Novatians to Donatists and Melitians.

[88] Cf. on this topic H.-I. Marrou, Décadence romaine ou antiquité tardive (Paris: Seuil, 1977).
[89] Cf. M. Heinzelmann, Bischofsherrschaft in Gallien (Munich: Artemis, 1976).
[90] Frend, The Rise of Christianity, ch. 9.

The acceptance – or was it a usurpation? – of the teaching profession by the bishops in the debate with the *gnosis* prevented an individualizing drifting apart into religious clubs characterized by patrons' wealth and education and their philosophical systems derived from diverse literary favourites.[91] Likewise, the episcopate managed to keep together the broad mass of church followers and the church of martyrs and to embrace them all in the way I have described using the idea of the church of martyrs. Its public prestige increased not least due to the means employed by the bishops for that purpose: discipline. It was Augustine who would first provide a theory.

Seen by many as too lenient, but on the whole in fact successful, the disciplining of this new mass movement 'Christian church' was then also able to bring about the change in the imperial religious policy from tolerance and persecution to legalization and its known consequences in the imperial church. In this we also find the century's answer to Tertullian's in many ways misinterpreted question: 'What has Athens to do with Jerusalem?'[92] In this, R. A. Markus rightly sees 'evidence not so much of a tip of submerged iceberg of hostility to secular culture as of a need felt to strengthen at a time of rapid assimilation which seemed to pose a threat to it'.[93]

As the church found followers from every class of Roman society in the remainder of the third century, and especially in its second half, and as it increasingly got into a process of assimilation in terms of lifestyle, culture and education (since they were part of the process of civilizing the members of the urban Roman upper classes), the unity of the church and its identification, indeed definition, as a church of martyrs became the greatest achievement of the bishops. With a lasting public result, such disciplining effectively assumed prestige and authority for the office, to an

[91] Cf. H. G. Kippenberg, 'Versuch einer soziologischen Verortung des antiken Gnostizismus', *Numen* 17 (1970), 211–31; K. Rudolph, *Gnosis: The Nature and History of an Ancient Religion* (Edinburgh: T&T Clark, 1983).

[92] Tertullian, *De praescriptione haereticorum*, 7.5. For its date (AD 203), see T. D. Barnes, *Tertullian*, 2nd edn (Oxford: Clarendon Press, 1985), 55, 210, 332f.

[93] Markus, *End of Ancient Christianity*, 27; cf. idem, 'The Problem of Self-Definition: from Sect to Church', in E. P. Sanders, ed., *Jewish and Christian Self-Definition* I (London: SCM Press, 1980), 1–15, 217–19.

extent which is difficult to describe, and for the bishop himself. He was responsible for the discipline of his *militia christiana* and, under the circumstances, he could be compared with the emperor if the bishop as martyr, like the emperor in his *natale*, shares a comparable *donativum*.[94]

Imperial and Jesuanic motifs were linked in the account of Bishop Cyprian's martyrdom, bringing about the possibility of identification on the part of the listener of the Acts. This not only pointed to the public effect of a large church forming in the third century, but also determined anew its self-perception and its view of the public, the *saeculum*. This was indeed just as important as the great achievements of the century's theologians, though little can be said here of them, or of the philosophical opponents of Christianity. From Clement and Tertullian to Lactantius and Arius, from Irenaeus to Dionysius of Alexandria and to Eusebius, and not forgetting Origen who towers above all: to what extent these had any external effect would require a precise examination, likewise the question of how strongly each of them was shaped individually by the problems which we have illustrated in our outline. There should be no argument, though, that they were parts of their church and children of their times. They, too, played their part in shaping the public image of this church of the people, which saw itself as a church of martyrs.

The theology of this church is, and remains, Bible theology. This is common to all theologians, and on the way, they have given it to the church of their day in its immense changes, as an indispensable ingredient and inheritance – and also for the future. The essential Christian self-definition is not the school of a philosopher, not a way of life, not a connection to a holy place, not the exclusivity of a social stratum or of a nationality, but concentration on the reinterpretation, at the time, of a binding relationship to the Bible's Old and New Testaments.[95]

---

[94] Cf. Wischmeyer, *Golgatha*, 203 n. 132.

[95] Here we find the importance of the history of the canon, its diversity and especially its closing. Cf. H. von Campenhausen, *Die Entstehung der christlichen Bibel* (Tübingen: Mohr, 1968); J.-T. Kaestli and O. Wermelinger, *Le canon de l'Ancien Testament* (Geneva: Labor et Fides, 1984); H. Y. Gamble, *The New Testament Canon* (Philadelphia: Fortress Press, 1985); A. M. Ritter, 'Die Entstehung des neutestamentlichen Kanons', in A.-J. Assmann, ed., *Kanon und Zensur* (Munich: Fink, 1987), 93–9; B. Lang and P. Hofrichter, *Neues Bibel-*

As such it was more than an episode in a debate among philosophers when Porphyry compared Ammonius and Origen:

> Ammonius was a Christian brought up in Christian ways by his parents, but when he began to think philosophically, he promptly changed to a law-abiding way of life. Origen on the other hand, a Greek schooled in Greek thought, plunged headlong into un-Greek recklessness; immersed in this, he peddled himself and his skill in argument. In his way of life he behaved like a Christian, defying the law; in his metaphysical and theological ideas he played the Greek, giving a Greek twist to foreign tales.[96]

Lexikon 8 (1992), 440–50 (Lit.). The *Muratorian Canon*, traditionally dated about AD 200, can possibly be seen as a fourth-century product, and there are many philological and historical reasons for a new dating that will fit very well into our context. Cf. A. C. Sundberg, Jr, 'Towards a Revised History of the New Testament Canon', *Studia Evangelica* 4.1 (1968), 452–61; idem, 'Canon Muratori: A Fourth-century List', *Harvard Theological Review* 66 (1973), 1–41; G. M. Hahneman, *The Muratorian Fragment and the Development of the Canon* (Oxford: Clarendon Press, 1992).

[96] Eusebius, *HE*, 6.19.

Chapter 5

Early Christian Features Preserved in Western Monasticism

EOIN DE BHALDRAITHE, OCɪsᴛ.

With the coming of Christendom, in which membership of the church and of civil society were almost identical, conditions of church membership, which had been stringent, became accommodating. But monastic communities in the West give clues as to what the church was like in the early centuries. Early Christian communities contained celibate and married people, who shared prayer in common assemblies and who sought to be obedient to Christ, as is evidenced in first-century Corinth, second- to fourth-century Syria and Rome, and Basil's Cappadocia. In the later fourth century, patterns of Egyptian monasticism, influenced by Neo-Platonic thinking, spread across East and West and brought a division between the 'perfect' Christians – celibate and living in poverty and non-violence – and the ordinary believers. The *Apostolic Tradition*, along with later church orders and canonical material, shows the spread of the understanding that Christians may take part in military violence; for this, Augustine of Hippo provided a theology. Rooted in assumptions coming from the Egyptian tradition, medieval monasticism saw itself as a state of perfection, lived in poverty, chastity and obedience and withdrew from parishes into separate assemblies.

Early in the fourth century Christians were accorded freedom of worship in the Roman Empire. By the end of the century all non-Christian worship was forbidden and even heresy was outlawed, leaving Catholicism as the established religion. This empire we know as Christendom. At the end of another four centuries a further phase developed in the West with the constitution of the Holy Roman Empire. This reached its peak when the Pope assumed supreme authority in the high Middle Ages.

The fact that all were expected to be Christian had an effect on the church itself and how it conceived its membership. Briefly, we believe that conditions for membership were reduced drastically in order to accommodate all people. This went much further in the West than the East. The more ancient conditions of membership now applied to monks and clerics only. Indeed the monastic communities of the West give us some idea of what the church itself was like in the early centuries.

In this paper we look at some of the less well-known aspects of early Christian communities and the place occupied within them by those called to remain unmarried. Then we will outline the main theological ideas which were to lead to a very different understanding. Finally by quickly reviewing the well-known features of medieval communities, we shall realize how many of them were features of the main church in the early period.

I. EARLY CHRISTIAN COMMUNITIES

We shall begin by looking at the primitive church in Corinth since we have some detail on the place occupied in it by celibate men and women. Then we shall select three examples of communities from the second to fourth centuries which seem to preserve strong continuity with the early ideals.

Corinth: monogamy and celibacy as charisms

The church in Corinth, according to Charles Kinsgley Barrett, 'evidently consists of a group of persons who will assemble to read (or hear) Paul's letter'.[1] They were 'called into communion' with Jesus Christ (1 Cor. 9). The community included married and unmarried people as we see in chapter 7. Paul told them that both states of life were gifts from God, literally charisms.

[1] C. K. Barrett, *A Commentary on the First Epistle to the Corinthians* (London: A&C Black, 1976), 32.

Though some doubt if Paul meant to describe marriage as a charism,[2] it would seem that this view is in line with the broader tradition as we meet it in Matthew 19. The disciples react to the Lord's words on monogamy by saying, 'If this is the situation between a husband and wife, it is better not to marry' (Mt. 19:10). There follows the *logion* about the eunuchs for the sake of the kingdom of heaven. Both monogamy and celibacy can be accepted 'only by those to whom it is given' (Mt. 19:11).[3]

Paul then would be in line with this tradition if he were saying that like celibacy, monogamy was a charism, a gift of the Holy Spirit to those who share the life of the Risen Lord.

In 1 Corinthians 7:25–40, Paul gives advice to the 'virgins'. It is a good thing to remain unmarried, yet 'if a virgin marries, it is not a sin' (v. 8). Here 'virgin' means someone unmarried and apparently with some intention of remaining so. The term includes both men and women. There were a number of them in the church at Corinth. A reason given for remaining celibate is that 'the time is short' (v. 29). Paul expected the *parousia* soon, but all through the letter there is a realized eschatology.[4] From this it seems to follow that Paul saw not only matters such as faith and the eucharist but also virginity as an anticipation of the eschaton.

Paul does say that the married man is 'divided' (1 Cor. 7:33). We cannot conclude from this, however, that he is only a 'half-Christian',[5] for Paul goes on to say that the virgin is anxious 'how to be holy in the body as well as in the Spirit' (v. 34).[6] All Christians were holy in Spirit as is clear from the previous chapter (6:17–20); indeed this holiness flowed over into the body too. Married people

---

[2] E.g. Barrett, *First Corinthians*, 158–9.

[3] 'Contemporary Biblical Criticism of Matt 19:12 and 1 Cor 7:32–35', and 'The Eunuch Saying on the Lips of Jesus', in F. J. Moloney, *Disciples and Prophets: A Biblical Model for the Religious Life* (London: Darton, Longman & Todd, 1980), 105–14.

[4] Barrett, *First Corinthians*, 40.

[5] 'The married person ... was almost of necessity a "half-Christian", disqualified from becoming one spirit with the Lord.' Peter Brown, *The Body and Society: Men, Women and Sexual Renunciation in Early Christianity* (London: Faber & Faber, 1989), 56.

[6] The Greek could be translated simply 'holy in body and spirit', but this is unlikely as holiness in the Spirit is presumed for all.

are certainly included here. The fact that the virgin abstained from sexual intercourse was one way of extending the sanctification of the Spirit to the body.

Paul also says that the married person is 'anxious about the things of the world' (1 Cor. 7:33). This would become 'secular' as opposed to 'religious' in medieval times. However it is important to emphasize that the whole Corinthian community is separated from the world. They mix with people in the world but exclude members who sin seriously. This separation will be stated emphatically in 2 Corinthians 6:14–18.

1 Corinthians 7:37–38 almost certainly refer to a spiritual marriage in which there is no physical relationship. The *New English Bible* adopted the translation 'partner in celibacy'.[7] It is hard to see how anything else can make sense of the passage.[8] Most translations now use the word 'betrothed' which makes good sense in public reading.[9] It presumes, however, that 'virgin' has a different meaning here and includes no intention of permanency. We surely have here the beginning of the institution later to be known as *virgines subintroductae*.

As we pass on to chapter 11, Paul deals with the Christian assembly and the eucharist. It is clear that all were to take part. The virgins mentioned were simply a part of the assembly. There, many charisms were recognized, the greatest of all being love, and the charisms of virginity and monogamy added to the variety.

It is important to outline this early Christian scene at Corinth as it will be repeated in so many churches of the early centuries.

Syria: committed virgins within congregational life

We find a system in Syria which corresponds very closely to the situation in Corinth. There are four terms found in the writings of Ephrem and Aphrahat. *Bthula* is a virgin, male or female. *Qaddisha*, 'holy' is a married person who abstains from sexual

---

[7] *The New English Bible* (Oxford and Cambridge University Presses, 1970). In the revision this translation goes into a footnote while the word 'betrothed' is used in the main text (*The Revised English Bible* [same presses, 1989]).

[8] J. S. Ruef, *Paul's First Letter to Corinth* (Harmondsworth: Penguin, 1971), 67–9.

[9] For example, *Traduction oecuménique de la bible* (Paris: Cerf, 1972) has *fiancée*, but with a note saying that the word is literally *'vierge'*.

intercourse. *Ihidaya* means 'single' or 'unique'. It translates *monogenes* which is the 'unique' rather than 'only-begotten' (Son of God). As applied to humans it means 'single-minded' and also 'celibate'. The fourth term is *qyama* or 'covenant'. This seems to designate the decision for celibacy by either the virgins or married people. Together those formed 'the sons and daughters of the covenant'.[10]

Aphrahat wrote his *Demonstrations* between 337 and 345. The sixth treatise is on the *ihidaya*.[11] Those live singly or in twos and threes among the rest of the Christian community. 'They were essentially a feature of town and village life, a far remove from the Egyptian monastic model of *anachoresis*, or withdrawal to the desert.'[12]

They may use money but not take interest. They are, however, involved in vigils and liturgical service. Aphrahat complains about some celibates losing their celibacy. Yet he allows a son and daughter of the covenant to marry publicly rather than to practise sexual intercourse in secret.[13]

The *Testamentum Domini* describes the ceremony of baptism.[14] Those who have decided on virginity are baptized first but all are together as part of the one congregation. This is so similar to Aphrahat's seventh *Demonstration* that it is one reason for

---

[10] S. Brock, *The Luminous Eye: The Spiritual World Vision of Saint Ephrem* (Kalamazoo: Cistercian Publications, 1992); cf. ch. 8 on 'Syrian proto-monasticism: a forgotten tradition', 131–41. The following is from Ephrem's hymn 8 on the Epiphany.

Hâ 'amdîn w-haweyn | btûlê w-qaddîsê
da-nhet(w) 'ªmad(w) wa-lbes(w) | l-haw had Ihîdayâ.

This is the transliteration of R. Murray, 'The Exhortation to Candidates for Ascetical Vows at Baptism in the Ancient Syriac Church', *New Testament Studies* 21 (1974), 59–80 (64). We easily recognize three of the terms explained. It translates as:

See (people) being baptized and becoming virgins and holy ones, having gone down, been baptized and put on the single 'Only One'.

[11] *PS*, 1.239–312; *Nicene and Post Nicene Fathers* (Grand Rapids: Eerdmans, 1978), ser. 2, 13.362–75; cited hereafter as *NPNF*.

[12] Brock, *Luminous Eye*, 136.

[13] G. Nedungatt, 'The Covenanters of the early Syriac-Speaking Church', *Orientalia Christiana Periodica* 39 (1973), 190–215; 419–44 (437).

[14] G. Sperry-White, *The Testamentum Domini: A Text for Students* (Bramcote: Grove, 1991), 2.5–10.

ascribing the *Testamentum* to Syria.[15] This is the passage which induced Arthur Vööbus to regard the community as totally celibate. It is rather an exhortation to those who have departed from celibacy to return.[16]

Though there has been some development, this system of celibacy is remarkably close to the New Testament. With the great prestige of Egyptian monasticism which was brought to Syria at the end of the fourth century, a virtual re-founding of the church occurred and the earlier tradition was forgotten.[17]

The most recent monograph is by Shafiq AbouZayd, a Catholic Maronite.[18] The author continually emphasizes that there is no major difference between the celibate and the married person. Holy marriage was a charism like virginity. The Sons and Daughters of the Covenant, as described by Aphrahat, did not follow a special rule; they simply lived the spirituality of their church.

Fornication destroys virginity as adultery destroys holy marriage. Marriage, however, does not mean a betrayal of virginity, no doubt following the words of Paul, 'If a virgin marries, it is not a sin.' Because of this AbouZayd says that 'virginity meant a time of preparation for marriage'. This perhaps overstates the case, as he tells us later that the virginity of the Sons and Daughters of the Covenant was not necessarily seen as leading to marriage. He continues by saying that, 'Virginity signifying lifetime celibacy was no more than an individual commitment for a limited number of people'. 'Commitment' is a good description of what was involved. 'Vow' is too strong, though our author occasionally uses it. Our Western expression 'profession' (of chastity) is nearer to the original idea.

---

[15] Sperry-White (ibid., 6) suggests Asia Minor.

[16] *PS*, 1.341–4; A. Vööbus, *Celibacy, a Requirement for Admission to Baptism in the Early Syrian Church* (Stockholm: Estonian Theological Society in Exile, 1951); Murray, 'Exhortation to Candidates', 60–2.

[17] Brock, *Luminous Eye*, 131–2. Brown, *Body and Society*, 96–7, deals with this material, citing Murray and some early work of Brock, but he seems to be misled by Vööbus into thinking it was a matter of totally celibate communities. However, depending on Nedungatt he describes the situation correctly on pages 101–2.

[18] Shafiq AbouZayd, *IHIDAYUTHA: A Study of the Life of Singleness in the Syrian Orient from Ignatius of Antioch to Chalcedon 451 AD* (Oxford: Oriental Institute, 1993). AbouZayd did his doctorate under Brock and this book is the result. It presents the Syrian teaching very thoroughly, if not always as systematically as a Westerner would wish.

John Chrysostom was the first to say that a monk or virgin who married committed adultery.[19] This teaching eventually prevailed in the church but it is clear that for the early church, 'virginity and holy marriage were in harmony'.[20] 'The Monastic understanding of devout celibacy helped to encourage a restricted, physical interpretation of the idea of virginity and to impose it on Christian theology.' By 'Monastic' here AbouZayd means the influence derived from Egypt. Under this influence also, the native Syriac word *ihidaya* came to mean 'hermit'.[21]

The *Apostolic Tradition*: spouses and virgins in a separated community

In the document we usually refer to as the *Apostolic Tradition* (*AT*) we get an indication of the liturgical regime of an early Christian community and of the celibates within it. It was generally ascribed to Hippolytus around AD 215.[22] Today we would be more careful.[23] The earliest portions, as we shall see, go back to the second century while some parts may be as late as the fourth century.[24]

It is a collection of church regulations which in its surviving variants may not represent any particular community. Its regulations were taken over and adapted in the many related documents. So while it is hard to say if all its rules were observed in any particular church, they do represent the general approach of many early communities.

[19] Ibid., 275; quoting John Chrysostom, *An Exhortation to Theodore after His Fall*, 10; *PG*, 47.289–90; *NPNF* ser. 2, 9.98.

[20] Ibid.

[21] Ibid., 271.

[22] B. Botte, *Hippolyte de Rome: La Tradition Apostolique*, SCh. 11 bis (Paris: Cerf, 1968); G. J. Cuming, *Hippolytus: A Text for Students* (Bramcote: Grove, 1987).

[23] M. Metzger, 'Nouvelles perspectives pour la prétendue *Tradition Apostolique*', *Ecclesia Orans* 5 (1988), 241–59; idem, 'Enquêtes autour de la prétendue *Tradition Apostolique*', *Ecclesia Orans* 9 (1992), 7–36; idem, 'A propos des règlements ecclésiastiques et de la prétendue *Tradition Apostolique*', *Revue des sciences religieuses* 66 (1992), 149–61.

[24] M. E. Johnson, 'The Postchrismational Structure of *Apostolic Tradition* 21, the Witness of Ambrose of Milan, and a Tentative Hypothesis Regarding the Current Reform of Confirmation in the Roman Rite', *Worship* 70 (1996), 16–34. Johnson has been able to use some of the unpublished conclusions of Paul Bradshaw.

We gather from the document that the community lived among a large number of pagans. As we shall see, this was most probably Rome. It was necessary to exclude many different kinds of people from baptism and eucharist. In a later section we shall deal with the exclusion of the soldier.

This community had fixed times for prayer. 'The people' assemble on the Lord's day for the ordination of the bishop. They also assemble like this every Sunday, as there are instructions on how to distribute communion to 'all the people'.[25]

There is an assembly in church on some mornings. The faithful are to go there to hear the 'verbal instruction' which is 'the word of God'. Otherwise they are to pray at home. In the shorter Latin version, there follow instructions on receiving the reserved eucharist at home before the main meal.

In the Coptic version there is an exhortation to read the Bible at home if there is no instruction in church.[26] People are recommended to pray three times in the day and three times at night. Those are clearly private prayers, as is stated for the midnight prayer of one married to a pagan wife. The series jumps from afternoon to bedtime prayer. So it seems to presume the evening prayer in common which is dealt with in chapter 25.[27]

At this evening service, blessed bread rather than the eucharist is distributed to 'the faithful who are present'. It seems clear that not all are expected to attend as at the Sunday eucharist. The ceremony begins with a blessing of the lamp and some 'alleluia' psalms. We know of a similar agape from Tertullian who speaks of prayers at the beginning and end of the meal. He mentions the 'lights' and the individual leading prayer in the centre.[28]

AT tells us that after supper 'the boys and the virgins' shall say psalms. This probably means male as well as female celibates. It is quite similar to Egeria's description of the office in Jerusalem. There the *monazontes* and *parthenae* performed a vigil office while the ordinary faithful came only for the main morning and evening

---

[25] Botte, *Tradition* 22 (not preserved in the Latin).

[26] Ibid., 41.

[27] R. Taft, *The Liturgy of the Hours in East and West* (Collegeville: Liturgical Press, 1986), 26–7.

[28] Tertullian, *Apologia*, 39.17–18; *PL*, 1.477; *The Ante Nicene Fathers* (hereafter *ANF*) (Grand Rapids: Eerdmans, 1978), 3.47.

service.[29] While Paul's *parthenos* could be a man or a woman, here we see later tradition trying to find a separate term for the male variety. The Western church would call them *monachi et virgines*.[30]

In the Coptic version we are also told that a virgin is not ordained as her 'choice' alone makes her a virgin. It seems to refer to women only. Apparently the Greek is simply transliterated here, so we can see that the original is *proairesis, propositum* in Latin.[31]

We gather then from the *Apostolic Tradition* that the community is emphatically separated from pagans, especially at its Sunday assembly. The practice of virginity is still very close to the New Testament except that a distinction is now growing between the male and female. There is an assembly in church on most weekday mornings where 'the word of God' can be heard. Those who cannot be present should read the Bible at home. The reserved eucharist is received before the main meal. The evening service includes the blessing of the lamp and responsorial psalms. There are about six times of private prayer during the day while the virgins are expected to devote more time to saying the psalms.

Basil: obedience, simplicity, non-violence for all Christians

There is a treatise on baptism attributed to Basil of Caesarea. Julien Garnier, whose introductory notes appear in Migne, doubted if it was written by Basil while Prudent Maran who completed the edition argued in favour. Umberto Neri has recently defended its authenticity.[32]

---

[29] J. Wilkinson, *Egeria's Travels to the Holy Land* (Warminster: Aris & Phillips, 1981), 123, 125.

[30] St Patrick, writing about AD 450, witnesses to the usage of the British church; see L. Bieler, *Libri Epistolarum Sancti Patricii Episcopi* (Dublin: Royal Irish Academy, 1993), 81, 97.

[31] Botte, *Tradition*, 12.

[32] U. Neri, *Basilio di Cesarea: Il Battesimo* (Brescia: Paideia, 1976), 23–53 claims to arrive at 'conclusioni definitive'. His arguments are accepted by J. Ducatillon, *Basile de Césarée: Sur le baptême*, SCh., 357 (Paris: Cerf, 1989). P. Rousseau retains a 'cautious scepticism', but he does not refer to the arguments of Neri (*Basil of Caesarea* [Berkeley: University of California Press, 1994], 130). For an English translation of Basil, see M. Wagner, *Saint Basil: Ascetical Works*, The Fathers of the Church 9 (Washington, DC: Catholic University of America Press, 1950), 339–430.

This treatise shows the original ideal surviving largely intact. Baptism was for adult catechumens who were still being carefully selected. The story of the rich young man is used to show the catechumen what is necessary to be a disciple of Christ. First keep the commandments; then sell all; finally follow Christ. The 'sell all' is for all the baptized. Repeatedly the saying about giving up all possessions (Lk 14:33) is quoted. The following text will illustrate.

> Not only should we not endeavour to increase our possessions and to acquire greater gains, as do people of the world, but we should not even lay claim to the property which has already been acquired and is our own. Let us be zealous in giving to the needy . . . including hostile and wicked people also in our acts of kindness.[33]

This was not absolute poverty, as one's own needs had to be supplied, but after that, superfluities were to be given away. It is a good illustration of a common doctrine of the patristic age.[34]

The quotation mentions 'people of the world'. For Basil it is the baptized (and not the 'monks' as an Egyptian might say) who are 'separated from the world'. Elsewhere in the treatise he refers to the baptized as 'set apart from all who live according to this world'.

For Basil all Christians were bound to non-violence or non-resistance:

> Surely we walk in newness of life and achieve a justice more perfect than that of the Scribes and Pharisees when we obey these words of the Lord: 'It was said to them of old: An eye for an eye and a tooth for a tooth. But I say to you not to resist evil . . .' Not only are we to refrain from revenge for offences first committed against us, . . . but

---

[33] *PG*, 31.1544; Neri, 212–13; Wagner, 364.

[34] W. J. Walsh and J. P. Langan, 'Patristic Social Consciousness: The Church and the Poor', in J. C. Haughey, ed., *The Faith That Does Justice* (New York: Paulist Press, 1977), 113–51; C. Avila, *Ownership: Early Christian Teaching* (London: Sheed & Ward, 1983). W. M. Swartley claims that this patristic teaching is implicit in the New Testament concept of *koinonia* which includes relationships with God and the community, the eucharist and mutual aid ('Mutual Aid Based in Jesus and Early Christianity', in D. B. Kraybill and W. M. Swartley, eds, *Building Communities of Compassion: Mennonite Mutual Aid in Theory and Practice* [Scottdale: Herald Press, 1999]).

we should show a forbearance greater than the offence and show in advance our readiness to sustain other wrongs of equal or even greater gravity.[35]

Note how he says that 'we obey these words of the Lord'. This is the obedience which binds all, and elsewhere he says that 'by obeying the Lord, we become illuminated with his light and so are accounted worthy of understanding and power' and this obedience lets our light shine before people.[36]

The 'profession' terminology of medieval religious life is used of baptism. 'We promise to be crucified, to die, to be buried with Christ'; 'we profess, through baptism, to be crucified with Christ'; 'we are consecrated to God by baptism'; 'we make and keep covenants which the apostle ratifies' in Romans 6.

Inside this church of Basil the monks or ascetics take their place with no special ideals of perfection.[37] In his book on Basil's church, Paul Fedwick uses the so-called 'monastic' rules of Basil as applying to the whole church. He quotes Neri as saying, 'For Basil, none of the essential categories which traditionally characterized the monastic life were exclusively proper to that state.' Baptism includes definitive renunciation of the world, total consecration to God, a promise to fulfil the gospel perfectly.[38] Philip Rousseau 'wholly supports' the position of Fedwick. 'The ideals he [Basil] defended were suited to all Christians, to be fulfilled within the church in the broadest sense, rather than simply within more limited and segregated communities.'[39]

II. THE FAITHFUL AND THE PERFECT

Though it is hard to pin-point one particular aspect, it seems that the introduction of Greek philosophy was the main factor in the transformation of the original ideal. Charles Munier claims

---

[35] *PG*, 31.1545; Neri, 214–15; Wagner, 364.

[36] *PG*, 31.1544; Neri, 210–11; Wagner, 363.

[37] J. Gribomont, 'Le monachisme au sein de l'Église en Syrie et en Cappadoce', *Studia Monastica* 7 (1965), 7–24.

[38] P. J. Fedwick, 'The Background of the Basilian Ascetics', in his *The Church and the Charisma of Leadership in Basil of Caesarea* (Toronto: Pontifical Institute, 1979), 161–5.

[39] Rousseau, *Basil*, 192. He regards the *Moralia* as early (228), apparently unaware that Fedwick had argued that it is Basil's last work, fully scriptural and directed to all Christians.

that even in the second century, while the persecutions were still in progress, Justin wrote of the special favour Christianity deserved from the state. Tatian also took this line which was finally incarnated in the edicts of 380 and 392 which outlawed the Arian heresy and recognized Catholicism as the only religion of the Empire. Athenagoras and Theophilus were more restrained and their view found expression in the Edict of Milan (313): simple toleration.[40]

The spread of Egyptian monasticism, rooted in Neo-Platonism

The sixth-century life of St Ephrem has him visit Egypt and bring back monasticism to his native Syria. This is simply a story to explain how by this time Egyptian ideas had swamped the native Syrian proto-monasticism which was forgotten. *Ihidaya* now meant a hermit. This was the period of the recluses who lived isolated from human society, their most remarkable expression being the Stylites.[41]

What made this kind of monasticism so different was its Neo-Platonic content. Some cite Arsenius, who avoided even his brothers in the desert, saying, 'I cannot live with God, if I live with people'.[42] Yet more ominous for the formation of Christendom was the gnostic theology inherited from Clement of Alexandria.

We could sum up as follows his argument in the *Stromata*. There are two kinds of Christians (1 Cor. 3:2). If perfect love casts out fear, then some Christians act with faith and fear, while the perfect are motivated by love. The love of God is poured out in the hearts of the perfect, not the beginners. They receive a hundredfold, the perfect an inconceivable reward. The upper-class Christian is a gnostic, a contemplative, possesses the spirit, is forbearing, passionless, infallible in virtue and sees God. The beginner is also called

[40] C. Munier, 'Les doctrines politiques de l'Eglise ancienne', *Revue des sciences religieuses* 62 (1988), 177–86; also in C. Munier, *Autorité épiscopale et sollicitude pastorale (IIᵉ–VIᵉ siècles)*, Collected Studies 341 (Aldershot: Variorum, 1991) II.

[41] 'Recluses, Open-Air Life, Stylitism', in AbouZayd, *Ihidayutha*, 322–77.

[42] B. Ward, *The Sayings of the Desert Fathers* (Kalamazoo: Cistercian Publications, 1975), 9. The saying of Arsenius is an echo of the last phrase of *The Enneads*, 'alone with the Alone'. Cf. S. McKenna and J. Dillon, eds, *Plotinus: The Enneads* (Harmondsworth: Penguin, 1991), 549.

'faithful' while the perfect receives knowledge and love. This perfect charity is synonymous with purity of heart and contemplation and is very close to the *apatheia* of the Stoics. Clement tells us that he admires those philosophers while he accepts fully the teaching of Plato.[43]

Most remarkable is Clement's treatise on the salvation of the rich. This is his exegesis of the parable of the rich young man. Selling possessions means getting rid of the passions of the soul. Then 'becoming virtuous and good, he may be able to make good use of these riches'. He must only get rid of what would use possessions badly, 'and these are the infirmities and passions of the soul'.[44]

William Walsh and John Langan interpret this too benignly when they accept Clement's idea of the Christian as 'affluent and poor in spirit'. It is simply out of line with the mainstream patristic teaching which insisted that superfluous property did not belong to oneself but rather to the poor.[45] The emphasis on 'poor in spirit' leads to an image of the real poor as inept and rapacious.[46] Now the way was open for the rich to enter the church with an easy conscience. Poverty was good but, like celibacy, it was only for some.

Clement's gnostic was not a recluse for all that. Peter Brown calls him 'a monk without a desert'.[47] The doctrine develops in this direction, however. We can follow the line through Origen, Evagrius and Cassian.[48]

Cassian applies Clement's distinction between the believer and the perfect to the lay Christian and the monk. Using his exegesis of 1 Corinthians 3:2, he says that the fervent monk (as distinct from the 'lukewarm') is the spiritual man while the carnal is 'the secular and the pagan'.[49]

[43] Eoin de Bhaldraithe, 'Faith in the Rule of St Benedict', *Regulae Benedicti Studia* 12 (1983), 89–110 (105).

[44] *Quis Dives Salvetur?* 14–15; PG, 8.617–20; ANF 2.595.

[45] Walsh and Langan, 'Patristic Social Consciousness', 120–1. C. Avila agrees that Clement does not attack 'wealth as such' (*Ownership*, 35). Avila seems, however, to confuse the Christian *koinonia* of believers with the Stoic *koinonia* of all men and women; ibid., 40.

[46] *Quis Dives salveteur?* 12–13; PG, 8.616–17; ANF 2.594.

[47] Brown, *Body and Society*, 131.

[48] O. Chadwick, *John Cassian: A Study in Primitive Monasticism* (Cambridge: Cambridge University Press, 1950), 100–7.

[49] Cassian, *Conference*, 4, chs 18–19; PL, 49.605–6; NPNF ser. 2, 11.336–7.

Àgain he says that the monk practises 'evangelical perfection' as he renounces marriage, property and retaliation. The lay person is bound only by the law of Moses which encourages marriage, asks only for tithes and allows retaliation. This time the non-monk is equated with the Jew.[50] Monastic renunciation rather than baptism has become the great divide of the human race.[51]

A similar distinction is also found in Eusebius, presumably dependent on Origen. There are 'two ways of life' in the church. The first excludes marriage and property; the second involves marriage, government, soldiering and even farming.[52]

How much this ideal has become part of the Egyptian mind-set is seen in one of the most famous stories of conversion, Athanasius' account of Anthony's call to the desert. Anthony was already a devout Christian when he heard the parable of the rich young man in church one day. 'If you would be perfect, go sell what you have and give to the poor.' So, desiring to be perfect, Anthony followed the gospel advice.[53]

This presupposes that the sharing of possessions is not for all the baptized but only for the perfect, in practice the monks. We remember that for Basil the parable was used in preparation for baptism, as all were to share their possessions and be perfect.

III. ACCEPTING THE SOLDIER

How to deal with soldiers was a crisis for the early church. Indeed, changing attitudes towards the military illustrate the developing ideals of Christendom. The *Apostolic Tradition* has a special article on soldiers who wish to become Christians. The text has survived

---

[50] Cassian, *Conference*, 21, chs 31–2; *PL*, 49.1209–11; *NPNF* ser. 2, 11.516.

[51] 'Autant dire que la grande ligne de démarcation entre les hommes est moins le baptême que la profession monastique.' 'Le séculier, tout baptisé qu'il est, retombe sous le joug de la loi ancienne. Nous l'avons vu tout à l'heure assimilé au païen. Le voici maintenant confondu avec le Juif!' A. de Vogüé, 'Monachisme et église dans la pensée de Cassien', *Théologie de la vie monastique* (Paris: Aubier, 1961), 213–40 (227, 229); English translation: 'Monasticism and the Church in the Writings of Cassian', *Monastic Studies* 3 (1965), 19–52 where the translation of those phrases is not satisfactory.

[52] Eusebius, *De Demonstratione Evangelica* 1.8; *PG* 22:76–77; cf. Brown, *Body and Society*, 205–6.

[53] *PG*, 26.841–44; *NPNF* ser. 2, 4.196.

only in the Coptic or Sahidic (S), Arabic (A) and Ethiopic (E) versions. The Latin translations of Jean Michel Hanssens with our own English translation of his Latin follow on pages 168–9.[54] When one sets the phrases in parallel, the additions and omissions become clear.

Apostolic Tradition: prohibiting killing but admitting soldiers

When we compare the texts we see that the E is the most rigid. The second section (29) mentions the 'prefect who has the sword'. 'The soldier of the prefect' (28) then would be his servant and probably his executioner. Such a person is not to be admitted. Then there follows what seems to be a first correction: 'if he is (admitted, presumably, and then) told to kill he must refuse to do so or be rejected'. This relaxes the strict prohibition on not admitting him. The next section (29) deals with an ordinary soldier who wishes to become a Christian. He is simply to cease soldiering or be rejected. This is consistent with the first part of (28), but sits uncomfortably with the correction in the second part.

A is more lenient: the prohibition on not admitting the high-class soldier is replaced by a command to the man himself not to kill. This makes the paragraph more consistent. In the next section, the prohibition on the ordinary soldier remains. If we can rely on Hanssens' translation, however, it now applies only to one of the faithful who would decide to *become* a soldier. Again this is an advance in consistency but the text is simply anticipating what will appear in the next section.

In S the prohibition against the ordinary soldier disappears. The prefect's soldier becomes simply 'a soldier in power', apparently meaning any soldier. S will accept him for baptism if he promises not to kill. A new note is introduced when he is reminded not to take the oath.

In the third section all three texts stipulate that one who is already accepted as a catechumen or actually baptized may not join the army. Such people have despised God (S), departed from God (A), or departed from Christ (E).

[54] J. M. Hanssens, *La Liturgie d'Hippolyte: Documents et Etudes*, Orientalia Christiana Analecta 155 (Rome: Gregoriana, 1970), 100–1, kindly supplied by Alan Kreider.

Sahidic	Arabic	Ethiopic
9. Miles, qui est in potestate,	27. Miles domini [alicuius]	28. Militem praefecti ne admittant,
ne occidet quemquam; si iubetur,	ne occidat, et si iubetur occidere, ne faciat id;	et si iussus erit caedem [facere], ne faciat;
ne properet ad rem, neve iuret;		
	et si is destiterit, [esto];	
cum autem non vult, reiciatur.	sin minus, exeat.	sin autem non desierit, reiciatur.
	28. De sumptuose vestito purpura vel [de] eo qui fit miles ex fidelibus, vel astrologus, vel magus, vel alia praeter illud, exeat.	29. De hominibus aliis. Sive qui est miles e fidelibus, sive astrologus, sive incantator, et quod ei simile est,
10. Aliquis qui habet potestatem super gladium vel magistratus urbis, qui induit se ipse purpura, aut desinat aut reiciatur.	Dominus super gladium, vel caput civitatis, et qui purpuram induit, desinat aut exeat.	et praefectus qui cum gladio est, vel caput praefectorum, et qui vestitus coccino desinat aut reiciatur.
11. Catechumenus vel fidelis, si volunt fieri milites, reiciantur, quoniam contempserunt deum.	Catechumenus vel fidelis, si volunt fieri milites, exeant [ambo]. Procul decesserunt [ambo] a deo.	Novellus christianus vel fidelis, si voluerint fieri milites reiciantur; nam decesserunt a domino.

EARLY CHRISTIAN FEATURES PRESERVED

Sahidic	Arabic	Ethiopic
9. A soldier in power	27. The soldier of any lord	28. The soldier of a prefect they shall not admit,
is not to kill anybody; if ordered,	is not to kill; if ordered to kill	and if he is ordered to (do) killing
let him not approach it nor is he to swear;	let him not do it;	let him not do it;
	and if he desists, (let him be);	
if he does not agree, let him be rejected.	if not, let him go out.	if he does not desist let him be rejected.
	28. On luxurious purple clothes or one of the faithful who becomes a soldier or astrologer or magician or some other besides, let him go out.	29. Of other people. If one of the faithful is a soldier or astrologer or charmer or similar to that
10. Anyone with power over the sword or a city magistrate who dresses in purple, let him desist or be rejected.	A lord over the sword or the head of a city who wears purple, let him cease or go out.	and the prefect who has the sword, or the head prefect who wears purple, let him desist or be rejected.
11. A catechumen or faithful, if they wish to become soldiers, let them be rejected, for they have contemned God.	A catechumen or faithful, if they wish to become soldiers, let them (both) go out. (Both) have departed far from God.	A new Christian or faithful, if they wish to become soldiers, let them be rejected; for they have departed from the Lord.

169

These words on the soldier belong to a section of the document on forbidden occupations. The brothel keeper, the pagan priest, the magistrate (seven trades in all) are named and briefly described. There follows the quasi-refrain, 'let them cease (the trade) or be rejected'. The words are applied by E to the soldier, by A to the faithful-become-soldier, and confined by S to the magistrate.

The application of the refrain to all the trades is a literary construction. When A and E apply it to the soldier, it could not be that they are departing from the reality that was S and construing an imaginary and more rigid situation. The only setting in which E could have been composed is a reality which corresponded to its literary expression. It must then have been the primitive E that was corrected into A and S.

The Ethiopian version is an example of peripheral conservatism. The most ancient ruling survives on the periphery of a large institution, while the centre 'modernizes' itself.[55]

Tertullian: witness to gradually increasing leniency

The closest parallel is to be found in the works of Tertullian. In his treatise *De Corona* he tells how a soldier suffered martyrdom for not wearing his laurel crown in honour of the gods.[56] There were other Christians in the army who had no scruples about the crown. When the oath is taken, they do not say any words but Tertullian insists that the crown on their heads is a response.[57]

He goes on to suggest that military service is not proper for Christians at all (*an in totum christianis militia conveniat*).[58] Even those who were soldiers already when they came to the faith should still abandon the army as many have done. In his treatise *On Idolatry* he distinguished between a believer becoming a soldier and a soldier becoming a believer 'even if he is a member only of the rank and file who are not required to take part in sacrifices or capital punishments'.[59]

---

[55] J. M. Hornus, *It is not Lawful for Me to Fight: Early Christian Attitudes toward War, Violence and the State* (Scottdale: Herald Press, 1980), 164–6.

[56] Tertullian, *De Corona*, 1; PL, 2.76; ANF 3.93.

[57] *De Corona*, 13; PL, 2.94; ANF 3.101.

[58] *De Corona*, 11; PL, 2.91; ANF 3.99.

[59] Tertullian, *De Idolatria*, 19; PL, 1.690; ANF 3.73.

So Tertullian here is fighting a lost cause. There are already many Christians in the army. Some have even joined after baptism. Sometimes they are present at a swearing ceremony but do not say the words. Our author is unhappy with this procedure. He is aware of the distinction between becoming a soldier before and after baptism, but his preference is that even those who were soldiers before conversion should leave the army. We also see the distinction between the two classes of soldiers, one of which was obliged to administer capital punishment.

The way Tertullian would wish things to be is well expressed in E, without the correction. Soldiers should leave the army when they become catechumens and the baptized may not join.

The first correction (in E) allows a high-ranking soldier to remain in the army provided he does not have to kill. It is done simply by inserting a few words (eight in Latin) which do not blend well with the rest of the text.

A generalizes the possibility of the soldier remaining in the army. This, however, involves considerable manipulation of the text. The words on not admitting the prefect's soldier have been removed. The section on soldiers in general is confined to those who would join the army after baptism. No doubt the redactor was satisfied that he now had a more consistent text.

S makes further major alterations in the text. The result is that any soldier may remain in the army. There are so many of them now that the practice of swearing must also be regulated. We saw that one way of doing this was not to say the words during the ceremony.[60] Tertullian knew that some Christians actually joined the army but this is forbidden by all three texts.

We see then three major corrections of the text. So we may presume that some authority altered the primitive text at various times so that the law would follow life.

De Corona is generally thought to have been written about AD 210. The S correction then must have been made some time before this as the situation has developed beyond it. The A correction must be considerably earlier, and the E correction earlier still. Before that there was the original E.

---

[60] Cuming, *Hippoloytus*, 16, says that A and E omit mention of the oath implying that S is more primitive. Rather S is much more lenient in allowing Christians to stay in the army, so it needs to regulate the oath.

We would like to make our own tentative suggestions on dating as a contribution to the current debate. It seems that an old rule cannot be changed officially until those responsible for it have passed on and a new generation comes into control. This generally takes about thirty years. So if the S correction was made some time before AD 200, A would be before 170, the corrected E earlier than AD 140 and the original at the beginning of the second century.

If our reasoning is right, we have a new perspective on the genesis of this church order. Metzger argued that the *Apostolic Tradition* could not have been written in Rome as its Christian population was much larger in AD 250 than that presupposed in *AT*.[61] The situation around AD 100 would be much more in line. Then the mention of gladiators and charioteers corresponds much better to Rome itself than to most other cities of the Empire. It is possible then that the title *Ordinatio Clementis*, found on some versions, could be original.

Later church orders and canons

We see a further stage in the *Canons of Hippolytus (CH)*.[62] The magistrate who has power of the sword may now, like the soldier, stay in the church provided he does not actually kill. If a soldier does shed blood, 'he is not to partake of the mysteries, unless he is purified by a punishment, tears, and wailing'.

The exclusion from church and eucharist is traditional, but there is now a system of penance by which one may return. We may compare Basil's canonical letter:

> Homicide in war is not reckoned by our fathers as homicide. I think from this that we should forgive them. However it is good advice that those with unclean hands should abstain from communion for three years.[63]

Basil means the 'fathers' who preceded his own generation. They apparently did not exclude soldiers who killed in war. Basil is also prepared to forgive but imposes a precise period of penance. The letter dates from about 375 so Coquin's date of 340 for the *CH*

[61] Metzger, 'Enquêtes', 29–30.
[62] P. F. Bradshaw, ed., *The Canons of Hippolytus* (Bramcote: Grove, 1987), 17–18.
[63] Basil, *Letter* 188.13; *PG*, 32.681; *NPNF* ser. 2, 8.228.

would be consistent with an earlier stage of development: penance prescribed but no precise period.

The *Apostolic Constitutions* belongs to the late fourth century. The soldier is now told to 'do no injustice, accuse no one falsely and be content with his wages'.[64] This was the advice of John the Baptist (Lk 3:14). It would be used twice by Augustine with a certain satisfaction as if at last there was a text to justify soldiering.[65]

Another related document is the *Testamentum Domini*. Here, however, the original ideal is preserved. The main text is in Syriac, so it seems to come from the church of the East which was cut off from the West and conserved many traits of primitive Christianity. Its office, for instance, is regarded as the most ancient form to survive. So the *Testamentum* may be similar. In two articles it says that the soldier cannot be baptized unless he leaves his trade, and a believer who joins the army has left the things of the Spirit for the flesh.[66] Like the Ethiopic *AT* it is another example of peripheral conservatism.

Augustine: developing a theology of violence

The East did not develop much beyond the canonical letters of Basil and the *Apostolic Constitutions*. In the West, however, Augustine developed a theology of violence which did not affect the East, and was later to cause tension between the two. During the crusades, the Western church, following Augustine, was 'less enlightened', according to Steven Runciman. The virtual pacifism of the Byzantine empire caused most of the misunderstandings with the crusaders.[67]

Augustine elaborated his own theory of persecution while dealing with the Donatists. His 'two full justifications of coercion' are well known.[68] Here we seek to emphasize his theological arguments.

[64] *Apostolic Constitutions*, 8.32; ANF, 7.495.
[65] Augustine, *Letter* 189.4; *PL*, 33.855; NPNF ser. 1, 1.553; idem, *Contra Faustum*, 22.74; *PL*, 42.447; NPNF ser. 1, 4.301.
[66] J. Cooper and J. A. Maclean, ed. and trans., *Testament of Our Lord* (Edinburgh: T&T Clark, 1902), 118; cf. Hornus, *It is not Lawful*, 166.
[67] 'Holy Peace and Holy War', in S. Runciman, *A History of the Crusades*, 1 (Cambridge: Cambridge University Press, 1951), 83–92.
[68] P. Brown, 'Religious Coercion in the Later Roman Empire: The Case of North Africa', *History* 48 (1963), 283–305 (297).

Augustine's men once captured a Donatist priest and brought him to a Catholic church. In a letter to his hostage, Augustine explained that they were only drawing him away from error and forcing him towards the good. On the basis of the Old Testament he says that corporal punishment is justified especially as the heretics have received baptism but have strayed.[69]

Even though Jesus had told his disciples that they were free to go away, this was humility on his part. The fact that Augustine seeks to refute this view can only indicate that it was commonly used at the time, and surely represents an early understanding of John 6:67.

He continues by saying that when the church got stronger it would not only invite but coerce people to what was good. He finds support for this view in the parable of the banquet where the servants went on to the highways and byways to 'compel' people to come in (Lk 14:23).[70]

In a letter to the tribune Boniface, he argues in favour of persecution. '"Blessed are those who suffer persecution for justice's sake", said the Lord' (Mt. 5:10). But Augustine added, 'not those who are persecuted for iniquity or for breaking the unity of the church'.[71] Thus does Augustine justify the coercion of heretics by the power of the state. This would be followed closely in the West until our own day.

'Do not resist the evil one' (Mt. 5:39) did not cause him much problem either. This refers not to the body but to the heart which is 'the chamber of virtue'.[72] Presumably he takes his cue from adultery of the heart (5:28). Thus does he allow

[69] Augustine, *Letter* 173; *PL*, 33.754; *NPNF* ser. I, 1.544. E. Lamirande, *Church, State and Toleration: An Intriguing Change of Mind in Augustine* (Philadelphia: Villanova University Press, 1975); R. A. Markus, 'St Augustine's views on the "just war"', in W. J. Shiels, ed., *The Church and War*, Studies in Church History 20 (Oxford: Blackwell, 1983), 1–13; D. A. Lenihan, 'The Just War Theory in the Work of Saint Augustine', *Augustinian Studies* 19 (1988), 37–70.

[70] Ibid., *PL*, 33.757; *NPNF* ser. 1, 1.546–7. As the church spreads more widely, *tanto majore utitur ecclesia potestate, ut non solum invitet, sed etiam cogat ad bonum.*

[71] Augustine, *Letter* 185; *PL*, 33.796; *NPNF* ser. 1, 4.636.

[72] Augustine, *Contra Faustum* 22.76; *PL*, 42.448; *NPNF* ser. 1, 4.301.

'objective atrocities' accompanied by subjective love.[73] It seems clear, however, that the penitentials continued to prescribe a period of abstinence from the eucharist for homicide, as we have seen in the *Canons of Hippolytus*. Those continued in West and East till the Middle Ages.[74]

As a kind of postscript we may mention the letter of Hugh of St Victor to the Knights Templar where he justifies warfare on an Augustinian basis. Attacks on the enemy must be accompanied by love. Hatred must be avoided. Soon thereafter St Bernard wrote his more famous treatise to the same people. He departed from the Augustinian norm. Relying on many examples from the Old Testament he recommended hatred of the enemies of God.[75]

IV. MEDIEVAL MONASTICISM

We may deal with the situation in medieval communities more briefly as it is generally well known. Our aim is to show the connection with features which were common to the whole church in primitive times. Today we would distinguish between monks (mainly Benedictines) and friars (such as the Franciscans). In medieval usage, however, all were regarded as 'monastic'. For example, Martin Luther, a friar, called his treatise on the vows of religious, *De votis monasticis iudicium*. Thomas Aquinas used the term 'religious' as applying to all who took the vow of chastity.

Evangelical perfection for monks, not laity

The theology of John Cassian, which he inherited from Clement of Alexandria, formed the basis of medieval understanding of

[73] Lenihan, 'Just War', 56–7. This study shows an interesting struggle by a Roman Catholic to come to terms with the teaching of this 'saint of peace and love'.

[74] F. H. Russell, *The Just War in the Middle Ages* (Cambridge: Cambridge University Press, 1975) believes that the pacifism of the church lasted till the crusades.

[75] Eoin de Bhaldraithe, 'Jean Leclercq's Attitude Toward War', in *The Joy of Learning and the Love of God: Studies in Honor of Jean Leclercq* (Kalamazoo: Cistercian Publications, 1995), 217–38 (224–5).

monasticism.[76] Religious were called to perfection, while layfolk were simply 'the faithful' or 'seculars'.[77] This latter meant they belonged to the world. It was based on 1 Corinthians 7:33 on the married man concerned for the world, but all the texts which applied to the church herself as separated from the world in the early period were now applied to religious. Indeed it would have been nonsense to claim that the medieval church was separated from the world since in theory it included everybody.

For Cassian there were three qualities observed by the monks: chastity, poverty and non-violence.[78] In the medieval monastery this latter became obedience. But the teaching that non-violence was not obligatory was carefully preserved on the understanding that Matthew 5:48 prescribed it only for the perfect. Even obedience was mutated. It was now the special quality of religious whereas we have seen that for Basil obedience to the Lord was for all Christians.[79]

Chastity became a vow. Aquinas said the celibacy of a priest could be dispensed with, but not that of a monk.[80]

Poverty was also a theme of perfection, so as a result the laity were allowed to own as much as they wished. Access to the church remained open to all the rich.

Monasteries become separate assemblies

One of the most mysterious mutations was how religious came to have their own churches and eucharist. The rule of Benedict witnesses to a state where the monks form part of the local church. It appears that it was the meeting of the Celtic and Roman systems on the continent that engendered the change. A Celtic abbot was always a 'parish' priest, as we would say. The European abbots of the ninth century decided to seek ordination to the presbyterate

[76] Thomas Aquinas, *Summa Theologica*, II–II q. 186 a. 1, on the state of perfection, quotes Cassian's teaching on perfect charity.

[77] E.g. ibid., a. 10.

[78] Cf. n. 50 above.

[79] Eoin de Bhaldraithe, 'Obedience to Christ in the Rules of Benedict and the Master', *Studia Patristica* 13 (1975), 437–43; idem, 'Obedience: The Doctrine of the Irish Monastic Rules', *Monastic Studies* 14 (1983), 63–84 (on Basil and Cassian 67–69).

[80] Aquinas II–II q. 88 a. 11.

but without pastoral care of layfolk. Thus did the male monastery become an almost independent church.[81]

The ceremony of monastic profession took on features which formerly belonged to adult baptism. Yet it is clear from the sources presented by Edward Malone that the aspect of renunciation received greater prominence, while the positive aspect of determination to follow Christ remained largely undeveloped.[82]

When the members of the poverty movement were accepted into the church as 'friars' they also were allowed ordination in order to be able to preach. This meant taking on the practice of private mass which further divorced the presbyterate from the Christian community. Ordination thus superseded monastic profession and became 'the new fullness of Christian initiation and the preferred way to perfection'.[83]

Non-violence remained only for presbyters; other monks and lay brothers were not bound by it, the most notable example being the military monks. St Bernard says in his treatise for them that he would wield the stylus, since he was not allowed to wield the lance. The 1917 Code of Canon Law in the Roman Catholic Church laid down that a judge who had pronounced sentence of death could not be ordained. Neither could anybody who helped to carry out an execution (c.984). This is a remarkable survival of the 'prefect' and his soldier of the Ethiopic *Apostolic Tradition*. There were other similar fossilized survivals.[84]

The official prayer times became the preserve of religious in the West even though they were originally for all. The little hours

---

[81] Eoin de Bhaldraithe, 'Daily Eucharist: The Need for an Early Church Paradigm', *The American Benedictine Review* 41 (1990) 378–440 (esp. 'Priests in monasteries', 410–14). For the earlier period, see J. M. Garrigues, J. Legrez, *Moines dans l'assemblée des fidèles à l'époque des Pères – IVᵉ–VIIIᵉ siècle* (Paris: Beauchesne, 1990).

[82] E. E. Malone, 'Martyrdom and Monastic Profession as a Second Baptism', in A. Mayr, J. Quasten and B. Neunheuser, eds, *Vom Christlichen Mysterium: Gesammelte Arbeiten zum Gedächtnis von Odo Casel* (Düsseldorf: Patmos, 1951), 115–34.

[83] E. Foley, *Rites of Religious Profession* (Chicago: Liturgy Training, 1989), 18; Eoin de Bhaldraithe, 'Private Mass, Parish Mass', *Religious Life Review* 33 (1994), 233–8.

[84] Eoin de Bhaldraithe, 'St Bernard, Thomas Merton, and Catholic Teaching on Peace', *Word and Spirit* 12 (1990), 54–79 (58).

which were originally intended as private prayers were now done in church. Morning and evening prayer, meant to be the public prayer of all the church, was lost in the middle of the long monastic office. This is typical of a 'clericalized' obligation.[85] Some laity still came to the office but it was considered so unimportant that the Counter Reformation virtually eliminated the office for the people.

We saw the remarkable recommendation in the *Apostolic Tradition* that the faithful should read the Bible regularly at the third hour each day. This of course became the preserve of educated priests and monks in the Middle Ages.

Those aspects of the medieval monastic community are well known. That they were features of the general church in the early period is not always appreciated.

[85] Robert K. Taft, *The Liturgy of the Hours in East and West* (Collegeville: Liturgical Press, 1986), 362.

Chapter 6

Charism and Office in a Changing Church

CHRISTINE TREVETT

The central area of debate between the New Prophecy (Montanists), and their Catholic co-religionists had to do with authority. But this was not a new debate: in the first two centuries it was widespread throughout the churches. Was authority vested in those who possessed certain charismata (glossolalia, exorcism, teaching and especially prophecy)? Or was it above all vested in occupants of ecclesiastical offices, notably bishops? This question is present by implication in the *Didache*; and it was at issue between groups in the church in Rome associated with Hermas and with Clement. Ignatius of Antioch, himself a prophet, argued in prophetic voice – against considerable opposition – that authority should properly reside in the bishops. Many congregations even into the third century, assumed that there should be a correlation between church office and spiritual gifts. However, in the course of the third century, prophecy and glossolalia largely disappeared, while exorcism came to be performed primarily by the lower ranks of the clergy. The decline in the charismata ran parallel with a silencing of women and an increasing emphasis upon order and office-holding.

'We too must receive the spiritual gifts.' These words were recorded by Epiphanius of Salamis in the late fourth century, making use of an anonymous source. He was reporting on a key doctrine of the New Prophecy (later known as Montanism, after the male Prophet who was one of its founders) and his source had probably been contemporaneous with other early anti-New Prophecy writers, such as Apollonius in Asia and Hippolytus in

Rome.[1] The words (given in *Pan.* 48.1.4) had allegedly figured in the *early* New Prophecy, and the Prophets claimed to have separated from the church 'because of spiritual gifts' (*Pan.* 48.12.1). The New Prophecy offers a good starting point for the subject under discussion, for charism and office were matters at issue within it.

By the time of Epiphanius the Prophets' language must have suggested a dangerous democratization. The church of the fourth century and later feared the implications of the New Prophets' teaching and for a long time it had declared that their claims to authority were spurious. By the fifth century, 'Montanism' was known through a number of groups called variously Cataphrygians (after the New Prophecy's place of origin), Pepuzians, Quintillians, Taskodrougites, Tertullianists, Priscillians, and so on.[2] Not only was 'Montanism' diverse but there were now heterodox elements within it. It had not been heretical at the outset, however,[3] but was criticized on other grounds.

Among the 'aberrations' which had come to characterize the Prophecy/Montanism there was the giving of clerical office to women.[4] This accorded well with its teaching about the outpouring of the Spirit (Joel 2:28ff.; Acts 2:17f.) and the Prophets had felt free to appeal to visions and angelic communication when propagating apparently novel teaching.[5] Some of the teaching had

---

[1] On the anonymous source, see P. de Labriolle, *Les Sources de l'Histoire du Montanisme* (Paris: E. Leroux, 1913); R. A. Lipsius, *Zur Quellenkritik des Epiphanios* (Vienna: W. Braumüller, 1865); H. G. Voigt, *Eine verschollene Urkunde des antimontanistischen Kampfes* (Leipzig, 1891).

[2] C. Trevett, *Montanism: Gender, Authority and the New Prophecy* (Cambridge: Cambridge University Press, 1996), ch. 5; eadem, 'Fingers up Noses and Pricking with Needles: Possible Reminiscences of Revelation in Later Montanism', *Vigiliae Christianae* 46 (1995), 256–69.

[3] I argue this in *Montanism*, and in recent decades other writers have begun to argue similarly.

[4] Epiphanius, *Pan.*, 49.2.1–5; Ambrosiaster, *Comm. in Ep. 1 ad Tim.*, 3.8–11; Augustine, *De Haer.* 27; 86, and epigraphy support such claims. See my *Montanism*, ch. 5 (5.1.4).

[5] C. M. Robeck, 'Canon, *Regula Fidei* and Continuing Revelation in the Early Church', in J. E. Bradley, R. A. Muller, eds, *Church, Word and Spirit, essays in Honor of G. W. Bromiley* (Grand Rapids: Eerdmans, 1987), 65–91; F. de Pauw, 'La justification des traditions non écrites chez Tertullien', *Ephemerides Theologicae Lovaniensis* 19 (1942), 5–46; H. Paulsen, 'Die Bedeutung des Montanismus für die Herausbildung des Kanons', *Vigiliae Christianae* 32 (1978), 19–52; Trevett, *Montanism*, 2.2.4; 3.9.

allowed them to claim the moral high ground. This was especially the case where Christian discipline was concerned, in such matters as fasting and the forbidding of digamy,[6] for their own requirements were more demanding than those of their Catholic co-religionists. Such things, together with the New Prophets' claim to receiving Paraclete revelation through their leaders (which formed the basis for their claims) might be seen as a threat. They were a threat to the right of *officers*, and *male* officers, properly appointed in churches, after Catholic fashion, to determine on disciplinary and other measures.[7]

In my opinion, the most significant debate between the New Prophets and their Catholic co-religionists was not about the right mode of martyrdom, or the relation of ecstasy to traditional Christian prophecy (though both these subjects *were* debated). It was about authority and about the who and the how of exercising it. Many other matters followed from that issue.[8]

G. Salmon in the late nineteenth century *Dictionary of Christian Biography* (III, 'Montanus') summed up neatly what many commentators have thought about the danger that Montanist-type charismatics thus posed to sound, male-led, Catholic teaching:

> If Montanus had triumphed, Christian doctrine would have developed not under the superintendence of the Christian teachers most esteemed for wisdom, but of wild and excitable women.

Charism and power

The Epiphanian Anonymous, writing probably in the first decades of the third century, was surely familiar with the apostolic teaching about receipt of spiritual gifts. He chose, nevertheless, to use the

---

[6] Fasting: Eusebius, *HE*, 5.18.2; Hippolytus, *Refut. Omn. Haer.*, 8.19, cf. 10.25; Tertullian *De Jej.*, 1; 10; 12–15 and *passim*; *De Monog.*, 15. Digamy: Tertullian, *De Exhort. Cast.*, 8; 13; *De Monog.*, 3; 14; 17 and *passim*; Epiphanius, *Pan.*, 48.9.5–8; Germanus of Constantinople, *Ad Antimum*, 5; Augustine, *De Haer.* 86.

[7] Cf. Hippolytus, *Refut. Omn. Haer.*, 18:19: 'They devise new feasts, fasts and the eating of dry food and cabbage, declaring that these things have been taught by those females' (i.e. the New Prophecy leaders Priscilla and Maximilla). Translated by R. E. Heine, *The Montanist Oracles and Testimonia* (Macon: Mercer University Press, 1989), 57.

[8] Trevett, *Montanism*, 3.10.

New Prophets' language ('We too must receive the spiritual gifts') as part of a process of denying their claims to the Spirit. The Anonymous acknowledged that the Spirit was intended to be an ongoing reality in churches. But if that was so, then the lack of New Prophets after the demise of Maximilla must mean that their claims were suspect.[9] The manner of their prophesying was suspect too, he claimed. These things were part of the polemic on the Catholic side.

On the New Prophecy/Montanism side there came to be a history of polemic against Catholic clergy. This concerned (among other things) their alleged lack of spirituality. The Catholics were numbered amongst the 'psychics', by contrast with the Montanist *pneumatikoi*.[10] One of Tertullian's most memorable statements, after his conversion to the New Prophecy, was that the church which pronounced forgiveness of sins should be the church of the Spirit-endowed, not that of bevies of bishops: '. . . *ecclesia spiritus per spiritalem hominem, non ecclesia numerus episcoporum*' (*De Pud.* 21.7). Such sentiments did not win many friends in Catholic circles. Nevertheless Tertullian and his fellow 'Tertullianist' (New Prophet) Carthaginians probably never separated from the Catholic circle in Africa but remained an irritant within it.[11]

Montanists were not hostile to clerical office *per se*. In fact the hierarchy of officialdom which Montanism developed, and the way in which it functioned, showed it to be conservative in some respects.[12] Montanists wanted office to be associated clearly with such manifestations of the Spirit as they knew and valued. Nevertheless it is clear from a number of sources that the question

[9] C. Trevett, 'Eschatological Timetabling and the Montanist Prophet Maximilla', *Studia Patristica* 31 (1996), 218–24; eadem, *Montanism* 2.2.4 and 3.2.5 on debates about the Age of the Paraclete. Maximilla proved not to be the last significant prophet.

[10] Tertullian, Clement of Alexandria, Praedestinatus and others confirm the use of the derogatory 'psychics'. Epigraphy suggests that Montanists regarded themselves as *pneumatikoi*.

[11] So too D. Powell, 'Tertullianists and Cataphrygians', *Vigiliae Christianae* 29 (1975), 33–54; D. Rankin, *Tertullian and the Church* (Cambridge: Cambridge University Press, 1995) among others.

[12] F. E. Vokes, 'Montanism and the Ministry', in F. L. Cross, ed., *Studia Patristica* 9 (Texte und Untersuchungen 94, Berlin, 1966), 306–15. J. Ysebaert's study of *Die Amtsterminologie im Neuen Testament und in der alten Kirche* (Breda: Eureia, 1994) oddly does not discuss the Montanist situation.

of the relation of charism to office figured in disputes between Montanists and Catholic Christians. Pacian of Barcelona, writing in the fourth century, reported that Montanism had brought a plethora of arguments. There had been disputes about the Paraclete, about penitence, about the apostolic and the prophetic (here probably referring to the New Prophets' appeals to *prophetic* succession, as well as apostolic).[13] Even the very term 'Catholic' had been in dispute (*Div. Haer. Lib.* 49).[14] And when Jerome wrote to Rome, to Marcella who was in contact with Montanists there, he noted that in the distinctive Montanist clerical order *bishops* appeared *third* in a list, after patriarchs and *koinonoi* (a term which itself may be related to charismatic endowment).[15] This, he hinted, was a deliberate snub to proper office, on the principle of 'the first (with the catholics) shall be last (with the followers of the New Prophecy/Montanism)'.

Given such a history of dispute, we may assume that the early Prophets' observation that 'we too must receive the spiritual gifts' had lost many of its positive and apostolic connotations by the time Epiphanius quoted it. No longer was it about positive empowerment, a mark of Christian enjoyment *already* of one, at least, of those things which would characterize the Future Age. To claim the widespread availability of spiritual gifts, and the necessity of manifesting them, was potentially to challenge the validity of office-holders. For it was with them, as the Christian centuries passed, that charism had come to be especially associated.

The erosion of *charismata*

Such positive connotations had been present in many second-century congregations and third-century ones too (notably Carthage of the third century), in respect of prophecy, at least.[16] Indeed it

---

[13] Eusebius, *HE*, 5.17.3–4 (Anonymous); cf. Epiphanius, *Pan.*, 8.1–6. Jerome seems to imply that Montanists lacked interest in apostolic succession (*Epp.*, 41 *Ad Marc.*). I suspect that this was not so.

[14] When anti-Montanist writers called it the *Cataphrygian* heresy were they trying to rob it of any claims to catholicity?

[15] See Trevett, *Montanism*, 5.1.4–5. Cf. W. Tabbernee, 'Montanist Regional Bishops: New Evidence from Ancient Inscriptions', *Journal of Early Christian Studies* 1 (1993), 249–80.

[16] C. M. Robeck, *Prophecy in Carthage: Perpetua, Tertullian and Cyprian* (Cleveland: Pilgrim Press, 1992).

would be hard to account for the success and rapid spread of the New Prophecy, through Asia Minor, to Rome, North Africa and elsewhere, had not charismatic phenomena been understood and associated with spiritual renewal for the churches. In Rome, Christian prophecy was far from dead.[17] Eusebius made just such a point when he aligned chronologically the martyrdoms in Lyon and Vienne and the rise of the New Prophecy (HE, 5.3.4):

> Just then the disciples of Montanus . . . first published among many their opinions about prophecy (for the many wonders of the divine charisma still being accomplished up to that time in various churches caused many to believe that those men too prophesied).

But within just a few decades of its beginnings, Catholic critics of the New Prophecy were appealing to 'times and seasons'. The New Prophets had spoken of 'promises' and their fulfilment *in their own people* (Eusebius, HE, 5.16.9; cf. Jerome, *Epp.*, 41.2; Origen, *Comm. in Matt.*, 15.30). The New Prophecy had appealed to great happenings in the *present* time, with an outpouring of the Spirit/Paraclete. At the start of the third century, however, the Montanist editor of the *Passio Perpetuae et Felicitatis* (1.3ff.) shows us that as part of the debate anti-Montanists were denying the kinds of things to which the charismatics were appealing. Such things, it was being argued, should be understood as limited to 'times and seasons'. Claims about the fulfilling of the Paraclete promises had evidently fuelled a debate about dispensationalism. The question of dispensationalism was also approached in the (probably Alexandrian) *Dialexis* (the so-called *Dialogue between an Orthodox and a Montanist*)[18] but was never properly addressed in that source.

Eusebius, of course, another fourth-century source, took it for granted that the wealth of charismatic phenomena which were known by, and were commonplace to, Irenaeus (cf. HE, 3.39.8–9

[17] J. S. Jeffers, *Conflict at Rome: Social Order and Hierarchy in Early Christianity* (Minneapolis: Augsburg Fortress, 1991), esp. 145ff. (this study concerns 1 Clement and *The Shepherd* of Hermas); J. Reiling, *Hermas and Christian Prophecy: A Study of the Eleventh Mandate*, Suppl. to *Novum Testamentum* 37 (Leiden: Brill, 1973). Cf. also Eusebius, HE, 5.16.8.

[18] For the text see Heine, *Montanist Oracles*, 112–27; G. Ficker, 'Widerlegung eines Montanisten', *Zeitschrift für Kirchengeschichte* 26 (1905), 447–63.

contrast *Adv. Haer.*, 3.11.12) were not to be expected in his own day. Irenaeus had reported that:

> Some drive out demons with certainty . . . some have foreknowledge of things to be, and visions and prophetic speech, and others cure the sick by laying on hands. The dead have been raised and remain with us for many years.

In the decade of the 240s Origen had written only of 'some measure' of miraculous powers remaining, and by his day, gifted individuals, such as teachers, were being incorporated into the ranks of the clergy (*Hom. Lev.*, 6.6; *Hom. Num.*, 16; and cf. *Did. Apost.*, 2.32.2–3; 2.34.4). Prophecy was not dead, however, as the situation in Carthage indicates, and as Origen's hostility to public female prophetic activity shows (*Catenae in Sancti Pauli Epist. ad Cor.* [on 1 Cor. 14:36]). The account of (probably Christian) prophets in *Contra Celsum* 7:9, which relates to the decade of the 170s, suggests activity which in some respects matches what we know of New Prophecy practice. Those concerned were not necessarily of the Prophecy, however, which was not unlike Christian prophecy generally in most respects. This was a time in which, as Irenaeus said,

> It is not possible to tell the number of the gifts which the church throughout the world . . . uses each day . . . we hear many brethren in the church who have gifts of prophecy, and who speak through the spirit with all manner of tongues and who bring hidden things of men into clearness (Eusebius, *HE*, 5.7.4–6; cf. *Adv. Haer.*, 5.6.1).

Yet 'so much', concluded Eusebius, 'on the point that variety of gifts remained among the worthy (*para tois axiois*) up till the time spoken of' (*HE*, 5.7.6). Evidently it was no longer true.

Over time, prophecy and glossolalia,[19] both of which had figured in congregational settings, moved towards near-extinction. Miracles and the control of demons did not. Christian practice, so Julian the Apostate declared, was best characterized by making the sign of the cross and hissing at demons (*Epp.*, 19 to a priest). But all such things came increasingly to be associated with approved 'classes' of practitioners. In the East, for example, one

[19] M. Parmentier, 'Das Zungenreden bei den Kirchenvätern', *Bijdragen, Tijdschrift voor Filosofie en Theologie* 55 (1994), 376–98; Trevett, *Montanism*, 3.2.3.

might find in some congregations that an approved widow functioned as a designated visionary/prophet. Some versions of the *Canones Ecclesiastici* (Statutes of the Apostles) indicate this. In others, official exorcists existed in the lower ranks of the hierarchy, along with doorkeepers.[20]

Thus when Epiphanius wrote of the existence of formalized congregational (female) prophecy among the Quintillians, he regarded it as an aberration, though it seems to have involved precisely the 'bringing hidden things into clearness' of which Irenaeus had written (Epiphanius, *Pan.*, 49.2). Possibly such Quintillian (Montanist) women were regarded as office-holders. There is insufficient evidence to be sure. But it is clear from epigraphy that a woman of this time might be acknowledged in stone as a prophet, for her ability to commune with angels, and acknowledged in a language, and in a setting which make it not implausible that she was a loyal *Catholic* woman.[21] It brought Epiphanius no consolation that the female Quintillianists' prophecy had the power to reduce its hearers to tears and seemingly to repentance.[22]

'A fundamental type of conflict'

In the rest of this paper I shall concentrate mostly on one of the *charismata*, as illustrative of trends and tensions. This is the gift of prophecy. There is much which could be said of other *charismata*, notably about teaching and exorcism, but prophecy is well-documented. Concentration on this will allow me to look

---

[20] The first reference to the official exorcist appears (along with reference to miracles and a female prophet-teacher) in an Asian source: a letter between Firmilian of Cappadocia and Cyprian of Carthage (Cyprian, *Epp.*, 75). See Trevett, 'Spiritual Authority and the "Heretical" Woman: Firmilian's Word to the Church in Carthage', in H.-W. Drijvers, J. W. Watt, eds, *Portraits of Spiritual Authority* (Leiden: Brill, 1999), 45–62. See too, Robin Lane Fox, *Pagans and Christians* (Harmondsworth: Penguin, 1986), 327–30.

[21] E.g., the woman Nanas in Phrygia (*Montanism*, 4.4) and see Lane Fox, *Pagans and Christians*, 747 n. 11. Since writing *Montanism* I have grown to doubt that Nanas must have been a Montanist. See '"Angelic Visitation and Speech She Had": Nanas of Kotiaeion', in P. Allen *et al.* eds, *Prayer and Spirituality in the Early Church* (Brisbane: Centre for Early Christian Studies, 1999), 2, 259–78.

[22] Epiphanius, *Pan.*, 49:2.

particularly at the *second* century as one in which the seeds of difficulty (in relation to charism and office) were sprouting. It was in that century that so much of *change* in the church was accelerated. Some of my examples will be taken from the East, as well as the West.

The decline in manifestations of *charismata* in churches ran in parallel with increasing emphasis on male office-holding and good order.[23] The history of Montanism encapsulated many of the challenges and fears associated with the collision of charism and office and it had made very public what Robert Eno described as 'a fundamental type of conflict'. The collision had not first been manifest with the New Prophecy, however. Other, and earlier, documents preserve accounts of the tensions or hints that they were there. And as the influence of officialdom grew, prophets, in particular, had felt themselves marginalized and undermined. Conflict, Eno suggested, was 'an unhappy constant' accompanying the development of church structure. For reasons which seemed good to those concerned, and which promised Christian communities which were more ordered and less alien to the understanding of the Graeco-Roman world, increasingly hierarchically controlled churches became the norm. Order and continuity were preferred above freedom for the Spirit and spontaneity. This, as Eno observed, was despite the fact that 'charismatic movements usually settle down rather quickly'.[24]

J. L. Ash, charting 'the decline of ecstatic prophecy' wrote of a developing view of office and of authority in which the episcopate claimed spiritual empowerment for itself – prophecy included - used the charisma 'for its own ends and rendered it powerless in the hands of others'.[25] There is some truth in the statements of Ash and Eno. But the question of the relation of charism to office

[23] Cf. H. von Campenhausen, *Ecclesiastical Authority and Spiritual Power in the Church of the First Three Centuries* (London: A&C Black, 1969), chs 8 and 10; S. E. McGinn, 'The New Prophecy in Asia Minor and the Rise of Ecclesiastical Patriarchy in Second-Century Pauline Tradition', PhD dissertation, Northwestern University, Evanston, 1989.

[24] R. B. Eno, 'Authority and Conflict in the Early Church', *Église et Théologie* 1 (1970) 47.

[25] J. L. Ash, 'The Decline of Ecstatic Prophecy in the Early Church', *Theological Studies* 37 (1978), 234, 250.

is not a simple one. Neither a picture of authoritarian quashing of the Spirit nor the monopolization of gifts by the clergy does justice to a complex and varied pattern of practice and change.

Disclaimers and warnings

Some disclaimers are necessary, and a variety of warnings with regard to the study of charism and office in this early period. There is very much which cannot be done in this paper, but certain factors deserve to be mentioned as being important for a fuller study.

1. Failure to acknowledge fully the diversity in early Christianity may lead to inappropriate 'labelling' of documents and passages. Unlike some writers, for example, I would not assume that the circle addressed by Hermas in Rome was the same as, or identical in congregational practice with, the circle out of which the Roman 1 Clement (*Ad Cor.*) came. Looking to the East, I would hesitate to identify the martyrs spoken of in John's Apocalypse as paradigms of Catholic martyrdom – though other writers have done so. On the contrary, I would surmise that the kind of congregations which the Seer addressed in Asia[26] would have contained precisely the kinds of Christians who proved troublesome to Ignatius of Antioch and his fellow bishops 'Catholic' (*Smyrn.*, 8) in exactly the same locations, perhaps no more than a decade later.[27] Nor should it be assumed that anything which is not evidently 'Catholic' is not normative and hence is necessarily either heterodox or in some other way suspect. In other words, sources must not be forced into preconceived ecclesiological niches.

2. Writers need to take care in assuming parallels between documents or progression from one source to another, as though trajectories were easily to be traced. There is much that we do not know. In fact there is still a dearth of studies which try to make sense of relationship (literary, occasional, theological, of

[26] Both Ignatius and John wrote letters to Ephesus, Philadelphia and Smyrna.
[27] C. Trevett, 'The Other Letters to the Churches of Asia: Apocalypse and Ignatius of Antioch', *Journal for the Study of the New Testament* 37 (FS David Hill, 1989), 117–35; eadem, *A Study of Ignatius of Antioch in Syria and Asia* (Lewiston and New York: Mellen, 1992), ch. 5.

opposition, etc.) between sources which originated in the same area (no such overarching study exists with regard to Christian Asia Minor, for example).

3. We need to recognize that there never was a simple distinction between the charismatic and the one to whom office was granted. Paul knew that. And the histories of people such as Irenaeus in Lyon, bridge-builder between East and West in the second century, and Cyprian in Carthage in the third century, are notable. They indicate that episcopal office in the developing Catholic tradition (and despite some of Tertullian's strictures in his New Prophecy phase) was not necessarily devoid of, opposed to or feeling threatened by charismatic gifts such as might be present in congregations also.[28]

4. As for the disclaimers, this paper is not addressing the progress and fate of individual charismata in relation to developing ideas of office and order, prophecy excepted. A fuller study would do so and would consider, also, theories of the routinization of charisma and of patterns of institutionalization in religious groups.[29] It would also address such important questions as (a) Were developments in ecclesiastical office and order, in different parts of the Empire, associated with particular views of 'progress' and/or of accommodation with secular patterns of social organization?[30] (b) Were clashes in which charism and office figured sometimes related, also, to regionalism and nationalism? and (c) Did the development of a cult of martyrs much influence churches' understanding of the relation of charism to office?[31]

---

[28] A. d'Alès, 'La doctrine de l'Esprit en Saint Irénée', *Recherches de Science Religieuse* 14 (1924), 497–538; A. Mehat, 'Saint Irénée et les charismes', in E. Livingstone, ed., *Studia Patristica* 7 (Oxford, 1982), 719–24; C. M. Robeck, 'Irenaeus and Prophetic Gifts', in P. Elbert, ed., *Essays on Apostolic Themes* (Peabody: Hendrickson, 1985), 104–14.

[29] See e.g. Jeffers, *Conflict at Rome*, 145ff.; H. O. Maier, *The Social Setting of the Ministry as Reflected in the Writings of Hermas, Clement and Ignatius* (Waterloo: Wilfrid Laurier University Press, 1991).

[30] W. Kinzig, *Novitas Christiana: Die Idee des Fortschritts in der alten Kirche bis Eusebius* (Göttingen: Vandenhoeck & Ruprecht, 1994).

[31] See especially F. C. Klawiter, 'The Role of Martyrdom and Persecution in Developing the Priestly Authority of Women in Early Christianity: A Case Study of Montanism', *Church History* 49 (1980), 251–61.

Warnings and disclaimers complete, I turn to the bishop and the prophet.

The bishop and the prophet

We see in one person the combination of episcopal authority and prophetic and other powers when we look at Polycarp of Smyrna. Here was prophet and teacher, martyr and bishop, according to the *Martyrdom of Polycarp* (16.2; 19.1), a document originating in Smyrna.[32] But Polycarp had not always been described so positively, when as a younger man he encountered Ignatius of Antioch.

A less flattering picture of the younger man emerges in the letters of Ignatius, written from one 'bishop' to another.[33] And the advice given to Polycarp, as the Syrian travelled through Asia *en route* to his martyrdom in Rome, tells us quite a lot about Ignatius's understanding of episcopal office and tells us something, also, of tensions in relation to office and the possession of *charismata*.

Ignatius wanted to foster loyalty to bishops, both among the laity and among the presbyters. Such loyalty was a vital element in his wider vision of congregations united harmoniously and acting as bastions against theological error. A significant exception to this picture was in his letter to Rome, but I shall return to that later.

The Ignatian letters are often treated as evidence for the rise of monepiscopacy or even as proof (and wrongly, I think) of the triumph of full-blown monarchical episcopacy (sometime pre-111 CE).[34] They are important sources for early Christianity in Asia Minor, as well as Syria (from which Ignatius had emerged) and preserve interesting christological insights. I have an eye on the opposition, however, though my opinion of tensions in some of the congregations to which Ignatius wrote, between him, his protégé Asian bishops and those I take to include charismatics, is

[32] B. Dehandschutter, 'The *Martyrium Polycarpi*: A Century of Research', *Aufstieg und Niedergang der Römischen Welt*, II.27.1 (Berlin: Walter de Gruyter, 1993), 483–522.
[33] Ysebaert, *Amtsterminologie*; G. Schöllgen, 'Monepiskopat und monarchisches Episkopat: Eine Bermerkung zur Terminologie', *Zeitschrift für die Neutestamentliche Wissenschaft* 77 (1986), 146–81.
[34] I argue this in my *A Study of Ignatius of Antioch*.

a minority opinion. By reading between the lines of the debate in these letters, and pinpointing the rhetorical strategies, there may well be insights into communities in transition, and some of their disagreements concerned charism and office.

There were plenty of *charismata* in the church of Smyrna when Ignatius wrote to Polycarp (*Smyrn.*, Inscr.). But *convulsions* (Greek *paroxysmos*; cf. Acts 15:39 for the disagreement between Paul and Barnabas in Antioch) existed there, too.

Ignatius thought that Polycarp, bishop in Smyrna, was not forceful enough. He was not sufficiently conscious of his office (*topos* in *Pol.*, 1.2) and might fall prey to 'plausible' people or to troublesome ones (*Pol.*, 2.1). Polycarp needed to be 'an anvil that is smitten', an athlete experiencing the gruelling punishment of his calling, a prudent reliever of convulsions, as well as a leader who controlled finances, who alone held the secret of the one sworn to celibacy and gave consent to marriages between Christians. Elisabeth Fiorenza has also suggested that the *widows* were a source of problems and were insufficiently under Polycarp's control for Ignatius's liking. So issues related to sex may have fed congregational tensions.[35] In this instance I have never been convinced.[36] But Ignatius certainly advocated that Polycarp should be more diligent and was solicitous that the younger man should 'lack no gift'. So Polycarp should pray that 'the things invisible' (*aorata*) might be revealed to him (*Pol.*, 2.2). It is interesting, too, that in other letters Ignatius took care to present his own credentials as a man of prophetic insight.

Ignatius himself (significantly, perhaps, a man 'in bonds') had knowledge of 'things seen and unseen'. He said so to Christians in Tralles (*Trall.*, 4, 5). He also offered support to those bishops who were described, enigmatically, as 'silent' (*Eph.*, 6; *Phld.*, 1). This, I believe, related to the perception of some Christians that officials were lacking in certain charismata. His criticism of those who distanced themselves from bishops, while holding their own eucharists and agape gatherings (neither valid nor 'catholic', he

[35] E. Schüssler Fiorenza, *In Memory of Her: A Feminist Theological Reconstruction of Christian Origins* (London: SCM Press, 1983), 313–15.

[36] Trevett, 'Ignatius and the Monstrous Regiment of Women', *Studia Patristica* 21 (1989), 202–14. It seems, nevertheless, that Polycarp was being called to exercise the control of an (episcopal) *paterfamilias*, and the matters of money, dealing with slaves and oversight of women came into this.

asserted, *Trall.*, 3:1; *Smyrn.*, 8) should probably be taken in conjunction with his other criticism of those who believed that 'one or two' could achieve 'a mighty prayer'. How much more a congregation gathered round the bishop, he asserted (*Eph.*, 5.2–3; cf. *Magn.*, 7–8)! It would seem, then, that the kind of unified Christian community Ignatius envisaged, unified behind its bishop, presbyters and deacons, was less of a reality in western Asia Minor than he would have wished.[37]

Philadelphia, with its 'silent' bishop, seems to have been home to the most troubled and divided community. It is no coincidence, I think, that it was in the presence of Philadelphian Christians that Ignatius, bishop and confessor-under-guard,[38] prophesied!

Ignatius the prophet bishop

Ignatius insisted that he had prophesied while fulfilling all the conventions of Christian prophecy. He had been no burden (*barys*) on the community. He had spoken 'with a loud voice' and had cried out using an authorization formula.[39] (Interestingly his prophecy seems to have been poetic in form.) Such things did him no good.

The prophecy had been tested and found deficient. It had concerned the necessity for obedience to the (silent) bishop! This spoke to some of his advance knowledge of troubles in the community, rather than of direct inspiration from God. In the letter which followed his encounter with Philadelphian Christians, Ignatius insisted that 'the Spirit was speaking'. It is unlikely, however, that his critics, clearly well-versed in the conventions of prophecy, would have been convinced.

This passage (*Phld.*, 6–8) is of considerable interest, not least because it illustrates that in some congregations at least, at this

---

[37] H. Chadwick, 'The Silence of Bishops in Ignatius', *Harvard Theological Review* 43 (1950), 169–72. Cf. Trevett, 'Prophecy and Anti-Episcopal Activity: A Third Error Combated by Ignatius?' *Journal of Ecclesiastical History* 34 (1983), 1–18. Judaizing and/or docetic Christians are usually cited as the opponents. Recently Michael Goulder has revived a nineteenth-century suggestion that they were Ebionites: 'Ignatius's "docetists"', *Vigiliae Christianae* 53 (1999), 16–30.

[38] *Eph.*, 1; 11.2; 21.2; *Trall.*, 5.2; 12.2; *Rom.*, 4.3; *Smyrn.*, 4.2; 10.2.

[39] See my 'Prophecy and Anti-Episcopal Activity' and *A Study of Ignatius*, ch. 4, on *Phld.*, 6–8.

early point in Christian history, a bishop might be expected to manifest those same *charismata* which graced other members of the flock, and might be tested, by some Christians at least.

It was not that Ignatius was claiming to be set apart from the congregation as a special spirit-bearer.[40] But this confrontation with some Philadelphian Christians, from a church which was divided (*merismos* and related words occur nine times in the Ignatian letters, six of them in the letter to Philadelphia), may also shed light on the passage in the letter to Ephesus (*Eph.*, 6) where he insists that a bishop should be received as the one (God) who sent him. The Ephesian bishop, too, was probably 'silent' and some Christians in Ephesus did not join in 'the common assembly' and opposed the bishop (*Eph.*, 5.3), just as in Philadelphia some were not 'with the bishop' (3.2). In Ignatius's opinion this meant that they were out of unity with the church.

In Philadelphia there may well have been accusations of a personal nature. Ignatius insisted that its bishop had not achieved his office due to vanity or human machinations. It had come from love of God. And as for the bishop's 'silence', it achieved more than the words which came from others (*Phld.*, 1)! His praise of the (unnamed) Philadelphian bishop was suspiciously fulsome.

Given this evidence of tensions and tribulations in the Christian communities concerned, it is not surprising that Ignatius should advise Polycarp in terms which promote denying ammunition to the opposition. It was important to 'lack no gift' lest 'troublesome' Christians question the basis of your authority.

From the *Didache* to 1 Clement

The writer of the Pastoral Letters had offered guidance on the qualities and functions of bishops, deacons and *presbyteroi* (1 Tim. 3:1–13; 5:17–19; cf. Tit. 1:7–9; 2:1–5). Timothy's own rise to leadership, he wrote, had been accompanied by 'prophetic utterances' (1 Tim. 2:18; 4:13; cf. 4:1; 2 Tim. 1:6 and 14). Such statements indicate clearly that in some congregations, where the

[40] So too Reiling, *Hermas*, 150 n. 2. And cf. J. B. Malina, 'The Social World implied in the Letters of the Christian Bishop-Martyr (Named Ignatius of Antioch)', in P. J. Achtemeier, ed., *SBL Seminar Papers* 78/2, Missoula, 1978, 71–119; Maier, *The Social Setting of the Ministry*, ch. 5.

roles of the bishop and his fellow officers were not challenged (so far as we know), the prophetic was not separated radically from the clerical. Presumably the bishop in Philadelphia had received no such prophetic acknowledgement, otherwise Ignatius would surely have used the fact as ammunition!

It was not only in the Ignatian letters, however, that such concerns about charism and office emerged during the second century.

In the East, at much the same time, the Didachist had written for a readership in which some Christians needed persuading that the appointment of bishops and deacons was not an inferior option. He tried reassurance, in the light of changing circumstances. The ministry of bishops and deacons, he insisted, matched that of the teachers and prophets (itinerant and settled) who were now less in evidence than in the past. Both were honourable, so they should appoint bishops and deacons who performed the same ministry as teachers and prophets. 'Do not despise them' (*Did.*, 15:1–2). Much more of that document, however, was given over to the leadership shown by apostles, prophets and teachers of older type.

Ignatius's stance was closer to the Pastor than to the Didachist. He may well have known the work of the latter, for some of the sentiments of the *Didache* find modified echo in his own letters.[41] This is not surprising. Both writers belonged to Syria and *Didache*-type tradition may also be reflected at a later date in the writings of Justin Martyr, Clement of Alexandria and Cyprian.[42] Writings and writers got around in those days!

Ignatius echoed and countered the concerns of the *Didache* when writing to churches far from Syria. But we cannot know how many Christians in the towns to which his letters were addressed shared fully his opinions or understood some of the allusions he was making. Certainly (and unlike some readers to which the *Didache*

---

[41] C. Trevett, 'Prophecy and Anti-Episcopal Activity'; C. N. Jefford, 'Did Ignatius of Antioch Know the Didache?' in Jefford, ed., *The Didache in Context: Essays on its History and Transmission* (Leiden: Brill, 1995), 330–51. There is insufficient evidence to show whether Ignatius knew this multi-layered document in the form in which we have it. Scholars debate whether the Didachist was addressing his reforms to *presbyters* in congregations. R. A. Campbell, in *The Elders: Seniority within Earliest Christianity* (Edinburgh: T&T Clark, 1994), 256; cf. 245, suggested that Ignatius's fulsome support for elders served to disguise the fact that under the reforms he was supporting, the elders had nothing to do.

[42] Jefford, *The Didache in Context*, bibliography.

was addressed) Ignatius had no doubt that 'the bishops, who have been appointed throughout the world, are by the will of Jesus Christ' (*Eph.*, 3.2; cf. *Phld.*, Inscr.). But as I have shown, some of those in Philadelphia, at least, had doubts about their own bishop, even though Ignatius insisted he had obtained the ministry 'neither from himself nor through men, nor for vainglory', adding 'as many as belong to God and Jesus Christ they are with the bishop' (*Phld.*, 1:1–2; 3.2). Despite the strictures of the Pastoral Letters, there were still Christians in Asia Minor who were less than convinced that hierarchical control and the associated ordering of Christian life and practice were proper (see too, *Eph.*, 5.2–6, 1; *Magn.*, 4; 6.1–2; *Trall.*, 2.1–3.2; *Smyrn.*, 8.1–9.1).

Looking beyond the Ignatian letters and the *Didache*, I would suggest that there is a good example of disaffection related to charism versus office in the second-century Christian interpolation which is 3.13–14.22 (especially 3.23ff.) in the accounts of the *Martyrdom and Ascension of Isaiah*. This is a work in the character of an Apocalypse.[43] The canonical Apocalypse too, speaks (or so I have argued elsewhere) of an understanding of Christian expectation, of congregational life and of the ongoing role for *charismata* within it, which makes it likely that the kinds of Christians for which the Seer had written in Asia were just those who would have been among Ignatius's opponents.[44] At a later date the success of the New Prophecy and the fact that it quarrelled with the Catholic side 'because of spiritual gifts' indicates that unanimity had not easily or quickly been established. The apocalyptic Isaiah passage includes these words:

> In those days there will be many who love office, although lacking wisdom. And there will be many wicked elders and shepherds who wrong their sheep ... and many will exchange the glory of the robes of the saints for those who love money ... and the Holy Spirit will withdraw from many.[45] And in those days there will not be

[43] But not Montanist in origin, I think, *pace* de Labriolle.

[44] Trevett, 'The other letters'; eadem, 'Apocalypse, Ignatius, Montanism: Seeking the Seeds', *Vigiliae Christianae* 43 (1989), 313–38. The seeds of appeal to prophetic insight and tradition as well as apostolic may be in evidence amongst some of Ignatius's opponents also (*Phld.*, 5.1–2). This became a feature of the New Prophecy later. I plan to develop this theme in a future publication.

[45] Cf. too Origen on bishops' love of status and power and their alienation from the 'little ones'; von Campenhausen, *Ecclesiastical Authority*, ch. 10.

many prophets, nor those who speak reliable words . . . except one here and there in different places . . . And among the elders there will be great hatred towards one another . . . they will make ineffective the prophecy of the prophets who were before me, and my visions also . . .[46]

This did not match the Ignatian view, of course. He was aligned with that strand of Syrian tradition which at some point had been incorporated into the pro-episcopal *Didache*, 15. He was also sympathetic to the sentiments of Clement of Rome in the letter to Corinth (95–100 CE). And that is significant I think. It is time to turn to 1 Clement.

Clement had appealed, and in detail, to Jewish, pagan and Christian precedents in support of his view of Christian community and harmony. Divine inspiration and prophecy had their part. It was these things which identified and tested people for appointment as bishops and deacons, he asserted (42.2; cf. Acts 20:28; 1 Tim. 1:18 and 2 Tim. 1:6). But such acknowledgment of *charismata* apart, above all he was, as Jeffers remarked, 'seeking to legitimize a new ideology of leadership by attributing it to earlier Christian tradition'.[47] It was a view with which Ignatius seems to have concurred. Nevertheless Clement did not represent the only Roman view on such matters.

By contrast, but also in Rome, Hermas wrote out of revelation, appealing to his visions and writing them down under command (*Vis.*, 2.1.4; 2.4.2; 5.5). Like the critic in the *Isaiah* document, Hermas saw contemporary leaders (those who liked to have 'chief seats') as uncorrected people, without peace among themselves (*Vis.*, 3.5.1; 3.9.7–10). In the eleventh *Mandate* Hermas contrasted the true and the false prophet. The former was meek, unpolluted by the world, poor and speaking only at the prompting of the Spirit. The latter exalted himself, desired the *protokathedria*, enjoyed luxury and prophesied for gain. *The Shepherd* contained a critique of wealth and worldly-mindedness and a challenge to leaders in the Roman churches.

[46] Translated by M. A. Knibb in J. H. Charlesworth, ed., *The Old Testament Pseudepigrapha* (London: Darton, Longman & Todd, 1985), 161. See too Trevett, 'Is the Bishop Also Among the Prophets? A Look at a Second-Century Concern', *Theology Wales*, Spring 1999, 25–40.

[47] Jeffers, *Conflict*, 152.

Clement had written of those in Rome 'who dissent from us' (*Ad Cor.*, 47.7; 39.1). Similarly Hermas knew of more than one kind of Christian group in Rome. But according to *The Shepherd*, Hermas the visionary was, in his day, the one worthy of receiving God's word. By implication others were not (*Vis.*, 3.4.3).

If the Clement of *Vis.*, 2.4.3 was he who penned *Ad Cor.* (and Hermas described him as the one whose task was to write to the churches), then clearly the circle around Hermas was not radically estranged from the one around Clement. It is important to recognize that while Christians and their groups might differ from each other in some respects, we should not assume a high degree of hostility during this relatively early period of Christian history. Similarly some of those who excited Ignatius's suspicions (and not docetists, who were beyond the pale altogether) were in contact with 'catholic' congregations and might be expected to influence them. Similarly the New Prophets were within Catholic-type congregations until driven from, or seceding from them (Eusebius, *HE*, 5.16.10; Epiphanius, *Pan.*, 48.12.1).

Ignatius knew Clement's letter to Corinth. Clement's condemnation of dissent and of the deposing of officials (presbyters) there would have appealed to him, though not once did the Roman indicate what the cause of such things might have been (cf. 1 Tim. 5:19). Maier has described this Corinthian letter as 'an attempt to legitimate a certain pattern of institutionalized leadership', and Clement had indeed painted a picture of *Homonoia*/concord in a Christian community which related to submission to the community's leaders. This was the purpose of his letter. The challenge to the prevailing leadership in Corinth had shattered the peace (*Ad Cor.*, 2:2; 2:6; 3:4).[48]

All this would have been music to the ears of Ignatius who was interested in 'the commandment' (cf. *Magn.*, 4, where some

---

[48] Maier, *The Social Setting of the Ministry*, 87–146, esp. 135. See too Jeffers, *Conflict*, 63–105 and the literature there; K. Beyschlag, *Clemens Romanus und der Frühkatholizismus* (Tübingen: Mohr 1966); J. Fuellenbach, *Ecclesiastical Office and the Primacy of Rome* (Washington, DC: Catholic University of America Press, 1980); P. Mikat, *Die Bedeutung der Begriffe Stasis und Aponoia für das Verständnis des 1 Clemensbriefes* (Cologne: Westdeutscher Verlag, 1969). In a forthcoming study of *Women and Christianity in the Second Century*, I examine the possibility that prophets were among the dissenters in Corinth.

recognize the bishop in name but disregard him in practice),[49] and in the establishment of peace in Antioch. Such things, together with his exceedingly high regard for the Roman Christian community to which he was writing ('you taught others', *Rom.*, 3:1) tell of his knowledge of 1 Clement. Moreover I have argued that he made clear reference to the letter from Rome to Corinth, in his own letter to Rome.[50]

It is reasonable to conclude, then, that Ignatius's own understanding of what constituted right ordering and loyalty to a properly constituted hierarchy of officials had been fed by the teaching of the Roman Clement. This brings me back to the question of charism and office in Rome, for the power of 1 Clement and of Roman teaching to influence other Christians in far reaches of the Roman Empire should not be taken to indicate that *Rome* had achieved a uniformity of belief and practice without difficulty.

Charism and office in Rome

Roman Christianity is a reminder to us that we have to think in the plural. If Clement was (pre-Ignatius) an advocate of Ignatian-type loyalty to officials, then Hermas's *The Shepherd* (another work which embraces the Apocalypse form) should be seen as a document of dissent.

Jeffers is surely right to think in terms of different types of Roman house churches, involving also Christians of different social classes. Analysing on the basis of Weber's and Wilson's studies of the sect, Jeffers observed that 'Clement's congregation had evolved beyond its original self-definition and ... developed a more world-embracing attitude, as it sought to redefine its identity in a world it no longer considered a threat to its existence'. As for the *Shepherd*, the nature of the church which is defended in that work 'resembles Wilson's notion of the classic form of the sect'.[51] It represents, Jeffers suggests, 'a narrower sectarian response to the world',[52] and one of its characteristics was that it did not have

---

[49] Cf. *Trall.*, 7.1; 13.2.

[50] C. Trevett, 'Ignatius "To the Romans" and 1 Clement liv–lvi', *Vigiliae Christianae* 43 (1989), 35–52.

[51] Jeffers, *Conflict*, 166. Both the *Didache* and *The Shepherd* were much read in the early church.

[52] Jeffers, *Conflict*, 74.

Clement's great concern for admission to leadership. In the on-going debate about the relation of charism to office in the changing churches we must not overlook the significance of class and of economic disempowerment, of attitude to 'the world' and expectations about the world's end.

Leadership (as Clement defined it in 43–4) was apostolic in origin and was self-perpetuating. The Apostles had known that there would be *eris* (strife) for the role of bishop and for that reason they had left instructions for the appointment of 'approved' men (44.2). No blameless holder of such office was to be removed (44.2–3; 44.6). Clement knew only of Apostles of the past, not of itinerant 'apostles' as in the *Didache*. Prophets, similarly, were for him something from the past. By contrast, for Hermas they were a living reality in congregations. And Hermas did not share Clement's advocacy of uncritical loyalty to church leaders.

Hermas did not regard church leaders as set apart, in the way which Clement seemed to. But at the same time (as would be the case with the New Prophets no more than a few decades later), he was not objecting to officialdom *per se*. In *The Shepherd* he too wrote of leaders (*prolegoumenos*), of teachers, prophets and also bishops, presbyters and deacons. His objections concerned leaders' lifestyles and a compromise with the world which a true charismatic could discern. In its response to the world, so one study has claimed, Clement *Ad Cor.* had gone 'well beyond anything in the New Testament and prepared the way for later Christian ideas'.[53]

Other factors, too, helped to determine an understanding of the community and the exercise of power within it. Clement did not share the otherworldly orientation or the expectation that the end was near, which informed Hermas (*Sim.*, 9.12.3). Similarly Ignatius, despite his assertion that 'these are the last times' (*Eph.*, 11) was less interested in ideas of 'warfare in heaven' (*Eph.*, 13.2; cf. Rev. 12:7; 13:7) than in promoting the unity of Christians behind their leaders. It was that which ensured peace, in his view (*Eph.*, 13.2; cf. 4.2; *Magn.*, 6; cf. *Phld.*, 10.2; *Smyrn.*, 10.2). Lack of unity would 'give occasion to the heathen' (*Trall.*, 8.2). Other Christians who encountered Ignatius had a different outlook, and

---

[53] R. M. Grant and H. H. Graham, *First and Second Clement* (New York: Thomas Nelson & Sons, 1965), 96.

they may well have considered that this would be unity at too great a cost.

The outcome

It was Clement's view which won, of course. But just as the Ignatian pattern of church order did not have an easy passage in Antioch, I think,[54] so too in Rome it struggled to achieve supremacy. Ignatius could name no bishop in his letter to Rome, and given his determined support for named bishops (and for unnamed 'silent' ones), and his admiration for the Roman Christians, this seems a remarkable omission. Nor did Hermas write of any such individual. We should not assume the triumph of monepiscopacy in Rome before the mid-second century. To achieve the unifying of congregations and 'for Clement's view to predominate in Rome', Jeffers concluded, 'it had to overcome the views of Christians such as Hermas'.[55]

Even with the triumph of episcopacy, prophecy did not die completely or suddenly, as the rise of the New Prophecy, the histories of Tertullian's Carthage, of Cyprian and perhaps of Hippolytus in Rome indicate too.[56] By the third Christian century, however, the die was cast and the tide could not be turned back. The struggle then was to ensure that *charismata* were not exercised in ways which might threaten established clerical authority. They had not ceased to exist,[57] but there was preference for a less untrammelled channelling of power, and in time (unlike what had

[54] Trevett, *A Study of Ignatius of Antioch*.
[55] Jeffers, *Conflict*, 198.
[56] Some argue that prophecy was a live issue in Hippolytus's day. Certainly he believed that ecclesiastical office depended on, and stemmed from, the Spirit's endowment. See J. E. Stam, 'Charismatic Theology in the *Apostolic Tradition* of Hippolytus', in G. Hawthorne, ed., *Current Issues in Biblical and Patristic Interpretation* (Grand Rapids: Eerdmans, 1975), 206ff. For Cyprian *visions* played a role in clerical appointment (*Epp.*, 33.1,4; 34; 44.4; 62.1).
[57] See e.g. Robeck on the later shift of *charismata* from the mainstream church into the monastic movement, in 'Ecclesiastical Authority and the Power of the Spirit', *Paraclete* 12/3 (1978), 17–23; idem, *Prophecy in Carthage*; idem, 'Hippolytus on the Gift of Prophecy', *Paraclete* 17/3 (1983), 22–7 (Hippolytus's treatise on the charismata is not extant); J. W. Trigg, 'The Charismatic Intellectual: Origen's Understanding of Religious Leadership', *Church History* 50 (1981), 5–19; Trevett, '"Angelic Visitations and Speech"', *passim*.

happened to Ignatius) there was less need for the office-holder to assert his credentials as a charismatic when seeking support.

Montanism in Rome and in Africa, as well as in Asia Minor, may have played some small part in mobilizing opinion. There was consolidation of the catholic position on authority and office. But it is too simple a picture to present the second century New Prophecy *only* in terms of charism against clericalization, as many have tended to do.

> It may be called a democratic reaction against the clerical aristocracy which from the time of Ignatius had more and more monopolized all ministerial privileges and functions. The Montanists found the true qualification and appointment for the office of teacher in direct endowment by the Spirit of God, in distinction from outward ordination and episcopal succession. They everywhere proposed the supernatural element and the free motion of the Spirit against the mechanism of a fixed ecclesiastical order.[58]

However, this ignores the existence of 'ecclesiastical order' in Montanism too, and there was more to the New Prophecy than this, just as there was more to the Patristic Age than the dry formalism which John Wesley described:

> I was fully convinced of what I had long suspected: (1) that Montanists . . . were real, scriptural Christians and (2) that the real reason why the miraculous gifts were so soon withdrawn was not only that faith and holiness were well nigh lost, but that dry, formal, orthodox men began even to ridicule whatever gifts they had not themselves and to decry them all as either madness or imposture.[59]

There is no doubt, however, that the exercise of charismata in congregations declined. Phenomena such as glossolalia, miracle-working and prophecy in heretical (e.g. Gnostic) groups may have helped to seal their fate, as also the failure of the New Prophets to make sufficient impact while also alienating many. When the

---

[58] P. Schaff, *History of the Christian Church* (Grand Rapids: Eerdmans, reprint 1981) II, 424.

[59] T. Jackson, ed., *The Works of John Wesley*, 3rd edn (London, 1829–31) II, 204. Hippolytus, though he decried the New Prophecy, hoped that the *charismata* of believers would assess those who were 'at the head of the church'. If he had omitted to say anything, Hippolytus knew that God would reveal it to the worthy (*Ap. Trad.*, 5, 43). See von Campenhausen, *Ecclesiastical Authority*, 191.

post-Nicene Fathers asked themselves why the decline had happened, they explained it in terms of the growth of undue pride and of schisms which charismatics had fostered (Chrysostom), or of such gifts having been products of a special Age, replaced now by brotherly love (Augustine). Theodore and Chrysostom alike saw them as having flourished at a time when faith was being established. No longer were they needed, as 'fatherly' control and guidance prevailed, and a view of eligibility which made it unlikely that the laic or non-appointee would prophesy, heal, speak in tongues or exorcise.

A final word

The gifts of the Spirit had functioned to manifest the ongoing work of Jesus Christ in the churches. Thus they had played a role in winning others to the Christian camp. The *charismata*, Origen had affirmed, demonstrated the truth of the gospel (*Contra Celsum*, 1.2) and so played a role in its proclamation.[60] Others came to see them as provoking arguments and unrest internal to Christianity. Such things were not conducive to good order or to the churches becoming institutions comprehensible to the Roman and Greek onlooker. Without unity behind office-holders, Ignatius had affirmed, it was more difficult to meet the opposition which 'the heathen' and the heretic represented (*Trall.*, 8.2; *Phld.*, 2.2; 3.2–3; 6.1; cf. *Eph.*, 13.1). *Merismos* ('division'), however caused, was an evil (*Trall.*, 13.1; *Phld.*, 2.2; 6.1; 7.2). Properly constituted, unified Christian communities – with teaching which carried the weight of their (apostolic) founders and with patriarchal and hierarchical leadership – would indeed be more comprehensible to the wider world. This, then, became the dominant direction for second-century thought. The church should be one which knew how to conduct itself soberly, in 'respectable' fashion.

The New Prophets, and probably others of which we are not aware, had objected that *prophecy* was no less apostolic in origin and that its line of succession was no less traceable. There was

[60] On the evangelistic function of exorcism and miracle-working, see e.g. Irenaeus, *Adv. Haer.*, 2.32.4; Tertullian, *Apol.*, 23, 28; Pseudo-Clement, *De Virg.*, 1.10; Origen, *Contra Celsum*, 7.18; A. Kreider, *Worship and Evangelism in Pre-Christendom*, Joint Liturgical Studies 32 (Cambridge: Grove Books, 1995), 14, including discussion of the Ramsay MacMullen–Robin Lane Fox debate.

continuity after more than one fashion and great past teachers of more than one kind to appeal to. They had objected 'we too must receive the spiritual gifts' and that possession of the Spirit was the proper determinant in dealings with sinners.

The Holy Church of God, said Epiphanius's anonymous source, by way of response, does of course accept the *charismata*. But it depended . . . The Holy Church received 'the veritable *charismata*'. He might have added, but didn't, that such a distinction ensured that 'Christian teachers most esteemed for wisdom' determined doctrine and not 'wild and excitable women'.[61] The debate is not yet ended.

---

[61] This study takes for granted the existence and validity of 'diverse ministry' and of 'tension between charisma and institutionalization'. This is a 'fashion' condemned by Alan Brent in 'Pseudonymity and Charisma in the Ministry of the Early Church', *Augustinianum* 27 (1987), 347–76; idem, *Cultural Episcopacy and Ecumenism: Representative Ministry in Church History from the Age of Ignatius of Antioch to the Reformation* (Leiden: Brill, 1992), 92f.

Chapter 7

Women in the Christianization of the West

ANNE JENSEN

Until recently, historians of the early church have ignored, marginalized and anonymized women. However, close examination of the sources demonstrates that women were active participants in the spread of Christianity. Some women – such as Mary Magdalene, Junia and the legendary Thecla – were active as apostles. Others, including Ammia of Philadelphia and several leaders of the 'New Prophecy', were prophets. In Rome Philomena demonstrated the possibility of being a theologically creative teacher, while Blandina, Perpetua and Felicitas were exemplary martyrs. Some Christian women developed the possibilities of a celibate life, in a manner unique in the ancient world, while others chose to remain with their families. The life history of the younger Melania and her husband Pinian embodied this tension; asceticism was victorious, and Melania was founder of many religious communities. The theologian and poet Faltonia Betitia Proba, on the other hand, was happily married; in her Virgilian *Cento de Christo* she created an unsurpassed synthesis between a Roman spiritual tradition and the biblical message.

There are few sources on the lives and activities of Christian women in late antiquity, so it has been hard to restrict myself to the West in this paper. But fortunately, of the four extant sources written by women of this period, three are Western: the prison diaries of the martyr Perpetua of Carthage (†AD 203); the Christ poem by Faltonia Betitia Proba of Rome (written *c.* AD 360);

and Egeria of Gaul's diary of her travels to the holy places of Christianity in Palestine and Asia Minor.[1]

For more information on women, we must refer to sources written by men. Women's studies of history have shown that women were often completely ignored in historical writing due to the male historians' lack of interest in them. If women were mentioned, they were often marginalized. This is clearly evident in the anonymization of women, which occurs even to the 'heroines' of a story. Examples (unfortunately Eastern) of this include the anonymous woman involved in the Christianization of Georgia[2] and the courageous but unnamed Christian woman in Edessa who prevented a massacre.[3] Both accounts are depicted in great detail in the ecclesiastical histories of Rufinus, Socrates, Sozomen and Theodoret.

The most effective way of making women invisible has always been, of course, to ignore them. This was a practice particularly favoured in cases where women, or certain women, did not fit into the author's philosophical mindset. Sozomen, for example, makes no mention whatsoever in his church history of the fact that there were numerous women among the desert ascetics he so admired. Here we can detect the tendentious reporting of the author, since we know the source he used for his reporting – 'The Paradise' (or the *Lausiac History*) by Palladius, who talked of many women and explicitly stressed that he attached equal importance to spiritual fathers and mothers. It should be noted here that modern translations (starting with the Latin) contribute considerably to making women invisible. The wisdom of the 'old' (*die Alten*, a masculine plural which can include women) becomes the wisdom of the 'fathers' (*die Väter*, which cannot include

[1] Cf. Patricia Wilson-Kastner *et al.*, eds, *A Lost Tradition: Women Writers of the Early Church* (Washington: University Press of America, 1981). This contains all four writings, translated into English, with a commentary.

[2] This story has been handed down in the following church histories: Rufinus, 1.10; Socrates, 1.20. Sozomen, 2.7; Theodoret, I. 24. Cf. Anne Jensen, *Gottes selbstbewußte Töchter: Frauenemanzipation im frühen Christentum?* (Freiburg: Herder, 1992), 165–73; English translation: *God's Self-Confident Daughters: Women's Liberation in Early Christianity?* translated by O. C. Dean, Jr (Louisville: Westminster/John Knox Press, 1996). Hereafter referred to as Jensen, *Gottes selbstbewußte Töchter*.

[3] Rufinus, 2.5; Socrates, 4.18; Sozomen, 6.18; Theodoret, 4.17. Cf. Jensen, *Gottes selbstbewußte Töchter*, 92f.

women): *Vita patrum*; *Apophthegmata patrum*, etc. However, we must not ignore the fact that even in his introduction, Palladius himself refers to 'male and female fathers'.

A less accentuated form of rendering women invisible is *marginalization*: the activities of women are not so much concealed as they are minimized. Again, this is exemplified by the previously mentioned anonymous female missionary in Georgia. In Theodoret's church history, this woman barely spoke at all; she converted others through her prayers (I, 24)! In the earliest report by Rufinus, in contrast, she gave speeches with a theological content. However, even this author is reductive; the anonymous woman teaches that 'Christ is God . . . as much as a woman has any right to do so' (I, 10).

The history of the suppression and repression of women, and of their activities, will not be the main topic of this paper. Yet we cannot turn a blind eye to the dismal state of women's history at the end of the first six centuries of Christianity. According to the texts of the New Testament, women were involved in all levels of community life at first – naturally not equal in numbers to men, but nowhere were they fundamentally excluded, even if tendencies to do this soon began to appear. By the end of the sixth century, women in the West were being refused entry to all ecclesiastical offices. The celibate life, which opened new areas of activity and was chosen by many women, became increasingly restricted to a secluded life behind cloister walls. Even today, strict rules of seclusion are applied to women in a completely different way than to men belonging to the same Order.

In this paper, a positive perspective will dominate. This will involve: (a) bringing to light the fact that women were active participants in preaching the gospel; and (b) finding out, wherever possible, what specific contribution women made to the shaping of Christianity and to its spread in the West. As Christians, they belonged – in the long run – to the victors; as women, they belonged perhaps to the losers. This aspect will be considered wherever possible. I will begin with the women apostles in the New Testament.

Women apostles

Treating the Twelve as 'the' Apostles had dire consequences for women, not least in terms of iconography, where these twelve men often appear as the sole representatives of both male and female disciples, or of the church. At most, Mary may be seen alongside the Apostles in depictions of the Pentecost. In my church (the Roman Catholic), as well as in the Orthodox tradition, this circle of the Twelve is used even today to justify the exclusion of women from the priesthood. Women apostles in the New Testament, such as Mary Magdalene, Priscilla and Junia, were therefore seen from the outset as second-class apostles, like many of their male counterparts. Only Paul became an Apostle *per se*, even though he himself did not belong to the Twelve.

In several gnostic texts, there is an interesting deviation. Here, we find several women disciples alongside the men. For example, in the introductory verses of the 'Sophia of Jesus Christ', the Twelve and seven women gathered in Galilee after the death of Jesus to meet the risen Christ. While even here there is a numerical imbalance, we are nevertheless dealing with a significant female presence, or at least a significant awareness of a female presence. We may indeed question whether there lay, behind such symbolic numbers, a truly egalitarian practice, but in many gnostic circles this was in fact the case.[4]

My task here is not to examine the New Testament, but I would like to refer to chapter 16 of Paul's Letter to the Romans, which presents some of the clearest evidence of women's apostolic engagement in early Christian times. It may provide evidence of circumstances in the West, providing that this closing section of the letter did not originally belong to a letter to the Ephesians, as some exegetes suspect. In any case, whether Eastern or Western in origin, Paul addressed twenty-eight people: all eighteen men, and eight of the women, by name; two other women remain anonymous and are defined by their relationships to men (mother of, sister of). Presumably, three of the women addressed were married. Four of the women were expressly mentioned in conjunction with the word *kopian* – to work hard (as an apostle). Junia (alias Junias),[5]

---

[4] Cf. Klaus Koschorke, 'Gnosis, Montanismus, Mönchtum: Zur Frage emanzipatorischer Bewegungen im Raum der alten Kirche', *Evangelische Theologie* 53 (1993), 216–31.

[5] Cf. Leopold Zscharnack, *Der Dienst der Frau in den ersten Jahrhunderten der christlichen Kirche* (Göttingen: Vandenhoeck & Ruprecht, 1902), 102; Marie-Joseph Lagrange, *L'Epître aux Romains* (Paris: Gabalda, 1950), 365f.; Bernadette J. Brooten, 'Junia – hervorragend unter den Aposteln (Rom. 16.7)',

who has recently been re-identified in the West (as she was always recognized in the East) as a woman, was referred to as 'outstanding amongst the apostles', and Phoebe, who delivered the letter, was described as *diakonos* and *prostatis*. Priscilla was not explicitly referred to as an apostle, but according to evidence in the New Testament, she would have truly earned the title.

In Romans 16, we are obviously dealing with historical facts. In other accounts from early Christianity, this is less clear. We learn nothing, in canonical writings, about the apostolic activities of individual women disciples from Jesus' direct circle. In non-canonical writings, however, we come across a few of these women, in particular those who stood at the cross or were at Jesus' tomb, and who were therefore regarded specifically as witnesses to his resurrection. In ecclesiastical tradition, Mary Magdalene has even received the title of 'apostle to the Apostles'. There are also mentions of Salome which refer to Egypt: in the preserved fragments of the 'Egyptian Gospel' she speaks with the risen Christ. In the 'Gospel according to Mary' (Magdalene) there is also a particularly informative passage, in which there is an argument as to whether Mary could have received a revelation, and in which Peter appears as an adversary of women, for which his brothers strongly rebuke him. But above all, Mary Magdalene was the one person who gave courage to the disciples who felt resigned after the death of Jesus – courage to make a new start. Even here, then, the involvement of apostolic women was not undisputed.[6]

As explained, not much of this is certain historical territory, but it is to be assumed that after the death of Jesus, these women did indeed carry on preaching the gospel like their male counterparts. In the gnostic tradition, Mary Magdalene was even elevated to mythological status: together with John, she was described as the greatest of the disciples.[7] Here, then, we are dealing with a remarkable representation of Christian discipleship in both a female and a male form. This recollection that women historically

---

Frauenbefreiung (1978), 148–51, and others. In Greek patristics and in Orthodoxy, Junia has always been venerated as a female apostle.

  [6] Cf. Wilhelm Schneemelcher, ed., *Neutestamentliche Apokryphen*, 1: *Evangelien*, 5th edn (Tübingen: J. C. B. Mohr, 1987), 174–9, 313–15.

  [7] *Pistis Sophia*, 96.

belonged to Jesus' circle of disciples found a late echo in some church orders, where women were allowed to speak alongside male disciples so as to legitimize certain church regulations as belonging to 'apostolic tradition'.[8]

We must also enter the realm of legend, or rather of the novel, to trace another woman who was likewise an active apostle and who, as a result of her preaching, fell victim to the persecution of Christians but survived: Thecla of Iconium.[9] Hers was the most important women's cult of Christian late antiquity, but it was gradually superseded by the veneration of the Virgin Mary. According to a late legend, Thecla even travelled underground to Rome to be close to her teacher, Paul. This is obviously a cult legend, which perhaps gave authorization to speak of Thecla as Western though it is obviously an Eastern tradition. (In my opinion, the division of East and West for the first three centuries makes little sense.) Incidentally, Thecla had already become so famous in second-century Carthage that women could refer to her whenever their right to teach or to baptize was brought into question. This is attested to by Tertullian, who strongly fought against such activities by women and classified them as heresy.[10]

As 'protomartyr of women', Thecla was the female equivalent of the male protomartyr Stephen. Even today she is celebrated in the Eastern church as the 'Apostles' equal'. Unfortunately, the peculiarity of the West is that it, even more strongly than the East, has praised Thecla almost exclusively as a model of ascetically motivated virginity. Her apostolic role fell into oblivion, and eventually so did she, so much so that the Second Vatican Council deleted her name from the martyrology in a fit of historicist hyper-zealousness. The Thecla account, I must add, is a testament to

[8] For example Martha and Mary in the 'Canons of the holy apostles'; Theodor Schermann, *Die allgemeine Kirchenordnung, frühchristlichen Liturgien und kirchliche Überlieferung* 1–3, Studien zur Geschichte und Kultur des Altertums, suppl. vol. 3 (Paderborn: F. Schöningh, 1914–16), 1, 12–34. Ironically, apostolic women were given a voice here to justify the exclusion of women from priestly functions!

[9] *Thekla die Apostolin: Ein apokrypher Text neu entdeckt*, Anne Jensen, trans. and ed., Frauen-Kultur-Geschichte 3 (Freiburg: Herder, 1995; Gütersloh: Gerd Mohn, 1999). Greek text: *Acta Apostolorum Apocrypha*, ed. Ricardus Adelbertus Lipsius and Maximilianus Bonnet, vol. 1 (Leipzig: Hermann Mendelssohn, 1891).

[10] Tertullian, *On Baptism*, 17; *Prescription against the Heretics*, 41.

remarkable solidarity among women in late antiquity: during the trial and also in the arena, the women protested vehemently and publicly against the 'disgraceful verdict'.

Women prophets

If Thecla can be styled an 'itinerant woman apostle', then similarly there were 'itinerant women prophets'.[11] The high regard for prophets, and their activities, are particularly well documented in the *Didache*, though it makes no explicit mention of women prophets. However, one name from the early Christian period has been handed down to us: Ammia of Philadelphia.[12] The connection between name and place indicates this woman's great significance and the esteem in which she was held, but we know no details about her. She was mentioned by a second-century opponent of the Phrygian prophecy movement who denied that movement the right to refer to Ammia.[13] She was therefore equally recognized from an ecclesiastical as well as from a prophetic standpoint. It should be noted that I am trying to avoid the stereotypic division between the 'church' (or the 'orthodox') and the 'heretics'. Early Christianity was characterized by very different strands of development. In my opinion, three of these were especially important: prophetism, gnosticism, and 'ecclesiasticism' (by which I mean the movement oriented towards the institution of the church and its hierarchy).

With regard to the Phrygian prophecy movement, we should of course mention the two outstanding women, Priscilla and Maximilla, as well as the male organizer, Montanus.[14] Once again we find ourselves in the East, and, once again, we are dealing with a movement which also gained a footing in the West. The official

---

[11] Luise Schottroff, 'Wanderprophetinnen: Eine feministische Analyse der Logienquelle', *Evangelische Theologie* 51 (1991), 332–44.
[12] Eusebius, *HE*, 5.17. Cf. Jensen, *Gottes selbstbewußte Töchter*, 67f.
[13] Loc. cit.
[14] Cf. Jensen, *Gottes selbstbewußte Töchter*, 268–352. Cf. Christine Trevett, *Montanism: Gender, Authority and the New Prophecy* (Cambridge: Cambridge University Press, 1996), of which I had only the advance notice. With regard to the sources: Pierre de Labriolle, *Les sources de l'histoire du montanisme*, Collectanea Friburgensia 24 (Paris: Ernest Leroux, 1913); Ronald E. Heine, ed., *The Montanist Oracles and Testimonia*, Patristic Monograph Series 14 (Macon: Mercer University Press, 1989).

recognition of New Prophecy (alias 'Montanism')[15] by the Bishop of Rome had already been signed and sent by the time an opponent of the movement succeeded in changing the Bishop's mind.[16] Tertullian is known to have endorsed the New Prophecy and he, who otherwise advocated female subservience, attributed the greatest authority to the prophet Priscilla. He made the following reference to her, in parallel to the Apostle Paul: 'through the holy prophetess Prisca the Gospel is thus preached'.[17] The following logion of Priscilla concerns purity and inner harmony which make prophetic experience (visions and voices) possible: '"For purity," says she, "is harmonious, and they see visions; and, turning their face downward, they even hear manifest voices, as salutary as they are . . . secret."'[18] Tertullian understood this purity, though, as sexual abstinence. He had previously interpreted Paul in much the same way.[19]

According to the extant logia of Priscilla, Maximilla and Montanus, and according to the information which we can sift from polemical distortions, charismatic experience accompanied by charismatically-based authority lay at the heart of this movement.

Contrary to the emerging monepiscopate, this movement wanted to retain the old egalitarian value system of prophecy. From this Phrygian tradition emerged an extremely remarkable vision of Christ, who appeared in female form so as to accord wisdom to the woman prophet – Christ, then, as holy Wisdom, as the incarnation of the divine Sophia. According to Epiphanius, the saying may also be attributed to the woman prophet Quintilla, about whom nothing else is known. However, I (along with Kurt Aland) take this logion to be Priscilla's. It is a sort of vision of the woman prophet's calling, through which the cult centre of Pepuza is to be explained: 'In the form of a woman in a white gown, Christ came

[15] The modern term 'Montanism' is meaningless and misleading, for Montanus was not the head of the movement. 'New Prophecy' on the other hand corresponds to its self-perception; cf. Jensen, *Gottest selbstbewußte Töchter*, 272; eadem, 'Prisca – Maximilla – Montan: Who was the Founder of "Montanism"'?, Papers of the 11th International Oxford Conference on Patristic Studies, 1991, *Studia Patristica* 26 (1993), 147–50.

[16] Tertullian, *Against Praxean*, 1.

[17] Tertullian, *Exhortation to Chastity*, 10.5.

[18] Ibid.

[19] Cf. Jensen, *Gottes selbstbewußte Töchter*, 316.

to me and instilled wisdom in me; he revealed to me that this place is holy and that Jerusalem will descend here from heaven'.[20]

In this movement, according to Epiphanius, there were even women presbyters and bishops.[21] We find here, then, both an egalitarian ethos and signs of a spirituality of wisdom which seems to be coupled with one of prophecy. Such short texts must not be overworked into a modern feminist theology. They are, however, *tesserae* connoting women in the midst of a theological tradition which is dominated by men.

Women teachers

Here, at last, we have clear evidence of a significant woman from the West: Philomena,[22] who lived in Rome in the second century, seems to have been a rival of Marcion, for it is said that she won over many of his followers to her moderate views. Among these former Marcionites, we find Apelles, who recorded her *phaneroseis*. The term *phaneroseis* is not best translated as 'revelations', since it presents a supersensory, but not actually supernatural, form of knowledge (gnosis). The word 'apophthegms' is used for the sayings, a term which also does not suggest prophetic revelations, possibly in a state of ecstasy. This must be emphasized, since the sources describe Philomena as a prophet. The later interpretation readily saw a woman prophet as a woman ecstatic. Yet the title of teacher is much more appropriate to Philomena, because her arguments were very rational. Leopold Zscharnack himself pointed out that Eastern prophetic and Western philosophical elements pervaded in gnostic tradition.

We have virtually no biographical information about Philomena, other than that she belonged to an order of virgins.[23] Yet we do

---

[20] Epiphanius, *Panarion*, 49.1.3; cf. Jensen, *Gottes selbstbewußte Töchter*, 320ff.; Kurt Aland, 'Bemerkungen zum Montanismus und zur frühchristlichen Eschatologie', *Kirchengeschichtliche Entwürfe* (Gütersloh: Gerd Mohn, 1960), 122.

[21] Epiphanius, *Panarion*, 48:19–49:2.

[22] To Philomena, cf. Jensen, *Gottes selbstbewußte Töchter*, 373–426; Roman Hanig, 'Der Beitrag der Philumene zur Theologie der Apelleianer', *Zeitschrift für antikes Christentum* 3 (1999), 241–77.

[23] Only polemical statements are extant; the most important are from Rhodon (Eusebius, *HE*, 5.13) and from various writings of Tertullian, who had known the *Phaneroseis* which have meanwhile been lost.

have some knowledge of her doctrines, which would perhaps seem odd to us today but do present rather moderate views in comparison with other beliefs of the period.[24] She refused to accept Marcion's extreme dualism which played the good God of Jesus Christ off against the evil God of the Old Testament. Together with Apelles,[25] she rehabilitated the idea of angelic mediation, so as to make the idea of the creation of an incomplete world by a totally good God acceptable to hellenistically-educated Christians. She portrayed this in three degrees: the creator of the world was the demiurge, the revealer of the Old Testament was the fiery angel (of the burning bush), and the fallen angel was the creator of evil. In this way, she was able to depict the world and the writings of the Old Testament as incomplete without having to reject them as evil. She developed a qualitative criterion for Scripture: one had to discern what had been inspired by the heavenly Christ in every writing (not just in the books of the Bible).

She dealt with human corporeality in a similarly complex fashion, particularly in christology. Once again she rejected Marcion's docetism: Christ's corporeality was real. It could not, however, be attributed to a half-natural, half-unnatural virgin birth. Rather, the heavenly Christ, on descending, had taken on earthly matter which he then relinquished upon ascension. In the world of God, a body made no sense. Resurrection should not be (mis)understood as plainly physical.[26] There is one further point of interest here: contrary to the widespread opinion that the body was male or female, whereas the soul was genderless, she maintained the opinion that gender had its place in the soul and therefore continued to exist after the resurrection.[27]

The theological system of Philomena and Apelles was too complicated to be accepted by a large number of people. Yet both belonged to those who made a decisive contribution to bridging the gap between the hellenistic and the biblical worlds of thought.

---

[24] Cf. also the previous confession from her school in Epiphanius, *Panarion*, 44:1, 42:8.

[25] The contribution of each to this idea is no longer ascertainable; however, Philomena was definitely the originator and Apelles the pupil.

[26] Cf. Tertullian, *Against Marcion*, 3.11.2; *On the Incarnation of Christ*, 6:1f. as well as Epiphanius, op. cit.

[27] Tertullian, *On the Soul*, 36.3.

They were accused of 'impudent rationalism'.[28] But do we not often have to accuse devout belief in revelation and church dogmatism of being 'impudent irrationality'?

Philomena was both a woman and a head of a theological school – a circumstance which in her day was not the rule but was nevertheless possible. This level of involvement required education, and this was a set component of the Roman ideal of women. In Christianity, however, a trend developed which set itself against both education and philosophy. In itself lamentable, this trend had a particularly damaging effect on women and contributed much to their increasing incapacitation in the centuries to follow. It was not until the late Middle Ages that a woman's voice raised against this low opinion of the female sex became impossible to ignore: the voice of Christine de Pisan (1365–1430).

Women martyrs

Among the women who helped to shape early Christianity, we must in particular discuss martyrs and confessors (the terms were, as we know, synonymous at the time and did not presuppose death, rather only persecution). Pliny, in an official letter to Trajan, mentions two *ancillae ministrae*, whom he had tortured in order to obtain information on the cult of the Christians.[29] Obviously these two female slaves played an important role in the Christian community. Additionally, in the trial and massacre of Christians at Lyon (AD 177), we find in Blandina a female slave at the very centre of events. She was repeatedly subjected to terrible tortures in the arena and was eventually the last one to die; such was her resilience that people compared her to the Maccabean mother who encouraged her seven sons to strive for martyrdom and saw them die before she herself died.

In AD 203, Perpetua and Felicitas died in the arena in Carthage together with four male fellow-sufferers. For a long time, the characterization of Felicitas as *conserva* of Revocatus led one to conclude that she was a slave. Yet the term *conserva* can also be used to denote a Christian wife, which is considerably more

---

[28] Adolf von Harnack, *Marcion: Das Evangelium vom fremden Gott: Eine Monographie zur Geschichte der Grundlegung der katholischen Kirche*, Texte und Untersuchungen 45, 2nd edn (Leipzig: J. C. Hinrichs, 1924), 179.

[29] Pliny, *Letters*, 10.96.

probable in this case.[30] We should take care not to idealize the church of martyrs in terms of the equality of masters and slaves, or of men and women. However, a tendency towards a more radical practice of equality is, indeed, to be noted.

This becomes particularly clear in Saturus's dream vision, in which the bishop of the divided Christian community in Carthage asked the martyrs, and in particular Perpetua, for the service of reconciliation. Both male and female martyrs possessed a high, charismatic authority (similar to the male and female prophets), which occasionally came into conflict with episcopal authority, when concerned with the reconciliation of the *lapsi*.

For women, martyrdom from time to time was associated with an additional form of cruelty, since those accused of religious offences could be forced into prostitution.[31] Such experience of sexual abasement may well have contributed to female 'honour' no longer being measured by physical virginity alone, but rather by its spiritualization. This is certainly an example of progress in Christianity against the rigid Roman sexual morality, according to which suicide was preferable to rape.

In prison, Perpetua wrote down her experiences and, more importantly, her dreams – or rather dream visions – until the day of her execution. The tender tone with which Perpetua records her love for her baby is both moving and almost comforting. Felicitas, too, was a pregnant young woman, whose new-born child would be cared for by a fellow Christian woman. Perpetua's dream visions reflected her previous experience of baptism and the impending martyrdom – the animal fight in the arena. In an impressive way, the dreams helped her to come to terms with her fate. But the images of baptism were firstly a struggle with the dragon and then with the Egyptian. In order to conquer him, Perpetua became a man in the dream, if only for a short time. It is not surprising that the woman dreamt this before her martyrdom. It is not the combat metaphor as such that should be queried, but

[30] Cf. Georg Schöllgen, *Ecclesia sordida? Zur Frage der sozialen Schichtung frühchristlicher Gemeinden am Beispiel Karthagos zur Zeit Tertullians* (Münster: Aschendorff, 1984), 248f.

[31] Cf. Friedrich Augar, *Die Frau im römischen Christenprozeß: ein Beitrag zur Verfolgungsgeschichte der christlichen Kirche im römischen Staat*, Texte und Untersuchungen 28 (Leipzig: J. C. Hinrichs, 1905); Jensen, *Gottes selbstbewußte Töchter*, 185–95.

its dominance in the Christian tradition, because this dominance is dangerous not only for women but also for men. In reality, it has occasionally led to a hostile attitude towards life. In Perpetua's dream visions, however, life-affirming counter-images were included throughout.

Marriage and celibacy

The metaphor of combat discussed here was adopted whole-heartedly by the ascetical tradition: men and women followed Christ, the ultimate athlete, as well as male and female martyrs, and they struggled against Satan in the desert not just for forty days, like Christ, but rather for their entire lives. Thus, there seems to be a great danger here of defeminizing women, for there is no lack of references to the ascetical praising of 'male' women.[32] It is doubtful, however, whether this refers to the way in which women see themselves. Alongside the 'Assimilation Model' (virgins are like men), upon which literature expounded greatly, there was also in asceticism the 'Transcendence Model', which was based on equality: men and women strove to overcome their sexuality and to live beyond sex, without, however, giving up their actual sexual identity.[33]

It is doubtlessly one of the most conspicuous trends in women's history during late antiquity, that such a great number of Christian women turned away from marriage and tried out various forms of celibate existence. We know the most about these women, because the ascetical-celibate idea prevailed in the end, although the Pastoral Epistles fought against it and wanted to commit women once again to marriage or remarriage and to the bearing of children. All biographies of women in late antiquity come from the ascetical tradition.

---

[32] Cf., for example, Gregory of Nyssa, *The Life of Macrina*; *The Life of Olympias*; *The Life of Synkletike*, etc. Cf. also Kari Vogt, '"Devenir mâle": Aspect d'une anthropologie chrétienne primitive', *Concilium* 202 (1985), 95–108; eadem, '"Becoming Male": A Gnostic and Early Christian Metaphor', in Kari Elisabeth Børresen, ed., *Image of God and Gender Models in Judaeo-Christian Tradition* (Oslo: Solum, 1991), 172–86; Kerstin Aspegren, *The Male Woman: A Feminine Ideal in the Early Church*, Acta Universitatis Upsaliensis, Uppsala Women's Studies, A. Women in Religion, 4 (Uppsala: Academia Upsaliensis, 1990).

[33] Cf. Jensen, *Gottes selbstbewußte Töchter*, 110ff.

The sources make it terribly difficult to do justice to the other group of women – the wives and the mothers – who were certainly at least as important in the spread of Christianity as the women ascetics. They were often the first to show interest in the new religion and bring its tidings into the home. From the controversy surrounding Jerome, we at least know of Christians such as Helvidius and Jovinian, who called for the parity of married and celibate lifestyles.[34] Presumably, this remained the opinion of the majority, at least in making a practical decision on lifestyle. But abundant propaganda at the time favouring a celibate lifestyle was dominated by the view that virginity was superior to marriage. Again it was women who were particularly affected by this devaluing, since they were seen to a great extent as sexual beings.

There is sometimes a tendency in feminist theological literature to regard virgins and widows collectively as a kind of women's movement or emancipation movement in late antiquity. To a certain extent this is correct, but only provided that married women are not degraded as unemancipated 'housewives' in the process. Roman women lacked political rights; but in the *usus*-marriage which was customary in the Roman Empire, they were not under the *manus* of their husbands, and they had control over their own finances. There is also some evidence in the extant texts that women in no way regarded themselves as subordinate to men. In Proba's adaptation of the story of Eden, which is otherwise true to the Bible, there is no mention of birth pains or subordination.

The aversion of many women (and of many men as well) to marriage in late antiquity was also a widespread tendency outside Christianity, yet nowhere else did women develop and practise a celibate life in the same way. Because of this, even Emperor Julian, as part of his attempt to restore the old Roman religion to its erstwhile rightful place, made efforts to create cloister-like places for men and women following the Christian model.[35] The first women's conflict in the Christian communities flared up over widows who did not want to remarry. They were obviously active

[34] Cf. Jerome, *Against Jovinian*; idem, *Against Helvidius*; David G. Hunter, 'Resistance to the Virginal Ideal in Late-Fourth-Century Rome: The Case of Jovinian', *Theological Studies* 48 (1987), 45–64; Elizabeth A. Clark, 'Theory and Practice in Late Ancient Asceticism: Jerome, Chrysostom, and Augustine', *Journal of Feminist Studies in Religion* 5 (1989), 25–46.

[35] Sozomen, *HE*, 5.16.

in the community, whereas the author of the Pastoral Epistles wanted to restrict them to a secluded life of prayer. The *Didascalia Apostolorum* (3.5–12) bore witness to a similar conflict, where widows again became the object of an extremely debasing polemic. According to the author's wishes, all of these rebellious women should be replaced by a single female deacon, who would be obliged to be most strictly obedient to the bishop.

In the *Apostolic Tradition* 11, also, there are signs of a similar conflict. The instructions regarding widows are not found with those for virgins (who did not receive ordination), but rather are to be found after those for the presbyters and deacons, and for the confessors, who had the same rank. However, the author refused ordination for widows. He polemicized against women who were supposedly incapable of abstinence and listed many things that widows should not do. They should only pray. An order with such restrictive clauses would hardly have been necessary if the widows had not already been carrying out completely different duties, which in the East eventually led to official recognition through the ordination of women deacons. There are many churches in which widows had these duties and were also ordained for them.[36] Once again, then, we have an example of women in the West being more severely restricted than they were in the East.

Yet women chose both lifestyles, that of the ascetic and that of social involvement. The two were not automatically linked. However, community ministry was later often tied to life in an ascetical community. If women decided in favour of an ascetical lifestyle, they could choose between the loneliness of the desert and the common life of a group of like-minded people. Alternatively, they could simply stay with their families – which they sometimes reconfigured into ascetical communities – or live alone in their own houses.

Furthermore, it is remarkable that many women lived a 'spiritual marriage' in sexual abstinence, possibly with their own husbands, but above all as virgins of the church or autonomous women

---

[36] Cf. especially *Testamentum Domini*, 1.40–3. See also Bonnie Bowman Thurston, *The Widows: A Women's Ministry in the Early Church* (Minneapolis: Fortress Press, 1989); Ute E. Eisen, *Amtsträgerinnen im frühen Christentum, Epigraphische und literarische Studien* (Göttingen: Vandenhoeck & Ruprecht, 1996).

ascetics with a male ascetic cleric. The denial of sexuality, then, was primarily a denial of fertility and progeny, since these would once again inevitably have entangled the parents in worldly life. As time passed people increasingly challenged this form of coexistence. The phenomenon of female ascetism cannot be reduced to a common denominator, but it was the achievement of the early Christian women to have broken through the one-sided determination of their lives by marriage and motherhood.

Between world-rejection and world-affirmation

In fourth-century and fifth-century Rome, it was not difficult to name women who embodied the ascetical ideal.[37] Two of the best known were Melania the Elder, a friend of Rufinus, who was widowed at the age of twenty-two, and her granddaughter, Melania the Younger, of whose life we have a *Vita*.[38] This biography sheds light on the real circumstances of choosing abstinence, and how this came to affect a young couple. Melania married Pinian when she was fourteen and he was seventeen. By this time, she was already insistent on renouncing sex; in compensation she offered Pinian her immense wealth. Yet Pinian hesitated: he only wanted to practise abstinence after they had had two children who could inherit their possessions. Soon afterwards they had a daughter, whom they immediately dedicated to virginity. In her second pregnancy, Melania's life was threatened by a premature birth, and the child died soon after birth. Shocked by these events, Pinian consented to the 'angelic life', which they led from then on. It is remarkable that Melania occasionally appears as the spiritual mother of her 'brother'.

The second act of their ascetical life together consisted of the disposal of their worldly goods, some of which they gave to the poor, naturally in the face of considerable familial protest. At

[37] Cf. Anne Ewing Hickey, *Women of the Roman Aristocracy as Christian Monastics*, Studies in Religion 1 (Ann Arbor: UMI Research Press, 1987); Griet Petersen-Szemerédy, *Zwischen Weltstadt und Wüste: Römische Asketinnen in der Spätantike*, Forschungen zur Kirchen und Dogmengeschichte 54 (Göttingen: Vandenhoeck & Ruprecht, 1993); Christa Krumeich, *Hieronymus und die christlichen feminae clarissimae* (Bonn: R. Habelt, 1993).

[38] Cf. the fully annotated translation by Elizabeth A. Clark, *The Life of Melanie the Younger*, Studies in Women and Religion 14 (New York: Edwin Mellen Press, 1984).

the same time, they devoted much of their energy to looking after the poor and sick. If social engagement were not the primary motive for ascetical life, it does appear from the evidence that it was indeed an important factor in individual as well as communitarian ascetical life. When Alaric entered Rome, Melania and Pinian had already gone to Africa, and they remained in Thagaste for seven years. As in many other places, they founded and financed two large cloisters there (one for eighty monks and one for one hundred and thirty virgins), and it is very clear that Melania won over great numbers of young men and women to the ascetical lifestyle. After seven years they both departed for Jerusalem, and except for a few journeys (to visit the ascetics in Egypt and to Constantinople) they remained in the Holy Land for the rest of their lives. Once again Melania founded a cloister (for which Pinian was charged with 'gathering up' ninety virgins) and she joined the community herself this time, without being their leader. She did, however, manage to interfere in her own way.

In seeking to concentrate on *Western* Christianity in this paper, I find that many of the ascetical Roman women present us with a particular problem: they left the West and settled in the East. This was the case for Melania the Elder, who in AD 372 was the first aristocratic Roman woman to choose the path of asceticism, firstly in the Egyptian desert and later in a cloister of fifty virgins which she had founded in Jerusalem. She was at work there with Rufinus, who had likewise founded a cloister in the area. Paula, the friend of Jerome, did the same. She was a widowed mother of five children when she began her ascetical life in AD 378. In AD 385, she and her daughter, Eustochium, left for Palestine, never to return.

The confusion brought about by the migration of the peoples might have contributed to this emigration, but it does not appear that women such as Melania were greatly concerned to retain Roman customs or introduce them into the ascetical way of life.[39] We come across a similar phenomenon in the pilgrimage of Egeria, who did not remain in the Holy Land but did, as it were, go to school there, not only to gain a better understanding of the Bible but also to visit the ascetical sites. It is thanks to her that we have a description of the great Thecla shrine in Seleucia, and she mentions, almost in passing, that her friend, the deacon Marthana,

---

[39] Cf. Clark, *Life of Melania*, 119–29.

was in charge of both male and female cloisters.[40] All of the women named, therefore, were, like the men of their time, heavily engaged in the transfer of spiritual ideas from East to West.

Yet not all female ascetics went to the East. Some remained, according to Jerome, to build a new Jerusalem in Rome.[41] Among them was Marcella, who was the first upper-class Roman woman to dare to break with all conventions and live an ascetical life in the city itself.[42] She gathered many like-minded women around her in the process, women who did not, however, live together in a fixed community. One point must be emphasized: Marcella led a life of *moderate* fasting and moderate forms of prayer. Another of her particular characteristics was her intense scholarly interest in biblical interpretation, which brought her into contact with Jerome. This direction of intellectual resources upon the study of the Scriptures was also characteristic of Melania the Younger and Egeria. We know that Marcella had 'become the leading exegetical authority in Rome'.[43] Furthermore, she was the driving force behind the condemnation of Origenism in the disputes within the city of Rome. I will not comment on whether the fixation on the Bible and the struggle against 'heretics' could also be viewed as unfortunate developments. In any event, the person of Marcella commands great respect. 'One should not forget Marcella when naming Benedict of Nursia as the founder of occidental monasticism',[44] for much of the wise *discretio* of his *regula monachorum* – which were to have a lasting effect on the West – can be found in the lifestyle she practised.

Faltonia Betitia Proba – theologian and poet

Faltonia Betitia Proba represents a quite different paradigm of Christian existence. She is the only Christian woman of late

[40] Egeria, *Pilgrimage* 23, 1–5.
[41] Jerome, *Letters*, 127.8.
[42] Jerome, *To the Virgin Principia on the Life of the Holy Marcella* (*Letter* 127); Karin Sugano, 'Marcella in Rom: ein Lebensbild', in Michael Wissemann, ed., *Roma renascens: Beiträge zur Spätantike und Rezeptionsgeschichte. Festschrift für Ilona Opelt* (Frankfurt/New York: Peter Lang, 1988), 355–70; Silvia Letsch-Brunner, *Marcella – discipula et magistra: auf den Spuren einer römischen Christin des 4. Jahrhunderts* (Berlin: Walter de Gruyter, 1998).
[43] Sugano, 'Marcella in Rom', 364.
[44] Ibid., 368, n. 36.

antiquity from whom a theological work has remained completely preserved.[45] I wish to conclude my paper by discussing her and her Virgilian *Cento de Christo*, for she created a synthesis between the spiritual tradition of Rome and the biblical message which remains unsurpassed. At the same time, Proba was a counterfigure to the many male and female ascetics of her time, a witness for a Christianity which held a positive attitude to the world and celebrated life. She was obviously happily married, a mother of three sons (the natural mother of two), and her entire work exudes a positive view of all facets of earthly existence. However, further details of her biography are not known. She must have died before her husband, Adelphius (†AD 379), as the epitaph for his *'uxori incomparabili'* remains intact.

We detect the theological author Proba (along with an entire circle of like-minded men and women) in a section of a letter from Jerome, in which he railed against three things: (1) against men who learned from women; (2) against the authors of centos on biblical material; (3) against those who 'made Virgil into a Christian without Christ'.[46] Paulinus of Nola, the recipient of the letter, was not impressed by that, and continued to write in hexameters. But the later *Decretum Gelasianum*, which often refers to Jerome, grouped the 'Virgilian Christ Cento' with the apocrypha – without mentioning Proba's name, which Jerome, too, had avoided. This curious condemnation, which did not prevent Isidore

---

[45] Elizabeth A. Clark and Diane F. Hatch, eds, *The Golden Bough, the Oaken Cross: The Virgilian Cento of Faltonia Betitia Proba*, American Academy of Religion, Texts and Translations Series 5 (Chico: Scholars Press, 1981); G. Ronald Kastner, Ann Millin, Jeremiah Reedy, 'Proba', in Kastner, *A Lost Tradition*, 33–69. Elizabeth A. Clark, 'Faltonia Betitia Proba and Her Virgilian Poem: The Christian Matron as Artist', in eadem, ed., *Ascetic Piety and Women's Faith*, Studies in Women and Religion 20 (Lewiston: Edwin Mellen Press, 1986), 124–52; Elizabeth A. Clark and Diane F. Hatch, 'Jesus as Hero in the Virgilian Cento of Faltonia Betitia Proba', op. cit. 153–71; Anne Jensen, 'Faltonia Betitia Proba – eine Kirchenlehrerin der Spätantike', in Herlinde Pissarek-Hudelist and Luise Schottroff, eds, *Mit allen Sinnen glauben: feministische Theologie unterwegs* (Gütersloh: Gerd Mohn, 1991), 84–94; Anne Jensen, 'Prophetin, Poetin, Kirchenmutter: Das theologische Werk von Faltonia Betitia Proba (Rom, 4. Jh.)', *Frauen Gestalten Geschichte* (Frankfurt: Lutherisches Verlagshaus, 1998), 33–53.

[46] Jerome, *Letters*, 53:7.

THE ORIGINS OF CHRISTENDOM IN THE WEST

of Seville from including Proba as the only woman among the *viros ecclesiasticos*,[47] need not concern us here. Rather, we can be pleased to confirm that this Latin work was also received in the East: Emperor Arcadius (AD 395–408) had a copy made for himself.

The copier's proem uses the frequently quoted expression of the 'improved Virgil' (*Maronem mutatum in Melius* – 3f.) to characterize Proba's work. However, it is not appropriate to the entire work and it devalues the Roman author. In contrast, Proba wrote that Virgil 'sang the praises of Christ's good works' (*Vergilium cecinisse loquar pia munera Christi* – 23), and through his verses this should once again occur in the '*carmen sacrum*' (9) of the Christian woman prophet: '*Proba vatis*' (12) – as she called herself. Everything that the 'old people' had praised, whether they belonged to the Jewish people or the Roman Empire, was to be placed for better or for worse on the same level, in view of the 'new' represented by Christ. 'The old' – for Proba this was above all war (319–33); the 'new', in contrast, was the anticipated, everlasting kingdom of peace. For Proba, the legendary founding of the Roman Empire by the Trojan hero and demigod Aeneas, which Virgil praised, was the *typos* of the kingdom of God brought about by Jesus. And Aeneas, the epitome of the *pietas* in his love for his father, was himself a *typos* of the Saviour sent by God. Both had a divine mission, both were tempted, both descended into the realm of the dead, both carried out their task despite all difficulties. Proba puts the following sentence, with which Anchises greeted his son in the underworld, into the mouth of the resurrected Christ: *Vicit iter durum pietas* (664).

Indeed this typological interpretation of the Roman epic was a considerable theological achievement. It is almost more impressive that Proba succeeded in expressing the Christian ideas of the Trinity and the incarnation of God in the language of gods and goddesses: for example, the ceremonial salutation in the Christ doxology *Nate patris summi* (32) was spoken in Virgil by Juno. Women (and men) like Proba are to be thanked for making many aspects of the old religion – which we should not dismiss as 'heathenism' – productive again in the new religion. For the divine was not only represented by the biblical Yahweh but by the hellenistic pantheon

<hr>

[47] Isidore of Seville, *Of Famous Men* V, ed. Carmen Codoñer Merino (Salamanca: Colegio Trilingue de la Universidad, 1964).

as well. And the Christian theology of incarnation was barely conceivable without the Greek theology.

In both of the old religions, Proba was able to take up an orientation towards the life in this world in contrast to the ascetical tradition of her time. In her epic of salvation, she integrated the stories of creation and salvation, the former peaking in a small, enchanting love-scene in paradise with the blessing *Vivite felices* (139). Corresponding with this beginning was the morning of the resurrection, with creation flourishing anew and Christ's urgent message of peace (675f.). Proba described Mary as a gentle and, at the same time, wise mother, who predicted the murder of the infants in Bethlehem and therefore organized her family's escape (372–9).

The characterization of Christian discipleship also shows that the old Roman ideals concerning the family continue to be valid for the author of the cento. As an example of this, she did not choose one of the famous scenes of calling, but rather the encounter with the rich young man (505–30). And here she not only left something out (such as subordination and birth pains in the story of Eden); but she also changed the text: the young man was not asked to leave everything, but rather to support the poor. This story, therefore, stressed the chasteness (*pudicitia*) which should govern his house, for he was thought of as the father of a family. One can certainly argue over whether we are dealing here with a watering-down of the gospel or a realistic reinterpretation of a utopian appeal. Whichever, this was certainly a clear counter-position to the ascetical world-view.

It also seems liberating that sexuality and love were without exception positive for Proba. The story of the temptation had no erotic connotations whatsoever for her, but rather both Eve and Adam were led to fall by the desire for power. Although Eve was seen to be far more active in this than Adam, both bore the same responsibility and suffered the same fate.

If the vision of a Christian kingdom was the key to all understanding in Proba's cento, then we again encounter the close connection between Eastern and Western – that is to say Greek and Latin – theology. For the idea of the kingdom came to characterize the Byzantine tradition, while, in the Western investiture controversy, church and state ended up opposed to each other. Here, too, Proba seems to me to represent a Christianity which had not yet divided into East and West.

Conclusion

It is not possible at this point to discuss this material further. I would like to have addressed some further aspects of female apostlehood, aspects which I would at least like to name: the 'Mission through Charity' is of great importance and was to a great extent, though by no means exclusively, performed by women. No doubt one of the strengths of Christianity up to the present lies in its social engagement. I have not considered the 'indirect mission', that is women's exertion of influence on their husbands and children, especially in religious education. Due to the state of the sources, though, it is very difficult to identify this specific form of theological culture, which Jacques Delumeau has named *la religion de ma mère*. The influence of Christian empresses should also be examined. Finally, I would like to have examined the role of those women, who, in the 'no-man's-land' between late antiquity and the Middle Ages, receive little attention, although they had been of great importance to the West: the women in the mission of Irish-Scottish monasticism such as Brigid of Kildare. But I have restricted myself to the Graeco-Roman sphere.

In summary, then, there is only a little material extant on the activities of women in early Christianity. The little that there is, though, is enough to demonstrate that they were active participants in the spread of Christianity, not only in missionary preaching and catechesis, but also – and perhaps above all – in the shaping of the culture out of which the Christian West emerged.

PART THREE

Liturgy and Christian Formation in the Advent of Christendom

Chapter 8

Catechesis and Initiation

EVERETT FERGUSON

Catechesis was central to the initiation of new Christians in the early centuries of Christianity. In the pre-Constantinian writers, evidence about the content of catechesis is sketchy. But Justin indicates that in mid-second-century Rome training in Christian lifestyle was as important as the teaching of doctrine. In Gaul a few years later, Irenaeus shows that an emphasis upon moral training in the Sermon on the Mount tradition was still strong, but evidently less prominent than doctrinal instruction. Cyprian's *Testimonia* demonstrate his concern in mid-third-century Carthage to establish a biblical basis for historical, doctrinal and moral instruction. In the large and rapidly growing church of the fourth and early fifth centuries, the evidence for catechesis becomes much fuller, and its focus appears to have altered somewhat. Cyril in Jerusalem concentrated on giving an exposition of the creed, with a post-baptismal emphasis upon mystagogy; moral instruction was present, but was incidental to instruction in orthodox doctrine. In Milan, Ambrose's catechesis similarly concentrated on doctrine and mystagogy; his homilies instructing catechumens in Christian lifestyle were based especially on Old Testament materials – the proverbs and the examples of the patriarchs. Augustine's many catechetical materials covered the entire span of the catechumenate and dealt with matters of doctrine, prayer and morals in eschatological perspective; the balance of materials was tilted towards doctrine, although Augustine was concerned that the new Christians in North Africa live lives of sexual chastity.

Lewis Rambo in his book *Understanding Religious Conversion*[1] identifies seven overlapping stages, or I might call them components or aspects, of conversion. These are context, crisis, quest (or search), encounter, interaction, commitment, and consequences. Of these stages, interaction describes the catechumenate of the ancient church. The goal of interaction between the potential convert and the group to which he or she is being converted is encapsulation.[2] The sphere of influence created by encapsulation involves four dimensions, according to Rambo: relationships, rituals, rhetoric, and roles.[3] The relationships that 'create and consolidate emotional bonds to the group and establish the day-by-day reality of the new perspective'[4] remind us of the sponsors, who introduced to the teachers those who came 'to hear the word' and who 'bore witness' to their readiness to be instructed.[5] Rituals would have included such practices as the teacher's prayer and laying on of hands in blessing;[6] exorcism, which dramatized the process of a change of realms in which the convert lived;[7] and fasting.[8] By rhetoric, Rambo means 'the language of transformation' that the new convert is taught; in the ancient church this was done by attendance at services of the word and instruction over a period of time,[9] and to this practice we shall return shortly. Roles, the enactment of the activities associated with the new life, included in the practice of the ancient church such items as prayer, renouncing Satan, and reciting the creed.[10] Rambo discusses Christian baptism as an example of commitment, and he includes in commitment

[1] Lewis R. Rambo, *Understanding Religious Conversion* (New Haven and London: Yale University Press, 1993).

[2] Ibid., 103–8.

[3] Ibid., 107–23.

[4] Ibid., 197.

[5] *Apostolic Tradition*, 16 (Gregory Dix, *The Treatise on the Apostolic Tradition of St Hippolytus of Rome*, 2nd edn [London: SPCK, 1968]), 23. In spite of the doubts about the authorship of this treatise (see n. 16), it remains a valuable source for what was done by some in the early third century.

[6] *Apostolic Tradition*, 19.

[7] *Apostolic Tradition*, 20.3–4, 8; Thomas Finn, 'Ritual Processes and the Survival of Early Christianity: A Study of the Apostolic Tradition of Hippolytus', *Journal of Ritual Studies* 3 (1989), 69–90.

[8] *Apostolic Tradition*, 20.8.

[9] Ibid., 17; 20.2.

[10] Ibid., 18.1 (prayer by the catechumens), 21.9 (renunciation of Satan), 21.12–18 (profession of faith).

adopting the story of a group as one's own,[11] but he does not discuss the early church's catechetical practices. This is the aspect of conversion, namely its rhetoric, that I want to consider.

What instruction did the early church, especially in the West, consider important to give to new converts? My purpose is to answer the question, What was taught to catechumens? Or, more broadly, how was the convert 'formed' into a Christian? 'Christian formation' certainly included ceremonies, actions, and practices as well as words, but the limitation to teachings is still quite ambitious.

Changes in emphasis may tell us something about both the changing circumstances of the church and changing understandings about Christianity itself. Conclusions must be drawn cautiously because we must allow for accidents of preservation. There is something capricious about what was preserved, but that is what we have to deal with. Moreover, preservation was not wholly capricious. Not only must we work with what we have, and for the fourth and fifth centuries that is rather considerable, but also we must assume that one factor in what was preserved was recognition by some persons that the contents of a document were important.

Therefore, I propose to take seriously what remains from the past. As historians we lament the fact of destroyed and lost source material. We speculate about what it would tell us. But also, there is a reason why we have many of the things we do. Contemporaries thought they were worth saving. That in itself tells us what they thought was important. Sometimes that favourable decision was made by later centuries and so may tell us more about the later century than an author's own time. Yet for the later century to transmit the material, it had to have been preserved to that day. So, with due allowance made for arbitrary and accidental features in the transmission, I conclude that what we have tells us something about what was important in a given period. That permits us in turn to make some tentative inferences concerning the thinking and concerns of people.

An observation on terminology is perhaps worth making at the outset.[12] The early church had a verb for giving instruction

---

[11] Rambo, *Understanding Religious Conversion*, 127–9, 138.

[12] André Turck, '*Catéchein* et *catéchèsis* chez les premiers Pères', *Revue des Sciences philosophiques et théologiques* 47 (1963), 361–72.

(*katēcheō*), a noun for the instruction itself (*katēchēsis*), a noun for the teacher (*katēchetēs*), the participle as a technical term for the one being instructed (*katēchoumenos*), and eventually a noun for the place where the instruction occurred (*katēchoumenion* or *katēchoumenon*). There was no word, however, for catechism. Greek did not create a word for it from the *katēch*-root.[13] Ecclesiastical Latin borrowed the Greek terminology, and in addition did create the word *catechismus*. Initially it had the same meaning as *catechesis*, the act of teaching, and not a formalized content. The first occurrences of *catechismus* are in Augustine.[14] Perhaps I am making too much of the late occurrence of the word and then only in Latin, but I find it corroborative of the fact that there was no fixed content to the instruction. Certainly there were common themes and subject matter, and the 'Rule of Faith' and eventually the baptismal creeds provided an outline of doctrinal instruction for many catechists, but there was no fixed catechism such as emerged in the Medieval and Reformation churches. Hence, I have chosen the word 'catechesis' for my title instead of 'catechism'.

Because of the limitation of my subject to the content of instruction to new converts, I omit the *Apostolic Tradition* from my survey, since it does not discuss the content of instruction during the three-year catechumenate it provides for.[15] There have been recently revived doubts about the title *Apostolic Tradition* and its

[13] A search of the Thesaurus Linguae Graecae reveals no occurrences of *katēchismos* or *katēchesmos*. Nor is such a word to be found in the lexica of H. G. Liddell and R. Scott, *Greek–English Lexicon* (Oxford: Clarendon Press, 1940), with *Supplement* (1968); G. W. H. Lampe, *A Patristic Greek Lexicon* (Oxford: Clarendon Press, 1968); E. A. Sophocles, *Greek Lexicon of the Roman and Byzantine Periods* (New York: Ungar, 1870); and D. Demetrakou, *Mega lexikon, oles tes Ellenikes glosses* [Greek] (Athens: Dome, 1964).
[14] The CETEDOC Library of Christian Latin Texts reveals none before Augustine, and lists four from him, all from *On Faith and Works*: 9.14 'those things to be said in catechizing'; 18.33 'rigorously disciplined by inculcation of precepts and catechizings'; and 19.35 'in the catechizings of candidates for baptism' are clearly the act of catechizing; 13.19 inclines more toward the content, referring to 'all the teachings'.
[15] The *Apostolic Tradition* does stress the moral qualifications for admission to the catechumenate (chs 16, 17, 20) and implies scriptural (chs 20, 35), doctrinal (chs 21; cf. 23.13 – 'you have already been instructed concerning the resurrection'), and liturgical (chs 23, 32) teaching.

attribution to Hippolytus of Rome as part of the observation that the work represents the genre of living institutional literature in the ancient church.[16] These doubts do not remove the importance of the work for the development of the catechumenate.[17] In this regard, we will refer to it once more in our conclusion.

Justin Martyr: training to live in a distinctive community

Justin Martyr, although coming from Palestine and converted in the East, is arguably our first witness to Christian initiatory practice in the West, since he spent his later years in Rome and did his writing there.[18] He, as the other apologists, was concerned to define

[16] Marcel Metzger, 'Nouvelles perspectives pour la prétendue *Tradition apostolique*', *Ecclesia Orans* 5 (1988), 241–59; idem, 'Enquêtes autour de la prétendue "*Tradition apostolique*"', *Ecclesia Orans* 9 (1992), 7–36. L. Edward Phillips, 'Hippolytus and the So-Called "Apostolic Tradition": Evidence for Authorship Reconsidered', a paper presented to the North American Patristic Society, Chicago, 30 May 1996, reported support for a connection with Hippolytus based on the appearance of phrases in the *Apostolic Tradition* that occur also in other works attributed to Hippolytus but not elsewhere (or rarely) in the first four centuries.

[17] For book-length surveys of the content of catechetical instruction, see André Turck, *Évangelisation et catéchèse aux deux premiers siècles* (Paris: Cerf, 1962) and Jean Daniélou with Régine du Charlat, *La catéchèse aux premiers siècles* (Fayard-Mame: Institut superieur de pastorale catéchétique, 1968); older points of departure for study include G. Bareille, 'Catéchèse', *Dictionnaire de Théologie Catholique*, ed. A. Vacant and E. Mangenot (Paris: 1905) 2, cols 1877–95, and H. Leclercq, 'Catéchèse, Catéchisme, Catéchumène', *Dictionnaire d'archéologie chrétienne et de liturgie* (Paris: Letouzey et Ané, 1925) 2, cols 2530–79. For the catechumenate itself, a brief overview is by Michel Dujarier, *A History of the Catechumenate: The First Six Centuries* (New York: Sadlier, 1979); still standard is P. de Puniet, 'Catéchuménat', *Dictionnaire d'archéologie chrétienne et de liturgie*, 2, cols 2579–621; cf. Th. Maertens, *Histoire et pastorale du rituel du catéchuménat et du Baptême* (Bruges: Biblica, 1962), esp. ch. 3; still useful, covering both the stages and the instructions given, is Lawrence D. Folkemer, 'A Study of the Catechumenate', *Church History* 15 (1946), 286–307, reprinted in E. Ferguson, *Studies in Early Christianity* 11: *Conversion, Cathechumenate, and Baptism in the Early Church* (New York: Garland, 1993), 244–65; bringing new material and perspectives is R. M. Grant, 'Development of the Christian Catechumenate', in *Made, Not Born: New Perspectives on Christian Initiation and the Catechumenate* (Notre Dame: University of Notre Dame Press, 1976), 32–49.

[18] For introductions to Justin, see L. W. Barnard, *Justin Martyr: His Life and Thought* (Cambridge: Cambridge University Press, 1967); E. F. Osborn, *Justin Martyr* (Tübingen: Mohr-Siebeck, 1973).

the Christian community over against both the pagan world and Judaism. The *Acts of Justin* give some information of Justin's teaching activities in Rome: 'Anyone who wished could come to my abode and I would impart to him the words of truth.'[19] The prefect who examined Justin and his companions thought Justin converted them, but the answers by the students indicate that Justin was teaching those already Christians. Justin may have engaged in evangelistic and catechetical work as well as more advanced instruction, for catechesis and apologetics have much in common. He does give us information about conversion and how one became a Christian.

Justin explained to his intended imperial readership 'how we dedicated ourselves to God and were made new through Christ'. 'As many as are persuaded and believe that the things taught and said by us are true and promise to be able to live accordingly' pray and fast in preparation for their baptism. He continues with another twofold statement about faith and life: the person baptized is 'one who chooses to be regenerated and who repents of his sins'.[20] Later he speaks of the one baptized as the one 'who has been persuaded and agreed entirely with our teachings' (1 *Apol.*, 65.1). The eucharist is for 'the one who believes the things which have been taught by us to be true, and was washed with the washing for the remission of sins and for regeneration, and lives in the manner Christ taught' (1 *Apol.*, 66.1). It is evident that for Justin faith, baptism, and conduct belong together. These statements may look back to the New Testament requirements of faith and repentance accompanying baptism[21] or forward to catechetical instruction in faith (doctrine) and morals; or Justin may be seen as linking both.[22]

---

[19] *Acts of Justin*, A 3.3; H. Musurillo, *The Acts of the Christian Martyrs* (Oxford: Clarendon Press, 1972), 45.

[20] Justin Martyr, 1 *Apol.*, 61.2, 10. Cf. the summary of Justin's evidence for practice in Rome before the introduction of a more formal catechumenate at the end of the second century by D. B. Capelle, 'L'introduction du catéchuménat à Rome', *Recherches de Théologie ancienne et médiévale* 5 (1933), 131–3.

[21] Acts 2:38; 18:8.

[22] Justin's characterization of the instruction prior to baptism as concerning faith and life is matched in the accounts found in the Apocryphal Acts – André Turck, 'Aux origines du catéchuménat', *Revue des sciences philosophiques et théologiques* 48 (1964), 24–6.

What Justin meant by the teachings about things to be believed
and about how to live may be reflected earlier in his *First Apology*.
Accepting an obligation to 'furnish an account of [Christian]
life and doctrine', Justin sets as his task to make possible for all to
examine 'our life and teachings' (1 *Apol.*, 3.2, 4). As a summary
of Christian doctrine, Justin refers to Christians offering the
worship of 'prayer and thanksgiving', 'ceremonies and hymns' to
the 'Creator of the universe'. 'Our teacher . . . is Jesus Christ, who
was crucified under Pontius Pilate, the governor of Judea in the
time of Tiberius Caesar. Having learned that he is the Son of the
true God, we will show that with reason we honour him, holding
him in the second place, and also the prophetic Spirit in the third
rank' (1 *Apol.*, 13).[23] Justin permits us to see the principal points
in teaching to pagans: condemnation of idolatry; unity of God;
existence of Father, Son, and Holy Spirit; creation; proof of the
divinity of Christ – Son of God, incarnate, crucified, and raised;
and eternal recompense.[24]

In addition to the brief summary of the *kerygma* about Christ
inserted into the doctrinal statement in *First Apology* 13, Justin
gives another brief reference in chapter 61 and a more extensive
account in chapter 31.[25] Moreover, it has been pointed out that
Justin arranges the heathen analogies to Christ according to the
items of the *kerygma* in chapters 21 and 22.[26] Similarly the
prophecies of Christ, with interruptions, are constructed according
to the *kerygma* in chapters 32–5, 40, 41, 45 and 47–53.[27]

Justin gives more attention at the beginning of his apology to
the teachings about Christian conduct, because he was concerned
to rebut charges of Christian immorality. The summary of
Christian doctrine in *First Apology* 13 is followed by a description
of the changed life by converts in chapter 14 and a detailing of the
moral teachings of Christ in chapters 15–17. These teachings cover

[23] Other trinitarian statements of Christian belief occur in 1 *Apol.*, 6 and in
connection with baptism in 61 (twice) and with prayer in 65 and 67.
[24] Bareille, 'Catéchèse', col. 1880.
[25] Kerygmatic statements are also found in Justin's *Dialogue with Trypho*,
30.3; 63.1; 132.1.
[26] R. Way-Rider, 'Justin Martyr's Use of Some Pagan and Jewish Material',
an unpublished paper read at the Seventh International Conference on Patristic
Studies, Oxford, 10 September 1975.
[27] As is done by Irenaeus in his *Demonstration of the Apostolic Preaching*.

chastity (*sophrosune*), love for all, giving to the needy, patience, not swearing oaths, and paying taxes.[28] This use of moral teaching in the instruction of converts preparatory to baptism may be fleshed out further from the 'Two Ways' in *Didache* 1–6, a document with which Justin otherwise seems to be familiar.[29] The moral teachings in Justin's account are followed by an eschatological sanction (chapters 18 and 19).

The Christian life served as an important part of the argument by second-century apologists, both to counter slanders against Christians and also to give a positive proof on the divine origin of Christian teaching.[30] Christ himself was the connection between doctrine and life, for he was both the object of worship as the Son of God and was the teacher of Christian conduct.[31]

The two subjects of doctrine and morals continued to be central to Christian catechetical instruction. This subject matter is related to a larger frame of reference in Irenaeus's *Demonstration of the Apostolic Preaching*.

Irenaeus: training to live in a community in the history of salvation

Beginning with Irenaeus, the authors of catechetical works in this survey are all bishops. Irenaeus was concerned to define orthodox

---

[28] The quotations from the teaching of Jesus are drawn primarily from the traditions found in the Sermon on the Mount/Plain in Matthew 5–7 and Luke 6. I have shown in 'Love of Enemies and Non-Retaliation in the Second Century', in Rodney L. Peterson and Calvin Augustine Pater, eds, *The Contentious Triangle: Church, State, and University: A Festschrift in Honor of George Huntston Williams* (Kirksville: Thomas Jefferson University Press, 1999), 81–95, the use of this material in the instruction of new converts (especially in the *Didache*).

[29] M. A. Smith, 'Did Justin Know the Didache?' *Studia Patristica* 7 (= Texte und Untersuchungen 92 [1966]), 287–90 discusses only the liturgical parallels, many of which were common Christian material. For the continued use of the *Didache* in catechesis, cf. Athanasius, *Festal Letters*, 39. For the use of the 'Two Ways' in catechesis, see A. Turck, *Évangélisation et Catéchèse*, 23–48, who concludes that the theme of two ways was current in catechesis but that it was not specifically a baptismal catechesis, and J. Daniélou, *La catéchèse*, 127–30, who describes it as the preponderant but not the only element in ancient moral catechesis.

[30] See my *Early Christians Speak*, 3rd edn (Abilene: ACU Press, 1999), 189–202.

[31] Justin Martyr, 1 *Apol.*, 13.3; 23.2.

Christianity over against various heresies, especially those of the Marcionites and Gnostics.[32] In order to do this he stresses the unity of God, the unity of the Lord Jesus Christ, and the unity of the plan of salvation. The new covenant in Christ is superior to God's earlier covenants with people, but is in continuity with them.[33] Irenaeus's favourite word for the plan of salvation is 'economy'.[34] His *Demonstration of the Apostolic Preaching* sets forth this unified view of Christian teaching as based on one continuous history of God's saving acts.

I have argued that the *Demonstration of the Apostolic Preaching* was catechetical, not apologetic, in purpose and was perhaps indeed written as a guide for catechists.[35] Among the catechetical motifs are the possible technical reference to 'hearers' ('those who wish to hear' – ch. 1), the use of the imagery of the two ways (ch. 1), and the association of the teaching with baptism (ch. 3). Hence, I would suggest that the title could be translated 'Presentation of the Apostolic Preaching'. In this work Irenaeus repeats the emphasis on doctrine and morals. He puts 'truth in the soul' and 'holiness in the body' together at the beginning of the treatise (ch. 2). Chapter 3 gives as twin emphases the keeping of 'the rule of faith' and carrying out 'the commands of God'. 'Our faith', he says, provides a 'way of life' (ch. 6). 'The preaching of the truth' and 'good works and sound moral character' come together again at the end of the treatise (ch. 98). Faith in God and love for neighbour recur in combination (chs 41, 87, 95).

[32] For introductions to Irenaeus, see André Benoit, *Saint Irénée: Introduction a l'étude de sa théologie* (Paris: Presses Universitaires de France, 1960) and D. Minns, *Irenaeus* (Washington, DC: Georgetown University Press, 1994).

[33] E. Ferguson, 'The Covenant Idea in the Second Century', in W. Eugene March, ed., *Texts and Testaments: Critical Studies on the Bible and Early Church Fathers* (San Antonio: Trinity University Press, 1980), 135–62 (144–8 on Irenaeus).

[34] J. Barthoulot, trans., *La prédication des apôtres et ses preuves ou La foi chrétienne* (Paris: Desclée de Brouwer, 1977), 24.

[35] 'Irenaeus' *Proof of the Apostolic Preaching* and Early Catechetical Instruction', *Studia Patristica* 18.3 (1989), 119–40, *contra* the conclusion of Joseph P. Smith, whose translation I use: *St Irenaeus: Proof of the Apostolic Preaching*, Ancient Christian Writers 16 (New York: Newman, 1952), 20. If Smith's translation, 'those who look after the salvation of souls', in ch. 1 is correct (see his n. 6, p. 132), this could be a confirmation that the work is intended for catechists.

The distinctive feature of the *Demonstration of the Apostolic Preaching* is that faith and morals are integrated into a historical framework. The introduction is a doctrinal/creedal summary (chs 1–6). The last section is a moral/practical application (chs 87–98). The largest part of the work is the telling of the history of salvation from creation to judgement. This biblical/historical body of the work functions on two levels: a historical narrative followed by the meaning of the history. The latter is Christological. Prophecies in the Old Testament are arranged according to the story of Christ.[36] Some of the distinctive concerns of Irenaeus are shown in his assertion that the prophecies in Deuteronomy were 'written about our Lord Jesus Christ and about the people and about the calling of the Gentiles and about the kingdom' (ch. 28). I rather think this biblical storyline was more central in early Christian teaching and preaching than is often realized,[37] appearing in other places than where it is as explicit as it is in Irenaeus.

The trinitarian ordering of the doctrinal statements appears to be a secondary imposition on the material, not consistently carried through. I gather from Irenaeus's references that the trinitarian structure of the instruction derives from the baptismal formula (chs 3, 7, 100). The 'rule of faith' (ch. 3; cf. ch. 6) is not a creed but the whole of the doctrinal content of Christian faith which the church teaches.[38] The christological centre is shown by the way in which the Spirit is treated as especially active in the prophets who foretold Christ (chs 6, 30, 49).[39]

Salvation, according to Irenaeus, is received not by the law but by faith and love, and love is defined by the two commandments

[36] See also Justin, *Dialogue with Trypho*; Cyprian, *Testimonies* (below); and Psuedo-Epiphanius, *Testimony Book*.

[37] Jean Daniélou, 'L'histoire du salut dans la catéchèse', *La Maison-Dieu* 30 (1952), 19–35 made it central; in his 'La catéchèse dans la tradition patristique', *Catéchèse* 1 (1960–1), 21–34 [reproduced in A. Hamman, ed., *L'initiation chrétienne* (Paris: B. Grasset, 1963), 7–20] he classified catechesis as biblical, dogmatic and sacramental (p. 26); but then he omitted the biblical-historical from his classification of the types of catechesis (dogmatic, moral and sacramental) in *La catéchèse*. J. Lupi, 'Catechetical Instruction in the Church of the First Two Centuries', *Melita Theologica* 9 (1956), 64 combined the items into four: historical, moral, dogmatic and liturgical.

[38] Turck, *Évangelisation et catéchèse*, 72.

[39] For Justin too, the Spirit is the 'prophetic Spirit' – 1 *Apol.*, 6; 13; 31.

to love God and the neighbour (ch. 87).[40] 'Through faith in [the Son of God] we learn to love God with our whole heart, and our neighbour as ourselves' (ch. 95). The double commandment to love is followed by a treatment of the Decalogue (ch. 96).[41] Irenaeus continues the use of the 'Sermon on the Mount' tradition in catechesis, taking up the commandments according to the interpretation in Matthew 5 but not in the Matthaean order. The moral teaching in Irenaeus's *Demonstration* is less prominent and less systematic than the doctrinal teaching. This work thus anticipates the ascendancy of doctrine and the decline of the moral element in catechesis evident in the fourth century. The biblical content continued to be important but not always as explicitly formulated in terms of God's saving history as it is in Irenaeus.

Cyprian: training to live in a community of martyrs

Cyprian guided the church of Carthage and North Africa through its greatest crisis, the Decian persecution and the accompanying mass apostasy among its members.[42] Although Quasten dates Cyprian's *Ad Quirinum* (*Testimoniorum libri III*) before 249, there is good reason to put book 3, which seems to be later than books 1 and 2, after the outbreak of the Decian persecution.[43] Even if this collection of biblical *excerpta*[44] does not directly reflect a martyr environment, it represents the teaching given on the eve of the Decian persecution. An early *topos* in book 3 is 'On the benefits of martyrdom' (3.16), and the following four *topoi* ('That what we suffer in this world is of less account than is the reward which is promised'; 'That nothing is to be preferred to the love of God

---

[40] Cf. *Didache*, 1.2; Justin, *Dialogue with Trypho*, 93.

[41] Daniélou, *La catéchèse*, 133–4.

[42] On Cyprian see M. M. Sage, *Cyprian* (Cambridge: Philadelphia Patristic Foundation, 1975); C. Saumagne, *Saint Cyprian, évêque de Carthage et 'pape' d'Afrique* (Paris: CNRS, 1975).

[43] J. Quasten, *Patrology* 2 (Westminster: Newman, 1953), 363. C. H. Turner, 'Prolegomena to the *Testimonia* and *Ad Fortunatum* of St Cyprian', *Journal of Theological Studies* 31 (1930), 230–1, however, dates only books 1 and 2 to 249, book 3 to Cyprian's retirement during the early months of AD 250 after the outbreak of the Decian persecution, and the *Ad Fortunatum* to AD 253.

[44] Antonio Quacquarelli, 'Note retoriche sui *Testimonia* di Cipriano', *Vetera Christianorum* 8 (1971), 181–209.

and Christ'; 'That we are not to obey our own will, but the will of God'; and 'That the foundation and strength of hope and faith is fear') are related to this theme.[45] The ensuing persecution occasioned a separate collection of *testimonia*, the *Ad Fortunatum de exhortatione martyrii*. Cyprian in his correspondence showed an interest in catechumens. He knew that the 'hearers' were in danger during persecution (*Epp.*, 18.2), and he declares that catechumens who were martyred received a baptism of blood (*Epp.*, 73.22).[46]

It has been suggested that Quirinus was engaged in the instruction of catechumens and had need of a manual collecting passages of scripture on various points.[47] Daniélou adds that there were two principal elements that gave structure to dogmatic catechesis: the formulas of faith or *symbola*, and collections of citations of the Old Testament or *testimonia*.[48] His suggestion that books 1 and 2 are dogmatic catechesis and book 3 is moral catechesis[49] I would like to revise and extend. Book 1 contains twenty-four topics on the theme of the church replacing the old Israel. This represents the historical framework of Christian teaching. Book 2 contains thirty topics on christology; this represents the central doctrinal affirmations of Christianity. Book 3 has a separate prologue and was apparently written later than the first two books; its 120 topics represent the moral duties of the Christian life. The preface to the first two books employs language consistent with a catechetical use. Cyprian addresses Quirinus as 'my beloved son', language used by teachers and by bishops to their clergy. Quirinus had requested 'divine teachings', whereby he might be 'led away from the darkness of error and enlightened by [the Lord's] pure and shining light' – definitely conversion language. Cyprian offers his treatise as advantageous 'for forming the first lineaments of your faith'. The thoroughly scriptural basis of the teaching is indicated by the encouragement to 'read through the complete volumes' of the 'Scriptures, old and new'.

[45] I use the translation of R. E. Wallis in the *Ante-Nicene Fathers* 5 (repr. Peabody: Hendrickson, 1994), 507–57.

[46] So *Apostolic Tradition*, 19.2.

[47] Quacquarelli, 'Note retoriche', 204.

[48] Daniélou, *La catéchèse*, 73.

[49] Ibid., 28; cf. his *The Origins of Latin Christianity* (London: Darton, Longman & Todd / Philadelphia: Westminster, 1977), 288–95.

Most of the *testimonia* in books 1 and 2 are quite traditional, as may be seen from *Barnabas*, Justin, Irenaeus, and Tertullian.[50] The history of salvation has taken a decidedly anti-Judaic turn in Cyprian's book 1. Chapters 1–4 deal with the faithlessness of the Jews; chapters 5–18 with the loss of Israel's privileges; and chapters 19–24 with the church of the Gentiles. His passages are selective, tendentious, and out of context.

Book 2 arranges the prophecies according to the same scheme as Irenaeus's *Demonstration*, beginning with the pre-existence of the Wisdom of God, continuing with his virgin birth, his titles, and his death and resurrection, and concluding with his coming again as judge and king. The passages collected under each heading follow the order of the biblical books. The presence of quotations from the New Testament, more frequent in book 2 than in book 1, shows that the work was not directed to Jews (at least not immediately).

Book 2.30 seems to prepare for Book 3, although the latter was written later and separately. There was a conscious effort to link the two parts, for 3.1 begins with Isaiah 58.1–9 on fasting, a topic which elsewhere appears in an anti-Judaic context, and contains a quotation of Matthew 25:31–46, with which book 2 ended. The contents of book 3 are mostly negative – what the Christian is not to do. The topics seem to be in random order, and there is no discernible order in which the texts are cited on each topic. However, I would note that brotherly love appears early (3.3) and is followed shortly by some of the topics from the Sermon on the Mount – anger (8), trusting God for material needs (11), not swearing oaths and cursing (12–13), not judging (21), and forgiving wrongs (22).

The prologue to book 3 states , 'You asked me to gather out for your instruction from the holy Scriptures some heads bearing upon the religious teaching of our school [*secta*]'. Several items might reflect a specifically catechetical context: The necessity of baptism and warning against sin after baptism (3.25–27); 'That we must hasten to faith and to attainment [*consecutionem*]', a word used in Latin Christianity for attaining grace in baptism (97);[51] 'That

[50] Daniélou, *The Origins of Latin Christianity*, 288–95.

[51] Cf. the inscriptions collected in E. Diehl, *Inscriptiones latinae christianae veteres*, 2nd edn (Berlin: 1961): 1523, 'obtained the grace [*gratiam consecuta*] of the glorious font on Easter day and survived after holy baptism five months'; cf. the phrase in 1524 and 1527; the verb form is used alone with '[baptismal] grace' understood in 1525, 1528, 1539, 1540.

the catechumen ought now no longer to sin' (98); 'That one ought to make confession while he is in the flesh' (114); 'That God is more loved by him who has had many sins forgiven in baptism' (116); and the call to take up the yoke of the Lord (119).

Cyprian's collection of scriptural *testimonia* may have served other purposes than catechesis and at best would represent a resource, a skeleton as it were for catechists to flesh out in their instruction. Nevertheless, it does remind us of the effort at a biblical basis for historical, doctrinal, and moral teachings in the early church.

Cyril of Jerusalem: training to live in an orthodox church

With the fourth century we enter the full light of day in regard to the catechumenate, as with many other subjects. No longer is it necessary to draw inferences from documents written for other purposes, or argue for the catechetical intent of works not explicitly so designated, for we have texts for that express purpose and the words of actual catechetical instructions. The fourth century presented a different situation for the church: no longer a persecuted church of martyrs, it was the triumphant church of the emperor. The development and refinement of the catechumenate was a major response to the changed circumstances. This fact raises problems for using the fourth century as a model from which earlier practice can be inferred. There assuredly was some continuity in practice, but just as assuredly there was adaptation to new needs. The development of a more organized catechumenate around AD 200 may have had, in part, the purpose of making sure that candidates were ready to make a deep commitment to the church and were persons who could be trusted in a crisis. The number of apostasies in the Decian and Diocletian persecutions showed how real the problem was and how decades of relative peace had caused a slackening of seriousness. The development in the fourth century of a series of catechetical lectures during Lent leading up to baptism at Easter apparently was designed to handle more efficiently the larger number of candidates for baptism and to make a serious effort at instructing them in the contents of the faith and at showing the special privileges of church membership for those who indeed took this step and did not delay their baptism, as many, following Constantine's example, did.

The surviving catechetical lectures of the fourth and fifth centuries are chiefly the instructions given during Lent and so are predominantly doctrinal. The fullest of these are from the Eastern realm, so I am going to stretch the meaning of 'Western' and illustrate this development from one of the Greek bishops of the fourth century, Cyril of Jerusalem. There is some justification for doing so in the extensive use made of his *Catechetical Lectures* in Rufinus's *Commentary on the Apostles' Creed*.[52] Cyril was active during the time of the trinitarian controversies between the Councils of Nicaea (AD 325) and Constantinople (AD 381). Cyril's *Catechetical Lectures* were delivered in about AD 348 while he was a presbyter who prepared candidates for baptism.[53] They are our earliest extant example of the full course of actual instruction of those preparing for baptism. Cyril became bishop in 350 or early 351. I am leaving aside the *Mystagogical Lectures* attributed to Cyril that were delivered on the Monday to Friday in the week after the Easter baptism so will not enter into the controversy over whether they come from Cyril or his successor John.[54]

The *Procatechesis* was delivered on Sunday at a public service. It is an exhortation to come not 'with soul bemired with sins' (4).[55] The candidates are given forty days in which to effect repentance for their sins. Fornication, uncleanness, and avarice are the specific sins mentioned; indeed, throughout the series sexual sin seems to be a special preoccupation, often taken as the representative sin.[56] Cyril warns about unworthy motives, but he

---

[52] J. N. D. Kelly, *Rufinus: A Commentary on the Apostles' Creed*, Ancient Christian Writers 20 (Westminster: Newman, 1955), 9–11.

[53] A. Paulin, *Saint Cyrille de Jerusalem: catéchète* (Paris: Cerf, 1959).

[54] Cyril's authorship is rejected in Victor Saxer and Gabriella Maestri, *Cirillo e Giovanni di Gerusalemme, catechesi prebattesimali e mistagogiche* (Milan: Paoline, 1994), but defended by Alexis Doval, *The Authorship of the Mystagogical Catecheses Attributed to St Cyril of Jerusalem* (Washington, DC: Catholic University of America Press, forthcoming). The mystagogical lectures are studied in Hugh M. Riley, *Christian Initiation: A Comparative Study of the Interpretation of the Baptismal Liturgy in the Mystagogical Writings of Cyril of Jerusalem, John Chrysostom, Theodore of Mopsuestia, and Ambrose of Milan* (Washington, DC: Catholic University of America Press, 1974).

[55] I use but update the wording of the translation of E. H. Gifford in *Nicene and Post-Nicene Fathers* Ser. 2, 7 (New York: 1894; repr. Peabody: Hendrickson, 1994).

[56] *Cat. Lect.*, 2.6, 9; 3.15; 4.2, 18, 21, 23, 24; 12.6, 26, 33–4; 18.1, 20.

welcomes all in the hope of making them alive (5), 'but one should beware of receiving the title of "faithful" but having the will of the faithless' (6). The flavour of the exhortation is indicated by some representative appeals: 'the water will receive, but the Spirit will not accept' the unrepentant (4); 'Cease from this day from every evil deed' (8); 'Prepare your heart for reception of doctrine, for fellowship in holy mysteries' (16). Thus a moral exhortation precedes the doctrinal instruction of the *Catechetical Lectures*, and even they begin with a discussion of repentance and confession of sin (*Cat.*, 1 and 2).

This order seems to be the pattern that had earlier emerged, moral training followed by doctrinal teaching, but the latter seems to have gained prominence over the former in the fourth century; at least the surviving catechetical works, although containing considerable moral teaching, show few examples of works devoted explicitly to moral instruction. Gregory of Nyssa (who puts the moral teaching at the end after the doctrinal in his *Catechetical Oration*) and John Chrysostom (whose *Baptismal Instructions* are permeated with moral teaching) illustrate the concern with morals but also the absence of a curriculum for moral teaching comparable to the creed for teaching doctrine and the liturgy for teaching sacraments. The *Procatechesis* is an appeal to true conversion and then a moral catechesis as part of the data of faith. Thus, Daniélou takes Cyril as an example of the unity of moral and doctrinal catechesis.[57] He seems to me to be putting the best face on the minor role of morals in many fourth-century catecheses when he claims that the moral catechesis in the fourth century is only the moral aspect of the doctrinal catechesis. Morals were a part of the faith itself, its practical application in daily life.[58] One could wish for more evidence that more of those baptized got the point.

The eighteen *Catechetical Lectures* proper were distributed during the following forty days that began on Monday and ended on the night of Good Friday, except that *Catechesis* 18 was delivered a day later on the Saturday evening before Easter Sunday. *Catechesis* 1 is a general encouragement to the hearers to be faithful to their calling.[59] They are to 'prepare for new birth' by confessing

---

[57] Daniélou, *La catéchèse*, 161–2.
[58] Ibid., 157–8.
[59] Note the references to faith: 1 (twice), 2 (twice), 3 ('believer'), 5 (twice).

sins, devoting time to exorcisms, catechizings, ascetic exercises, forgiving others, attending church assemblies, and nourishing their souls with sacred readings. *Catechesis* 2 concentrates on repentance. Biblical history is employed in support of the topic by giving examples of sin and repentance in their biblical order. The conclusion summarizes the lecture: 'Having therefore, brothers and sisters, many examples of those who have sinned and repented and been saved, do you also heartily make confession to the Lord, that you may both receive the forgiveness of your former sins and be counted worthy of the heavenly gift' (2.20).

Catechesis 3 discusses the doctrinal meaning of baptism. Cyril repeatedly connects the effectiveness of baptism with faith and repentance (3.2, 15); his conception of faith, however, may be inadequate, since he often means by faith the creed. The confession of faith for him is the reciting of the creed (3.10). Baptism is necessary for salvation (except for the martyrs – 3.10) and brings forgiveness of all sins (3.15). He emphasizes the necessity of bringing forth the fruits of good works (3.8, 16).

Catechesis 4 begins the doctrinal discussion proper with a summary of the principal points of Christian doctrine. Cyril defines godliness as consisting of two things, 'pious doctrine and virtuous practice' (4.2), and he concludes the doctrinal survey with a statement of Christian living, especially avoiding pagan, Jewish, and heretical practices (4.37). The emphasis, however, lies on doctrine, and he develops the doctrinal points with more relish.

Catechesis 5 discusses faith, almost with the sense of 'faithfulness'. Cyril has in mind especially keeping the 'dogmatic' faith, professing what is delivered by the church (5.12). He identifies two kinds of faith: the 'dogmatic, involving an assent of the soul on some particular point', and the faith which is 'a gift of grace', which 'works things above human power' (5.10–11). Neither seems to be faith in the Pauline and Johannine sense of personal trust in the promises and work of God in Christ.

Catecheses 6–9 take up the phrases in the creed concerning the one God (especially directed against heretics – 6), Father (7), Almighty (8), and Maker of heaven and earth (9). Cyril's method is on each article of the symbol to collect the 'proof out of the Prophets' (13.23) for the teaching.[60] Throughout he uses passages

[60] Daniélou, 'La catéchèse dans la tradition patristique', 28.

and incidents from the Old and New Testaments, so the biblical content is quite extensive, although arranged topically and not historically or 'biblically'. The principal concern of Cyril's lectures is, as a commentary on the creed, doctrinal, as expressed by the phrase, 'the saving doctrines of the true faith' (7.1). He does add that it profits nothing to have the title of Christians unless the works also follow (7.14) and uses the title of God as Father as an occasion to teach the necessity of honouring parents (7.15–16).

Lectures 10–15 discuss the 'one Lord Jesus Christ' (10), the 'only begotten' (11), 'incarnate' (12), 'crucified and buried' (13), who 'rose on the third day and ascended' (14), and who is coming again in judgement (15). There seems to be more of the sense of 'trust' here in the call to believe in Christ and not to let him be blasphemed because of the hearers' conduct (10.20). Faith is accepting what the prophecies say about Christ, but this gives a trust and commitment, for 'You have taken your stand on the rock of the faith in the resurrection' (14.21). Nevertheless, there is the warning against falling away from Christ (14.30).

The discussion of the articles pertaining to Christ often contain anti-Judaic statements (10.2, 8, 16; 12.2, 13, 28; 13.7; 14.1, 15, 26). Cyril gives a survey of Old Testament history from Adam onward, including quotations from the prophets in order to demonstrate human sin and God's sending Christ as the remedy (12.5ff.). The use of the Old Testament throughout this section of the lectures is comparable to that of Irenaeus. Testimonies to the passion are collected (13.9ff.) and to the resurrection (14.3ff.). Those concerning the resurrection are particularly arbitrary and unconvincing to the modern reader, but the method is significant. The scriptures are read from the standpoint of the experience of Christ, and every word that has any reference to a 'rising up' or the like is understood of the resurrection of Christ. There is a recurrent pattern involving the citing of Old Testament prophecies and then recording the witnesses or testimonies to the event.[61]

The concluding admonition of *Catechesis* 15, 'Flee all heretical error' (15.33) sums up Cyril's principal concern in his dogmatic catechesis. The heretics are sometimes specifically the Gnostics

[61] On the resurrection, the prophecies are collected in 14.3–20 and the witnesses in 14.22–3; on the ascension, prophecies in 14.24, 27–8, testimonies in 14.29.

(11.21); the Manichees, a special concern in *Catecheses* 4 and 6, appear in this section also (14.21). Sabellian and Arian teachings are opposed as contrasting errors, but not by name (e.g. 11.13–17; 15.9); for the most part Cyril deals with contemporary doctrinal issues through a positive exposition of his own understanding. The discussion of Christ's coming in judgement provides occasion to bring in the moral dimension by warning against immoral acts and, with reference to Matthew 25 (as in Cyprian), by giving the exhortation, 'Let the light of your good works shine' coupled with the repetition of the admonition, 'Let not Christ be blasphemed on your account' (15.23, 26).

Catecheses 16 and 17 instruct about the Holy Spirit. The same characteristics observed in the previous lectures obtain here too. The biblical content is pervasive. Passages about the 'One and same Holy Spirit' who spoke in the Law and the Prophets and in the Gospels and Apostles (17.5; cf. 4.16 and 16.3–4) are collected: from the Old Testament in 16.25–31, and from the New Testament in 17 – the Gospels (17.6–12), Acts (17.13–31), and Paul (17.32–38). The hearers were expected to continue in 'the frequent reading of the sacred scriptures' (17.34). The thrust against the heretics remains strong; these include Sabellians, Gnostics, Marcionites, Montanists, and Manicheans (16.4, 6–10). The Spirit gives knowledge (16.17) and continues his work of enlightenment, a frequently mentioned feature of the Spirit's work,[62] and spiritual maturing in the present (16.22), but otherwise Cyril offers no discussion of the moral achievements by the Spirit.[63] Because baptism is the work of the Holy Spirit and not of the human administrator, one should not come to baptism in hypocrisy (17.35–36).

The last catechetical lecture in the series deals with the resurrection (18.2–21), the catholic church (18.22–27), and eternal life (18.27–31). Cyril affirms the hope of resurrection as the root of all good works (18.1). Fornication is once more the representative sin (18.1, 20). He declares again that the Jewish

---

[62] *Cat.*, 16.3, 12, 16 (three times), 17, 18, 22 (twice).

[63] For instance, the 'fruits of the Holy Spirit' in Galatians 5.22, 23 appears only in the closing doxology of *Cat.*, 17.38. Cyril's treatment of the Holy Spirit bears many points of contact with the treatment in Novatian, *De Trinitate*, 29 except that Novatian's briefer discussion offers proportionately more on the Spirit as effecting holiness through moral improvement.

church 'is cast off' and 'the churches of Christ are increased over all the world' (18.25). The heavy content of scripture quotation continues, and as Cyril forecasts the coming mystagogical cate-cheses, he says the newly baptized will 'receive proofs from the Old and New Testaments' about what they experienced on Easter Sunday.

During the fourth century a process that had begun with the Gnostic struggles of the second century reached a climax, namely to identify the true church more by correct doctrine than by manner of life.

The earliest of our surviving instructions on the sacraments of initiation are the *Mystagogical Catecheses* delivered on Monday to Friday after baptism on Easter Sunday and ascribed to Cyril of Jerusalem. However, to illustrate this aspect of catechetical instruc-tion we will return to the West to Ambrose of Milan.

Ambrose: training to live in a state church

Ambrose may be taken as representative of the situation in the church in the late fourth century when it was now the authorized state religion, receiving a multitude of new converts and struggling to incorporate them into its life and to accommodate itself to its new position. That often uneasy situation is well typified in the career of Ambrose. Coming directly from high government office to the bishopric of arguably the most important church in the West in his time, Ambrose found himself at the centre of the conflicts and tensions of his time, affirming the independence of the church and exerting its influence in the affairs of state.[64]

There are ascribed to Ambrose two sets of mystagogical catecheses, delivered during the week following baptism on Easter Sunday morning, the *De Mysteriis* and the *De Sacramentis*. There have been weighty objections to the common authorship of these works, but the argument in favour of Ambrose as the author of both works seems now to be in the ascendancy. I do not feel competent to address the stylistic arguments, but the content of the two works does not seem to me to be inconsistent with common

---

[64] For an introduction to Ambrose, see N. B. McLynn, *Ambrose of Milan: Church and Court in a Christian Capital* (Berkeley: University of California Press, 1994).

authorship.[65] They may represent the mystagogical instruction given by Ambrose on two different occasions, essentially the same but varied from year to year. The six addresses of the *De Sacramentis* are certainly not so well organized as the *De Mysteriis*. They have the marks of oral delivery and may be notes on actual addresses only lightly retouched. The *De Mysteriis*, on the other hand, is more formal and exact; if not an epitome of the *De Sacramentis*,[66] it is a more polished literary presentation of the material.

The very terminology of 'mysteries' says something about the accommodation to Graeco-Roman religious conceptions.[67] The comparison of Christian initiation to initiation in the pagan mysteries served both pedagogic and hortatory purposes. It was a way of teaching the solemnity and seriousness of the Christian rites and of making full initiation more appealing to those inclined to maintain only a minimal association with the church. Ambrose himself offers two reasons for postponing instruction about the mysteries until after baptism: 'For if we had thought that such an account should be propounded before baptism to the uninitiated, we should be esteemed traitors rather than teachers; further, because it were better that the light of the mysteries should reveal itself unasked and unexpected than preceded by some discourse' (*Mys.*, 1.2).[68] In other words, what had once been only an analogy

[65] B. Botte, *Ambroise de Milan: Des Sacrements, Des Mystères, Explication du Symbole*, Sources Chrétiennes 25 bis (Paris: Cerf, 1961), 12–24; further bibliography in J. Quasten and A. Di Berardino, *Patrology* 4 (Westminster: Christian Classics, 1986), 171–2. Riley, *Christian Initiation*, uses both works for his comparative study.

[66] R. H. Connolly, 'The *Explanatio symboli ad initiandos*: A Work of Saint Ambrose', *Texts and Studies* 10 (1952), 39.

[67] H. A. Echle, 'Sacramental Initiation as Christian Mystery – Initiation According to Clement of Alexandria', and J. Daniélou, 'Le Mystère du culte dans les sermons de Saint Grégoire de Nysse', in A. Mayr *et al.*, eds, *Vom Christlichen Mysterium* (Düsseldorf: Patmos, 1951), 54–65, 76–93; J. D. B. Hamilton, 'The Church and the Language of Mystery: The First Four Centuries', *Ephemerides Theologicae Lovanienses* 53 (1977), 479–94.

[68] I use for the English translation of these works T. Thompson, *St Ambrose, 'On the Mysteries' and the Treatise 'On the Sacraments' by an Unknown Author* (London: SPCK, 1919), 45; cf. the discussion on xiii. As the full title indicates, this work (the introduction and notes were prepared by J. H. Srawley) concludes separate authorship.

to the mysteries (as I think is the case with Clement of Alexandria) had become by the fourth century a controlling imagery with the resultant conviction that only after initiation should full secrets be revealed. This is given the further pedagogical justification that one can understand better after experiencing the initiatory rites than only hearing about them.[69]

Contemporaries and successors of Ambrose preserved the *De Mysteriis* and *De Sacramentis* in numerous manuscripts, because they found them useful and/or distinctive, at least containing what was not expressed so well elsewhere. This was an important part of his teaching and represents certain tendencies in him and his age, but the mystagogical catechesis was not all there was to Ambrose's preparation of new converts, so before discussing its contents, I want to say something about what preceded it in the ceremonies of initiation at Milan.[70]

Ambrose begins the *De Mysteriis* with this reminder: 'On questions of right conduct we discoursed daily at the time when the lives of the patriarchs or the precepts of the Proverbs were being read, in order that, trained and instructed thereby, . . . you might, after being renewed by baptism, continue to practice the life which befitted the regenerate' (1.1). The lives of the patriarchs provided appropriate models to imitate, and the Proverbs provided basic moral principles.[71] There survive several works by Ambrose on the lives of the patriarchs, the written texts of which appear to be revised, polished, and generalized versions of originally preached sermons. They may have been preached in the liturgical assemblies during Lent and so have been intended for the faithful as well as the *competentes*. The *De Abraham* contains express reference to the candidates for baptism during Lent.[72]

---

[69] Daniélou, *La catéchèse*, 175.

[70] D. G. Michiels, 'L'initiation chrétienne selon saint Ambroise', *Les Questions Liturgiques et Paroissiales* 34 (1953), 109–14, 164–9 gives a popular survey of the three components: catechumenate, sacraments of initiation, and the post-baptismal catechesis.

[71] William Harmless, *Augustine and the Catechumenate* (Collegeville: Liturgical Press, 1995), 94–5.

[72] Ambrose, *De Abraham*, 1.4.25 ('you who are proceeding to the grace of the Lord'); 1.7.59 ('you who are proceeding to the grace of baptism'); 1.9.89 ('you daughters who are proceeding to the grace of the Lord'). The first two statements are in passages teaching against adultery; cf. what is noted above about Cyril's concern with sexual sins.

Ambrose's biblical sermons at the beginning of Lent draw moral lessons from the stories of the patriarchs.[73] The introduction to *De Ioseph* provides a summary: 'In him [Joseph] there shone forth above all the mark of chastity. In Abraham you have learned the undaunted devotion of faith, in Isaac the purity of a sincere heart, in Jacob the spirit's signal endurance of toils. For it is right that after the treatment of virtues in general you should give attention to moral principles in their specific kinds'.[74] Joseph served as a type of Christ (*De Ioseph*, 2.8 and *passim*) as well as a 'mirror of purity' (ibid., 1.2).

Ambrose makes frequent use of Canticles (or Song of Solomon). He comments on Canticles 8.6,

> Christ is the seal on the forehead, the seal in the heart – on the forehead that we may always confess Him, in the heart that we may always love Him, and a seal on the arm, that we may always do His work. Therefore let His image shine forth in our profession of faith, let it shine forth in our love, let it shine forth in our works and deeds so that, if it is possible, all His beauty may be represented in us (*De Isaac*, 8.74).[75]

As this quotation indicates, there is a fair amount in these sermons on confession.

De Iacob et vita beata develops the theme of 4 Maccabees that reason rules the passions. Biblical examples are given of various virtues, and Ambrose goes through Jacob's life in detail with spiritual lessons drawn. Thus the biblical framework serves as the basis for moral instruction. Ambrose lays out the history of salvation in three periods: there was the natural law, which was not kept, so the law of Moses was added to it, and now with Christ grace has come (*De Iacob*, 1.6.20, 22).[76] 'Happy indeed', he says, 'is the young man who leads a good life, but happy also is the old man who has led a good life. What the young man hopes for, the old man has obtained' (*De Iacob*, 2.8.35). Other biblical illustrations of the happy life are introduced (ibid., 2.9.41ff.) before Ambrose returns to 4 Maccabees for his conclusion.

[73] Daniélou, 'La catéchèse dans la tradition patristique', 30.

[74] Michael P. McHugh, trans., *Saint Ambrose: Seven Exegetical Works*, Fathers of the Church 65 (Washington, DC: Catholic University of America Press, 1972), 189.

[75] Ibid., 59.

[76] Cf. *De fuga saeculi*, 3.15 for a natural law in the heart and a written law.

De bono mortis uses 2 Esdras extensively. It was probably intended as two sermons (1–29; 30–57), perhaps for catechumens awaiting baptism.[77] If so, there is a wide-ranging allegorical exegesis applied to death, as *De Isaac* does with the soul. *De fuga saeculi*, another sermon apparently delivered during Eastertide, was influenced by Philo and adduces numerous biblical examples.[78] 'The flight consists in this: to keep away from sins, to take up the rule of the virtues unto the likeness and image of God, to enlarge our strength unto the imitation of God according to the limit of our potentiality. For the perfect man is the image and glory of God' (*De fuga*, 4.17).[79] Ambrose particularly urges his hearers to flee immorality, avarice, and unbelief.

As Cyril drew moral instruction from the creed, Ambrose drew it from scripture. It could also be drawn from the sacraments, as in John Chrysostom's catechetical lectures.[80] I observe, and leave what its significance may be as a point to be pondered, that Ambrose draws his moral instruction from the Old Testament rather than from the teachings of Jesus, as earlier catechists had done.

Since we have given more extensive treatment of doctrinal catechesis in discussing Cyril of Jerusalem, we may treat it more briefly in Ambrose, by reference to his brief *Explanatio symboli ad initiandos*. This short address accompanied the delivery of the creed to the candidates for baptism following the scrutinies (exorcism) and was delivered on the Sunday before Easter.[81] Cyril expounded the baptismal creed of the Jerusalem church, which was similar to the creed that was the basis of the Nicene Creed. Ambrose delivered the 'Apostles' Creed', as was common in the

---

[77] McHugh, *St Ambrose: Seven Exegetical Works*, 69.

[78] Hervé Savon, *Saint Ambroise devant l'exégèse de Philon le Juif* (Paris: Études Augustiniennes, 1977), 1, 329–76.

[79] McHugh, *St Ambrose: Seven Exegetical Works*, 295.

[80] Daniélou, 'La Catéchèse dans la tradition patristique', 30; idem, *La catéchèse*, 162–70.

[81] Connolly, 'The *explanatio symboli ad initiandos*'. Ambrose, *Epp.*, 20.4: '[On Sunday] when the catechumens were dismissed, I was teaching the creed to certain candidates in the baptistery of the basilica'. The same letter (20:14, 25) refers to the reading of the books of Job (cf. Ambrose's sermon *The Prayer of Job and David*, translated in Fathers of the Church 65 [1972], 327ff.) and Jonah at the season leading up to Easter.

Western church.[82] He instructed his hearers not to write it down (ch. 12), for it was part of the 'secret' that belonged to the initiated alone. In his explanation of the name 'symbol', Ambrose either confused *symbolum* ('token', 'watchword') with *symbola* ('contribution') or made a play on the former by interpreting it in the latter sense. There are twelve pronouncements in the creed, as there are twelve Apostles (ch. 11). He justifies inclusion of the articles on the church, forgiveness of sins, and resurrection on the grounds that to believe in the Author is to believe in his works (ch. 9). He affirms, 'This whole sacrament is concerned with your resurrection'; what is the 'sacrament' here – baptism or the symbol?

The contents of the *De Mysteriis* and *De Sacramentis*, like the *Mystagogical Catecheses* of Cyril, are explanations after the event of what was experienced in the initiation on Easter. Ambrose in the former address calls on his hearers to 'open their ears', for they were obligated to remember the answer of faith they had professed (1.3). When they descended into the font, they gave a pledge by their own voice, giving answer that they believed in the Father, in the Son, and in the Holy Spirit (5.28; cf. 4.21).[83] There is much use of scripture with the intention of showing the analogy of the acts of God in scripture and in the sacraments of the church.[84] Ambrose adduces Old Testament types of baptism – creation, Noah's ark, Israel's crossing of the Red Sea, the bitter waters of Marah made sweet by the rod of Moses, Naaman's cleansing of leprosy (3.9–18, all quite traditional and familiar

[82] Ambrose refers to the doctrinal instruction of baptismal candidates in his *Expositio Evangelii secundam Lucam*, 6:104–9: 'When some from the Gentiles are called to the church, we must produce a series of precepts, so that at first we teach one God to be the maker of the world and all things . . . When you are persuaded there is one God, then by his disclosure you add on the salvation given to us by Christ' (104); 'Wherefore the catechumen who is proceeding to the sacraments of the faithful must receive initial instruction. It must be said that there is one God, from whom are all things, and one Jesus Christ, through whom are all things . . .'. (107).

[83] The creed was interrogatory, 'Do you believe in . . . ?', to which the candidate answered, 'I believe'. The baptismal questions are more fully quoted in *Sacram.*, 2.7.20.

[84] Elisabeth Germain, 'Baptême et éducation de la foi dans l'église ancienne', *Catéchèse*, 22 (1982), 117.

from other sources);[85] and of the eucharist – Melchizedek, the manna from heaven, and water from the rock (8.43–49, likewise traditional).

The *De Mysteriis* concentrates on baptism and the eucharist. The newly baptized now have the 'innocence of a dove' (*Mys.*, 4.25). Regeneration by the Spirit in baptism is compared to and validated by the Spirit's generation of Christ in the virgin Mary (*Mys.*, 9.59). The eucharist is not bodily food, but spiritual (*Mys.*, 9.58). In support of the bread and wine becoming the body and blood of Christ, Ambrose adduces biblical incidents where a blessing produced a miraculous transformation (several of which are baptismal types here used of the eucharist): the rod of Moses, the Red Sea becoming dry land, the turning back of the Jordan, water from the rock, the bitter waters of Marah, and Elisha's axe-head that floated (*Mys.*, 9.50–52).[86] Little is said about the unction, but it is affirmed that 'we are all anointed with spiritual grace unto the kingdom of God and the priesthood' (6.30).

The *De Sacramentis* covers much the same ground but contains some significant additions to what is found in the shorter treatise. It begins with an explanation for delaying the interpretation of the initiatory rites that is couched in more 'Christian' terms than in terms of the mysteries, 'for in a Christian, faith must come first' (*Sacram.*, 1.1.1). The explanation begins with the rite of *Ephpheta* ('opening') on Saturday night (1.1.2), only alluded to in *De Mysteriis* (1.3–4). The renunciation of 'the devil and his works', and of 'the world and its pleasures' is stated (1.2.5) and is interpreted as a binding promise before Christ (1.2.6, 8). The reason for Christ's baptism is stated to be that he might cleanse the flesh of our nature and set a pattern for us (*Sacram.*, 1.5.16).[87]

---

[85] *Sacram.*, 1.5.13–1.6.23 refers to the exodus, Naaman, and the flood, and adds from the New Testament the healing of the paralytic at the pool (2.23–2.3.9).

[86] Cf. *Sacram.*, 4.4.17–20 for miracles of transformation. The argument is similar to that of Gregory of Nyssa in a baptismal context, *De baptisma Christi* (Gregorii Nysseni opera [henceforth GNO] 9:225, 10 – 227, 4). *De Sacram.*, 1.3.9–10; 1.5.15 similarly asserts that the water of baptism is more than water.

[87] For the treatment of the baptism of Jesus in patristic literature, see Robert L. Wilken, 'The Interpretation of the Baptism of Jesus in the Later Fathers', *Studia Patristica* 11 (1972), 268–77; Jean Doignon, 'La scène évangélique du Baptême de Jésus commentée par Lactance (*Diuinae institutiones*, 4.15) et Hilaire de Poitiers (*In Matthaeum*, 2, 5–6)', in J. Fontaine and C. Kannengiesser, eds,

Ambrose contrasts the 'one baptism' of Christians with the baptisms of the Gentiles and Jews (*Sacram.*, 2.1.2).[88] The efficacy of baptism is ascribed to the cross (*Sacram.*, 2.2.6; 3.4.11–13),[89] to Christ (2.2.7; 2.7.23), to the name of the Trinity (2.3.9; 2.4.10–13; 2.5.14; 2.7.20–22), and to the Holy Spirit (2.5.15). The water of baptism is associated with the earth, so the font 'is, as it were, a burial' (2.6.19).[90] Baptism is a resurrection and a regeneration (*Sacram.*, 3.1.2); in it 'all guilt is washed away' (3.1.7).

More is said in this treatise about the unction, but less than is said by Cyril's *Mystagogical Lectures*. The 'sealing' brings the seven gifts of the Spirit (3.2.8–10). Of greater concern is the justification of the ritual footwashing (*Sacram.*, 3.1.4–7; cf. the stronger justification in *Mys.*, 6.31–33), which Ambrose knew was not part of the Roman baptismal ceremony.

On the eucharist, Ambrose joins Cyril of Jerusalem and Gregory of Nyssa in making the earliest explicit arguments that the consecration effects a change in the elements themselves and not just in their use (*Sacram.*, 4.4.14 of the bread; 4.4.19 of the wine and water).[91] Each communion is said to bring a remission of sins (*Sacram.*, 5.3.17). There continues to be much use of scripture in Ambrose's instructions; quite striking in discourse 5 is the use of Canticles.

Epektasis: Mélanges patristiques offerts au Cardinal Jean Daniélou (Paris: Beauchesne, 1972), 63–73; Kilian McDonnell, 'Jesus' Baptism in the Jordan', *Theological Studies* 56 (1995), 209–36.

[88] Cf. Basil, *Exh. bapt.*, 1–2 (*PG*, 31.425A-428B); idem, *De Bapt.*, 1.2 (*PG*, 31.1532C–1533C); John Chrysostom, *De Bapt. Chr. et Epiph.*, 2–3 (*PG*, 49.366).

[89] Cf. the wording of the baptismal interrogation, unique to these two treatises, 'Do you believe in our Lord Jesus Christ and in his cross?' (*Sacram.*, 2.7.20; *Mys.*, 5.28).

[90] Cf. the different yet similar comparison of burial in the earth of Jesus and in water of the convert by Gregory of Nyssa, *Bapt. Chr.* (GNO 9.228, 9–22); idem, *Catech. Or.*, 35.

[91] William R. Crockett, *Eucharist: Symbol of Transformation* (New York: Pueblo, 1989), 61–2, 88–98; C. W. Dugmore, 'Sacrament and Sacrifice in the Early Fathers', *Journal of Ecclesiastical History*, n.s. 2 (1951), 24–37; reproduced in E. Ferguson, ed., *Studies in Early Christianity*, 15: *Worship in Early Christianity* (New York: Garland, 1993), 178–91; E. Ferguson, 'The Lord's Supper in Church History: The Early Church through the Medieval Period', in Dale R. Stoffer, ed., *The Lord's Supper: Believers' Church Perspectives* (Scottdale: Herald Press, 1997), 21–45.

Another new feature of *De Sacramentis* is the instruction on prayer, beginning with an exposition of the Lord's prayer (5.4.18–30). The sixth discourse, after a brief review of earlier material, continues with instructions on how and where to pray (6.3.11 – 6.4.19) and on the order of contents of prayer (6.5.22–25).

Daniélou identified three types of mystagogical catechesis: commentary on the rites, biblical theology of the sacraments (types from the Old Testament), and response to theological difficulties.[92] Ambrose (as also Cyril of Jerusalem) structures his instructions as a commentary on the rites, but includes within that commentary biblical typology and argumentation on theological points. The prominence of the liturgical catechesis following baptism shows the extent to which the process of salvation had become a drama, and the extent to which membership in the church was identified with a performance and an understanding of the ceremonies that were part of a state church. We must not forget what motivated much of this development. There was the worthy concern to make church membership meaningful and to incorporate the large numbers of new members into a new (for them) cohesive social community. Yet there was almost inevitably associated with these developments an emphasis on externals, in spite of the diligent efforts by church leaders to emphasize the spiritual. Their repeated affirmations along this line only confirm the need and the difficulty of achieving a truly spiritual formation.

Augustine: training to live in the Heavenly City

Augustine as Bishop of Hippo sits astride two ages, at the end of the ancient church and the beginning of the medieval church. He is usually remembered as a towering intellectual genius, the apex of Latin patristic theology and the seminal genius and authoritative church father of the Latin Middle Ages. Our concern here is with one aspect of Augustine's pastoral work,[93] his activity as a catechist.

---

[92] Daniélou, *La catéchèse*, 61.

[93] For brief introductions to Augustine, note Henry Chadwick, *Augustine* (Oxford: Oxford University Press, 1986) and Henri Marrou, *St Augustine and His Influence through the Ages* (New York: Harper & Brothers, 1957), text reprinted without the selections in E. Ferguson, *Studies in Early Christianity* 1: *Personalities of the Early Church* (New York: Garland, 1993), 271–352. For his pastoral work, see F. Van der Meer, *Augustine the Bishop: Church and Society*

For this, we are fortunate to have an admirable recent synthesis by William Harmless, who looks at Augustine's material from an educator's point of view.[94] As the Roman world in which he had been educated and lived was coming to an end in the West under the force of the migration of Germanic peoples, Augustine directed attention to the 'City of God', present as a spiritual reality in this world but having as its goal the future heavenly city. Although Augustine gave much attention, as we shall see, to life in the present world, his catechetical work is infused with a much more futuristic eschatology than is found in the Antiochians, John Chrysostom and Theodore of Mopsuestia, who present an almost realized eschatology in their baptismal catecheses.[95]

Augustine is the only church father from whom there survives a sampling of material from each of the four periods of initiation into the church: (1) pre-catechesis or evangelization (*On Catechizing Beginners* [or *Cat. rud.*]);[96] (2) the catechumenate proper (*Sermon* 132; *Exposition of the Psalms*, 81 [Lt. 80]; *Tractates on the Gospel of John*, 4, 10, and 11); (3) Lenten instructions to the *competentes* (*Sermons*, 56–59; 212–218); and (4) mystagogy (*Sermons*, 224–229; 260; 272).[97]

---

at the Dawn of the Middle Ages (London: Sheed & Ward, 1961), esp. pp. 347–87 on Christian initiation according to Augustine.

[94] Harmless, *Augustine and the Catechumenate* (n. 71 above), to whose presentation my summary is greatly indebted. Benedictus Busch, 'De initiatione christiana secundum sanctum Augustinum', *Ephemerides Liturgicae* 52 (1938), 159–78, 385–483 covers this material but with primarily liturgical interests. The same applies to R. De Latte, 'Saint Augustin et le baptême: Étude liturgico-historique du rituel baptismal des adultes chez saint Augustin', *Questions liturgiques* 56 (1975), 177–223, who organizes his study according to the two steps of first making one a catechumen and then making that person one of the faithful. For an overview of the North African catechumenate in the time of Augustine with an emphasis on the power of ritual, see Thomas M. Finn, 'It Happened One Saturday Night: Ritual and Conversion in Augustine's North Africa', *Journal of the American Academy of Religion* 58 (1990), 589–616.

[95] Arthur B. Shippee, 'Antioch's Separate Catechetical Classes and Curricula', unpublished paper read at the annual meeting of the North American Patristic Society, Chicago, 31 May 1996.

[96] If we had the letter that Ambrose wrote to the queen of the Marcomanni in response to her request for information on what belief in Christ involved, we would have a sample of Ambrose's instruction at this stage (Paulinus, *Vita Ambrosii*, 8.36).

[97] Harmless, *Augustine and the Catechumenate*, 29.

Augustine's *On Catechizing Beginners*, written perhaps in 399,[98] has been much studied, because, while revealing his 'pedagogical acumen and psychological sensitivity'[99] it also offers both a long and a short sample of instruction.[100] I find it particularly noteworthy that Augustine's recommendation of the content of the preliminary instruction (*Cat. rud.*, 6.10) and both his long (16–25) and short (26.51–27.55) samples take the form of a survey of biblical and Christian history. This historical framework allows the catechist to adapt the presentation according to the needs of the hearers (*Cat. rud.*, 15). Giving a salvation history overview was traditional, going back to Jewish roots,[101] and recognition of this common method of presentation may to some extent account for the way many fathers make abundant use of the scriptures, assuming their hearers will have a framework into which to put their frequent references. Augustine, moreover, extends the biblical history to include the church up to his time (*Cat. rud.*, 6.10; 24.44–45).[102] He repeats some of his characteristic themes: the division of human history into seven ages (*Cat. rud.*, 17.28; 22.39);[103] and

[98] L. J. Van der Lof, 'The Date of the *De catechizandis rudibus*', *Vigiliae Christianae* 16 (1962), 198–204.

[99] Harmless, *Augustine and the Catechumenate*, 108.

[100] Note J. Touton, 'La méthode catéchétique de St Cyrille de Jérusalem comparée à celles de St Augustin et de Théodore de Mopsuestia', *Proche-Orient chrétien* 1 (1951), 265–85; J. B. Allard, *La nature du De catechizandis rudibus de S. Augustin* (Diss.: Rome: 1976); J. Belche, 'Die Bekehrung zum Christentum nach Augustins Büchlein De catechizandis rudibus', *Augustiniana* 27 (1977), 26–69, 333–63; 28 (1978), 255–87; 29 (1979), 247–79.

[101] Harmless, *Augustine and the Catechumenate*, 127. For Christian practice, see Irenaeus, *Demonstration of the Apostolic Preaching* (see my study cited in note 35); *Apostolic Constitutions*, 7.39; Egeria, *Travels*, 46 (the practice referred to by Egeria of the Bishop of Jerusalem going 'through the whole of scripture' could explain why Cyril was able to draw so fully from Old Testament examples and prophecies in his creedal exposition). Joseph P. Christopher (whose translation I use), *St Augustine: The First Catechetical Instruction*, Ancient Christian Writers 2 (Westminster: Newman, 1952), 7, concludes that the resemblances in these works indicate that all 'derive from an original, well-defined catechetical model'.

[102] Both Justin, 1 *Apol.*, 39; 45; *Dial.*, 109–10, and Irenaeus, *Dem.*, 91–5, had included the mission of the apostles and calling of the Gentiles in their summaries of the Christian faith.

[103] *Civ. Dei*, 22.30; *Serm.*, 259.2; *Enarr. in Ps.*, 93 [Lt. 92].1; *Tract. in Ioh.*, 9.6; 15.9.

the division of humanity into 'two cities' *(Cat. rud.*, 19.31), which is comparable to the 'two ways' in earlier catechetical instruction and better known from his apologetic work, *The City of God*.[104] True Christians, he says, are 'citizens of the heavenly Jerusalem' (*Cat. rud.*, 7.11). Most characteristic is Augustine's emphasis on the two commands to love God and love neighbour: all scripture depends on them (*Cat. rud.*, 4.8); the narration of God's dealings with humanity all relate to the goal of love (6.10); the Decalogue can be reduced to these two commands (23.41); and they are the duties enjoined on Christians (27.55).[105] Augustine's concern for 'steadfast faith and a good life' (*Cat. rud.*, 25.47) prompts several warnings about the new converts being led astray by the various classes of sinners, the 'chaff' in the church who were Christians in name only (*Cat. rud.*, 7.11; 14.21; 25.48; 27.55). His advice to close with an eschatological exhortation (*Cat. rud.*, 7.11), although common enough in early Christian instruction, high-lights the way in which the eschatological theme permeates the whole instruction – 16.24–25 ('rest that is hoped for after this life'); 17.27–28 (eternal blessedness in the seventh age); 24.45 (judgement); 25.46 (defence of the resurrection); 25.47–48 (sample exhortation).

Augustine's sermons on the Psalms and on the Gospel of John were addressed to 'all', including catechumens, to whom he made a number of references.[106] The sermons on John focused more on

[104] Harmless, *Augustine and the Catechumenate*, 144–7.

[105] Raymond Canning has written a series of articles on the two commands. See his 'The Distinction Between Love for God and Love for Neighbour in St Augustine', *Augustiniana* 32 (1982), 5–41; repr. in E. Ferguson, *Studies in Early Christianity*, 16: *Christian Life: Ethics, Morality, and Discipline in the Early Church* (New York: Garland, 1993), 103–39; 'Love of Neighbour in St. Augustine: A Preparation for or the Essential Moment of Love for God?', 33 (1983), 5–57; 'The Augustinian *uti/frui* Distinction in the Relation Between Love for Neighbour and Love for God', 33 (1983), 165–231; ' "Love Your Neighbour as Yourself" (Matt xxii,39): St Augustine on the Lineaments of the Self to Be Loved', 34 (1984), 145–97; 'Augustine on the Identity of the Neighbour and the Meaning of True Love for Him "As Ourselves" (Matt. xxii,39) and "As Christ has Loved Us" (Jn xiii,34)', 36 (1986), 161–239; 'The Unity of Love for God and Neighbour', 37 (1987), 38–121.

[106] E.g., *Tract. in Ioh.*, 4.13; 10.10; 11.1, 2, 4. See Harmless, *Augustine and the Catechumenate*, 158–9 for *Enarr. in Psalm.*, 119–33 [Lt.] and *Tract. Ioh.*, 1–12 as an intertwining series of sermons preached between December and the opening of Lent, probably AD 406–7.

doctrine and an intellectual understanding of the faith; those on the Psalms focused on spirituality and an affective grasp of the faith.[107] Augustine saw himself as a minister of the word, whose task was to 'feed the [spiritually] hungry' with the bread of life. The biblical text controlled his expositions.[108] Scripture has a moral core; its purpose is to cleanse the soul for the journey home to God.[109]

Augustine repeats many themes expressed by the Greek fathers in their Epiphany sermons and their exhortations to catechumens to receive baptism.[110] After developing the common interpretation of Israel's crossing the Red Sea as a baptism in which past sins (= the Egyptians) are destroyed, Augustine challenges his hearers, 'Why do you fear to come?'[111] He too contrasts Christian baptism with that of John the Baptist and explores the reasons for Christ's baptism. One purpose was to serve as an example: 'If I [Jesus] have received the baptism of the servant [John], do you disdain to be baptized by the Lord?'[112]

Like his Eastern counterparts, Augustine complains that the public entertainments were more popular than church: 'For there are many that live not worthily of the baptism which they have received. For how many that are baptized have chosen rather to be filling the circus than this basilica'.[113] He often complains of the

[107] Harmless, *Augustine and the Catechumenate*, 194, 206.

[108] Ibid., 160-1, 180-1.

[109] Ibid., 186 with reference to *De doctrina christiana*.

[110] E. Ferguson, 'Preaching at Epiphany: Gregory of Nyssa and John Chrysostom on Baptism and the Church', *Church History* 66 (1997), 1-17, and 'Exhortations to Baptism in the Cappadocians', *Studia Patristica* 32 (1997), 112-20. There are a fair number of exhortations to baptism embedded in Augustine's various sermons and letters – Harmless, *Augustine and the Catechumenate*, 191 for a listing – but Augustine's Epiphany sermons (*Serm.*, 199–204) do not treat baptism, for they follow the Western understanding of the feast as connected with the visit of the Magi to the infant Jesus.

[111] *Enarr. in Psalm.*, 81.8; cf. *Tract. in Ioh.*, 11.4. Augustine knew the same problem of the delay of baptism by those 'more fearful of future sins than present ones' (*Serm.*, 97A.3; cf. 339.8) – Harmless, *Augustine and the Catechumenate*, 187.

[112] *Tract. in Ioh.*, 4.12-14; quotation from 4.13. The treatment has many similarities to John Chrysostom. For literature see n. 87.

[113] *Enarr. in Psalm.*, 81.2. 'Crowds fill the churches on feast days of the Christians which likewise fill the theaters on the ritual days of the pagans' (*Cat. rud.*, 25.48); many came to church for the great feasts but at other times filled

many Christians who live evil lives and pull the church down.[114] One of the key themes of the sermons on Psalms and John is that Christ as the inner Teacher exhorts to ascend to the heavenly Jerusalem by good works (*Enarr. in Psalm.*, 122 [Lt 121]).[115] 'The people of God are the city of God' (ibid., 125 [Lt 124.10]), so they have a foretaste of the heavenly joy; however, they remain exiles returning home (ibid., 126 [Lt 125.4]).[116]

Augustine alludes to activities of those undergoing the immediate preparation for baptism. Before coming to the water, there are fastings, tribulations, and prayers (*Enarr. in Psalm.*, 81 [Lt. 80].10). The renunciations are given a moral thrust: as well as rejecting the realm of the devil, the candidate renounced 'thefts, plunderings, perjuries, manslayings, adulteries, sacrileges, abominable rites, curious arts' (ibid., 81.18). The catechumens 'do not eat the flesh or drink the blood of the Son of Man', for they 'know not what Christians receive' (*Tract. in Ioh.*, 11.3, 4). So, we turn to Augustine's Lenten instructions to the *competentes*.

In several works Augustine offered summaries of the Christian faith according to the baptismal creed. His *Enchiridion*, or *Faith, Hope, and Love*, written c.421, remains the best single introduction to his thought. The bulk of the work is a commentary on the 'Apostles' Creed' (the faith: 9–113); the remainder takes up the Lord's Prayer (hope: 114–16) and the command to love (117–21) – the faith, prayer (liturgy), and love (morals) were his handbook summary of Christianity. *On Faith and the Creed* was a model explanation of the Apostles' Creed delivered while he was still a presbyter to the North African bishops in synod (AD 393). At each article, the address takes note of the false teachings refuted by the Creed. *On Christian Combat* also covers the Creed in terms of positions to be rejected (13.14–33.35). Other summaries of the creed occur in sermons addressed to the *competentes* at the occasion of the delivery of the creed to them (*traditio symboli*)

---

the theatres and arenas (*Sermons*, 301A.8 [= Denis 17]. Cf. Gregory of Nyssa, *Bapt. Chr.* (GNO, 9, 221, 6–9, 18) and John Chrysostom, *Bapt. Chr.*, 1 (PG, 49.363).

[114] *Serm.*, 248; 250. Augustine lamented that those converted in appearance were greater in number than those truly converted (*In Psalm.*, 40.10).

[115] Harmless, *Augustine and the Catechumenate*, 207–13.

[116] Ibid., 225–6.

two weeks before their baptism (*Sermons* 212–14 and *On the Symbol to Catechumens*) and their recitation of it (*redditio symboli*) a week before their baptism (*Sermon* 215).

Sermon 214 is much more theological than 213. Augustine's rhetorical flair for the paradoxical is evident in his characterization of the first nativity of the Son of God (from eternity) as of the Father without a mother; his second (on earth) as of a mother without a father (6). Another striking phrase is the description of the last resurrection as an end without an end (213.9). He describes the contents of the Creed as 'arranged in a fixed order and condensed', so as not to tax the memory of what the initiates are accustomed to hear in scripture and in sermons in church (1).[117] As part of the *disciplina arcani*, they are admonished not to write down the Creed but to learn it by oral repetition (1; cf. 212.2).[118]

Although Ambrose and Cyril of Jerusalem interpreted the Lord's Prayer after baptism, Augustine (as Theodore of Mopsuestia) did so before baptism, delivering the text of the prayer accompanied by a sermon of instruction on the same day as the first *redditio symboli* a week before baptism. 'You have been taught the Creed first, so that you may know what to believe, and afterwards the Prayer, so that you may know upon whom to call ... It is the believer's prayer that is heard' (*Serm.*, 56.2; cf. 57.1).[119] The first three petitions, he says, will never cease for all eternity; the remaining petitions have to do with life on this earth (19). Even these first three petitions are not for God but for one's self. For example, the prayer for the kingdom to come is a petition that it come within us so we may be found within that kingdom. It is a prayer that a person lead a good life so as to partake of the kingdom that is to come (6).

The treatise *On Faith and Works*, written in 413, refutes the error that faith and baptism alone are sufficient for salvation

---

[117] Mary Sarah Muldowney, trans., *Saint Augustine: Sermons on the Liturgical Seasons*, Fathers of the Church 38 (New York: Fathers of the Church, 1959).

[118] R. De Latte, 'Saint Augustin et le baptême', 201 observes that in *Serm.* 212.2 Augustine bases the prohibition not on the rule of secrecy but on Jeremiah 31.33, 'written on the heart'.

[119] Denis J. Kavanagh, trans., *Saint Augustine: Commentary on the Lord's Sermon on the Mount with Seventeen Related Sermons*, Fathers of the Church 11 (New York: Fathers of the Church, 1951). *Sermons* 57–9 also concerned the delivery of the 'Our Father'.

without good works (*Retractationes*, 2.38) and that instruction for baptism should consist only of doctrines to be believed, with morals to be taught afterwards (*Faith and Works*, 1.1).[120] The particular concern of Augustine's opponents in this treatise is adulterers, viz., those who were married to persons who had been previously married (passim, but esp. 19.35). Erroneous teaching and practice often expose the points of weaknesses that occasion the errors, and it may be that the position opposed in *On Faith and Works* grew out of the church's practice of giving more attention to instruction in the faith and little explicit attention to morals. Augustine responds that repentance requires quitting one's sins (8.12). When Paul affirmed salvation by faith, he did not mean that good works are unnecessary nor that it is enough to profess the faith and no more (14.21). Those to be admitted to baptism are those who believe in the Trinity (as in the Creed) *and* do penance for their sins (20.36). The one being prepared for baptism was to be zealous in attending instructions, exorcisms, and scrutinies (6.9). Augustine insisted that faith and morals belong together; one must have faith in order to live a good, Christian life (7.11). Those preparing for baptism are to be taught not only what to believe but also what to do in the Christian life (27.49). In practice, however, it seems that most of the moral teaching was done by way of the ceremonies of scrutiny and exorcism[121] and not by systematic exposition. Moreover, it must be said that although Augustine protested against these laxists who said to make people Christians first and then teach them how to live, his support of coercion against the Donatists and support for infant baptism had the effect of establishing that very approach. In his argument against the Donatists and Pelagians, who in different ways held to an elitist view of the church as made up of the pure, he began 'to edge, in carefully measured ways, towards a Church of the many'.[122]

Augustine, like Theodore of Mopsuestia and John Chrysostom, did not wait until Easter week to explain baptism and eucharist,

---

[120] Gregory J. Lombardo, trans., *St Augustine on Faith and Works*, Ancient Christian Writers 48 (New York: Newman, 1988).

[121] R. De Latte, 'Saint Augustin et le baptême', 196–9.

[122] Harmless, *Augustine and the Catechumenate*, 250, with reference to R. A. Markus, 'Augustine: A Defense of Christian Mediocrity', in his *End of Ancient Christianity* (Cambridge: Cambridge University Press, 1990), 52–5.

for there are many explanations of its significance in the works already surveyed.[123] He gave private catecheses on the eucharist to the newly baptized on Easter Sunday morning before they received it (*Serm.*, 229 and 229A before the prayer; 227 and 272 before communion).[124] One of his Easter Sunday sermons says that he has treated the sacrament of the creed, the sacrament of the Lord's prayer, the sacrament of the font and baptism; now it is time for the sacrament of the holy altar (228.3).[125]

Augustine's sermons delivered on Easter Sunday contain many direct references to those 'reborn in Christ Jesus', no longer *competentes* but now *infantes* (*Serm.*, 224.1, 4; 225.4; 228.1, 2). He gave attention to sins to abstain from; adultery is prominent (224), but also mentioned is drunkenness (225.4). The older believers are admonished not to set a bad example, and the newly baptized are exhorted: 'If you do not find what you may imitate, then be what somebody else may imitate' (228.1, 2).

During the Octave of Easter, eucharistic liturgies were held daily, and Augustine preached twice daily to the older and the newer believers. His sermons explored especially the meaning of the resurrection, a doctrine closely associated with the theme of the city of God. Thus, Augustine's mystagogy was not so much liturgical (as in other fourth-century representatives) as it was eschatological. To be incorporated into the church was not enough, for the church was a mix of wheat and chaff; hence Christians must keep their eyes fixed on the eschaton. A comparison of Augustine's mystagogy with that of other fourth and fifth-century teachers shows a much greater emphasis on the endtime.[126]

Hence, we have treated Augustine's catecheses as 'Training to Live in the Heavenly City'. This, as should be evident from even this brief survey, did not mean that Augustine had his head in the clouds. On the Sunday after Easter, he concluded his instructions to new converts on a practical moral note. 'You have to return to

---

[123] Harmless, *Augustine and the Catechumenate*, 306.

[124] Ibid., pp. 316–17. One of these is studied in H. R. Drobner, 'Augustinus, Sermo 227: Eine österliche Eucharistiekatechese für die Neugetauften', *Augustiniana* 41 (1991), 483–95.

[125] For Augustine's doctrine of the real presence see my paper referred to in n. 91.

[126] Harmless, *Augustine and the Catechumenate*, 324–8, 338–9, 364–5; De Latte, 'Saint Augustin et le baptême', 223.

the people; you have to mingle with the faithful; beware of imitating wicked believers'. Among his admonitions, the one that is elaborated on is, 'Preserve your chastity'; other sins are only mentioned (*Serm.*, 260).

Concluding observations

The catechumenate all along served an evangelistic function,[127] but in the course of the fourth century it became more didactic. At the beginnings of the organized catechumenate the concern seems to have been how to keep the unworthy out of the church. It established clear boundary lines, and its rituals marked the transition to a new community.[128] The fourth-century catechumenate was still concerned with boundaries in a new situation, but the principal concern seems to have become how to get the worthy into the church.

The former concern is exhibited in the *Apostolic Tradition*, which provided for a three-year catechumenate (ch. 17). Persons in certain occupations were excluded; others were told to cease their circumstances or be excluded (ch. 16). A rigorous moral examination preceded admission to the catechumenate. In the *Apostolic Tradition* the catechumens, although in the process of making a transition to the church, still in some sense belonged to the 'enemy' and so were subject to frequent exorcisms.[129] By the fourth century the rituals such as exorcism were still there, but the emphasis had shifted from the separation between the two realms of the world and the church to preparation for assuming a place in the church.

Maertens notes that what the *Apostolic Tradition* puts at the beginning – the moral instruction – Augustine puts at the end.[130] On Augustine's behalf, I would say that he does put a testing of motives first (*Cat. rud.*, 5.9), and moral exhortation in the form of

[127] E. Glenn Hinson, *The Evangelization of the Roman Empire* (Macon: Mercer University Press, 1981).

[128] Finn, 'Ritual Process', 69–90 finds the rituals of the catechumenate as providing a powerful influence in developing the social stamina of Christians in Rome. The social dimension of the catechesis is noted by Germain, 'Baptême et éducation de la foi', 113.

[129] Finn, 'Ritual Process', 75, 79.

[130] Maertens, *Histoire et pastorale*, 118.

the two commandments to love is part of the first instruction. Nevertheless, he places the main moral instruction later. *On Faith and Works* says training in the faith and the pattern of the Christian life goes on during the time of the catechumenate and becomes more intensive during the candidates' time as *competentes* (6.9). Elsewhere he states, 'It is faith that first makes souls subject to God. Next come the precepts for right living'.[131] And even in these later stages, I must observe, there is regrettably no systematic moral exposition comparable to the creedal and liturgical instructions. Daniélou explains the change in timing by saying that at the beginning of the church, moral catechesis had to come first to mark the rupture with pagan customs; in the fourth century it was at the end as the flowering of all life in the grace of the Holy Spirit.[132] Both statements are true, but the former is a sociological observation, the latter a theological affirmation. Were not morals rooted in doctrine in the second century? Was there not still a need in the fourth century to make the rupture with pagan society evident?

The space allotments in Augustine's 'Handbook' (*Enchiridion*) may serve to illustrate the concerns in fifth-century teaching. One hundred and five sections discuss the creed, three sections the Lord's Prayer, and five sections charity (or love). There are likely practical considerations for this distribution, and I would not argue that it represents Augustine's ultimate priorities. Nevertheless, the disproportionate attention given to the creed over prayer and a life of love may serve as a symbol of the state of catechetical instruction in the West at the beginning of the fifth century.

The eagerness to include as many as possible in the church is illustrated by Augustine's terminology. Instead of treating catechumens as outsiders, he includes them in the name 'Christian', meaning 'anointed', because they were admitted to the catechumenate in a ceremony that involved being signed with the cross

---

[131] *On Christian Combat*, 13.14, translated by Bernard M. Peebles, *Saint Augustine*, Fathers of the Church 2 (New York: Fathers of the Church, 1947), 331. The passage continues, 'When these are observed, our hope is made firm, charity is nurtured, and what before was only believed begins to be clearly understood'. The same sequence of hearing, believing, hoping, and loving is found in *Cat. rud.*, 4.8; cf. the related statement in *Enchiridion*, 3.8, 'There is no love without hope, no hope without love, and neither hope nor love without faith'.

[132] Daniélou, *La catéchèse*, 126.

(*Tract. in Ioh.*, 44.2). He does maintain a distinction by declaring that catechumens are servants in the household but the baptized are sons (*Tract. in Ioh.*, 11.4), or in another image suggested by John 3:5, the catechumens are in the womb of the church but must be born of water and the Spirit (*Tract. in Ioh.*, 11.6; 12.3). I have sometimes illustrated the changed circumstances for the church by the observation that in the third century Christian authors wrote exhortations to martyrdom; in the fourth century, exhortations to baptism. There are a number of these encouragements in Augustine.[133] People were glad to be identified with the church to the extent of admission to the catechumenate, but they were not eager to assume the full duties of church membership.

We have seen that the fourth century offers us examples of instruction surveying the contents of the Bible (Augustine, *Cat. rud.*), explaining the articles of the Creed (Cyril of Jerusalem, Ambrose, Augustine, and others), and interpreting the rites of initiation (Cyril of Jerusalem, Ambrose, Augustine, and others). Although there are many scattered references to moral instruction and sermons having that as the principal content, there were no catechetical instructions on morals as such and no set place in the catechumenate for giving this instruction. There was no curriculum for moral teaching comparable to that supplied by the Creed and the liturgy. Daniélou explains the lack of a separate moral catechesis in the fourth century by saying that morals were taught from the scriptures, the creed, and the sacraments,[134] and he justifies this practice as avoiding the danger of cutting off morals from their doctrinal roots.[135] Such makes the best of the anomaly. The lack of balance and consistency here, I suspect, has a great deal to do with the failure of the Christianization of the West to penetrate more deeply into the behaviour of people. At some places a balance was maintained, and some did the job of Christian formation better than others. Ambrose and Augustine certainly tried. But I am left with the (to me) disturbing impression that even in these fathers a more concentrated and thorough job was done of doctrinal and liturgical (sacramental) instruction than was done with biblical and moral teaching. The emphasis had shifted from the earlier

---

[133] See notes 110–11.
[134] Daniélou, 'La Catéchèse dans la Tradition patristique', 29–30.
[135] Daniélou, *La catéchèse*, 158.

days of the church. The new centre of gravity for catechesis in the fourth and fifth centuries perhaps reflected the prominence of doctrinal controversy in church life. Being a Christian was now defined primarily in terms of doctrine and not in terms of behaviour. It was left for the monks to maintain the witness to a distinctive Christian lifestyle. Was all this the price of becoming the church of the Empire?

Chapter 9

The Effects of the Coming of Christendom on Early Christian Worship

PAUL F. BRADSHAW

As Christendom developed, liturgical practices evolved gradually; they did not change suddenly as a result of Constantine's legalization of Christianity. But fourth-century liturgical elaborations, far from making for a golden age of Christian worship, in reality were expressions of the desperate attempts of church leaders to shape the Christian belief, behaviour and experience of an increasingly half-converted laity. As the fourth century progressed, earlier efforts to resist pagan influences were superseded by attempts to appropriate pagan understandings and practices to enable communication with the surrounding culture. This led to a heightening of the emotional temperature of the baptismal rituals and to an emphasis upon the 'awefulness' of the eucharist, resulting in both the withdrawal of many laypeople from the act of communion and in the clericalization of worship. In the fourth century, attempts to safeguard the orthodoxy of doctrine led to the standardization of liturgical practice and the disappearance of extemporized prayer.

The apparent conversion to Christianity of the Emperor Constantine early in the fourth century is usually portrayed as marking a crucial turning-point in the evolution of forms of Christian worship; and it is undoubtedly true that a very clear contrast can be observed between the form and character of liturgical practices in the pre- and post-Constantinian eras. However, scholars are now beginning to realize that one must be careful not to overstate this distinction between the two periods of ecclesiastical history.[1] A number of developments, the genesis of which has traditionally been ascribed to the changed situation of the church after the Peace of Constantine, can be shown as having roots that reach back into the third century, and in some cases even earlier still. Similarly, many of the differences that really do seem to be new creations in the fourth century first come to our attention in the second half of that century, and in some cases its final quarter, suggesting that they were not so much the immediate consequences of Constantine's conversion but rather part of a process that had certainly begun well before that momentous event, was intensified by it, but only issued forth in radical changes of practice through the interaction of a complex series of cultural and doctrinal shifts in the course of the succeeding decades.

Traditional scholarship has also tended to paint a picture of post-Constantinian forms of worship as constituting the classic expression of the Christian faith. Liturgy is viewed as gradually evolving from its inchoate roots in the New Testament through the refining processes of the second and third centuries and then bursting into full bloom in the light of the Constantinian era. It then threw off the shackles that persecution and poverty had put upon it, and became what it was always intended to be, reaching the zenith of form and articulation in this golden age, before beginning its long period of slow decline, disintegration and obfuscation in the course of the Middle Ages. Once again, while there is some truth to this perspective, it tends to be wildly overstated. On the contrary, many of the fourth-century liturgical developments were the responses of a church which had already passed its peak, was experiencing the beginnings of decline, and was trying to do something to stem the tide. Unfortunately, all too often the 'something' that was then done unwittingly carried within it the seeds of further destruction rather than the solution that would preserve the glories of the past.

It is the primary intention of my paper, therefore, to offer some illustrations of these two trends – the gradual and complex

---

[1] See, for example, Alexander Schmemann, *Introduction to Liturgical Theology* (London: Faith Press, 1966), 76: 'It is really impossible to speak of a "liturgical revolution" in the fourth century, if by this we mean the appearance of a type of worship differing radically from that which had gone before. It is also difficult, however, to deny the profound change which after all did mark the church's liturgical life beginning with the epoch of Constantine'.

evolution of liturgical practice rather than its sudden switch of focus, and the inbuilt tendency towards disintegration of that evolution rather than the full flowering of the Christian vision. Because space does not permit a comprehensive exploration of all the aspects of the subject, I have chosen to focus upon the two principal causes: paganism and the formulation of doctrine.

Resisting the influence of paganism

It is often said that early Christian worship felt little effect from the pagan world around, because Christians were anxious to keep their practices separate and distinct from what went on in the contemporary culture. They wanted to show that they were not a religion like other religions, that they had no temple or altar in the sense in which others did;[2] and the periodic accusations of atheism that came from their critics suggest that they were generally successful in this attempt. Thus, it is claimed, it was only when paganism ceased to be a threat to the integrity of the Christian faith in the fourth century that its adherents felt free to borrow and absorb the vocabulary and images of other religions to enhance the expression of its own liturgical worship. Now that the liturgy was functioning as a cultus publicus, seeking the divine favour to secure the well-being of the state, it was willing to see itself as the fulfilment of that to which those other religions had dimly pointed.

Although there are certainly some elements of truth in this account, the real story is by no means as simple as that. While the predominant external influence on the shape of Christian worship in the early centuries came from Judaism – both in terms of elements that had been preserved from Christianity's roots in that tradition and also in terms of its subsequent reaction against continuing practices that made it appear to be dependent upon Judaism – yet the effect of paganism prior to the Peace of Constantine must not be discounted. Anscar Chupungco, for example, has recently argued that many elements in the Christian baptismal rites of the second and third centuries were drawn from the surrounding pagan culture.[3] Similarly, the Christian church after the Peace of

---

[2] See Minucius Felix, *Octavius*, 32.
[3] Anscar Chupungco, 'Baptism in the Early Church and its Cultural Settings', in S. Anita Stauffer, ed., *Worship and Culture in Dialogue* (Geneva: Lutheran World Federation, 1994), 39–56, reproduced in elaborated form in Anscar

Constantine did not immediately open its arms to embrace paganism fully. Instead we see two parallel – and seemingly contradictory – trajectories, as Christians struggled to decide what their attitude should be.

On the one hand, pagan practices were still viewed as a threat to the integrity of the Christian faith, and ecclesiastical authorities felt it necessary to try to draw the faithful away from the temptation to participate in them. We can see this exemplified best with regard to pagan winter solstice celebrations. There are a number of signs that Christians were being encouraged to intensify their regular practice of fasting around this period of the year, apparently in an attempt to keep them from indulging in the excesses of the pagan feasting during this season. 1 January, for instance, was designated as a day of fasting by the church at Rome.[4] It soon became clear to the ecclesiastical authorities, however, that Christian feasts rather than fasts would provide more effective counter-attractions to the pagan delights. Although scholars still debate why 25 December was originally selected as the feast of the nativity of Christ at Rome,[5] its subsequent adoption in northern Italy can clearly be shown to be the result of a desire to rival the pagan solstice celebrations held on that date in the Julian calendar.[6] In Rome itself, 1 January was later changed from a fast-day into a feast in honour of the Virgin Mary, presumably for similar reasons.[7]

Chupungco, *Worship: Beyond Inculturation* (Washington, DC: Pastoral Press, 1994), 1–18. See also Elizabeth Leeper, 'From Alexandria to Rome: The Valentinian Connection to the Incorporation of Exorcism as a Prebaptismal Rite', *Vigiliae Christianae* 44 (1990), 6–24.

[4] See Thomas J. Talley, *The Origins of the Liturgical Year* (New York: Pueblo, 1986), 149–51; J. Neil Alexander, *Waiting for the Coming: The Liturgical Meaning of Advent, Christmas, Epiphany* (Washington, DC: Pastoral Press, 1993), 8–23.

[5] For an account of the debate, see Susan K. Roll, *Toward the Origins of Christmas* (Kampen: Kok Pharos, 1995).

[6] See Martin Connell, 'The Liturgical Year in Northern Italy (365–450)' (unpublished PhD dissertation, University of Notre Dame, 1995), 169–233.

[7] See Bernard Botte, 'La première fête mariale de la liturgie romaine', *Ephemerides Liturgicae* 47 (1933), 425–30; also J.-M. Guilmard, 'Une antique fête mariale au 1er janvier dans la ville de Rome?' *Ecclesia Orans* 11 (1994), 25–67.

Appropriating pagan practices to foster communication

On the other hand, at the same time as this was going on, the church was appropriating language, images, and ceremonies from pagan practice in order to serve its liturgical purposes and enable it to communicate more effectively with the surrounding culture. A good example of this trend is the major shift that the whole style of initiation practice underwent everywhere in the fourth century in imitation of pagan mystery rites. Edward Yarnold attributes the prime responsibility for this development to the Emperor Constantine himself.[8] The ceremonies surrounding baptism became highly elaborate, much more dramatic – one might even say theatrical – in character, and cloaked in such great secrecy that candidates would have no idea in advance what was going to happen to them. Only after they had experienced the celebration of baptism and the eucharist was an explanation of the meaning of the sacred mysteries in which they had partaken then given to them in what was called mystagogy – post-baptismal instruction, usually during the week following their initiation. The baptismal homilies of the period use expressions such as 'awe-inspiring' and 'hair-raising' to describe the sensational style of the ceremonial used, which included such things as dramatic exorcisms and multiple anointings with oil.[9]

A similar shift in the style of celebrations of the eucharist can also be observed at the same period. They became much more formal and elaborate; they used such things as ceremonial actions, vesture, processions, and music to an extent previously unknown; and in both word and action they stressed the majesty and transcendence of God and the divinity of Christ present in the eucharistic mystery.[10] At first, these notes were struck more in preaching and

[8] Edward Yarnold, *The Awe-Inspiring Rites of Initiation* (Slough: St Paul Publications, 1971), 55–62; 'Baptism and the Pagan Mysteries in the Fourth Century', *Heythrop Journal* 13 (1972), 247–67; 'Who Planned the Churches at the Christian Holy Places in the Holy Land?' *Studia Patristica* 18/1 (1989), 105–9.

[9] See further Yarnold, *Awe-Inspiring Rites*; H. M. Riley, *Christian Initiation: A Comparative Study of the Interpretation of the Baptismal Liturgy in the Mystagogical Writings of Cyril of Jerusalem, John Chrysostom, Theodore of Mopsuestia, and Ambrose of Milan* (Washington, DC: Catholic University of America Press, 1974).

[10] See Joseph Jungmann, *The Early Liturgy to the Time of Gregory the Great* (London: Darton, Longman & Todd, 1960), 122–74.

teaching about the eucharist than in the liturgical texts themselves. Thus John Chrysostom repeatedly speaks of the 'dreadful sacrifice', of the 'fearful moment' when the mysteries were accomplished, and of the 'terrible and awful table' that should only be approached with fear and trembling.[11] But Cyril of Jerusalem's directions to the newly baptized on the proper manner of reception of holy communion reveal a radical shift in practice from the simplicity and intimacy of earlier times:

> So when you come forward, do not come with arm extended or fingers parted. Make your left hand a throne for your right, since your right hand is about to welcome a king. Cup your palm and receive in it Christ's body, saying in response Amen. Then carefully bless your eyes with a touch of the holy body, and consume it, being careful to drop not a particle of it. For to lose any of it is clearly like losing part of your own body ... After partaking of Christ's body, go to the chalice of his blood. Do not stretch out your hands for it. Bow your head and say Amen to show your homage and reverence, and sanctify yourself by partaking also of Christ's blood. While your lips are still moist with his blood, touch it with your hands and bless your eyes, forehead, and other organs of sense.[12]

We can see here that not only are the eucharistic elements to be treated with great reverence when they are consumed but that they are also regarded as objects of power which can be used to confer blessing on a person's body and protect it against evil and sickness.

Many other examples could be cited of the tension between, on the one hand, the desire to make a clear distinction between pagan and Christian practices and ideas, and on the other hand, the desire to use the images and vocabulary of paganism to communicate to the world around the true meaning of Christianity as the fulfilment of everything to which other religions had dimly pointed. For instance, Christians were deeply sensitive to charges made against

---

[11] See Edmund Bishop, 'Fear and Awe Attaching to the Eucharistic Service', in R. H. Connolly, *The Liturgical Homilies of Narsai* (Cambridge: Cambridge University Press, 1909), 92–7; Joseph Jungmann, *The Place of Christ in Liturgical Prayer* (London: Geoffrey Chapman, 1965), 245–55; J. G. Davies, 'The Introduction of the Numinous into the Liturgy: An Historical Note', *Studia Liturgica* 8 (1971/72), 216–23.

[12] Cyril of Jerusalem, *Mystagogical Catechesis*, 5.21–22; English translation from Yarnold, *Awe-Inspiring Rites*, 94–5.

them by Manichaeans and others that because the disposition of their annual feasts was made in connection with the movement of the moon and the sun, they were worshipping those heavenly bodies; and various leading figures, among them Ambrose of Milan and Leo the Great, mounted defences against these attacks.[13] Yet, when Constantine embarked upon his ambitious programme of church building, Christians were quite willing to employ the language of 'temples' and 'sanctuaries' in relation to these edifices. Even the church's extensive use of public space in the cities for processions and other ceremonial acts ('worship on the town', as Aidan Kavanagh has termed it), can be seen both as an anti-pagan demonstration that it had conquered what was formerly pagan territory and also at the same time as an adoption of the very forms and practices of paganism itself.[14]

Disintegration of Christian worship: coping with the half-converted

If we ask why the church was willing, even eager, to adopt elements from pagan worship in its initiatory and eucharistic liturgies at the very same period when it was apparently still viewing pagan religion as a rival against which it had to defend itself, then we must turn to my second thesis: that fourth-century liturgical developments were often part of the process of disintegration of Christian worship rather than its full flowering. While it has been usual to view the elaborations of liturgical practice such as we have just noted as manifesting the classic or golden age of liturgical evolution, in reality they are symptoms of a church that was losing the battle for the hearts and minds of its followers and was desperately attempting to remedy the situation by whatever means lay to hand.

[13] See Charles Pietri, 'Le temps de la semaine à Rome et dans l'Italie chrétienne (IV-VI s.)', in Jean-Marie Leroux, ed., Le temps chrétien de la fin de l'antiquité au Moyen Age (IIIe-XIIIe siècles), Colloques internationaux du Centre Nationale de la Recherche Scientifique 604 (Paris: Éditions du CNRS, 1984), 72–3.
[14] Aidan Kavanagh, On Liturgical Theology (New York: Pueblo, 1984), 65; see also John F. Baldovin, The Urban Character of Christian Worship, Orientalia Christiana Analecta 228 (Rome: Pont. Institutum Studiorum Orientalium, 1987); Charles Pietri, 'Liturgy, Culture, and Society: The Example of Rome at the End of the Ancient World (Fourth-Fifth Centuries)', Concilium 162 (1983), 38–46.

Prior to the fourth century, one could reasonably assume that those who sought admission to the church, and were prepared to take upon themselves the attendant risks of social ostracism and even actual, if sporadic, persecution, were generally motivated by some genuine conversion experience that they were undergoing in their lives. In such a context, the initiatory rituals of Christianity served to give symbolic expression to a reality which already existed for the candidates. In the changed circumstances of the fourth century, however, not all those who sought admission to the church took the step because they had experienced an inner conversion: some did so from less worthy motives, such as the desire to marry a Christian or to please a master or friend, or because it promised to be advantageous to their career or political ambitions. Moreover, once having become catechumens, many people were in no hurry to complete the process of initiation. Since they were already regarded as Christians, they saw no need to proceed to baptism itself, especially as that would leave no second chance to obtain the forgiveness of sins that baptism was believed to convey. It seemed preferable, therefore, to delay the actual baptism as long as possible so as to be sure of having all one's sins forgiven and so of gaining salvation. Consequently, many parents enrolled their children as catechumens early in their life but delayed presenting them for baptism at least until after the passions of youth had subsided and there was less chance of them succumbing to temptation; and many adults deferred their own baptism until they became seriously ill and feared that they might die unbaptized.[15]

All of this had a profound effect on the nature of the baptismal process itself. The reluctance of candidates to proceed to baptism led to a tendency among the clergy to 'lower the hurdles' as far as possible to encourage them to come in. In their enthusiasm to win more members, they tended to welcome baptismal candidates without such a rigorous examination of the genuineness of their conversion and of their lifestyle as had earlier been customary. Consequently, rather than being the outward expression of an inner conversion that had already taken place, the rites now became instead the means of producing a powerful emotional and

---

[15] See further Michael Dujarier, *A History of the Catechumenate: The First Six Centuries* (New York: Sadlier, 1979), 78–111.

psychological impression upon the candidates in the hope of bringing about their conversion. The greater formalization of the time of the catechumenate, for example, with its periodic punctuation with ritual moments that might involve such things as exorcism or the tasting of salt, is not an advance upon the less formalized preparation for baptism of earlier centuries, but a sign that the process was no longer working properly and needed shoring up.

Similar factors were also at work in the changes that were taking place in the style of eucharistic celebration. Since many members of the church could be described as at best only half-converted and half-instructed, their behaviour both in their daily lives and at public worship often left a great deal to be desired. According to John Chrysostom, for example, they pushed and pulled one another in an unruly manner during the services; they gossiped with one another; young people engaged in various kinds of mischief; and pickpockets preyed upon the crowd.[16] Thus, the regular liturgies had to assume more of an instructional and formational role than heretofore. It was necessary to try to communicate through the style of liturgical celebration itself something of the majesty of God and the reality of Christ's sacramental presence, as well as of the appropriate attitude of reverence required before that divinity.

Severing the act of communion from the eucharistic action

Unfortunately, however, once again the cures chosen for these particular ills carried within themselves the seeds of further liturgical destruction. The ultimate aim was to secure the worthy participation of all in the Christian mysteries; the measure chosen towards this end was to exclude the unworthy. Thus, fourth-century preachers regularly warned their congregations against coming to communion while still leading sinful lives. John Chrysostom again was particularly vigilant in this regard, frequently emphasizing the sincerity and purity of soul necessary to approach the supper of the Lord: 'With this, approach at all times; without it, never!' He advised those who were guilty of sin to leave the service before the eucharistic action itself began.[17]

---

[16] For references, see Davies, 'The Introduction of the Numinous into the Liturgy', 222.

[17] John Chrysostom, *Hom. in Eph.*, 3.4.

The purpose of preaching such as this was of course not to discourage the reception of communion, but rather to encourage higher standards of Christian living and of behaviour in church. But, as so often happens, the results were exactly the opposite of the intentions of the preachers. Many people preferred to give up the reception of communion rather than amend their lives. Thus began the practice of non-communicating attendance at the eucharist. Contrary to Chrysostom's advice, many people apparently stayed until the time for communion and then left the church. The ecclesiastical authorities were eventually forced to accept this practice, and they began to make provision in the rites at the time of the communion for a formal blessing and dismissal of non-communicants in order to encourage a more orderly departure.[18]

Clericalization

This development had a significant effect upon people's understanding of the eucharist, since it severed the act of communion from the rest of the eucharistic action. It made it possible for them to think of the eucharist as complete and effective without the need for them to participate in the reception of the bread and wine, and thus helped to further the idea that liturgy was something that the clergy did on their behalf, which ultimately did not even require their presence. This notion, too, had roots that went back well before the age of Constantine. Already by the middle of the third century, the idea that the bishops with their clergy constituted a priesthood which would act on behalf of the rest had already made an appearance, and was beginning to break down the older concept that the whole people – ordained ministers and laity together – composed a royal priesthood functioning before God in their worship and offering the sacrifice of praise.[19] Thus,

[18] See Robert F. Taft, 'The Inclination Prayer before Communion in the Byzantine Liturgy of St John Chrysostom: A Study in Comparative Liturgy', *Ecclesia Orans* 3 (1986), 29–60.

[19] See, for example, Maurice Bévenot, 'Tertullian's Thoughts about the Christian "Priesthood",' in *Corona Gratiarum* I. *Miscellanea Patristica, Historica et Liturgica, Eligio Dekkers OSB XII Lustra Complenti Oblata* (Bruges: Sint Pietersubdij, 1975), 125–37; idem, '"Sacerdos" as Understood by Cyprian', *Journal of Theological Studies* 30 (1979), 413–29; John D. Laurance, *'Priest' as Type of Christ: The Leader of the Eucharist in Salvation History According to Cyprian of Carthage* (New York: Lang, 1984).

clericalism was not a novelty of the fourth century. But it certainly took a significant step forward then. The more professionalized clergy of this period increasingly dominated public worship, and the people were content to let them do it, the pure acting for the impure, the experts for the ignorant. Even Chrysostom's very assertion that there were some moments when there was no difference at all between the roles of priest and people in the eucharist is itself a tacit admission that there were other times when there most definitely was a difference:

> But there are occasions when there is no difference at all between the priest and those under him; for instance, when we are to partake of the awful mysteries . . . And in the prayers also, one may observe the people contributing much . . . Again, in the most awful mysteries themselves, the priest prays for the people and the people also pray for the priest; for the words 'with thy spirit' are nothing else than this. The offering of thanksgiving again is common: for neither doth he give thanks alone, but also for all the people . . .[20]

The influence of the formulation of doctrine

We must not assume, however, that the challenge posed by paganism was the only thing responsible for the changing character of the church's worship in the fourth century. As well as pressures from without, there were fears from within. The drive towards greater precision in the formulation of Christian doctrine played a significant part in reshaping liturgical practice in the Constantinian age. The need to distinguish true belief from false doctrine was of course nothing new at this time. It had existed ever since the first Christians tried to define their faith. But the problem of heresy was now posed far more acutely, as much for political and practical reasons as for theological ones: it was, for example, essential to be able to decide who were the rightful owners of ecclesiastical property. Thus the fourth century brought to the boil doctrinal issues that had been simmering for some time, and through the successive ecumenical councils of the period required all local churches to declare themselves clearly on one side or another of

[20] John Chrysostom, *Hom. in 2 Cor.*, 18.3; English translation from Philip Schaff, ed., *A Select Library of the Nicene and Post-Nicene Fathers of the Christian Church* 12 (New York: Christian Literature Company, 1889), 365–6.

the various debates. In such a situation, therefore, any tendency to persist in what appeared to be idiosyncratic liturgical observances was likely to have been interpreted as a mark of heterodoxy.[21]

Standardizing liturgical practice

Although earlier generations of scholars tended towards the view that there had always been a large measure of homogeneity, or even uniformity, in the liturgical traditions stemming from the apostolic age, more recent research points towards the conclusion that liturgical variety generally diminished rather than increased as the church developed.[22] Hence, the large measure of agreement in liturgical practice that can be seen in later sources is more often the result of a conscious movement towards standardization that did not begin until the fourth century – and frequently only in the second half of that century – rather than the survival of an ancient way of doing things that all Christians shared from the beginning.[23]

In the area of Christian initiation for example, it appears that the widespread adoption of Easter as the preferred baptismal season was a development of the mid-fourth century, and that prior to that time the custom was restricted to North Africa and Rome.[24] Similarly, the tendency to locate the action of the Holy Spirit in some form of post-baptismal ceremony began to spread during this century from what seems to have been its place of

[21] See, for example, Rowan Williams, 'Baptism and the Arian Controversy', in Michael R. Barnes and Daniel H. Williams, eds, *Arianism after Arius: Essays on the Development of the Fourth-Century Trinitarian Conflicts* (Edinburgh: T&T Clark, 1993), 149–80.

[22] See Paul F. Bradshaw, *The Search for the Origins of Christian Worship: Sources and Methods for the Study of Early Liturgy* (London: SPCK and New York: Oxford University Press, 1992); also published in French as *La Liturgie chrétienne en ses origines: Sources et méthodes* (Paris: Cerf, 1995).

[23] See further Paul F. Bradshaw, 'The Homogenization of Christian Liturgy – Ancient and Modern', *Studia Liturgica* 26 (1996), 1–15; also published in French as 'L'uniformisation de la liturgie chrétienne au IVᵉ et au XXᵉ siècle', *La Maison-Dieu* 204 (1995), 9–30.

[24] See Paul F. Bradshaw, 'Diem baptismo sollemniorem: Initiation and Easter in Christian Antiquity', in Ephrem Carr, Stefano Parenti, Abraham-Andreas Thiermeyer, Elena Velkovska, eds, *Eulogêma: Studies in Honor of Robert Taft, SJ*, Studia Anselmiana 110 (Rome: Centro Studi S. Anselmo, 1993), 41–51; reprinted in Maxwell Johnson, ed., *Living Water, Sealing Spirit: Readings on Christian Initiation* (Collegeville: Liturgical Press, 1995), 137–47.

origin in North Africa to other parts of the world.[25] At the very same time, the use of a baptismal formula to accompany the act of immersion was beginning a journey from its Syrian home, appearing in Egypt in the early fourth century, and later in Spain, Gaul and Rome.[26]

In the area of eucharistic worship, there is a similar convergence of practice. This can most clearly be seen with regard to eucharistic prayer itself. The apparently relatively simple local patterns of earlier centuries were expanded with new features, many of which – like the Sanctus, the narrative of institution, and epiclesis – were simply borrowed from the practice of other places and inserted into the native structures. Sometimes large portions of two prayers from different regions were combined to form a complex and composite anaphora, and sometimes whole prayers were exported from one ecclesiastical centre to become the standard liturgical fare of other localities.[27]

---

[25] See S. P. Brock, 'The Transition to a Post-Baptismal Anointing in the Antiochene Rite', in Bryan D. Spinks, ed., *The Sacrifice of Praise*, Bibliotheca 'Ephemerides Liturgicae' Subsidia 19 (Rome: Edizioni Liturgiche, 1981), 215–25.

[26] See further E. C. Whitaker, 'The Baptismal Formula in the Syrian Rite', *Church Quarterly Review* 161 (1960), 346–52; idem, 'The History of the Baptismal Formula', *Journal of Ecclesiastical History* 16 (1965), 1–12; P.-M. Gy, 'La formule "Je te baptise" (Et ego te baptizo)', in *Communio Sanctorum: Mélanges offerts à Jean-Jacques von Allmen* (Geneva: Labor et Fides, 1982), 65–72; Paul de Clerck, 'Les origines de la formule baptismale', in Paul de Clerck and Eric Palazzo, eds, *Rituels: Mélanges offerts à Pierre-Marie Gy, OP* (Paris: Cerf, 1990), 199–213.

[27] Among recent studies, see especially John R. K. Fenwick, 'The Missing Oblation': The Contents of the Early Antiochene Anaphora, Alcuin/GROW Liturgical Study 11 (Nottingham: Grove Books, 1989); idem, *The Anaphoras of St Basil and St James: An Investigation into their Common Origin*, Orientalia Christiana Analecta 240 (Rome: Pontificium Institutum Orientale, 1992); Bryan D. Spinks, *The Sanctus in the Eucharistic Prayer* (Cambridge: Cambridge University Press, 1991); Robert F. Taft, 'The Authenticity of the Chrysostom Anaphora Revisited: Determining the Authorship of Liturgical Texts by Computer', *Orientalia Christiana Periodica* 56 (1990), 5–51; idem, 'From Logos to Spirit: On the Early History of the Epiclesis', in A. Heinz and H. Rennings, eds, *Gratias Agamus: Studien zum eucharistischen Hochgebet. Für Balthasar Fischer* (Freiburg: Herder, 1992), 489–502; idem, 'The Interpolation of the Sanctus into the Anaphora: When and Where? A Review of the Dossier', *Orientalia Christiana Periodica* 57 (1991), 281–308; 58 (1992), 83–121; Gabriele Winkler, 'Nochmals zu den Anfängen der Epiklese und des Sanctus im

Again, in the area of the liturgical year, the adoption of Lent as a universal pre-paschal phenomenon appears to date only from the middle of the fourth century. Prior to that, the season seems have been unique to Egypt, and to have been located immediately after the celebration of the baptism of Jesus on 6 January.[28] What is even more clear is that before the late fourth century no church included both 25 December and 6 January in its liturgical calendar.[29] Indeed, the celebration of 25 December now appears to have originally been a peculiarity of Rome, and perhaps North Africa too. Even Milan may have celebrated 6 January and not 25 December prior to the episcopate of the romanophile Ambrose.[30] Yet within the space of less than half a century, both feasts became established features of all major centres of Christianity.[31] Above all, in spite of the Quartodeciman disputes of the second century, a common date for the celebration of Easter itself only became more of a reality as part of the Nicean settlement, and even after that some variation still persisted.[32]

Limiting extemporized prayer

Fear of heresy also began to place limitations around the practice of extemporizing public prayer. The almost total absence of extant liturgical texts prior to the fourth century is not because they were

---

Eucharistischen Hochgebet', *Theologische Quartalschrift* 174 (1994), 214–31; eadem, 'Weitere Beobachtungen zür Epiklese (den Doxologien und dem Sanctus). Über die Bedeutung der Apokryphen für die Erforschung der Entwicklung der Riten', *Oriens Christianus* 80 (1996), 1–18.

[28] See Talley, *The Origins of the Liturgical Year*, 163–230. The attempt by Charles Renoux, 'La quarantaine pré-pascale au 3ᵉ siècle à Jérusalem', *La Maison-Dieu* 196 (1993), 111–29, to posit the existence of a forty-day Lent in Jerusalem as early as the third century is not convincing.

[29] On the origins of 6 January see Talley, *The Origins of the Liturgical Year*, 103–33; Gabriele Winkler, 'Die Licht-Erscheinung bei der Taufe Jesu und der Ursprung des Epiphaniefestes: Eine Untersuchung griechischer, syrischer, armenischer und lateinischer Quellen', *Oriens Christianus* 78 (1994), 177–229.

[30] See Connell, 'The Liturgical Year in Northern Italy', 239–54.

[31] See Talley, *The Origins of the Liturgical Year*, 134–47.

[32] See Anscar J. Chupungco, *Shaping the Easter Feast* (Washington, DC: Pastoral Press, 1992), 43–50, 69–73. On the Quartodeciman controversy, see the recent contribution by Robert Cabié, 'A propos de la 'Question pascale': quelle pratique opposait-on à celles des Quartodecimans?' *Ecclesia Orans* 11 (1994), 101–6.

all destroyed by later generations, but because they did not exist in the first place. It was not part of the early Jewish and Christian traditions that liturgical prayers should be written down. Instead, they were passed on orally, and subject to development and modification in response to changing circumstances. But this freedom meant that individual bishops and other clergy might introduce unorthodox ideas into their prayers, whether consciously or unwittingly. In the more doctrinally sensitive climate of the fourth century, therefore, we see fences gradually being erected around such liberty. Not only do written eucharistic prayers now begin to appear,[33] but in some places steps are taken to censor the contents of all forms of public prayer. The earliest instances of this are in North Africa, where local ecclesiastical councils enacted legislation requiring the liturgical texts used by bishops and presbyters to be submitted to the scrutiny and approval of their colleagues.[34] The virtual disappearance of early Christian hymns and their replacement in liturgical worship by the canonical psalms at this period is another symptom of the desire to control doctrine. The Arian use of hymns to promote their beliefs caused a reaction against all non-canonical compositions among their opponents, and a strong preference for biblical psalms and canticles, the orthodoxy of which could be safely guaranteed.[35]

Doctrinal issues not only encouraged churches to adopt a similar liturgical appearance to one another, but were also responsible for determining the particular form that many of these shared expressions then took. For example, the fourth-century pneumatological debates influenced the specific shape of liturgy in a number of ways, including the development of the epicletic element in eucharistic prayers and of post-baptismal ceremonies related to the Holy Spirit.[36] Similarly, while the initial concept of a paschal

---

[33] See further Allan Bouley, *From Freedom to Formula: The Evolution of the Eucharistic Prayer from Oral Improvisation to Written Texts* (Washington, DC: Catholic University of America Press, 1981).

[34] See Edward J. Kilmartin, 'Early African Legislation Concerning Liturgical Prayer', *Ephemerides Liturgicae* 99 (1985), 105–27.

[35] See Paul F. Bradshaw, *Daily Prayer in the Early Church* (London: SPCK, 1981; New York: Oxford University Press, 1982), 90, 94, 113, 118.

[36] See John H. McKenna, *Eucharist and Holy Spirit*, Alcuin Club Collection 57 (Great Wakering, Essex: Mayhew-McCrimmon, 1975), 19–44; Taft, 'From Logos to Spirit'; L. L. Mitchell, *Baptismal Anointing*, Alcuin Club Collection 48

triduum seems to have its roots in a third-century shift in the Alexandrian theological interpretation of the feast from *passio* to *transitus*,[37] as part of the general tendency in that region to allegorize and de-historicize the Christian mysteries, and while its earliest liturgical expression in Jerusalem seems to have been primarily a response to popular piety, yet its further dissemination to other parts of the world appears to be not unrelated to the continuing christological controversies of the period. Homiletic material from northern Italy, for example, demonstrates the assistance that the emerging separation of the commemoration of Christ's death on Good Friday from the celebration of his resurrection on Easter Day gave to attempts to define the divine/human nature of Christ.[38] In the same way, anti-Arian concerns strongly influenced the content of the new feast of Christmas as a celebration of the incarnation of the pre-existent Son of God rather than merely a historical commemoration of Jesus' nativity. For it is not without significance that readings from both the Gospel of Luke and that of John are included in the earliest stratum of the lectionary tradition for this feast at Rome.[39]

Some of the consequences of this process of liturgical convergence cannot but be regarded as positive effects on Christianity. The church undoubtedly gained a greater sense of its own internal cohesion and was also strengthened in its defence of orthodoxy by the united liturgical front that it was thus able to present to its opponents and to the pagan world. Moreover, the adoption of different customs from other Christian traditions was for the most part a real enrichment of the liturgical life of the various local

---

(London: SPCK, 1966); Maxwell E. Johnson, 'The Postchrismational Structure of Apostolic Tradition 21, the Witness of Ambrose of Milan, and a Tentative Hypothesis Regarding the Current Reform of Confirmation in the Roman Rite', *Worship* 70 (1996), 16–34.

[37] Clement, *Stromata*, 2.11.51.2; Origen, *Peri Pascha*, 1; *Hom. in Exod.*, 5.2. See Paul F. Bradshaw, 'The Origins of Easter', in Paul F. Bradshaw and Lawrence Hoffman, eds, *Passover and Easter: Origin and History to Modern Times*, Two Liturgical Traditions 5 (Notre Dame: University of Notre Dame Press, 1999), 81–98.

[38] See Connell, 'The Liturgical Year in Northern Italy', 54–127.

[39] See Lester Ruth, 'The Early Roman Christmas Gospel: Magi, Manger, or Verbum Factum?' *Studia Liturgica* 24 (1994), 214–21.

churches, and it enlarged their earlier limited and often one-sided vision of the Christian faith.

On the other hand, this fourth-century development also had consequences which perhaps should not be viewed in such a positive light. The amalgamation of liturgical customs from different regions did not result in the preservation of everything from former times, but more often led to the dominance of certain ways of saying and doing things over others. Thus enrichment brought with it some impoverishment, as various local traditions were subordinated to others, reduced to a mere shadow of their former selves, or even entirely eliminated from contemporary practice. Furthermore, what emerged in the fourth century, although containing elements from a number of earlier Christian traditions, was itself identical to none of them. Local churches gave up their indigenous liturgical tradition and received back a mixed bag of native and foreign practices that did not fully reflect their own particular heritage and culture, but instead a more generic regional or universal concept of worship. Although, as we have said, this development succeeded in strengthening the unity and catholicity of the Church, the price paid was a loss of some sense of local self-identity.

Conclusion: the gains and losses of inculturation

Those responsible for shaping Christian liturgy in the fourth century thus found themselves caught between two opposing forces. One was the desire to remain counter-cultural, to draw a sharp dividing line between what was pagan and what was Christian, for fear of the dilution of distinctively Christian beliefs and of the confusion and misunderstanding that the adoption of practices resembling those of other religions might cause. The other was the need to communicate with the pagan world around in its own terms, to inculturate the church's liturgy in the context in which it was situated, to clothe its worship in the language and symbols that converts and potential converts would more easily understand, and by this means to lead them to full and right participation in the Christian mysteries.

After something of a struggle, the second force won the day, for the church did not know how otherwise to handle the growing flood of new members who lacked the understanding of the biblical background possessed by the earliest Jewish converts and the deep commitment to Christian discipleship possessed by the adherents of former, and less comfortable, centuries. But such a step was not only a tacit admission of defeat in the process of the full conversion of all its followers; it also carried with it the seeds of further destruction. While in one sense the process of liturgical evolution that then ensued helped to save the church from even worse consequences, it also led to the disappearance or transformation of many worship practices that had safeguarded and given expression to important aspects of the primitive Christian faith, which were consequently lost to later generations of believers.

A similar story can be told with regard to the effects of the crystallization of Christian doctrine. Once again, there was something of a struggle between traditional liturgical forms on the one hand and the demands of the new orthodoxy on the other. But eventually doctrinal correctness won; variety was reined in, and a more homogenized pattern of liturgy began to emerge, displacing many ancient local traditions. While this growing liturgical uniformity undoubtedly strengthened the church in its battle with heresy, it also contributed to the diminution or loss of a number of significant insights and emphases for the Christianity of later centuries. For, as Robert Taft has observed, the process of selective evolution led to 'the survival of the fittest – of the fittest, not necessarily of the best'.[40]

---

[40] Robert F. Taft, 'How Liturgies Grow: The Evolution of the Byzantine Divine Liturgy', *Orientalia Christiana Periodica* 43 (1977), 355; reprinted in Robert F. Taft, *Beyond East and West* (Washington, DC: Pastoral Press, 1984), 167. See also his article, 'Reconstructing the History of the Byzantine Communion Ritual: Principles, Methods, Results', *Ecclesia Orans* 11 (1994), 355–77, esp. 356–64.

Chapter 10

Augustine and the Transformation of Baptism

DAVID F. WRIGHT

Before Augustine of Hippo, baptismal practice and theology assumed the active participation of converts; baptism of infants and children took place, but far from routinely and perhaps primarily in cases of illness. Augustine's early writings show that he, like other Christians of his time, had done little theological thinking about infant baptism. On baptism they are neither passionate nor profound. A new clarity came to his treatment of baptism after *c*.410 in his anti-Pelagian writings. Theologically he came to believe that infant baptism was the sole cure for the guilt of original sin; practically he came to advocate the universal baptism of infants soon after their birth. The result was a devaluation of baptism in the West which did much to determine the contours of Christendom.

'The atmosphere at their [i.e. Patricius's and Monnica's] home was Christian, yet Augustine was not baptized.'[1] A simple enough sentence, one might think, from a recent distinguished study of Augustine's thought, but it is in fact not wholly unexceptionable. I would amend it to read '. . . and Augustine was not baptized'. John Rist's 'yet' implies an unfulfilled expectation, whereas in all the best Christian homes in the later fourth century – some of them patently more Christian than the maritally mixed ménage at Tagaste – one did not baptize babies, or young children

[1] John M. Rist, *Augustine: Ancient Thought Baptized* (Cambridge: Cambridge University Press, 1994), 2.

at all, for that matter. Whatever Augustine may later have believed, by these standards there was nothing incongruous in Monnica's not having had him baptized in tender infancy.

I have set out the evidence in outline elsewhere.[2] On the one hand one can cite a lengthy and impressive list of later-fourth-century churchmen and churchwomen nurtured in Christian families but not baptized until they were adults – normally in their twenties. It embraces not only all in the family circles of the Cappadocian Fathers and similarly those around Jerome and Rufinus, but also Ephraem Syrus, John Chrysostom, Paulinus of Nola and Ambrose. On the other hand, it is difficult, and perhaps impossible, to advance any counter-examples, that is, of named individuals born of Christian parentage in this era and known to have been baptized as infants. This problem in turn may be wrapped up in a larger question: who was the first Christian we can name who was baptized in infancy? Youngsters baptized clinically within sight of death would not qualify, but I forbear to pursue this surprisingly elusive enquiry further on this occasion.[3]

What is at issue here is not simply practice – were they, were they not, baptized as babies? More intriguing are the assumptions at work and the judgements passed, and here we encounter the distorting influence of the case of Augustine. There is no more prominent baptismal history in the whole early church than that of Augustine. It is known and read of all on the face of the *Confessions*, which means that generations of students have got used to perceiving it through Augustine's eyes. What have they learned about Augustine's baptismal story from the author of the *Confessions*?

Baptism in the *Confessions*

In the first place, Augustine passes over in silence the fact that he was not baptized soon after birth. We deduce it both from his being ceremonially registered as a catechumen straight from the womb and from his need to beg for baptism when as a young boy (*puer*) he fell gravely ill (*paene moriturus*). His mother prepared him for baptism but he suddenly recovered, whereupon 'my

[2] 'At What Ages Were People Baptized in the Early Centuries?', *Studia Patristica* 30 (1997), 387–92.
[3] See n. 2 above.

cleansing was deferred'.[4] Writing perhaps some thirty-five years after the event, Augustine laments the laxity still heard on all sides, 'Let him be, let him do it; he is not yet baptized'. Then the never-to-be-forgotten censure of his mother's negligence:

> How much better for me if I had been quickly healed and if, thanks to the diligent care of my family and my own decision [*meorum meaque diligentia*], action had been taken by which I received the health of my soul and was kept safe under the protection which you would have given me. Certainly much better.[5]

Augustine piously subsumes his mother's fault in the broader responsibility of his parents and himself. Much later, when he again fell perilously ill after arriving in Rome from Carthage (*iam ibam et peribam*), by contrast he had no desire for baptism. 'I did better as a boy when I begged for it from my devout mother, as I have recalled and confessed.'[6]

One of the most moving passages in the *Confessions* records Augustine's desolation at the death of a close, but unnamed, friend, whom he had converted from Catholic Christianity to Manicheism. While he lay mortally sick of fever, he was given Catholic baptism all unknowing. On recovering temporarily, he rebuffed Augustine's mockery of his unconscious baptism. Augustine's confusion was further confounded when the friend's condition relapsed and he died in his absence.[7] The episode is almost a reverse image of Augustine's boyhood frustration. Although the tale is told in the *Confessions* chiefly, it seems, to introduce a searching meditation

---

[4] *Confessions*, 1.11.17. Henry Chadwick translates *puer* 'a small boy' in his edition of Augustine's *Confessions* (Oxford: Oxford University Press, 1991), 13. The word elicits no comment in J. J. O'Donnell's three-volume edition and commentary (Oxford: Clarendon Press, 1992), but see 2, 52–6 on *pueritia* in Augustine's scheme of the 'ages of man'. See also n. 9 below. In *De Genesi ad litteram*, 10.13.23 Augustine rejects the opinion that personal sin should not be attributed to children before puberty at 14. But he is sure that this holds for infancy (10.14.23).

[5] *Confessions*, 1.11.18; Chadwick, 14. 'The story tells us much about the prevailing view of evil: on the one hand, it was felt that there was sin in the child which must be stilled; on the other that, if possible, each postulant to Catholicism should make his or her own, willed, profession through the medium of baptism.' Peter Cramer, *Baptism and Change in the Early Middle Ages, c.200–c.1150* (Cambridge: Cambridge University Press, 1993), 118.

[6] *Confessions*, 5.9.16; Chadwick, 83.

[7] *Confessions*, 4.4.8.

on human love, one might read it as reinforcing the mild, but real, criticism of Monnica. Even when totally unsought, baptism had the power to convert and establish firmly in the truth.

The uniqueness of Augustine's verdict on his failure to be given baptism lies here, that he alone of the sons and daughters of Christian households not baptized until their adult years is known to have found fault with his parent's or parents' omission. In all other cases known to me where biographical or autobiographical accounts are available, none blames parent or parents for not having secured them baptism as infants.

On the contrary, the more normal picture is that painted by Gregory Nazianzen, who depicts in glowing colours the godly nurture he and his siblings received, without a hint of their parents' remissness in not having them baptized. If we read these experiences as instances of the deferral of baptism, we owe that gratuitous insight at least in part to our familiarity with what has been called the most famous mother–son relationship in antiquity. Part of its perennial appeal lies in the dissonance between the two, of which Monnica's refusal to go through with his boyhood baptism is a signal example. But why should we privilege this baptismal history and make it the lens through which to view the spiritual life-stories of others?

All the other mentions of baptism in the *Confessions* relate to what I will call, if only by convenient shorthand, believer's baptism or perhaps better conversion-baptism: Monnica's hope for Augustine (6.13.23), the famously public baptism of Victorinus, 'an infant born at your font' (8.2.3–5), Verecundus' death-bed conversion and baptism (9.3.5), that of Nebridius (9.3.6), of Alypius with Augustine himself and his son Adeodatus (9.6.14), of Evodius (9.8.17), of Patricius his father (9.10.22), and even it seems of Monnica herself (9.13.34).[8] Together these instances remind us how consistently the *Confessions* bear witness to the

---

[8] Rist, *Augustine*, 4, strangely has Monnica baptized with Augustine in 387. O'Donnell does not comment on her baptism on 9.13.34. Monnica's baptism is relegated to a footnote in A. Mandouze, *Prosopographie de l' Afrique chrétienne (303–533)* (Paris: Éditions du CNRS, 1982), 758–62, *s.n.* 'Monnica'. This passing over baptism in silence is not unusual: see Wright, 'At What Ages . . . ?', 388, 392, and idem, 'Monnica's Baptism, Augustine's Deferred Baptism, and Patricius', *Augustinian Studies* 29:2 (1998), 1–17.

baptismal practice of the pre-Augustinian era, when the norm was for it to be deliberately sought by responsible believers. There is no allusion whatever in the *Confessions* to infant baptism. Monnica's advertised omission was not in failing to baptize the baby Augustine but in desisting from carrying through with the baptism he had himself importunately requested.[9]

The religious significance of Augustine's own reception of baptism at the hands of Ambrose is, to be sure, not easily reducible to the model of conversion-baptism *simpliciter*. He had reactivated his status as a catechumen after encountering Ambrose's preaching in Milan,[10] and delicate questions of continuity and discontinuity between his earlier spiritual and intellectual peregrinations and his Milanese experience press for an answer. George Lawless has the narrative of the *Confessions* on his side in arguing that the complex of conversion and baptism constituted more the choice of a particular religious vocation than anything else.[11]

Nevertheless, Augustine's own baptismal history must stand, by his own design in the *Confessions*, for the decisive transition from an old life to a new that marked early Christian baptism: the abandonment of his profession of rhetoric, and of all expectation of a successful career in the public eye; a final turning away from the pleasures of the flesh, within or without marriage; the divine remission of all his 'horrendous and mortal sins';[12] the ultimate reconciliation with his devoted mother,[13] sealed in the climactic

---

[9] Later, in *The Soul and its Origin*, 1.10.12, 3.9.12, Augustine would identify seven as the age at which children could first answer for themselves in baptism. See my article, cited n. 2 above, 390. He is described as having attained the 'age of reason' by the time of this unfulfilled baptism by J.-C. Didier, 'Saint Augustin et le baptême des enfants', *Revue des études augustiniennes* 2 (1956), 109–29 at 110, and by R. De Latte, 'Saint Augustin et le baptême: Étude liturgico-historique du rituel baptismal des enfants chez Saint Augustin', *Questions liturgiques* 57 (1976), 41–55 at 41 n. 2.

[10] *Confessions*, 5.14.25, 6.11.18.

[11] George Lawless, *Augustine of Hippo and His Monastic Rule* (Oxford: Clarendon Press, 1987), 11–12.

[12] *Confessions*, 9.2.4.

[13] Cf. *Confessions*, 9.13.37 (the sole mention of Monnica's name in Augustine's works). In *Confessions*, 9.9.22 O'Donnell's punctuation and reading (3, 121) are to be preferred to Chadwick's (170), which allow for the misunderstanding found in Rist (n. 8 above). Neither *vivebamus* nor *percepta gratia baptismi tui* includes Monnica.

vision of Ostia; the new delights of the Psalms, of the hymns and chants of worship in Milan, and fresh plans for a shared life in the service of God back in Africa.[14]

Comments on baptism in early works

Disentangling the densely interwoven threads of history and theology in the *Confessions* is a daunting – and surely unappealing – task. By the time he wrote them, some dozen years after his baptism, near the turn of the century, Augustine certainly intended his baptismal passage to be received as the dramatic turning-point of his life. But that was before he had got to grips with that nexus of theological challenges that would turn him into the most uncompromising champion of infant baptism – and effectively doom to obsolescence that model of conversion-baptism of which the *Confessions* made him so convincing an icon.

This metamorphosis took something over a decade. The immensity of the change involved is evident from what is probably Augustine's first mention of infant baptism, in *The Size of the Soul* written at Rome in 388. Discussing the stages by which 'true religion' binds the soul by reconciliation to God alone, he comments that 'the question what benefits the consecrations even of infant children [*etiam puerorum infantium*] may confer is a very obscure one, but we must believe that they have some benefit [*nonnihil . . . prodesse*]. Reason will find this out, when it falls to be investigated'.[15]

---

[14] *Confessions*, 9.4.8, 9.6.14, 9.8.17. On the central significance of Augustine's baptism, even within the text of the *Confessions*, see O'Donnell, 1, xxviii–xxix; 3, 72, 106–9; also David C. Alexander, 'The Emergence of Augustine's Early Ecclesiology (386–91)', PhD thesis, University of Edinburgh, 1995, 47–52, 250–1. The radical character of the rupture with his social and political aspirations is well stressed by C. Lepelley, 'Un aspect de la conversion d'Augustin: la rupture avec ses ambitions sociales et politiques', *Bulletin de littérature ecclésiastique* 88 (1987), 229–46.

[15] *De quantitate animae*, 36.80. Note the assumption of voluntary action in an earlier statement in this book (3.4): 'The injunction is rightly made in the sacraments that whoever wishes to be restored to such as God made him should condemn all things bodily and renounce this whole world, which, as we see, is bodily'. Augustine's difficulties are sketched by E. R. Fairweather, 'St Augustine's Interpretation of Infant Baptism', in *Augustinus Magister: Congrès International Augustinien, Paris, 21–24 Septembre 1954* (Paris: Études Augustiniennes, 1954),

A few years later, in his third book on *Free Will* written at Hippo as a presbyter or perhaps a newly-consecrated bishop, Augustine's understanding has advanced sufficiently to attempt an answer to the puzzling question 'what good the sacrament of Christ's baptism does to infants, since most of them [*plerumque*] die after receiving it before they can have known anything of it'. The 'pious and right belief' is that the infant is benefited by the faith of those who bring him to baptism. This is corroborated by the soundest authority of the church.[16] It is at best half an answer – responding in terms of 'how?' to the question 'what?' Later, of course, almost the whole burden of Augustine's promotion of infants' baptism would rest on their receiving it before they died. That the context of this short discussion in *Free Will* is infant death is noteworthy.

To Simplician on Various Questions was written, so Augustine tells us, at the very beginning of his episcopate, i.e. in 396. His grappling with Simplician's second question, on the interpretation of Romans 9:10–29, by Augustine's own acknowledgement effected a significant advance in his comprehension of grace. 'I had tried hard to maintain the free choice of the human will, but the grace of God prevailed.'[17] His commentators agree on the cruciality of the turning-point. 'The position is now reached in all its essential features which provoked the protest of Pelagius.'[18] Augustine had 'derived from a seemingly unambiguous text, an intricate synthesis of grace, free will and predestination. For the

---

II, 897–903, but his presentation fails to take account of development in Augustine's understanding. An able survey is given by B. Delaroche, *Saint Augustin lecteur et interprète de Saint Paul dans le De peccatorum meritis et remissione (hiver 411–412)* (Paris: Études Augustiniennes, 1996), 347–56.

[16] *De libero arbitrio* 3.23.67: *Ecclesiae . . . saluberrima auctoritas* is the tradition of baptizing infants (cf. Fairweather, 'St. Augustine's Interpretation', 898–900). It is important not to read into such brief phrases questionable assumptions about the frequency or normative character of the traditional practice. Such references are fully compatible, *ex hypothesi*, with an established tradition of the clinical baptism of dying infants. Cramer, *Baptism and Change*, 117, comments that 'Infant baptism has no obvious place' in the general argument of *Free Will*.

[17] *Retractationes*, 2.1.

[18] J. H. S. Burleigh, ed., *Augustine: Earlier Writings*. Library of Christian Classics 6 (London: SCM Press, 1953), 375.

first time, Augustine came to see man as utterly dependent on God, even for his first initiative of believing in Him'.[19]

But as John Rist notes, 'His first mature account of man's need for grace, worked out in the reply to Simplicianus, had inevitably focused on the sinfulness of adults, as was only to be expected since Christianity was originally a missionary religion, making adult converts'.[20] It is rather remarkable that, when the nettle to be grasped is the election of Jacob and the rejection of Esau before they were born, no connection is drawn between the priority of grace in election and the salvation of new-born babies through baptism. The whole tenor of the discussion suggests the domination of Augustine's mind by the paradigm of the responsible person coming to faith. In 399 or 400 Augustine would oblige Deogratias, a deacon at Carthage, by composing a short guide to *Catechizing the Uninstructed* with precisely such candidates in mind. In 393, when addressing the African bishops assembled in council in Hippo, this precocious presbyter had commented on the credal phrase 'in the remission of sins' without mentioning baptism at all.[21]

The Literal Meaning of Genesis

In the early years of the fifth century in two further discussions of the value of infant baptism Augustine leans heavily on the authority of church practice. The date of the tenth book of *The Literal Meaning of Genesis* has not yet been fixed with any certainty. He began this neglected *magnum opus* in 401 and completed its twelve books in 415. Most of it was written much nearer its starting than its terminal date, and book 10 indubitably before the onset of the Pelagian controversy. At issue is the origin of the soul, on which Augustine never came down decisively in favour of either of the two main competing theories, traducianism and creationism. Here he evinces a sharp awareness that the practice of parents 'rushing' (*curro*, 'run', is used twice, perhaps implying that clinical baptism is chiefly in mind) with infants to baptism is far easier to square with the derivation of the soul, and not merely the body, from Adam through the immediate parents. The infant in his own person has

[19] Peter Brown, *Augustine of Hippo* (London: Faber & Faber, 1967), 154.
[20] Rist, *Augustine*, 17; cf. 125.
[21] *De fide et symbolo*, 22.

done neither good nor evil, and his soul is spotless if it has not descended from Adam; what harm, then, would he (i.e. his soul) suffer if it left the body in death without baptism? If baptism benefits only the body, why not baptize dead bodies? It will be a marvel if anyone can show, on a non-traducianist supposition, why the soul of an infant dying unbaptized should be justly condemned.[22]

He proceeds to venture a creationist's response to this conundrum. In a nutshell, the soul that God creates anew for each individual either tames the flesh which is inherited from Adam already tainted by sin, or is tamed by it. 'Even an infant as long as he is alive should be baptized so that union with sinful flesh may not harm his soul.'[23]

Augustine is obviously not satisfied. The infant dying unbaptized is a different matter from the adult dying unbaptized, who will have unforgiven personal sins. Is the newly-created soul's contamination by contact with sinful flesh sufficient of itself to doom it if it fails, through parental unbelief or negligence, to win baptism before death? Perhaps the solution lies in God's foreknowledge, supplying 'the ministry of the saving waters' to each one whom, dying untimely young, he foreknows would have been a godly believer had he lived.[24] (The recourse to divine foreknowledge offers no escape. Towards the end of his life Augustine firmly rejects divine foreknowledge of future merits to explain why some infants receive baptism and others die without it.[25] But by then the framework of discussion had been drastically changed.) God foreknows vices as well as virtues, and if judgement covers not only what one has done while alive but what one would have done had one lived longer, the salvation of those who have died in good standing would become a prey to uncertainty. Augustine pleads again for any who, without resorting to traducianism, can reconcile Scripture (he has Romans 5.12, 18–19 in mind) or Scripture-informed reason with infant baptism to come forward to help him.[26]

Augustine rounds off his weighing up of the alternative explanations in *The Literal Meaning of Genesis* with the judgement that 'the weight of arguments and scriptural evidences would be

---

[22] *De Genesi ad litteram*, 10.11.19.
[23] Ibid., 10.14.24–25.
[24] Ibid., 10.15.26–27.
[25] *De praedestinatione sanctorum*, 24.
[26] *De Genesi ad litteram*, 10.16.28–29.

equal or nearly equal on each side' did not infant baptism lend greater weight to the opinion that derives souls from parents. For the moment Augustine cannot counter this view; subsequently he will not hesitate if God gives him something to say on it. He then adds a somewhat elusive sentence:

> Now, however, I give notice in advance that the witness of [the baptism of] infants is not to be despised, so that one fails to refute a position [on this ground], if the truth counts against it.[27]

Meantime, persistence in humble searching and knocking is certainly preferable to resting satisfied with present knowledge. In conclusion Augustine repeats himself with added emphasis.

> But the custom of mother church in baptizing infants is not in the least to be scorned and in no way to be regarded as irrelevant, nor to be believed at all unless it were an apostolic tradition. That tiny age, which won the distinction of being the first to shed its blood for Christ, bears a witness of great weight.[28]

Surely Augustine is speaking to himself. He would so obviously have loved to believe in God's fresh creation of a soul for each new life. Alas for him, the further deepening of his understanding of the relation between Adam's sin and babies would push this desirable apple even further beyond his grasp.

De baptismo

Augustine's only work to be called *De baptismo* was directed, as its longer title indicates, 'against the Donatists'. It has commonly

---

[27] Ibid., 10.23.39: '*Nunc tamen non esse contemnendum testimonium parvulorum, ut quasi refelli, si veritas contra est, negligatur, ante denuntio*'. The translation of J. H. Taylor, *St Augustine: The Literal Meaning of Genesis*, II, Ancient Christian Writers 42 (New York and Ramsey: Newman Press, 1982), 127, does not make coherent sense in context: 'Now, however, I want to state in advance that the argument from the baptism of infants is not to be so despised that we should neglect to refute it if the truth is against it.' It is difficult to imagine Augustine, in the early 400s, feeling the need to warn against so low an esteem for infant baptism that one did not even bother to expose its untruth. The final sentences of 10.23.39, cited in the text, will not tolerate Taylor's reading. The French translation by P. Agaësse and A. Solignac in *Bibliothèque Augustinienne* 49, 215–17, is nearer Taylor's than mine: '. . . *n' est pas à mépriser, si bien qu'on ne doit pas négliger de le réfuter en quelque sorte, s'il est contraire à la vérité*'. I remain unpersuaded.

[28] *De Genesi ad litteram*, 10.23.39.

been dated in 400/401 but has recently been brought forward to 405 at the earliest.[29] It may seem paradoxical in a paper devoted to exposing Augustine's transformation of baptism that this extensive treatise should have so little to contribute. In reality, here too, in the anti-Donatist polemic, Augustine was effecting *another* transformation of baptism (what versatility!) – and getting himself here too, in all manner of fixes.[30] The notion of baptismal character, with its corollary of the sundering of baptism from the church, was nevertheless less fateful than the transformation which is my present subject. The fact that De baptismo has little specific grist for this mill should remind us that the baptismal divide between Donatists and Catholics had nothing to do with infant baptism as such – which the magisterial Reformers' assimilation of Anabaptists to Donatists still sometimes obscures.[31]

Yet the one discussion of infant baptism in De baptismo is revealing. It arises in the sequel to a consideration of instances of persons who lacked baptism itself – e.g. martyred catechumens and the penitent thief – but indubitably received salvation. Likewise when the sacrament is given but faith and repentance are unavoidably absent, as with infants, salvation, according to 'the firm tradition of the universal church', is nevertheless present. Why, babies by screaming and girning even raise their voices in opposition to the words of the sacrament![32]

---

[29] A. Schindler in *Augustinus-Lexikon* I, 574; on the title, 573; F. Dolbeau, *Augustin d'Hippone: Vingt-six sermons au peuple d'Afrique* (Paris: Études Augustiniennes, 1996), 359 (= *Recherches augustiniennes* 26, 1992, 83).

[30] See my paper 'Donatist Theologoumena in Augustine? Baptism, Reviviscence of Sins and Unworthy Ministers', in *Congresso Internazionale su S. Agostino . . . Atti II* (Rome: Institutum Patristicum Augustinianum, 1987), 213–24.

[31] Cf. my paper 'The Donatists in the Sixteenth Century', *Auctoritas Patrum* II. *Neue Beiträge zur Rezeption der Kirchenväter im 15. und 16. Jahrhundert*, ed. L. Grane *et al.* (Mainz: Philipp von Zabern, 1998), 281–93. In *The Soul and its Origin*, 1.9.10–1.11.13, 2.9.13–2.12.16, 3.9.12–3.10.14, Augustine refutes the opinion of one Vincentius Victor that infants dying unbaptized entered the kingdom of heaven, but his error seemed unrelated to his former allegiance to Rogatist Donatism.

[32] *De baptismo*, 4.23.30. This must be the first appearance of this fatuous argument from the tears of babies at the font, vainly resisting irresistible grace, as it is often characterised. In *Epistle* 187, written in 417, as part of his response to Dardanus's question whether infants truly do not know God, Augustine is careful to absolve infants at baptism of any blame for appearing by crying and wriggling to fight against receiving the grace of Christ. 'They do not know what

Augustine proceeds to develop for the first time the parallel with circumcision, which, commanded first as a seal of Abraham's faith, was afterward decreed for all males eight days old. There is no problem when baptized infants come later to that 'conversion of heart', whose sacramental sign had gone before. But as with the thief God supplied what was lacking, so too in baptized infants who die young, we must believe that the same grace of the Almighty fulfils what, not by wilful perversity but by poverty of age, they could not – i.e. 'believe in their hearts for righteousness and confess with their mouths for salvation'.

Hence the responses made by others on their behalf, since they cannot answer for themselves, unquestionably avail for their consecration to God.[33]

This approach to infant baptism is eloquent enough. Augustine keeps close enough to the New Testament to assume faith- or conversion-baptism as the norm, in the light of which some vindication of infant (literally 'non-speaking') baptism is called for. Augustine's vindication is not wholly coherent; if the parallel with the thief on the cross holds good, God supplies the deficiency, presumably faith and confession, but it breaks down, and sponsors seem to supply it also. As we will see, neither explanation corresponds precisely to the liturgical reality.

---

they are doing and hence are not credited with doing it.' *Epistle* 187.7.25. Dardanus had been praefectus praetorio of the Gauls in 412–13; cf. J. R. Martindale, *The Prosopography of the Later Roman Empire*, II (Cambridge: Cambridge University Press, 1980), 346–7.

[33] *De baptismo*, 4.24.31. Augustine cites John 9.21, 'He is of age, let him speak for himself'. See the comment of J. H. Lynch, *Godparents and Kinship in Early Medieval Europe* (Princeton: Princeton University Press, 1986), 127. The earliest attested mark of differentiation between what so much of the tradition has defined in terms of ages – adult baptism and infant baptism – is the rubric in the Hippolytan *Apostolic Tradition* 21, distinguishing those who can speak for themselves from those who cannot. We await the collaborative edition of this text, whose traditional date and provenance are now seriously in question, being co-ordinated by Paul Bradshaw. If the provisional judgement assigns this paragraph to an early stratum of the work, it remains to be seen how far this verdict rests on criteria more secure than broader assumptions about baptismal development.

When Augustine says that *universa tenet ecclesia* the practice of infant baptism (*De baptismo*, 4.24.31), he presumably indicates its universal acceptance, not its routine invariability throughout the church.

The more general point to be made about *De baptismo* follows neatly: the whole of its discussion of baptismal cases, actual and hypothetical, presupposes persons of independent responsibility. It takes quite a leap of imagination to assume that in the congregations of Africa, whether Donatist or Catholic, infant baptism was in any sense normal practice. To be sure, this baptismal controversy, between Africa's two mainstream denominations, directed no attention to infant baptism as such. Nevertheless, when such extended argument with frequent citation of particular instances can be read from first to last – with the exception of two chapters – as though it was dealing with a squabble among African Baptists, we rightly sit up and take note.

It is in *De baptismo* that Augustine develops his theory of the reviviscence of sins (see n. 30 above). In response to the Donatists' charge that his view of their baptisms left him impaled on the horns of a dilemma, Augustine allowed that through Donatist baptism sins were indeed momentarily remitted (and the Spirit received, etc.) – but immediately returned on the baptized's heads because of their sinful persistence in schism. This is difficult, if not impossible, to apply to the infant-baptized.

Epistle 98

One further text falls to be considered before we reach the critical watershed in Augustine's baptismal understanding. In *Letter* 98 he responds to a series of questions relating to the baptism of infants, or baptized infants, addressed to him by an episcopal colleague named Boniface, probably Bishop of Cataquas not far from Hippo.[34] The letter is generally dated 408.[35] It comprises

[34] The precise location is unknown. On the identity of this Boniface, see S. Lancel in *Augustinus-Lexikon* I, 652, and Mandouze, *Prosopographie*, 148–50, *s.n.* 'Bonifatius 7'.

[35] But Mandouze, *Prosopographie*, 149 n. 10, thinks it probable that it belongs to the years of the Pelagian controversy, on the inadequate ground that it deals with infant baptism. Section 5 certainly has Donatist error in view. In my judgement, the answers of sections 9–10, reviewed in the text, are not redolent of that intense reflection on infant baptism that the Pelagians evoked from him. J. C. Didier places the letter in 411, just before Pelagius's arrival in Africa: 'Observations sur la date de la lettre 98 de S. Augustin', *Mélanges de science religieuse* 27 (1970), 115–17, in response to V. Grossi's hazardous argument for a date between 411/412 and 413, in *Augustinianum* 9 (1969), 30–61. M. F. Berrouard

Augustine's most extended treatment of infant baptism so far – despite Boniface's request that Augustine respond briefly, not citing the authority of tradition but furnishing a reasoned explanation.[36] All the questions were grounded in the relationship between the child, baptized or baptizand, and the parent or other sponsor – territory from which Julian in particular would fire off repeated salvos at Augustine's defences. The question that deserves to detain us in this paper is of interest not least because of what it reveals about one of the earliest adaptations of the baptismal liturgy to accommodate infants.

Whereas a candidate capable of answering the baptismal interrogations for himself was asked 'Do you believe ... ?', the question addressed to the promoter of an infant candidate was 'Does he(she) believe in God ... ?', and the reply expected was 'He(she) believes'.[37] There is no evidence of a variant practice. Boniface had expressed surprise that a confident answer could be given by parents or other presenters at that age of the child when he or she does not so much as know that there is a God. Moreover, they would not presume to answer other questions about the child's future character or conduct.

Augustine's response is less direct and subtler than his response to a not dissimilar problem in *De baptismo*. First he shows by analysis how sacraments take the name of the reality or transaction of which they are sacraments.

> Just as in a certain manner the sacrament of Christ's body is Christ's body ... , so the sacrament of faith is faith ... When, on behalf of an infant as yet lacking the capacity for faith, the response is given that 'He believes', this response means that he has faith because of the

holds to 408–10 in 'Similitudo et la définition du réalisme sacramental d'après l'Epître 98, 9–10 de S. Augustin', *Studia Patristica* 6 (1962), 277–93, at 277; Delaroche, *S. Augustin lecteur*, 353–6, holds to 408–11, as also does Lynch, *Godparents*, 128–32.

[36] *Epistle* 98.7.

[37] *Epistle* 98.7. See J. C. Didier, 'Une adaptation de la liturgie baptismale au baptême des enfants dans l' Église ancienne', *Mélanges de science religieuse* 22 (1965), 79–90; R. De Latte, 'Saint Augustin et le baptême: Étude liturgico-historique du rituel baptismal des enfants chez S. Augustin', *Questions liturgiques* 57 (1976), 41–55. For Pseudo-Dionysius's handling of this practice, see Lynch, *Godparents*, 138–9.

sacrament of faith, and the response that 'He converts to God' is made because of the sacrament of conversion, for the response itself belongs to the celebration of the sacrament.[38]

Not Augustine at his best, we must trust. He seems to have travelled no distance at all towards Boniface's testing ground. He tries a slightly different tack, still not without some unclarity.

Even though an infant as yet lacks 'that faith which rests upon the will of those believing' (does he then, one must interject, possess some other kind of faith?), nevertheless the *sacramentum fidei* makes him a *fidelis*, a believer, one of the faithful. Augustine is on safe ground; as the inscriptional evidence alone makes abundantly plain, very young baptized children were consistently called *fideles*. That Augustine's explanation of this fact is probably not historically secure need not detain us now.

Furthermore, though still lacking faith rooted in understanding, at least the infant does not obstruct it with an inimical understanding, and 'hence receives the sacrament of faith beneficially [*salubriter*]'. As the baptized *fidelis* matures, he or she grows into knowledge and faith. Before he is able to do so, the sacrament protects him against forces of evil, to such effect that if he dies before the age of reason, 'he is freed by Christian help from that condemnation which through one man entered the world, as the love of the church commends him through this very sacrament'.[39]

Augustine reckons that his responses will satisfy peaceable and understanding souls, but not the dull and argumentative. Boniface should obviously have asked for a longer answer. The answer that an historian today would have to give him would only exacerbate his anxiety, namely, that the practice of addressing questions about infants to their presenters in the third person is to be explained simply as a minor adaptation of a rite developed solely

---

[38] *Epistle* 98.9.
[39] *Epistle* 98.10. Augustine would have done better to refer Boniface back to part of his first answer, where he explains that the common possession of the Spirit by parent (or other presenter) and child alike enables the will (and presumably the words) of the parent to benefit the child. 'We are made partakers of grace along with others through the unity of the Holy Spirit' (*Epistle* 98.2). See the discussion of this letter in Cramer, *Baptism and Change*, 125–9, although Cramer fails to acknowledge that *Epistle* 98 by no means expresses Augustine's mature mind on infant baptism.

for self-respondent believers. At its best we may regard it as a strange device to maintain the unity of the baptismal observance.

The anti-Pelagian writings: a *bouleversement* in Augustine's thinking

This is a convenient point at which to make the transition to the anti-Pelagian phase of Augustine's reflection on baptism. For one of the tracks along which he chased Caelestius, in particular, led, claimed Augustine, to two kinds of baptism. If infants had no original sin, and no sins of their own commission, how could they be given the church's baptism 'for the remission of sins'? 'Shall we create another kind of baptism for infants, in which remission of sins does not take place'?[40] Eventually Caelestius was prevailed upon to grant that infants should be baptized for the remission of sins according to the church's universal custom. 'It is appropriate to confess this, lest we seem to be making different kinds of baptism'.[41] Pelagius got himself off the same hook by insisting that 'infants ought to be baptized with the same formula of sacramental words as adults'.[42]

Such concessions played into Augustine's hands, for it was a cardinal principle in his vindication of infant baptism against what he perceived to be Pelagian attack that the church's full understanding and practice of baptism applied no less to infants than to responsible adults. What this meant, in effect – and it emerges with crystal clarity at the moment of the baptismal questions – was that a sacrament formed around the active participation of converts was accommodated to passive silent infants, and in the process was transformed.

One route that Augustine did not travel was followed by many of the Greek Fathers of his generation – to distinguish between the two classes of baptismal candidates by recognizing that infants were baptized not for the remission of sins – for they had no sins to be remitted – but for the reception of the gifts of sanctification, adoption, strengthening against future sin, and so on. Such thinking

---

[40] Cf., e.g., *Sermon* 293.11. 'The theology determining Augustine's doctrine of infant baptism is identical with that of his theology of baptism in general', G. Bonner in *Augustinus-Lexikon* I, 592.

[41] *The Grace of Christ and Original Sin*, 2.5.5–6.6.

[42] *The Grace of Christ and Original Sin*, 2.1.1, etc.

meant that the clause in the Niceno-Constantinopolitan Creed 'one baptism for the remission of sins' cannot in its framers' minds have encompassed infant baptism – and in any case the 'one baptism' it affirmed was quite different from the 'one baptism' that Augustine thought the Pelagians threatened.[43] Through Julian of Eclanum, Augustine became aware of John Chrysostom's quintessential enunciation of the Eastern view, and spent most of the first book of *Against Julian* evading the plain sense of his words. What John had written was that infants had no sins; elsewhere in John's works Augustine thought he could demonstrate his belief in original sin.[44]

It was, of course, the doctrine of original sin that served as the springboard for the great leap forward that Augustine's apprehension of infant baptism experienced during the Pelagian contest. Already in his *Homilies on the First Epistle of John* in 407 Augustine could say *en passant*, 'If we are born with no sin, why is it that people rush [*curritur*] with infants to baptism for their release from it?' (We note again the tell-tale verb *curritur*, which may well echo the fear of early death that counselled speed in the baptism of many babies.) This brief text has often not been accorded its place in Augustine's developing baptismal understanding because for long these *Homilies* were dated later, after the onset of the Pelagian debates.[45] As Gerald Bonner puts it in his sympathetic article on 'Baptismus paruulorum' in the *Augustinus-Lexikon*, 'The problem [how baptism benefited infants] was eventually resolved for Augustine by the doctrine of Original Sin and the *massa damnata* . . . : infants share in Adam's guilt, from which they must be cleansed by baptism' (I, 592). This is much more familiar territory than Augustine's pre-Pelagian essays

---

[43] See my paper 'The Meaning and Reference of "One Baptism for the Remission of Sins" in the Niceno-Constantinopolitan Creed', *Studia Patristica* 19 (1989), 281–5. Cf. E. TeSelle, *Augustine the Theologian* (London: Burns & Oates, 1970), 280: 'Probably the germ of the [Pelagian] controversy was the now undisputed fact that differing explanations of infant baptism were held in the East and in the West.'

[44] *Against Julian*, 1.6.21–7.35.

[45] *Homilies on First Epistle of John*, 4.11. Augustine instinctively connects infant baptism with the dread of infant death: e.g. *Homilies on John's Gospel*, 38.6: 'Even the baby at the breast is brought in his mother's devout arms to the church, lest he depart this life without baptism and die in the sin with which he was born.' The correct reading is *sugens* (BA), not *surgens* (PL, CCL).

in resolving the puzzles of infant baptism, and needs no mapping here.[46] It must suffice to tease out some salient threads of argument to sustain my claim that at Augustine's hands baptism underwent a fateful transformation.

Gerald Bonner has written that 'the Pelagian theology of baptism was constructed on the model of adult baptism; the infant baptizand was, for them, the anomaly. For Augustine the urgency of the need for baptism made him the norm'.[47] But for Augustine it was not always so. We have seen sufficient evidence above to conclude that, until the latter years of the first decade of the fifth century, Augustine too worked with adult baptism (I prefer to characterize it without reference to age, as conversion-baptism or the like) as the norm. Which simply means that he was a man of his time.

I am myself convinced that the baptizing of infants was, until the era of Augustine and beyond, far more minimal and marginal, at least in the West, than is often assumed. It is perhaps easier to demonstrate this in terms of theology than of practice. One has only to look at an anthology of patristic texts on infant baptism to become starkly aware of Augustine's domination of the field. Thus in J. C. Didier's collection, documents from the first four centuries occupy forty-four pages (including ten of inscriptions) while Augustine is allotted sixty pages.[48] And in Augustine himself, discussion prior to the Pelagian dispute is a drop in the bucket compared with the oceans released by the Pelagian challenges. If Augustine became the catalyst for far-reaching change within the church at large, it was as a result of the *bouleversement* in his own understanding. Even Didier himself, who starts with a conviction of 'le fait extrêmement répandu du pédobaptisme' in

---

[46] See Bonner, *Augustinus-Lexikon* I, 592–602, and my brief discussion in 'How Controversial Was the Development of Infant Baptism in the Early Church?', in J. E. Bradley and R. A. Muller, eds, *Church, Word and Spirit . . . in Honor of Geoffrey W. Bromiley* (Grand Rapids: Eerdmans, 1987), 45–63 at 56–63. Rist, *Augustine*, 17 is wrong in asserting that not until *The Merits and Remission of Sins*, 2.20.34, in 411–12, does Augustine raise the question 'what sins had an infant committed, and when, and how?' He later recognizes that *Epistle* 98 does so, in 408 (p. 125), and, we should add, so does *The Literal Meaning of Genesis*, 10.

[47] *Augustinus-Lexikon* I, 596.

[48] *Le Baptême des enfants dans la tradition de l' Église* (Tournai: Desclée & Cie, 1959).

fourth-century Africa, is puzzled that in his ante-Pelagian years Augustine shows himself uninterested in establishing the necessity and even the legitimacy of infant baptism.[49]

As for practice, the evidence advanced at the outset of this paper in my judgement damagingly disrupts the standard graph of developments in the early centuries, plotted influentially by Joachim Jeremias.[50] This shows infant baptism present from very early days and becoming increasing commonplace until the fourth century, when for the first time postponement becomes a problem for some decades.[51] A far more plausible coherence can be discerned in the patchy evidence (I remember C. F. D. Moule commenting on Jeremias's monograph that it contained 'at least all the evidence'!) by something more akin to a single line tracing a fairly low trajectory until after Augustine.[52] Apart from any other considerations, such as the liturgical conservatism considered above,[53] the glaring *lacuna* of any agreed theology of infant baptism defies comprehension if the practice had been common, let alone standard, for centuries. At the very least it has to be acknowledged

[49] Didier, 'Saint Augustin', 110, 128.

[50] Joachim Jeremias, *Infant Baptism in the First Four Centuries* (London: SCM Press, 1960), with minor adjustments in his *The Origins of Infant Baptism* (London: SCM Press, 1963) following the challenge of Kurt Aland's *Did the Early Church Baptise Infants?* (London: SCM Press, 1963).

[51] The so-called vogue for 'postponing' baptism in the fourth and fifth centuries has not received the exhaustive investigation it merits. For the North Africans see E. Nagel, *Kindertaufe und Taufaufschub: Die Praxis vom 3–5. Jahrhundert in Nordafrika und ihre theologische Einordnung bei Tertullian, Cyprian und Augustinus*, Europäische Hochschulschriften 23:144 (Frankfurt am Main: Peter Lang Verlag, 1980). I have not yet seen Holger Hammerich, 'Taufe und Askese: Der Taufaufschub in vorkonstantinischer Zeit' (dissertation, University of Hamburg, 1994).

[52] In addition to the articles cited in nn. 2 and 46 above, see my 'The Origins of Infant Baptism – Child Believers' Baptism?', *Scottish Journal of Theology* 40 (1987), 1–23. For the late fifth or sixth century as the age when infant baptism first became the common practice, see Cramer, *Baptism and Change*, 138ff.; Didier, 'Adaptation', 85; T. M. Finn, *Early Christian Baptism and the Cate-chumenate: Italy, North Africa, and Egypt*, Message of the Fathers of the Church 6 (Collegeville: Liturgical Press, 1992), 91–2, 230.

[53] Cf. Cramer, *Baptism and Change*, 3: 'Thus one of the great questions posed by the history of baptism is how it was that even after the habit of infant baptism had become widespread in the churches of Latin Christendom, the *form* of adult baptism – of a rite of conversion celebrated either at Easter or Pentecost, and not just of passive or magical exorcism – continued largely to prevail.'

that the development remains in major respects puzzling, a fact which a loose undifferentiated use of 'postponement' has too often glossed over. No less a cause of the vulnerability of the Jeremias consensus has been the facile transition in its assumptions from the attested occurrence or acceptance of infant baptism to its general prevalence as the norm.

The necessity of infant baptism for infant salvation

Undoubtedly one's estimate of Augustine's role in baptismal change will be significantly shaped by one's conception of developments before his time. In this connection greater interest must attach to his own pre-Pelagian ruminations. Collectively they are hardly impressive. They give little hint of the floodgates that would open wide in 411. Not least marked is the contrast between his *Confessions* (apart from the isolated and, as we have seen, unparalleled criticism of his mother for not having had him baptized *in extremis* as a boy – not an infant) and his anti-Pelagian corpus.

So wherein did the Augustinian transformation of baptism consist? First and foremost, of course, in making infant baptism essential for infant salvation. Although to the end Augustine allowed that 'unbaptized infants, having only original sin and no burden of their own sins, will suffer the lightest condemnation of all',[54] it was still condemnation, not limbo or some middle ground between heaven and hell. In some ways, this placed infants in a harsher position than adults. 'Though unbaptized adults outside the sphere of the people of God may be saved by heeding cryptic admonitions from God, infants can be saved only through baptism'.[55] 'The need to baptise early, the necessity of infant baptism rather than its possibility or desirability, is perhaps the most obvious legacy of Augustine to the Middle Ages'.[56]

[54] *Against Julian*, 5.11.44.
[55] TeSelle, *Augustine the Theologian*, 323.
[56] Cramer, *Baptism and Change*, 125. Walahfrid Strabo (c.808–49) may have been the first commentator to link the transition from faith-baptism to infant baptism to clarification of the doctrine of original sin: see his *Libellus de exordiis et incrementis quarundam in observationibus ecclesiasticis rerum*, ed. and trans. Alice L. Harting-Correa, Mitellateinische Studien und Texte 19 (Leiden: Brill, 1996), 176–9 (ch. 27, 511–12), with 306 on Walahfrid's historical interest.

Augustine was not blind to the apparently fortuitous circumstances that left one baby dying unbaptized, albeit the child of pious parents, and another baptized in time, although the castaway of a promiscuous mother taken in by virgins.[57] He could not concede the decision to the play of chance. And so what he had come to believe about baptism as the sole cure for the guilt of original sin reinforced his doctrine of predestination. TeSelle appositely quotes Warfield:

> It was not because of his theology of grace, or of his doctrine of predestination, that Augustine taught that comparatively few of the human race are saved. It was because he believed that baptism and incorporation into the visible Church were necessary for salvation.[58]

But Augustine could not stop there. Divine judgement and providence must be involved. This is not to imply that Augustine tightly correlated predestination and the receiving of baptism as an infant. He did not, but the parent grieving the loss not only of a young child but one unbaptized through some unhappy accident should not draw the cold comfort of haphazard change: 'Often when the parents are eager and the ministers prepared for giving baptism to the infants, it still is not given, because God does not choose'.[59] When life expectancy was so precarious, baptism became burdened with a heavy incubus of doom.

---

[57] *Against Two Letters of the Pelagians*, 2.6.11; *The Gift of Perseverance*, 12.31. Cf. TeSelle, *Augustine the Theologian*, 324; Bonner, *Augustinus-Lexikon* I, 600–1.

[58] TeSelle, 323, from B. B. Warfield, *Studies in Tertullian and Augustine* (New York: Oxford University Press, 1930), 411.

[59] *The Gift of Perseverance*, 12.31. In a recent essay provoked by one of the newly discovered Mainz sermons of Augustine, Eric Rebillard has argued that the postponement of baptism did not constitute a pastoral challenge to Augustine. He dealt with it in his preaching only during Lent, the period of preparation for baptism. His sermons do not conjure up a picture of crowds of indifferent Christians waiting until their last days to be baptized. See 'La figure du catéchumène et le problème du delai du baptême dans la pastorale d'Augustin', in G. Madec, ed., *Augustin prédicateur (395–411): Actes du Colloque International de Chantilly (5–7 septembre 1996)* (Paris: Études Augustiniennes, 1998), 285–92. This may be an issue on which his preaching and his controversial treatises speak in discordant tones.

The effects of Augustine's baptismal revolution

Such a framework of belief could not tolerate a wait until the paschal season between Easter and Pentecost. Any time was ripe for baptism of a new-born of uncertain viability.[60] Inevitably, baptism, distributed randomly throughout the year, and indeed the days of the week, would become less of a celebration of the whole congregation. Changes such as these might take decades or centuries to unfold, but Augustine's baptismal revolution prescribed them.

By the same token, and for other weightier reasons, with infant baptism increasingly the norm, the baptismal ceremony would itself tend to shrink. The 'awe-inspiring rites of Christian initiation', as E. J. Yarnold has called them, whose dramatic richness can be glimpsed already in the Hippolytan *Apostolic Tradition* and discerned more clearly in the mystagogy of the fourth- and fifth-century Fathers, would become the midwives' routine of the Middle Ages and, on a longer perspective, the innocuous and colourless minirite of modern Western Protestantism lambasted by Karl Barth.

From another angle, baptism as a normative rite of early childhood lost much of the theological and spiritual creativity it had exercised in the early centuries. We easily lose sight of the success of early Christian baptism as the fruitful mother of many offspring: the catechumenate, and the rich catechetical homiletic harvest of the golden age of the Fathers; the stimulus to the elaboration of the paschal celebration; its provocation of the penitential system (not all of baptism's children turned out too well!); the deep fountain of imagery that bound baptism with martyrdom, that developed the motifs of passover and exodus, that linked up with the symbolism of the transition from seventhday sabbath to eighth-day, i.e. first-day Sunday, that exploited darkness and light, unclothing to nakedness and then reclothing in a new outfit, and so one could go on. When infant baptism became standard, baptism's productivity began to atrophy, and the consequences lived stubbornly on, through the Reformation into the modern era.

But the chief result of the metamorphosis of baptism of which Augustine was the most significant catalyst is to be found simply

---

[60] Cf. De Latte, 'Saint Augustin et le baptême', 50–1.

in the replacement of the experience of a willing and purposive heart and mind with helpless passivity. (Theologians ever since have not been above making capital out of the baby's physical immobility and bare receptacle-capacity.) The import of this greatest of all transformations of baptism has been suggestively, if not always fully coherently, explored by Peter Cramer's *Baptism and Change*:

> [T]his whole view of sacrament as meeting and dialogue ... apparently fades to nothing before Augustine's teaching – developed from *c*.406 onward – that mankind, and thus the child at birth, inherits the sin of Adam. In this perspective, baptism is suddenly exorcism again: it has the exact and negative function of removing the adverse judgement incurred by 'birth in Adam'. The rite loses all its ethical colour: instead of something done by the candidate, it becomes something done to him ... The combined effect of original sin and infant baptism thus appears to make the candidate a vessel, an involuntary being, a theatre of good and evil.[61]

Cramer discerns here ground for a conflict in Augustine's mind:

> [O]n the one hand he wants baptism (whether infant or adult) as part of the *cultus*, to be *transitus*, dialogue, meeting, a ritual expression of the soul's capacity for God; on the other hand, partly in response to the Pelagians, he presents it as a substitution of good for evil, with no reference to the personal will of the subject.[62]

As I read Augustine (although I acknowledge the need for further exploration of this front), the conflict was in essence resolved in favour of his anti-Pelagian stance. We are dealing more with successive phases in his thought than with coexisting alternatives. When infant baptism became the norm, as it undoubtedly did in his later theology, it cut baptism *in genere* down to the size of what may and must be believed about the baptism of infants. It has, I suggest,

---

[61] *Baptism and Change*, 113–14. Cf. also on the domination of Augustine's late conception of infant baptism by the theme of exorcism, H. A. Kelly, *The Devil at Baptism: Ritual, Theology and Drama* (Ithaca: Cornell University Press, 1985), esp. 112–13. On the profound change that baptism underwent by the shift to infant baptism, see the contributions by Paul de Clerck and others on the paper by Arnold Angenendt, 'Der Taufritus im frühen Mittelalter', *Segni et riti nella chiesa altomedievale occidentale*, I (Settimane di Studio 33; Spoleto: Presso la Sede del Centro, 1987), 275–336, at 325ff.

[62] *Baptism and Change*, 114.

ever been the case: infant baptism, when normative in practice as well as in church doctrine, has effected a massive baptismal reductionism.

I doubt if the Augustine of the 410s and 420s could have felt very comfortable rereading the portrayal of baptism he had scripted in the *Confessions*. We touch here, of course, on the large-scale transitions that Augustine's theological mind underwent from the 390s onwards and from *c*.410. It was not simply that Augustine's baptismal thinking revolved around infants and Pelagius's around converts. Augustine could no longer endorse what Pelagius believed about the decisiveness of baptism for the convert.[63] He had earlier been much closer to the Pelagian attitude; indeed, he had been a living exemplar of it himself. But the worm had turned, and the devaluation of baptism attendant upon its irreversible turn to the baby must apply to baptism *in toto*. The wider context in Augustine's shifting teaching has been sensitively exposed by Peter Brown.[64] In the process not only Augustine's understanding of baptism changed, but that change set in motion a far broader transformation that determined the contours of the Christianity of Christendom, in large measure to the present day.

[63] Cf. my brief review, 'Pelagius the Twice-Born', *Churchman* 86 (1972), 6–15.
[64] In both *Augustine of Hippo* and the essays on Pelagius reprinted in *Religion and Society in the Age of Saint Augustine* (London: Faber & Faber, 1972).

PART FOUR

Theology and Inculturation

Chapter 11

Defining Heresy

ROWAN WILLIAMS

Heresy's modern meaning – doctrinal deviance – took centuries to develop. *Hairesis* began its Christian history as a relatively neutral term for faction. With the passage of time, as anxiety about criteria of belonging developed, *hairesis* had begun to denote unacceptable behaviour threatening common adherence. Gradually a network of 'catholic' Christian communities emerged, with common books and commonly revered martyrs, and a system of mutual recognition took shape. *Hairesis* thus came to be seen as a body outside this network which must be teaching erroneous doctrine precisely because it was outside. In its early centuries the church needed to find ways of wedding a necessary element of continuity and stability to the disruptive element strongly present in Christianity's origins and literature. Thus Christians, who had been conscious of themselves as embodying conflict and contradiction, came to discover themes of universality and continuity in which doctrine mirrored the mechanisms of episcopal authority. As Christian leaders thus sought to reassemble a reliable world, heresy came to be seen as beliefs which threatened this. Fourth-century debates on heresy were carried on in terms of second-century concerns about disruption; the Arian debate reflected the earlier debate about gnosticism. These debates represent an ongoing task in Christian theology – to articulate the gospel with both scepticism and confidence.

Hairesis as a faction or party

Hairesis begins life as a relatively innocent term. In classical Greek, its sense of a 'school of thought' is widely attested (for example in the field of medical theory), and it carries no pejorative connotations.[1] Even in the New Testament, its sense remains neutral, a word that designates factions or parties: it appears in this way in Acts (5:17, 15:5 and 26:5), describing the Pharisaic and Sadducaic groups, and also as a Jewish term for Christians (Acts 24:5 and 14; 28:22). In 1 Corinthians 11:18, Paul mentions the prevalence of *haireseis* among the Corinthian congregations, and, while deploring factional bitterness, evidently considers a measure of variety among schools of opinion an inevitable and even, to some extent, a healthy phenomenon: only when a thousand doctrinal flowers bloom can truth be fully discerned, through the testing processes of debate. 'Heresy' is thus, at this period, not deviant and automatically suspect doctrine, but simply 'doctrine' itself, any teaching that is typical of one group over against others.

The rake's progress which brought *hairesis* to mean unacceptable deviance takes time to get under way. Second-century Christian usage preserves much of the earlier neutrality of sense. Justin Martyr, for example, speaks in precisely the same terms as the New Testament of *haireseis* as 'parties' among the Jews and of the Christian faith being described as a *hairesis* by its opponents.[2] At the end of the second century, Clement of Alexandria is still using the word in this way[3] – though there are passages in which a more unfavourable sense may be at work.[4] Two passages of Ignatius of Antioch, at the very beginning of the second century, have been adduced as evidence for an early sense of *hairesis* as deviant doctrine; but in fact this is not wholly clear. In *Ephesians* 6:2, Ignatius notes his pleasure that the Ephesian bishop Onesimus reports an absence of *hairesis* in his church; and in *Trallians* 6.1, believers are exhorted not to eat of 'strange herbage, which is *hairesis*'. The word clearly designates something undesirable, but it would make perfect sense to treat it as warning primarily against factionalism. Ephesus is free from *hairesis* apparently because all

[1] See the excellent study by Heinrich von Staden, 'Hairesis and Heresy: The Case of the *hairesis iatrikai*', in B. F. Meyer and E. P. Sanders, eds, *Jewish and Christian Self-Definition*, III, *Self-Definition in the Graeco-Roman World* (London: SCM Press, 1982), 76–100.

[2] Justin, *Dialogue*, 80.4; 108.2.

[3] Clement of Alexandria, *Stromateis*, 7.15.

[4] Ibid., 1.19; 2.15.

wish to hear about nothing but Jesus Christ. No 'parties' can appear. And in the *Trallians* text, I suspect that we should not read Ignatius as saying, 'Beware of strange herbage, i.e. heresy', but should treat *hairesis* as appositional to *botanē*, herbage, so that the sense is, 'Beware of strange herbage, i.e. strange opinion'. This is certainly disputable, but it seems better not to presuppose a straightforwardly negative sense for the word quite so early. The same ambiguity probably lies behind Justin's use of *hairesiōtēs*.[5] Not until Irenaeus do we have a clear identification of *hairesis* with false belief and *hairetikoi* with dissidents from the Catholic faith as Irenaeus defines it.[6]

This is not, of course, to say that first- and second-century Christians had no concept of doctrinal deviance or of unacceptable levels of hermeneutical pluralism. Ignatius certainly has plenty to say about false belief or teaching, especially as regards the nature of Christ's humanity. But one of the interesting aspects of Ignatius's rhetoric is precisely the idea that false belief has as one of its identifying symptoms deviant behaviour, some sort of offence against the tangible unity and coherence of the community. Ignatian dissidents either avoid or supplement the general gathering of the church around the bishop and his authoritative teaching; they have local loyalties of their own alongside their membership of the 'catholic' church, the assembly that is for everyone.[7] And this assembly is recognizable and validated in virtue of the presence of the publicly acknowledged teacher in its midst. Thus the 'factionalist', the *hairetikos*, in this context is the behavioural deviant; but his or her behavioural deviance gives grounds for suspecting deviant belief as well. It is worth noting that Justin can use *hairetikoi* for Christians who fail to keep the rules, who, for example, eat food offered to idols:[8] faction is *doing* different things before it is disputing beliefs; but the former is easily taken as a sign of the latter, and the slippage of *hairesis* towards its familiar negative sense is already beginning wherever this association is made.

---

[5] Justin, *Dialogue*, 80.4.
[6] As in the Greek fragment of Book III (iii.4) of *Adversus Haereses* preserved in Eusebius, *HE*, 4.14.
[7] See, for example, Ignatius, *Smyrn.*, 8.
[8] Justin, *Dialogue*, 35.

Haeresis as deviant behaviour threatening understandings of belonging

The modern student is always liable to ask of religious groupings, past or present, what they are 'meant' to believe, in trying to establish the difference between 'normality' and 'deviancy'. But often, then and now, this can be a misleading place to start. It may be better to begin with a question like, 'What sort of behaviour is counted as showing that you belong?' Where people have a reasonably clear sense of how that can be answered for their community, they will frequently assume that non-standard ways of behaving imply the conviction that the community as such is defective or misguided, and will thus begin to look for beliefs that might be used to legitimate the conclusion that the community is wrong or inadequate. Where separatism appears, the question is raised of how that is to be justified; and even where a separatist group or individual may have little or no developed theory that is consciously at odds with the parent or rival body, the fact of separation (even in the form of the supplementation of 'standard' activities) tends to be used as evidence that something radically different is being taught or believed. The whole process results in a heightened self-consciousness all round of distinctive and distinguishable beliefs. In other words, the history of the early Christian period suggests less a pattern of primitive ideological protest against a clearly defined orthodoxy than a story of the gradual fragmentation of communities originally rather loosely defined as far as commonly accepted belief goes: the fragmenting of community life urges the question of how both unity and dissidence are to be understood and justified; and the long-term result is the familiar picture of separation understood as the *effect* of ideological protest or disagreement.

Modern patristic scholarship has rightly insisted upon the misleading character of the typical heresiological story which depicts Christian history as the record of a single coherent belief-community from which dissident groups broke away because they believed different things.[9] The literary evidence suggests that

---

[9] Walter Bauer's classic *Rechtgläubigkeit und Ketzerei im ältesten Christentum* (Tübingen: Mohr, 1934; ET from the 2nd, 1964, edition, *Orthodoxy and Heresy in Earliest Christianity* [Philadelphia: Fortress Press, 1971; London: SCM Press, 1972]) set the terms of later debate, although his conclusions have been seriously

plurality of belief in the second century certainly involved exclusions and separations – above all in the desire to root out the varieties of gnostic teaching from the body of the 'true' Church; but my point is that it is seldom clear that differences of belief became a problem prior to or independent of the manifestation of deviant behaviour, separatism of some kind. And conversely, where divergent belief did not manifest itself in deviant behaviour, it seems as though anxiety about uniform theology was slow to develop. The implication of this is that it is as the criteria of visible belonging become harder-edged that separatism emerges as a problem or a challenge in a community's self-identification. As people become clear – in some quarters, anyway – as to what you have to do to 'count' as a Christian, or what you have to avoid, new disunities inevitably appear, and are interpreted, rightly or wrongly, as symptoms of deep divergences of belief. Something of the puzzlement attendant on this process appears in 1 John 2:19: the dissidents who have left the community 'never really belonged'. At some point, divergence has been recognized, and the split in visible communion is taken as a sign that those who have left must always have been secretly at odds with the remaining group – i.e., must have believed differently.

And of course the deduction was not always false. The most dramatic illustration is in the history of the Christian movement itself vis-à-vis the Jewish world. We have gradually shed the idea of a single normative Judaism in the first Christian century, a standard by which reform movements like those of the Pharisees, John the Baptist, the Dead Sea community or Jesus himself might have been judged.[10] Jewish religious practice in the Second Temple

---

challenged on numerous matters. For a survey, see Rowan Williams, 'Does it Make Sense to Speak of Pre-Nicene Orthodoxy?' in idem, *The Making of Orthodoxy* (Cambridge: Cambridge University Press, 1989), 1–23. Further discussion of the evolution of the terminology in Alain le Boulluec, *La notion d'hérésie dans la littérature grecque des IIᵉ-IIIᵉ siècles* (Paris: Études Augustiniennes, 1985).

[10] For the general picture, E. P. Sanders with A. I. Baumgarten and Alan Mendelson, eds, *Jewish and Christian Self-Definition*, II, *Aspects of Judaism in the Graeco-Roman Period* (London: SCM Press, 1981), especially the essays by Ferdinand Dexinger and Lawrence H. Schiffman; also Jacob Neusner, William S. Green and Ernest Frerichs, eds, *Judaisms and Their Messiahs at the Turn of the Christian Era* (Cambridge: Cambridge University Press, 1987), and Jacob

era was vastly diverse, and all the indications are that it took some time for Christians to be systematically excluded from various forms of Jewish 'belonging' (as opposed to being the occasional victims of political manoeuvring by the ruling priestly class, as in Acts and the records of the martyrdom of James the brother of Jesus). There is nothing odd or irregular about the participation of Paul in synagogue worship or even the Temple cult, in some of its aspects. But by the second century, Christians are the object of formal anathemas: it was well-known to Christians that they were daily cursed by pious Jews in their prayers. The *birkath ha-minim*, the Twelfth Benediction of morning prayer, associates Christians with apostates and hostile Gentiles; though even here we should note that what is at issue is not deviant doctrine but the rupturing or jeopardizing of the unity of the people of Israel. The word *minim* comes from a root that has to do with splitting or severing, and the traditional translation, 'Benediction of the Heretics', begs just the question we are here exploring.[11] However, it is clear from what we know of anti-Christian Jewish polemic that ideas or teaching have begun to be an issue, as there is evident anxiety about exegesis as an area of conflict. Sharper behavioural definition throws into relief what had been half-concealed disagreements, and, in the process of arguing for the justification or illegitimacy of particular practices, divergent ideas are in turn brought to light.

Hairesis turns to heresy: sectional interest challenges a network of normative communities

Why then does a moment come when divergency of practice becomes a new kind of problem? It arises when traditional markers

---

Neusner, *Jews and Christians: The Myth of a Common Tradition* (London: SCM Press, and Philadelphia: Trinity Press International, 1991).

[11] On the many problems associated with tracing the origins of the *birkath* and defining its exact character, see Reuven Kimelman, '*Birkat Ha-Minim* and the Lack of Evidence for an Anti-Christian Jewish Prayer in Late Antiquity', in Sanders, Baumgarten and Mendelson, *Jewish and Christian Self-Definition*, II, 336–44; William Horbury, 'The Benediction of the *Minim* and Early Jewish-Christian Controversy', *Journal of Theological Studies*, n.s., 33 (1982), 19–62; and T. C. G. Thornton, 'Christian Understandings of the *Birkath Ha-Minim* in the Eastern Roman Empire', *Journal of Theological Studies*, n.s., 38 (1987), 419–31.

of identity have been challenged or destroyed. To 'count' as a Jew in the Second Temple period had to do with a range of criteria; but all of them were fairly public and unproblematic. There was the bare fact of birth, the association, a bit vague but very powerful, with the land of Israel, and the sophisticated interweavings of ideological and economic loyalties connected with the Temple and its priesthood, involving the 'Temple tax', the festival system and, within the territory of Judaea, the (often grudging) acknowledgement of the High Priest's status as a sort of ethnarch. In the period after 70 CE, these markers have all been rendered ambiguous or inaccessible. There is no Temple; the Jews are, almost by definition, a scattered people; and there is a significant penumbra of ethnically Gentile sympathizers, participants in a religious practice (synagogue worship) with practically no connection to the Temple anyway. The achievement of the Tannaitic period is to separate Jewish identity from the historical cult and reconstruct it on the basis of a particular style of legal observance, universalized and rendered almost timeless in quality.[12] And exclusions become necessary because the criteria of belonging have shifted: the canopy beneath which certain kinds of pluralism once flourished has disappeared. In this process, the notion of 'standard' beliefs and actions inevitably develops; it becomes possible to speak about 'heresy' in the modern sense.

Pluralism in practice and teaching is a problem where there has ceased to be an accessible pragmatic answer to questions of identity (one might compare the ways in which the identity of the Anglican Church has become problematic in the wake of the disappearance of the 1662 Prayer Book as a standard of usage; people suddenly become unprecedentedly concerned with the public scrutiny of moral and doctrinal purity). More emphasis will then be laid on the defining role of practices (including verbal formulae) which formerly had a place within a wider and looser spectrum. And where these appear jeopardized or compromised, there is a clear incentive to identify the possible or assumed rationale for deviant behaviour, and to classify the contents of this rationale as deviant. This is how *hairesis* turns into heresy: when a sectional interest

---

[12] See Jacob Neusner, 'Mishnah and Messiah', in Neusner, Green and Frerichs, *Judaisms*, 265–82, for the characterization of Mishnaic Judaism as 'beyond history'.

or emphasis offends against hardening criteria of belonging, particularly in a period of general disorientation, the 'faction' or 'school' comes to be identified as an alien body – all the more dangerous for preserving some features of the 'parent' body that might lead the uninstructed observer to misunderstand the nature and identity of that body (Christians *look* like Jews, Gnostics *look* like Catholics and so on).[13]

This is not to prejudge the question of whether the 'factionalist' (*hairetikos*) is or is not really engaged in deliberate reconstruction of formerly held beliefs. As far as early Christian history is concerned, the student can only say that some probably were and some probably were not. The opponents of Ignatius of Antioch hold meetings apart from the episcopally-chaired assembly: did all of them necessarily hold the docetic views he ascribes to them? There is no certain answer. In the mid-second century, there can be no doubt that 'Catholics' believed some significantly different things from – say – Valentinians; yet gnosticizing groups could and did claim at times to stand in some sort of authentic continuity with the beginnings of Christianity. Again, what we know of the beliefs of Montanists or, later, of Messalians, from the fragments of their own teaching suggests very strongly that some of the views ascribed to them by the heresiologists are extrapolations from eccentric and potentially subversive practice: if this is what they do, they must believe things we don't, or disbelieve things we hold.[14] At the same time, the literature we call gnostic is itself marked by challenge and refutation of beliefs held by other Christians: it is a crude distortion to say that heresiology is nothing but malicious propaganda.

The process we must imagine is, I believe, something like this.[15] By 100 CE there exists a substantial number of groups in the urban Mediterranean world (as well as some more rural networks,

---

[13] Le Boulluec, *La notion d'hérésie*, 87. Origen has to explain in his refutation of the pagan apologist Celsus that there is a difference between orthodox and heretical Christian literature and that true Christians cannot be held responsible for gnostic views (*Contra Celsum*, 3.10ff.).

[14] On the question of Montanism, see the excellent monograph of Christine Trevett, *Montanism: Gender, Authority and the New Prophecy* (Cambridge: Cambridge University Press, 1996).

[15] I have outlined a similar scenario in 'Does it Make Sense to Speak of Pre-Nicene Orthodoxy?' (see n. 9 above), esp. 11–15.

inside and outside the Eastern frontier of the Empire) associating themselves with the name of Jesus. Their distinction from the synagogue has recently become more sharply focused as the Jewish communities in the same environment tighten their criteria of belonging and acceptability in the aftermath of the Jewish War. Many – though not all – of these groups are beginning to share a common literary deposit: texts are circulated through the various networks along major travelling and trading routes (Antioch through Asia Minor to Greece, Alexandria to Rome, Rome to North Africa, and – with rather different texts and traditions eastward to Edessa and Mesopotamia). As yet, there is no single common organization or 'creed': the identifying practices seem to include the initiation rite of baptism and the eucharistic meeting at which teaching is delivered. But anxiety about boundaries is beginning to take root. The coherence of these groups is fragile, and, under pressure from the state's hostility to secret societies (especially secret societies in direct opposition to the state cult), it becomes important to secure links and exchanges of information, partly for encouragement, partly to guarantee means of recognizing and legitimating people, particularly teachers, moving from one community to another. The effort is under way to establish bonds that have something about them of the tangible and public character of the written law in the Jewish world.

The idea of the normatively Christian thus emerges in a cluster of practices that embody the exchange of information and recognition – not least in the exchange of the records of martyrdom.[16] Sharing in the suffering of Christ is offered as a highly significant form of validation for the experience of a local Christian community: the martyred bishop in particular can be presented as united with the foundational sacrifice of Christ (hence the vivid eucharistic language that appears in Ignatius and in the account of Polycarp's death, for instance).[17] This is where continuity and recognizability can most dramatically be made visible. But this exchange of martyrdom narratives already presupposes the exchange of 'routine' experience, including advice about how to

---

[16] For example, the letter of the Church of Smyrna describing the martyrdom of Polycarp, and the letter of the Gallic churches on the martyrs of Lyon and Vienne, preserved in Eusebius, *HE*, 5.1.

[17] *Martyrdom of Polycarp*, 14.1–3; cf. Ignatius, *Romans* 4.

discern the legitimacy of wandering teachers. The *Didache* offers rules of thumb for testing the prophets, while still repeating traditional attitudes to the exceptional authority of the true prophet. And in all this, increasing significance is given to the role of tangible links with the history of Jesus and to the idea of a *universal* interpretation of the traditions about Jesus that can be applied from community to community across (and beyond) the Roman world. Thus the teacher outside the system of mutual recognition, at odds in some way with the bishop, especially the martyred bishop, making a bid for authority on grounds unrelated to these developing continuities, is more and more assumed by the emerging 'Catholic' network to be teaching something radically at variance with what has been received and accepted there. Whether they did or not is, as I have indicated, of less interest in the tracing of how heresy comes to be defined than the mechanisms by which the whole process worked; all we can usefully say is that some, but not all, 'dissident' teachers would have been content to be ruled out of the emerging normative communities, and that these were the people with the strongest doctrines of an internally or individually specified Christian identity in terms of belonging to a particular predefined sector of the human race, characterized as 'naturally' spiritual and free.

The content of Christian belief: disruption and continuity

So far all this is largely a matter of sociological commonplace – how pressures from outside and inside a group produce anxiety about criteria of belonging. But in order more fully to understand the processes by which heresy was defined, we need also to look at some issues of *content* in the Christian tradition, so as to grasp why certain questions recur over several centuries as central to this definitional task. How are these processes at work in a tradition which is itself problematic in some quite acute ways where issues of continuity or stability are concerned?[18] Christianity is self-consciously both innovative and universalistic; that is to say, it is aware of beginning in a rupture from existing systems of meaning,

---

[18] This is recognized tacitly in the concern of the second-century apologists to deal with the problem of the novelty of Christianity, and to argue that the Greek sages were familiar with the same Logos as became flesh in Jesus.

and it moves consistently and rapidly away from any localized, ethnic or political criteria for belonging. To be in this particular community as it encounters the sacred is to be involved with a specific person as represented in the community's language and practice, in a way that – at least – relativizes other loyalties or identities. More particularly, there is a basic problem about relating to the Jewish identity, to the extent that Jesus' relation to his own undoubted Jewish identity was not straightforward (he is at odds with the dominant paradigm of political Jewishness in his own lifetime, the ideology represented by the Temple and its hierarchy). But the universality that emerges awkwardly but irresistibly in *this* conflict creates further and harder problems with Roman imperial identity (not to mention the fact that Jesus suffered the death penalty under a Roman colonial administration): to be a Christian is to be more than a citizen or denizen of the Empire, and one's social bonds as a Christian have to do with factors quite unrelated to the quasi-divine status of the Emperor as focus of social loyalty. In short, Christianity is fundamentally disruptive of pre-existing forms of religious meaning and social belonging. It dissolves earlier worlds of symbolic understanding, and its foundational records are heavily moulded by images of paradox and irony, by a pervasive suspicion of the *appearances* of the sacred and the orderly. Jesus fulfils prophecy, but is rejected; Jesus fulfils prophecy but reconstructs it in fulfilling it. To be acceptable in the sight of God requires only fellowship with Jesus; to be holy requires not separation from the impure but association with the impure – with the polluted corpse of the crucified, with those whom the crucified welcomed into his company. The emissary of Jesus appears as a 'fool', as a prisoner displayed in another's triumph, as an exemplar of inarticulacy, squalor and helplessness (Paul in his Corinthian correspondence). And so on. The generative moment of Christian language and practice is one of dissonance and difficulty.

The initial Christian proclamation as reflected in the greater part of Christian scripture strongly suggests that the given environment, ritual, social and political, is inherently unreliable or deceptive. And the question thus posed to the emergent Christian *institution* is whether its language can survive as a constant re-enactment of the disruption in which it begins, suggesting a lasting and unhealable schism in the order of things, between the empirical world and the truth of Christian revelation, or whether there is another level of unity to be sought and discerned at a deeper level than hitherto. This latter option will, in effect, argue that the world can be 'reassembled' and that the appearance of rupture reflects prior error or distortion; now there is a new synthesis. The self-consistency and self-continuity of the community itself act as a kind of reassurance that order is somewhere restored and honoured; the unity of the community and its history affirms the unity of the universe and of the divine source of its meaning. If this reading is correct, second-generation Christianity has a particularly strong investment in tackling issues of continuity and stability, if only to explain how it locates itself in a world decisively disrupted and contradicted by what has been revealed, yet manifestly continuing.

It is in this context that the theological polarizations of the second century may begin to make more sense. The cluster of systems we call 'gnostic' generally represent a commitment to the fundamental unreliability of the empirical environment and of the god responsible for it (for contingency, matter, history and human authority, including the human authority involved in Christian community life). They remain with the disruptive moment, but systematize it into a theory of what it is tempting to call 'anti-history': there is always and necessarily a gulf between the world and the truth, between appearance and reality, between wisdom and convention or communal life. It is a schism deeper than the one envisaged by the Cynics, between nature and convention (a schism whose traces some have discerned in the teaching of Jesus himself);[19] it runs through what we think of as 'nature'. And in contrast the strategy typified in the apologists of the second century, for example, insists upon unsuspected unities, not only the unity of Christian revelation with the law of Moses, but its unity also with the theism of Socrates and Heraclitus; the history of divine action is one. And this dovetails neatly into the insistence on the

---

[19] There is a fairly substantial literature on Jesus as Cynic; see most conveniently John Dominic Crossan, *The Historical Jesus: The Life of a Mediterranean Peasant* (Edinburgh: T&T Clark, and San Francisco: HarperSanFrancisco, 1991), ch. 13; and F. Gerald Downing, *Cynics and Christian Origins* (Edinburgh: T&T Clark, 1992). For a sceptical reaction, see N. T. Wright, *Jesus and the Victory of God* (London: SPCK, 1996), 66–74.

unbroken witness of teaching and practice in the Christian community itself. It is no surprise to see the evolution side by side of the mechanisms of episcopal authority and the various 'rules of faith' that circulated in the Mediterranean churches by the end of the second century.[20]

The formulae of these rules invariably insist upon the unity of the Christian God with the God of 'the law and the prophets', and also frequently appeal to their own unbroken ancestry and/or universality.[21] Issues about authority and obedience are tightly interwoven with cosmology and hermeneutics. But in the second century it is in regard to Christology that the diverse questions around stability and meaning converge. For the 'gnostic', the redeemer must be a dual figure, essentially free from the material and historical environment even when using its phenomena as an instrument. He appears as what he is not: his identity is defined by something utterly other than the material world. In riposte, 'Catholic' polemic, from Ignatius onwards, can mount a powerful argument in defence of Christ's integral humanity (and thus real, historical suffering) as the foundation for order in the church and as an affirmation of the significance of the material and historical in general – an argument which receives perhaps its most sophisticated application in the eighth century debates about iconography, in which the trustworthiness both of material symbols of the divine and of the Byzantine political hierarchy is grounded in the brilliant syntheses of christological doctrine achieved in the sixth and seventh centuries.[22]

Resident aliens attempt to recompose a world

Yet this counter-position to the radical dualisms of the Gnostics was always an uneasy settlement. The radical conversionism, the witness to disruption, in a Paul or a Mark was always present, the

---

[20] Still useful on this is R. P. C. Hanson, *Tradition in the Early Church* (London: SCM Press, 1962); the fundamental study is D. van den Eynde, *Les normes de l'enseignement chrétien dans la littérature patristique des trois premiers siècles* (Gembloux: J. Duculot, 1933).

[21] A clear example is Irenaeus, *Adv. Haer*, 3.1–3.

[22] Judith Herrin, *The Formation of Christendom* (Princeton: Princeton University Press, 1987), esp. part III, is an admirable guide to the interlocking of politics, theology and social development in this period.

endemic mistrust of the world and its prince (and princes). Some
of the difficulties of early Christianity arise from elements of non-
negotiable tension in the Christian mind. And we should not forget
just how socially odd the early communities were in the terms of
the ancient world: prototypically sectarian groups with hardly any
prior analogues because they isolated, for certain purposes, the
criteria of cultic belonging from the ordinary criteria of social
identity. They claimed to be able to tell you who you were inde-
pendently of the ways in which the given socio-religious system
told you who you were, and thus laid claim to a loyalty potentially
at odds with that system. They made strong assertions about the
universality of the community, its normative status for the future
of the entire human race. Even those most preoccupied with unities
and continuities were bound to labour at marking the divisions
between church and not church with adequate sharpness, often
using the language already present in Christian scripture of the
'resident alien' community (the verb *paroikeō* and its cognates).[23]
The theological polarity runs *within* what came to be called
'Catholic' Christianity as well as between this and its competitors,
the groups defined as deviant.

'Heresy' in its familiar sense thus emerges as a concept in a
specific historical situation: not only is there the problem of a
community or network of communities faced with critical questions of self-definition; the community itself deploys a set of
foundational stories and images identifying it as disruptive or
discontinuous, and its social patterns are separatist, subversive
and universalist. For such communities to maintain a continuous
and coherent social presence over time, this disruptive foundation
had to be supplemented with a different conceptuality allowing
the basic ruptures to be transcended or resolved in some way. And
in this process, those who appeared to be reinscribing the primitive
separatism in radical ways were inevitably the cause of anxiety to
the emergent institution. Those who were struggling to establish a
normative Christianity were, we could say, struggling to recompose

[23] The word appears in the New Testament infrequently, though *paroikoi*
designates Christian believers in Ephesians 2:18 and 1 Peter 2:11; by the early
second century CE, *paroikountes* is becoming a standard term for Christians,
used in a variety of literature (the *Epistle* of Clement and the *Martyrdom of
Polycarp*, for example).

a *world*, a trustworthy social and ritual environment; heresy comes to be defined, tacitly or explicitly, as what splits this precariously achieved unity or coherence. Hence, as Christianity evolves through the third and fourth centuries, what makes people worried about various unfamiliar theological positions, and what is therefore the focus of polemic against them, is the possibility of making fissures in the universe – by dividing creator from redeemer, or old covenant from new; by emphasizing the distinction in Christ between divine and human agency; by dividing the Godhead into two *archai* (first principles); by dividing the created soul from the body; and so on. The second century is, in this sense, constantly being replayed. While it is part of anti-heretical polemic to insist that heresy is deliberate and malicious innovation, there is an equally powerful and regular convention of reducing a new doctrinal controversy to the terms of an older one: the same accusations are laid, and a genealogy of error is postulated – often to the great confusion of later generations of scholars, who have tended to assume that the heresiologist's analysis of the roots of a heresy is dependable history. There is a good example of this in the treatment of the origins of Arianism common in European scholarship well into this century; Alexander of Alexandria associates Arius with the Jewish-Christian Ebionite movement (about which we have very limited reliable information) and with the teachings of Paul of Samosata; neither association is plausible or demonstrable, but scholars regularly repeated the assertion, with notably muddling effects.[24]

Distinguishing deviant doctrine (heresy) from deviant forms of belonging (schism)

However, before looking at this in greater detail, there is one further point to note. By the middle of the third century another shift has occurred. Whereas in the second century separatism of any kind tended to carry the assumption that there were deep doctrinal differences involved, it had become possible by the middle of the third century to distinguish heresy from schism – i.e. to acknowledge that there were ruptures in the life of the church

---

[24] For some useful observations, see Rudolf Lorenz, *Arius Judaizans? Untersuchungen zur dogmengeschichtlichen Einordnung des Arius* (Göttingen: Vandenhoeck & Ruprecht, 1979), 128–35.

which, while threatening and troublesome, and extremely problematic in relation to structures of authority, were not perceived as threatening the coherence of the believer's imaginative universe, the 'reassembled' world of doctrine. In the famous debate between Cyprian of Carthage and Pope Stephen over the re-baptism of dissidents,[25] Cyprian in effect assimilates the status of dissidents over disciplinary issues to that of rebels against the faith as such; but the Bishop of Rome, in contrast, evidently takes it that there is some kind of unity in faith, symbolized in the fact of a common baptismal confession, that can survive the breaking of visible unity. Stephen's view generally prevailed among 'Catholics', and it suggests that the unity of the Christian community is being understood and constructed in a way slightly at odds with some of the assumptions of the preceding century. At one level there is less anxiety about the implications of separatism: the reconstructed universe depicted in the *regula fidei* and embodied in the sacramental system has become strong enough to withstand the threat posed by concrete division. Institutional loyalty to the 'right' authority certainly matters (enough to express itself in separation at the eucharistic table), and the protester against this loyalty is regarded as cut off from the *actual* benefits of membership in the church. But such a protester remains an *anomalous* Christian, still under the same canopy, not a 'parodic' Christian, as a second-century gnostic might have been seen. At the same time, the implications for the dissident are no more favourable; indeed, in a sense they are worse. The dissident is now an insider in a state of disobedience, subject to the law of the church, which may properly treat them as (so to speak) rebels against their acknowledged masters rather than citizens of an alien polity. The recognition of common baptismal faith and practice *intensifies* the dissident's guilt rather than otherwise. This is the position finally articulated with great dialectical brilliance by Augustine in his anti-Donatist works, and was long to remain the foundation for canonical attitudes in the Catholic Church towards separatists of relatively 'orthodox' belief.[26]

So the distinction between heresy and schism does not signify a move towards greater ideological flexibility – if anything, the

---

[25] See especially Cyprian's *Epp.*, 67–75.
[26] See in particular Augustine, *De Baptismo*, I, and 3.16.21ff.; also *Epp.*, 135.43.

contrary. Christian identity can be described in terms of the acceptance of a scheme of beliefs rather more clearly than it might have been earlier, to such a degree that the sharing of beliefs can to some extent be separated off from the sharing of the common life. As Augustine was to conclude, it might be possible to hold Christian beliefs, yet to be without the sanctifying power of the Holy Spirit's love, *caritas*.[27] Why exactly this development took place at a different rate in Rome and Carthage is by no means clear. Both churches had recent experience of theologies witnessing to the disruptive and discontinuous elements in Christian discourse. Marcionism in Rome left the Roman Church with a long legacy of suspicion towards any theology jeopardizing divine unity; Montanism, as a powerful presence in the North African churches, stressed the continuing importance of the prophet as against the regular congregational minister. It may simply be that, whereas Rome had faced and to some extent settled the issues about cosmology that Marcionism had raised, the African Church had had less experience of resolving strictly doctrinal debates and was therefore more likely to focus anxieties on the concrete 'chain of command' in the community. All this, however, is uncertain; what is important for this discussion is that part of the story of the development of the concept of heresy is the process by which deviant doctrine and deviant forms of belonging or loyalty gradually came to be distinguished from each other. And this fact tends to conceal from the student of the early Christian period the ways in which the agenda of doctrinal debate continued to be shaped, if not dominated, by questions about unity and stability.

Disruption and stability in the Arian controversy

This is best illustrated by examining the major doctrinal struggles of the Christian East in the fourth and fifth centuries. In the controversy provoked by the teachings of Arius at the beginning of the fourth century, it is very clear that the spectre seen by each side in the teaching of the other is residual Gnosticism. Arius accuses his bishop of implying either a Valentinian or a Manichaean view of God by teaching that there is a substantial continuity and co-eternity between the Father, the source of Godhead,

[27] Augustine, *De Baptismo*, 3, *passim*.

and the Son or Logos. If Bishop Alexander claims that such continuity exists, what he is *actually* doing is fragmenting the unity of God: the Logos must be either some sort of divine emanation – which is tantamout to Valentinianism – or a quasi-independent eternal principle – which opens the door to Manichaean dualism, the belief in two *ageneta*, two causeless first principles.[28] For Arius, the theology of a co-eternal and consubstantial pair or triad of divine agents presupposes a degenerate, materialistic model of God, as a substance capable of division. In contrast, Arius himself argues for a wholly free and immaterial divine agent who elects to act directly in revelation by the voluntary creation of a perfect (though finite) image of his glory: the single fully divine person (the Father) works through a single, uniquely privileged, mediator, who alone has the maximal vision of God's glory possible for any created being.[29] Arius consciously stands in a long and respectable tradition of philosophical and theological polemic against cosmological dualism.[30]

But within a couple of decades, Arius's most sophisticated opponent, Alexander's successor Athanasius, could reverse the accusation. It is the 'Arians' who are reviving gnostic errors: by insisting that God must freely generate the Logos by an act of will, not as an eternal reflection of his own nature, they drive a wedge between the mind of God and the will of God; they imply that God cannot generate simply by the action of his eternal thought, but needs something further, a determinate, punctiliar act of will, to achieve his purposes. Is not *this* a version of Valentinianism, dividing up the acts and attributes of God into a plurality of pseudo-entities between God and the world?[31] There are other arguments deployed by Athanasius, of course, about the risks of separating the work of redemption from the action of the creator in person, but this particular point is most germane to the present discussion because of its mirroring of Arius's own charges and its witness to a continuing concern in the fourth century over the agenda of the second. The interest of both parties in defending

[28] On anxieties over this, see Rowan Williams, 'The Logic of Arianism', *Journal of Theological Studies*, n.s., 34 (1983), 58–81, esp. 66–70.

[29] Further detail in Rowan Williams, *Arius, Heresy and Tradition* (London: Darton, Longman & Todd, 1987), 95–116.

[30] Ibid., 181–98.

[31] Athanasius, *Oratio contra Arianos*, 3.60, 64, 67.

the simplicity of the divine nature is again bound up with the characteristic Catholic concern to affirm the unity of divine action in creation and redemption and in the orderly life of the church in the present so that the controversy over Arius's teachings is also and very importantly a conflict not wholly unlike that of Cyprian with his rivals in Carthage, charismatic and exemplary confessors of the faith: a conflict about the relation between *exemplary* authority (martyr, confessor, learned ascetic) and what we might call *statutory* authority (bishop). Does the unity of the church depend on a unified story of legitimate succession or on the unity of moral or spiritual performance with the foundational patterns and narratives of the faith?[32]

At least one of Arius's supporters began to develop another model, influential for many centuries. For Eusebius of Caesarea, the unity of the cosmos is guaranteed by a hierarchy of monarchies, systems focused upon a single figure representing the higher order on which the system depends. The emperor is the focus of unity on earth, depending on *his* vision of the Logos, who is the focus of unity in the whole cosmos and in turn lives from his vision of the divine Father.[33] But this did not at once commend itself to a church still liable to be at odds with emperors on the 'wrong' side of the theological debate. What is interesting is that we still encounter accusations of gnosticizing in the later fourth century. Gregory of Nyssa, defending his brother Basil against the replies of Eunomius to Basil's attacks makes it clear that Eunomius was eager to convict Basil and his pro-Nicene supporters of (what else but?) Valentinianism.[34] The detail of the debate is quite complex: Basil had argued that human designations of God were not given directly in revelation but predicated on the basis of the acts of God in creation, and of the contrasts between what can be said of creation and what must be said of its transcendent creator. Thus we look back on the ages (*aiōnai*) past and see that God exceeds the range of all that can be remembered, and we look to the ages ahead and see that God can never cease to exist. On this basis we call God

[32] Williams, *Arius*, 82–91.
[33] Eusebius, *Oration in Honour of Constantine* (Tricennalia), 1–3.
[34] Eunomius's charges are preserved for us in Gregory of Nyssa's *Contra Eunomium* (the relevant passages are in Jaeger's edition of Gregory, I, 356–62). The text is discussed and summarized in Richard Vaggione's edition of *Eunomius, The Extant Works* (Oxford: Clarendon Press, 1987), 110–11.

'without beginning' or 'without generation' or 'indestructible'. Eunomius objects that this drives a wedge between God's properties and God's nature: we cannot surely say that God possesses his properties of indestructibility and so on in virtue of his relation to the 'aeons' of cosmic history, for either these are temporally limited (in which case God is not eternally the same) or they are eternal (in which case God is being treated as one of two eternal principles, the other being the world of change). If the latter is what Basil believes, then he must hold the error of the 'Greeks and Valentinians'.[35] Basil's casual use of 'aeons' here allows Eunomius the crude but potent debating point that Basil appears to be using typically Valentinian language about the self-diffusion of God's nature through the plurality of the powers of the cosmos which Valentinus had called 'aeons'. And more generally, Eunomius claimed that 'Valentinus, Cerinthus, Basilides, Montanus and Marcion' were the ancestors of Basil's doctrine of the ineffability of the divine essence in itself;[36] and we know from the *Apostolic Constitutions* that this was an anxiety in non-Nicene circles[37] beyond the relatively small group who supported the distinctive theology of Eunomius.

Second-century debates live on in the fifth

Thus in the most protracted and bitter theological conflict of the early centuries, we find the 'classic' themes of those initial conflicts in which heresy came to be defined surfacing again. To brand a doctrine heretical entails showing that it fragments the unity of God's nature or action: behind the disruption caused to the regular functioning of unifying authority in the church lies a deeper disruption, a threat to the restored and reconciled universe in which the dependability of God has been rather precariously rediscovered after the upheavals of a revelation of discontinuities and judgements. Further illustrations could be given of how heresy is identified as the postulating of division at various levels (Origen's belief in the separable soul would be a case in point; and it is intriguing to see how a skilful opponent of Origen's like Methodius

---

[35] Jaeger, I, 362; Vaggione, 111.

[36] Jaeger, II, 284; Vaggione, 125.

[37] *Apostolic Constitutions*, 6.11.1; in contrast to the teachings of Gnostics and Marcionites, God is not *agnōstos* and *alektos*.

can attach to him the charge of teaching two first principles);[38] but one last instance is worth looking at before we conclude. One of the major anxieties around gnostic theologies in the second century was evidently to do with the frequently recurring idea that the fleshly identity of Jesus was illusory or, at best, incidental to his saving mission and divine power. Consequently there is a recurring fear of any doctrine that appears to postulate 'two Christs'. By the beginning of the fourth century, this has become a staple of accusations of heresy. Paul of Samosata is apparently charged with teaching this late in the third century,[39] and it seems to have been revived in the charge sheet against Origen to which Pamphilus and Eusebius reply early in the fourth, with the association with Paul of Samosata itself now being part of the indictment.[40] Marcellus of Ancyra is similarly accused,[41] as is Asterius the Sophist;[42] and the charge features very prominently, of course, in the christological debate between Cyril and Nestorius. Cyril in his second letter to Nestorius indicates what he sees as the risk of distinguishing between a man *treated* as divine and the Word of God who is by nature divine.[43] Since Athanasius clearly associates the idea of two sons with gnostic theology (specifically with Valentinus),[44] we can plainly see how the second century lives on into the fifth; how what counts as heresy is still specified in relation to what I have suggested is the basic anxiety of the second century, the fear of opening up again the gulf between the empirical world and the truth of God which just

[38] Methodius, *De Autexousia*, 5 on the fallacies of two first principles; *De Resurrectione*, 1.27–28 on Origenian ideas that might imply the eternity of matter.

[39] According to the surviving texts from the Synod of Antioch that condemned him: see Henri de Riedmatten, *Les actes du procès de Paul de Samosate* (Fribourg: Éditions St-Paul, 1952), 146ff.

[40] Pamphilus's *Apologia pro Origene*, PG, 17.478C–597C for the accusations: Origen teaches that Jesus is *purus homo*, as does Paul; and he implies that there are 'two Christs'.

[41] Eusebius, *Contra Marcellum*, 2.4.24.

[42] Athanasius, *Oratio contra Arianos*, 1.32; 2.37–38. For a list of examples of this and other stock charges, see G. C. Stead, 'Rhetorical Method in Athanasius', *Vigiliae Christianae* 30 (1970), 121–37, esp. 132–3.

[43] Cyril's second letter to Nestorius, 6 (in Lionel R. Wickham, ed., *Cyril of Alexandria: Select Letters* [Oxford: Clarendon Press, 1983], 8–9); cf. the attached third letter, 5–8 (Wickham, 18–25), and the third to the eighth anathemas attached to this letter (Wickham, 28–31).

[44] Athanasius, *Oratio contra Arianos*, 3.64.

might be adumbrated by the disturbingly paradoxical character of Christianity's central narratives and the language of radical disjunction between God's action and our effort found in Paul. Heresy is whatever pushes Christian speech over from its precarious balance into a rhetoric of cosmic fragmentation.

The examples cited here make it clear that the same charges were made by people we now regard as orthodox against their opponents as were made by their opponents against the 'orthodox'. There were no instantly available criteria to determine which was the more dangerous in terms of this cosmic fragmentation. The extreme critic of Nicene theology, someone like Eunomius, appeared in the eyes of some to threaten the unity of the divine mind and action by his ruthless disjunction between the sole true God and the Son, 'unlike' God in essence; but a supporter of Eunomius, or even a less hard-edged observer in the anti-Nicene camp, found just as much to worry about in the Cappadocians' insistence on the utter ineffability of the divine essence shared by Father and Son, evoking as it did the formless abyss of divinity that gnostics had spoken of. To understand 'heresy', we must understand how orthodoxy itself unavoidably negotiates the same dangers as its critics, with comparably uneven success.

The ongoing task: engagement between scepticism and confidence

As we are so often reminded, issues about heresy are inextricably bound up with questions of power, the securing of the authority of Christian leadership; but I am suggesting that we need to be alert to why exactly such a securing of authority might matter so much. The answer seems to lie in the anxiety characteristically felt by communities self-consciously challenging the prevailing norms of meaning and coherence in the social and cosmic environment; and this helps, perhaps, to explain why it was these specific issues – the unity of first and second covenants, the unity of Father and Son, the unity of Christ's person – that provoked the most trouble. And if this is so, we have to recognize at the same time the fact that Christian language as such cannot avoid this risky area. The disruptive and (to borrow a word from Hannah Arendt) 'world-less' elements that cause anxiety in the early church continually resurface, from Gnosticism to medieval millennarianism to Luther's paradoxes about the hidden God to theologies of revolution and theologies of deconstruction. The actual Christian 'norm' is not so much in the steady overcoming of all this in a fully reconciled metaphysic, as in the continuing labour of engagement between the disruptive narrative and the conventions making for historical intelligibility – the institutionally positive aspects that make it possible to see the act of God in Jesus as fulfilling as well as overthrowing, aspects such as ministerial validation and succession, iconography, sacramental theologies and so on. Early heresiologists predictably represent their foes as malicious disrupters of a pre-existent harmony; yet they or their allies often tacitly or indirectly acknowledge (notably in the tradition of apophatic theology) that the defended tradition is distorted if its apocalyptic, utopian and discontinuous moments are wholly domesticated; in that sense at least, 'heresy' perpetually nudges the agenda of 'orthodoxy' away from inflexible ideological settlements.

A final reflection, pertinent to the whole question of mission in Western culture: Western Christianity, for a variety of reasons, ended up with a strong predisposition to emphasize the *un*-settlement of the Christian schema, expressing this first in the conflicts between papal and royal authority in the early Middle Ages, then in the Reformation, magisterial as well as radical, in the Enlightenment's challenge to visible mediations of meaning and authority, and in the fragmented maps of modernity and after. The 'heretical' impulse has done much to shape a culture, in the sense that it has obliged Western Christendom to pursue an intellectual history of intensifying disunity and scepticism. Divorced from the gospel of a 'saving' or reconciling work achieved through the ruptures of systems of meaning and location, this becomes a more and more hectic and violent pluralism. The challenge that missiology now has to confront, a challenge of extreme delicacy and difficulty, is how the articulation of the Christian gospel holds together scepticism and confidence in a way faithful to its foundational history, how it speaks adequately of both terror and gratitude, both silence and praise. To become able to see our task in some such light is one of the results to be looked for from a serious and engaged exploration of how heresy and orthodoxy came to be defined by our Christian forebears.

Chapter 12

Comparative Inculturations

ANTONIE WESSELS

Attempts to Christianize Western Europe were at times 'against culture', when Christians adopted understandings and methods which sought to eradicate prior cultural expressions. But the more profound efforts to Christianize the West involved a 'transformation of culture' by inculturating the Christian faith in the societies' matrix of myths which thereby served as vehicles for the Christian message. So Christians Christianized pagan holy places by building churches on them; they incorporated attributes of pagan divinities into Christian saints; and they adopted and transformed pagan festivals into high days in the church's calendar. Patrick in Ireland demonstrated the possibility of a positive inculturation of the faith in a Celtic setting. Such inculturation is inevitable, but it can be dangerous, so it must always be critically evaluated in light of the newness of the gospel. The use of myths may be a vehicle for authentic Christian witness in contemporary Europe.

Let me begin by saying something about myself. My original field of study was the history of religion. Later on I specialized in Islam and in questions concerning the relation between Islam and Christianity, especially in the Middle East. For years I also lived and worked in that area (particularly in Egypt and Lebanon). In 1978 I was appointed to the chair in missiology at the theological faculty of the Free University of Amsterdam, and later combined this with the chair in religious studies at the same university. I have always tried to make the knowledge of the one subject fruitful for the other. This has led me especially to concern myself with the study of the interaction between gospel and culture, not only globally, but also within Europe. From this first concern my book *The Images of Jesus: How Jesus is Perceived and Portrayed in Non-European Cultures* originated.[1] In this, I dealt with inculturations of Christology in Asia, Africa and Latin America, and to some extent in Europe as well, ending with the question whether there are criteria to determine what is and what is not authentic or acceptable as an image of Jesus Christ.

In Africa and Asia Christians are especially concerned with the question of how the Christian faith relates to other religions such as Hinduism and Buddhism. European Christians, however, do not often ask themselves the question how things stand in terms of the relation of their own Christian faith to the pre-Christian European religions. This latter question has come to interest me over the last couple of years. I was inspired to investigate this by a remark of Mircea Eliade, who said somewhere that the secret of the success of the early Christianization of Europe is related to the fact that the church managed to connect with the myths and stories of Europe. This led me to study the early Christianization of Europe, but nevertheless always to keep at the back of my mind the following questions: might the history of the fairly successful original Christianization of Europe contain lessons for rendering the gospel in the de-Christianized, secularized Europe of today? Can we learn from the interaction between gospel and myths in the past how to build a bridge between the gospel and the 'modern myths' and stories of today? Can the inculturations of the past be compared to possible inculturations in the present? This approach presupposes a greater appreciation of 'myth' and a certain view of the inculturation process.[2]

Argument

This paper reflects the point of view which I have just sketched. I offer the following argument:

[1] Grand Rapids: Eerdmans, 1990; London: SCM Press, 1990.
[2] I have devoted two of my publications to this subject: *Europe: Was it Ever Really Christian?* (London: SCM Press, 1994); and *Secularized Europe: Who is Carrying off Its Soul?* (Geneva: WCC Publications, 1996).

1. First, I would like to discuss the two ways in which the inculturation came about in the Christianization of Europe.

2. Furthermore, I would like to clarify my thesis about the meaning and use of myth.

3. Next, I will give examples of how the gospel has inculturated itself in various European cultures and contexts.

4. Then some evaluation: can it be said when an inculturation is authentic and when the gospel is being betrayed?

5. Finally, I will ask the question: 'Who will abduct Europe today?'

Two means of Christianization

In principle, there have been two means by which Europe became Christianized. On the one hand, at times Christians have adopted an antithetic approach which H. Richard Niebuhr has called 'Christ against culture'; in this approach, missionaries have required their converts 'to abandon wholly the customs and institutions of so-called "pagan" societies. . .'.[3] At other times, Christians have been open to an approach which Niebuhr called 'Christ the transformer of culture', in which the culture was, as it were, lifted onto a higher plane.[4]

Saint Martin of Tours (†397), the pioneering apostle of Europe, could be cited as an example of the first method. In the trail of the Franconian missionaries, churches named after him arose everywhere in Europe, including the Netherlands. Of this missionary, de Hamer (the Hammer) is kept in the Catharijnenconvent Museum in Utrecht. Sulpicius Severus (†c.420) in his Life of Martin reported that Martin used the hammer to demolish pagan temples; in their place he built churches and convents. The Latin inscription reads: 'The idols fall down, struck by Martin's axe. Let no one believe that those who fall so easily are gods.' Incidentally, scholars have noted that this stone axe does not show signs of wearing, so it was probably never really used as a weapon. It was specially made for ritual purposes.[5] However, even though this particular

[3] H. Richard Niebuhr, Christ and Culture (New York: Harper & Brothers, 1951), 41, 45.

[4] Ibid., 190, 195–6.

[5] Marieke van Vlieder, Willibrord en het begin van Nederland (Utrecht: Clavis, Museum Catharijnenconvent, 1995), 93.

hammer was never used for destruction, it is a fact that destruction was typical of Saint Martin's missionary work, and similar examples are known of other European missionaries. Boniface (†754), the apostle of the Germans, is an example of the literal carrying out of this 'Christ against culture' approach when he felled the Oak of Thor at Geismar.

In opposition to this antithetic approach, however, stands one which sought a greater degree of rapprochement. Willibrord (658–739), apostle of the Frisians, is an example of this through the connection he sought with wells. His name is explained as 'the one who strikes wells'.

Willibrord came to the Low Countries in 690 and received permission from Pippin II (†714) to preach among the Frisians. In 695 he visited the Pope in Rome, who consecrated him as archbishop; then he began his work of Christianization. Willibrord was a transitional figure. He was not, like the Franconian missionaries, a clear representative of Roman piety, as Boniface after him was to be. The two-sidedness of Willibrord's approach was reflected in the structure of his mission, which had two centres which were far apart and which greatly differed between themselves: a bishop's see (in Utrecht) and a convent (in Echternach).

For the Celts, wells represented the water that bubbles up out of '(mother) earth'. For the Germans, water symbolically represented the belief in reincarnation. This latter idea can also be found in the etymological relation between *bron* (well), *baren* (to give birth) and *geboren worden* (to be born). In the Low Countries churches are built near holy wells (such as Heilo). The word *dopen* (to baptize) stems from the Celtic *tobar*, which means well – fountain, spring, source. The word *doopvont* (baptismal font) combines this with *vont* (font), stemming from the Latin word *fons* 'well'.[6]

While the one approach discarded the pre-Christian religious practices as pagan, the other approach 'transformed' them. In contrast to the 'continental church fathers, the Irish never troubled themselves overmuch about eradicating pagan influences'.[7]

[6] Lucas Catherine, *De gelaagde religie: Over mythische verhalen en kritische atheïsten* (Antwerpen/Baarn: Hadewych, 1996), 16, 99.

[7] T. Cahill, *How the Irish Saved Civilization: The Untold Story of Ireland's Heroic Role from the Fall of Rome to the Rise of Medieval Europe* (London: Hodder & Stoughton, 1995), 148.

The use of myth

The church has often been antagonistic to myth. In order to explain what I mean by myths and in which way they were and could be used, I want to refer to the famous myth of the abduction of Europa. Europa was the daughter of the Phoenician royal couple Agenor and Telephasa. One day she was walking along the beach, where she was approached by none other than the god Zeus in the guise of a handsome bull. He fell in love with her and thought that he could come close to her in this way. When he knelt before her, she caressed him and dared to sit on him. The bull then leapt up, and rushed into the sea, abducting Europa to Crete. There, Zeus revealed himself in his true form and took her to a mountain where she became the mother of Minos, Rhadamanthys and Sarpedon.

The meaning of her name 'Europa' is uncertain. It may have been derived from 'evening' or 'the West'.

The explanation that one tends to give to this myth at first hearing is that it is one of the many examples of the low moral principles of the gods of the Greek pantheon. If this explanation is satisfactory, then we can dismiss the story as an indecent tale about an all too potent god.

Such a reading is to a large extent inspired by the way in which Greek philosophers often read and interpreted the myths. The early church gratefully took advantage of the philosophers' criticisms of the myths and mythologies to give weight to their own criticism and to expose the unreliability of the gods of the Greek pantheon. This then also fitted in with those Old Testament notions which have a strong anti-mythical tendency. The later approach of the fifteenth/sixteenth-century Christians to the other cultures and religions which they encountered outside Europe was strongly influenced by certain elements of the Old Testament teaching combined with Greek philosophical religious criticism. Their attitude towards the North American Indians, whom they saw as Canaanites and Edomites, is one of several examples of this.[8]

---

[8] Horst Gründer, *Welteroberung und Christentum: Ein Handbuch zur Geschichte der Neuzeit* (Gütersloh: Gerd Mohn, 1992), 189. Cf. Aloysius Pieris, *Love Meets Wisdom: A Christian Experience of Buddhism* (Maryknoll: Orbis Books, 1988), 23.

But we must ask whether this biblical, Old Testament criticism was not social rather than religious in essence. One probably opposed Baal less because he was a rain god – all sorts of characteristics were, after all, as it were, adopted by Yahweh. Passages such as 'he who rides the clouds' (Ps. 68:33), or Psalm 29 which praises the majesty of God's voice in the thunderstorm, were originally about Baal, and were then transposed to Yahweh. The prophet Hosea used imagery borrowed from Baal. Indeed, 'Baal' represented the 'baalization' of Yahweh which King Ahab used to 'add field to field' (Isaiah 5:8), as in the case of Naboth's vineyard (1 Kings 21). The fight against the Baals therefore had more to do with politics than with the fertility cult.

This story about the abduction of Europa was told, amongst others, by the Latin writer Apuleius (at the time of Emperor Hadrian), and also by Ovid (43–19 BCE) in his famous *Metamorphoses*. This work was translated into French in the fourteenth century under the title: *Ovide Moralisé*. In this book the abduction was explained as the leading of the soul to God. A similar interpretation was given by Carel van Mander (1548–1606), a (southern) Dutch painter, writer and poet, who translated classical works, in *Wtleggingh* (explanation) of Ovid's *Metamorphoses*.[9] This explanation, after blending with neoplatonic ideas, probably contributed to the popularity of the theme in the arts, and occurred frequently in the humanist culture of the Italian Renaissance.[10]

This is not the place to try to retrieve the origins and the most original explanation of this myth, if this were possible at all. One can at least say that Europa originally seems to have been a pre-Greek chtonic deity, who was mainly worshipped in Boetia. Certain holy places on Crete were associated with Europa's marriage to Zeus. It is clear that these myths did not come into being as piquant tales. It could be that the medieval interpretation – 'the leading of the soul to God' – was closer to the original intention of the myth than the explanation which we tend to give to it at first hearing.

---

[9] Van Mander's *Uitlegging op de Metamorphosen van Ovidius* (1604) remained a handbook for visual artists during the seventeenth century. A. van Duinkerken, *Beeldenspel van nederlandse dichters* (Utrecht, Antwerp: Het Spectrum, 1957), 75.

[10] E. M. Moormann, W. Uitterhoeve, *Van Achilles tot Zeus: Themas uit de klassieke mythologie in literatuur, muziek, beeldende kunst en theater* (Nijmegen: Sun, 1987), 95, 96.

Be that as it may, the church in her history in Europe did not simply follow certain Greek philosophers in condemning and writing off myths. She has also, as may be the case with the 'myth of Europa', used myths as a vehicle for her message. We could give many examples of this latter phenomenon. If we limit ourselves to Greek/Roman mythology we can think of the connections which Christians at times made between Christ on the one hand and Odysseus and Orpheus on the other hand.

To illustrate the same phenomenon it is worth referring to the theme of hospitality. Zeus and Hermes went around the world disguised as travellers to verify to what extent the people performed the duty of hospitality. They never encountered hospitality until they were welcomed and fed in a humble hut of an elderly couple – Philemon and Baucis – living in poverty in Phrygia. During the great flood which Zeus and Hermes called down upon the land, their hut was spared.

This story, which can be found already in Ovid, recurred in the literature from the Middle Ages onwards to serve as a counterpart to the story of Abraham and Lot and the hospitality they extended to (the angel of) God (Genesis 18–19) or of the story of Christ's presence in the hungry, thirsty, naked, sick, prisoner or stranger. The mystery of the offering of hospitality touches upon the mystery of the anonymous presence of God, as it is described in the Bible (amongst other places in Mt. 25:31–46; Heb. 13:2).

I believe that we should look for such 'connections' in our time. As an example of someone who in the twentieth century gained an eye for the value of the myth for rendering the gospel I would like to mention the renowned British scholar and writer – he also wrote children's books – C. S. Lewis (1898–1963). For this discovery, Lewis's friendship with the famous linguist and writer of *The Lord of the Rings*, J. R. R. Tolkien (1892–1973), was very important. In the 1930s the two scholars conversed about the meaning of the Gospels. Lewis remarked to Tolkien that he could not bring himself to find a meaning for the present time in the story about Jesus of two thousand years ago, except as a kind of useful example, and that he, while praying, wondered whether he was not 'sending letters to a non-existent address'. Tolkien, in reply, pointed out that his question revealed a lack of imagination. Lewis would have to learn to read the Christian stories as he read mythical texts. The story of Christ, Tolkien taught him, is a 'true myth'. It affects us in the same way as other myths affect us, with the major difference that this myth speaks of things which actually happened.[11]

European inculturations

When we talk about this interaction between gospel and European culture, we must never forget that within the European culture there is a distinction between the Old-European culture and the Indo-European culture (e.g. Greek/Roman, Celtic and German cultures), although these two can often no longer be separated. The Old-European culture had a matriarchal, earthly, peaceful and non-hierarchical agricultural religion;[12] while the Indo-European culture was patriarchal in its many expressions. The most important researcher in the field of Old-European culture was Marija Gimbutas; she mainly used archaeological finds. In the field of Indo-European culture, the leading expert is the French religious historian, Georges Dumézil. The distinction between the two cultures can most simply be characterized by referring to the title of Riane Eisler's book *The Chalice and the Blade*: for her the chalice or the Grail is the symbol of the Old-European feminine civilization, while the sword symbolizes the Indo-European masculine, aggressive culture.[13]

To those who think that Christendom mainly aimed itself *against* the existing cultures, it may be pointed out that Christendom has contributed a great deal to the preservation of the original, pre-Christian European culture. Much of the Celtic culture of Ireland would have been lost, if the monks had not written it down. The *Edda*, two anthologies of Old-Icelandic literature with their stories

[11] Sylvain de Bleeckere, *Shadowlands: Van woord naar beeld in menswording* (Kampen: J. H. Kok, 1995), 41. Cf. H. Carpenter, *The Inklings: C. S. Lewis, J. R. R. Tolkien, Charles Williams and Their Friends* (London: George Allen & Unwin, 1978); and Northrop Frye, *The Great Code: The Bible and Literature* (New York: Harcourt Brace Jovanovich, 1981); Walter Hooper, *C. S. Lewis: A Companion and Guide* (London: HarperCollins, 1996), 582–5.

[12] Cf. G. de Haas, *Publieke religie: Voorchristelijke patronen in ons religieus gedrag* (Baarn: Ten Have, 1994), 31. Cf. Helmut Uhlig, *Die Mutter Europas: Ursprünge abendländischer Kultur in Alt-Anatolien* (Bergisch Gladbach: Gustav Lübbe Verlag, 1991); and idem, *Am Anfang war Gott eine Göttin: eine Weltreligion des Weiblichen* (Bergisch Gladbach: Gustav Lübbe Verlag, 1992).

[13] Riane Eisler, *The Chalice and the Blade: Our History, Our Future* (San Francisco: Harper & Row, 1987).

of heroes and gods, would have remained unknown if it had not been for Christendom.

An important factor in the preservation and the formation of the European culture came with the translations of the Bible. The translation of the Bible into German by Martin Luther (sixteenth century) or the authorized Dutch Version sponsored by the States (seventeenth century) are two examples which could easily be multiplied. The translation of the Bible into Welsh in 1588 by Bishop William Morgan has been called a major turning point for both gospel and culture. Through this translation the gospel could be understood and celebrated in the Welsh language, but it also became an instrument to preserve the riches of Welsh language and culture.[14] What is true of Welsh would be equally true of many other European languages.

The church has managed to make a connection with the stories and myths about holy times, places and persons in the various cultures of Europe, be they Old-European or Indo-European. Some examples of each:

Holy places

What I have said of Wales would apply to countless places in Europe: churches were built at holy sites and for centuries served as places of pilgrimage.[15]

Holy persons

Sucellos, who is often pictured with a hammer, was the bringer of news who travelled around the world with crows on his shoulder. *Rukha* is Celtic for 'crow', and these sounds we later encounter again in the name of Saint Rochus of Montpellier (c.1295–1327), the patron saint of travellers who became popular in Western Europe as a protector against the plague and contagious diseases. He is counted as one of the fourteen 'helpers in times of need'.[16]

The *god Wodan* has lived on in the inventive hagiographies developed for various saints:

[14] Noel Davies, *Wales: Language, Nation, Faith and Witness*, Gospel and Cultures Pamphlet 4 (Geneva: WCC Publications, 1996), 13.
[15] Ibid., 51. Cf. several examples in my two books on Europe mentioned in n. 1.
[16] Catherine, *De gelaagde religie*, 18, 21.

- as god of the warriors in Saint Sebastian, a Roman martyr, who was an officer in the bodyguard of Emperor Diocletian, and who was killed by archers. He has become patron of the shooting associations.
- in Saint Martin, also a warrior, a Roman legionary. The attributes in which he lives on are: a grey and red cape, and a sword replacing Wodan's spear. On 11 November Martin brings the children presents and rides through the air and over rooftops.
- in Saint Nicholas, to whom these attributes were later ascribed,[17] and who furthermore accumulated other attributes of Wodan, such as the ring (*Draupnir*, the ring forged by dwarfs which brings wealth) and the book (of runes) in which everything is written down.

The *marzipan pigs* distributed in the Netherlands at St Nicholas (6 December) are a remnant of the offering of pigs to the god Freyr to whom this animal was dedicated.

Freya, Wodan's wife, goddess of marriage, lives on in the word *vrijen* (to make love) and in one of the days of the week: *vrijdag* (Friday). Balder, the son of Freya and Wodan, was married to Ostara. Balder is the god of spring and Ostara is the goddess of Easter. The German Ostern and English Easter are derived from her name. Freyr himself lives on in the story of Saint Anthony with the pig.[18]

Columcille, the 'dove of the church', was the pioneer Irish missionary saint. He lived in community with nature. He spoke to the animals in the forest, and had the first ever mentioned meeting with the Loch Ness monster which, at his command disappeared from the lake. As Cú Chulainn served as a model for prehistoric masculinity, so Columcille became the model for 'those who would deserve the victory in the end'. Missionaries such as Columcille set out in all directions and were unafraid of monsters. Some, such as the Irish saint and founder of convents Brendan, went to the North-West (Greenland and North America). The saga of his miraculous seagoing to the land of promise probably originated in the ninth century, mixing Celtic and Christian ideas.

[17] Louis Janssen, *Nicolaas, de duivel en de doden: Opstellen over volkscultuur* (Utrecht: Ambo, 1993).
[18] Catherine, *De gelaagde religie*, 18, 19, 21.

Beowulf, the great German-English hero, was a pagan warrior. He is depicted as a model of Saxon masculinity – loyal, brave, noble – who fights with the monster as a type of Christ fighting Satan.[19]

Holy times

One can think of many examples of inculturation from the Celtic culture. The 'pagan' festivals went on being celebrated in Ireland: Celtic holy times there obtained a place on the Christian calendar.

Samhain, the last night of October, marks the beginning of winter. That is the time when inhabitants of the underworld mingled with the people. On that night, the ghosts and other unfriendly creatures from the other world were allowed to scare the living. In 835, Pope Gregory IV determined that this would become the date of the feast of All Saints, hence Halloween.

Imbolc, 1 February, marks the beginning of spring. This became the saint's day of the holy Brigid and from then on was associated with Candlemas.

Beltine Beltain, 1 May, was a spring festival anticipating the beginning of summer. It was the feast of fire, the feast of the triumphant sun god Belenos, the Celtic Balder, and the mother goddess Danna, the Celtic Ostara. The animal with which she was associated was the hare, hence the 'Christian' *paashaas* (Easter bunny, literally Easter *hare*).

On the tower of Magdalen College in Oxford, choirboys sing to the rising sun every 1 May at six o'clock in the morning. This 'celebration' plays a part in the film *Shadowlands* about C. S. Lewis and his marriage. The latter calls it 'pagan, vulgar and foolish', but he admits that 'it works'. His wife reacts affirmatively by saying: 'The sunrise always works'.[20]

Since Christianization took place, the month of May was no longer dedicated to the mother goddess Danna, but to Mary. But folklore still carries the traces of Beltain: *meivuur* (may fire), maypole, the 'phallic symbol which is rammed into mother earth'. In the field of religion the Easter candles and the so-called candle processions in May hark back to the ritual fires for the sun god Belenos and to Beltain.[21]

---

[19] Cahill, *How the Irish Saved Civilization*, 185, 187, 203.
[20] De Bleeckere, *Shadowlands*, 33.
[21] Catherine, *De gelaagde religie*, 22, 23.

Lughnasa, 1 August, was pre-eminently the feast of Lugh, and was a harvest festival marking the beginning of autumn. In Kerry, a fertility festival in which a billy goat presides for three days and nights as Cernunnos (he is pictured in Buddha position on the famous kettle of Gundestrup) is still celebrated each August. It is a characteristically Irish pagan and Christian mixture which constitutes the theme of Brien Friel's play *Dancing in Lughnasa*. Lughnasa is also still celebrated in parts of Ulster.[22]

The Feast of Assumption, 15 August, is related to the 'elevation' of the feast of 'mother earth'. Mater Matuta (a temple to whom is located in Satrium) was the good mother, the Italian goddess of the dawn. She was portrayed with a child on her lap. According to G. Dumézil, she originally was the vedic morning goddess. Matuta really means 'of the morning'.[23]

Christmas is above all a matter of observing connections with existing feasts, such as that of the invincible sun (Mitras), which is celebrated in Rome on 25 December, and the midwinter feasts in the North of Europe. Jul, really Hjul, is Scandinavian for sun ring (although this interpretation is being challenged). The month of December is a month of offering to Freyr. During the sacrificial meal, pigs' heads and whole swine were sacrificed to him. All sorts of Christmas customs refer to this background: marzipan pigs, presents (sacrificial gifts).[24]

Patrick

A prime example of inculturation in this transforming sense is Patrick, the apostle of Ireland. Patrick worked outside the sphere of influence of where the Roman law ruled. His approach differed from the more Latin Christianization. Somewhere, Patrick spoke of a 'blessed woman of Irish descent, exceptionally beautiful, a true adult, whom I have baptized'. Who, asks Thomas Cahill, could imagine such outspoken admiration for a woman from the pen of Augustine of Hippo? According to Cahill, Patrick had a greater emotional grip on the Christian truth than Augustine:

[22] Cahill, *How the Irish Saved Civilization*, 149.
[23] Catherine, *De gelaagde religie*, 26.
[24] Ibid., 23.

Augustine looked into his own heart and found there the inexpressible anguish of each individual, which enabled him to articulate a theory of sin that has no equal – the dark side of Christianity. Patrick prayed, made peace with God, and then looked not only in his own heart but into the heart of others. What he saw convinced him of the bright side – that even slave traders can turn into liberators, even murderers can act as peacemakers, even barbarians can take their place among the nobility of heaven.[25]

Patrick was capable of penetrating the depths of the Irish psyche and imagination, warming and transforming it by making it more humane and nobler, while nevertheless enabling it to remain Irish. Not only was the baptismal water an effective sign of new life in God; new life was abundantly present everywhere. God's whole creation was good.

Certain things which are commonly said about Patrick cannot be historically verified. We cannot say with certainty whether he actually used the cloverleaf, with which his statue on Mount Croagh Patrick (in the far West of Ireland) is depicted, as a means of illustrating the Trinity. It is likely, however, that he confronted a king, possibly the King of Tara, about the right to commemorate the resurrection of Christ by lighting bonfires.

Similarly, it is not certain whether the great Irish prayer *Saint Patrick's Breastplate*, also called *The Deer's Cry*, which invokes God's protection against the forces of evil, really stems from him. According to Cahill, this prayer was written by a Christian Druid, and its spirit is entirely un-Augustinian.[26]

Patrick offered the Irish an alternative. It was possible to be brave, to excel, to be murdered, to be betrayed, to be carried away into slavery, and yet to be a 'man of peace and at peace'. The *difference* between Patrick's magic and that of the Druids was this: in Patrick's world all living creatures and events come from the hand of the good Lord, who loves the people and wishes them well.

Such spirituality, with such a feeling for the world as a holy and healing mystery full of divine messages, could never have come about in the Greek/Roman civilization, characterized as it was by a deep pessimism and the Platonic suspicion of the body as unholy

---

[25] Cahill, *How the Irish Saved Civilization*, 115.
[26] Ibid., 116.

and of the world as without meaning. From the spirit of the *Breastplate* springs the art and poetry of the medieval liturgy, the smiling angels, the funny demons, the sweetness of poets like Francis of Assisi, whose sun song could be held for a Celtic poem.

Patrick's gift to the Irish was his Christendom, the first de-Romanized Christendom, that completely inculturated itself in Ireland. By means of the Edict of Milan in 313 Christianity was received in Rome, but Rome was not received into Christendom. In the case of Patrick, Ireland was received into Christendom, which transformed Christendom into something new – a Christian culture in which slavery and human sacrifice became inconceivable and in which the waging of war, although impossible to eliminate altogether, diminished remarkably.[27]

You could, of course, ask yourself: what could be the aim of this connection with holy places, times and persons? Why did people have such a need for holy places? Perhaps it is better to ask oneself why apparently this need is less nowadays, at least in the Western world. The space and the world used to be holy, the landscape itself was holy, there was a holy geography, and humans experienced themselves to be part of nature, not as excluded from it. The Western perception, on the other hand, is very different: space is demystified, external to man; nature is neutral, quantitative and atomized; humans stand at a distance and try to control nature.[28] Monastic orders used to contribute significantly to the cultivation of Europe (agriculture). The point is this: we now live in a world in which we, although we know better, are polluting the air, the soil and the seas. The land we cultivated we mostly have not 'preserved', but we have exploited it more and more. 'The Christian doctrine of creation apparently could not prevent . . . a (positive) *demystification* of nature from degenerating into a (negative) *desecration* and exploitation of nature.'[29]

After the failure of the European and Western 'Christian' civilization, the contact with nature, with 'mother earth', will have

---

[27] Ibid., 108, 109, 115, 116, 128, 131, 133, 148.
[28] Ton Lemaire, *De Indiaan in ons bewustzijn: De Ontmoeting van de oude met de nieuwe wereld* (Baarn: Ambo, 1986), 292.
[29] D. Tieleman, *Geloofscrisis als gezichtsbedrog: Spiritualiteit en pastoraat in een postmoderne cultuur* (Kampen: J. H. Kok, 1995), 112.

to be rediscovered. Elements of the early contextualization and orientation to the theology of creation, such as the 'ecological' reading of Francis, could be of use.

Are there criteria for assessment?

According to Lucas Catherine, religions grow like trees. 'European Christendom is layered: around the marrow of Celtic and German religion, Christian annual rings grow'.[30] How should we look at this stratification of Christendom in Europe? Are the connections which I have listed with holy places, times and persons simply examples of syncretism? When is adaptation right and when is it a matter of betrayal of the message? Is it a process in which the actual authenticity of the Christian message is lost? Are there criteria on the basis of which one can explain when inculturation is non-authentic, in other words, when it is an example of betrayal of the gospel? Is there authentic and non-authentic contextualization?

In the first place I would like to observe that the history of religion in all sorts of respects is the history of syncretism. The history of the Christian religion is no exception to the rule. This means that a religious message is not available separated from context or culture. This is, of course, true of the biblical message. It always is about a process which uses material from the outside world as a vehicle for the new message. For example, the Creation narratives in Genesis, or the stories about the Great Flood, can be seen in the context of the stories as they were found in the cultures and religions in Mesopotamia.

However, it is often argued that although this is indeed the case, the biblical message has transformed these stories and thus stripped them of their original meaning: 'Christian life does not adapt to pagan forms of life, but possesses them and by doing so, makes them new'.[31]

Of course, no one will want to deny that the Jewish or Christian message has brought something new. However, we should bear in mind that their message was influenced by what came before them. That which precedes also influences what comes after it. But to

---

[30] Catherine, *De gelaagde religie*, 10.
[31] J. H. Bavinck, *Inleiding in de zendingswetenschap* (Kampen: J. H. Kok, 1954), 181.

this I would like to add the question: Who abolishes whom? Who takes possession of whom?

One could refer here to the image used by Aloysius Pieris, namely that of baptism. Twice, baptism is discussed in relation to Jesus. The baptism of Jesus by John the Baptist in the River Jordan (Mk. 1:9–11) and the baptism of Jesus on the cross (Mk. 10:35; Lk. 12:50). It expresses the most self-effacing act of Christ, first in the Jordan where he knelt before his predecessor (Mk. 1:9–11) and then on the cross (Mk. 10:38: 'Are you able to . . . be baptized with the baptism I am baptized with?', and Lk. 12:50: 'I have a baptism with which to be baptized, and what stress I am under until it is completed!'), where he ended his earthly mission in seeming failure as the suffering servant. However, who baptized whom? Here Jesus does not baptize John the Baptist, as you might expect, and as John himself expected (Mt. 3.14), but John the predecessor baptized the one who followed.

Pieris applies this thought to the relation of Christendom to other religions and cultures: Christians must dare to be baptized by their predecessors! They have to be humble enough to be baptized in the Jordan of Asian religiosity and brave enough to be baptized on the cross of Asian poverty. They must submerse themselves in the Jordan of these religions and come out with a new assignment, as Jesus did, and with a messianic awareness, which is worth listening to: Listen to him![32]

When arguing for a connection with the myth, one should never overlook the fact that myths can be false as well as benevolent. We should oppose false myths, such as the example from the thirties in Europe: *Der Mythos des 20 Jahrhundert: Eine Wertung der seelisch-geistigen Gestaltenkämpfe unserer Zeit* (Munich, 1938) by Alfred Rosenberg (1893–1946). Rosenberg, the star ideologist of German National Socialism whose work embroidered the racial theories of Joseph Arthur de Gobineau, thought he could demonstrate the inequalities of the races, and that he thereby could give anti-Semitism an appearance of scientific motivation. My reference to symbols and myths is not intended to argue in favour of a right-wing ideology. Nowadays, such old symbols are sometimes used by right-wing extremists (fairy rings in England, Wodan and Co. groups in Germany, the 'right-wing' abuse of the

[32] Pieris, *Love Meets Wisdom*, 40, 41.

Irish sun cross). It is therefore good to hold on to that double meaning of the word *opheffen* (elevate/abolish; *Aufhebung der Religion*). It is not only about lifting it onto a new plane, but also about abolishing, saying 'no', to that which is non-authentic. Herein lies the enduring relevance of the critical insertion of K. H. Miskotte in his renowned *Edda en Thora*.[33] In this he answered the 'command of the hour' of the 1930s by cutting across the false myth of the twentieth century, a danger which is not limited to Nazi Germany, considering the recent developments in the former Yugoslavia! Noel Davies cites R. Tudor Jones, who wrote about certain nationalists in Wales during this century:

> For them nationalism is a direct contradiction of the gospel emphasis on the centrality of love, a pernicious undermining of true inter-nationalism of Christianity, a retreat into nasty chauvinism, an attempt to transform Jesus Christ into a national mascot and plain treason against the message of reconciliation.[34]

The Torah (and the gospel) take a hard line against that kind of paganism. Cultural criticism will have to continue to be engaged in. It will need to be about the commitment to humaneness, to humanity.

You could ask yourself whether a *religious* appeal is needed or necessary for this? Is humanity alone not sufficient? Although it has to be said that the institutional forms of religion (church, synagogue, mosque, sangha) often contributed to inhumanity (discrimination against women; obscuring of their rights and opportunities), I nevertheless think that religious commitment is important and will continue to be so as a guarantee for true humanity. Religion, including the Christian religion, has stood and still stands for something for which it might be hard to find a motivation elsewhere. Why would life, the weak and handicapped as well, deserve protection? Why are we supposed to make a stand for the weak in society? In any case, the prophets, Jesus as a prophet as well, provided a source of inspiration for this.

To continue to voice the uniqueness, the newness of the gospel one can refer to knowing compassion (which is of course also

---

[33] K. H. Miskotte, *Edda en Thora: Een vergelijking van germaansche en israëlitische religie* (Kampen: J. H. Kok, 1983).
[34] Davies, *Wales*, 7.

present, for instance, in Buddhism), but which probably did not occur so much in Greek-Roman society (but then again Philemon and Baucis?). The characteristic which Christendom brought to Europe is the idea and practice of social activity, the care for the poor and the liberation of the prisoners. The fourth-century Roman Emperor Julian the Apostate said that the 'unpious Galileans do not only support their own poor, but ours as well'.[35] 'Blessed are the poor' – this belonged neither in the Greek-Roman conceptual universe, nor in that of the Germanic peoples. It was the church that brought about this change in awareness.

Who will abduct Europe?

When I make a plea for the use of 'myth' as a vehicle for an authentic Christian message today I am thinking of 'similarities' in the sense in which 'parable' is used in the New Testament.

The parables in the Bible have always had the character of a reflection of the everyday, which was potentially transparent and could lead to disclosure of a religious, divine reality.[36]

At the beginning of this paper, I cited the story of the myth of Europa. Why could this myth not serve as a vehicle for the message of the gospel in Europe today? Is Europe's soul being led to God? And if it is not, then to whom is it being led?

In a preparatory paper for a conference on church and economy in Utrecht, there was a reference which seized my imagination. It was a reference to the Juggernaut, an enormously heavy cart, on which a statue of the Indian God Krishna used to be placed. At times, motivated by religious devotion, fanatical worshippers would throw themselves under the wheels of the colossus and be crushed by it.[37] The question was asked there whether the modern world market is not such a colossus, propelled by humans, but which at the same time is adrift? Is it an immense social system built by humans, that will ultimately crush anything that gets under its wheels? Can this monster still be stopped? Are there possibilities

---

[35] Ramsay MacMullen and Eugene N. Lane, *Paganism and Christianity, 100–425 CE: A Sourcebook* (Minneapolis: Fortress Press, 1992), 270, 271.

[36] Tieleman, *Geloofscrisis als gezichtsbedrog*, 84.

[37] Cf. G. Bannock, *The Juggernauts: The Age of the Big Corporation* (London: Weidenfeld & Nicolson, 1971), xi, which refers the reader to the *Oxford English Dictionary* for this story.

and leads for steering the colossus? Does theology – the Bible – have a contribution to make to directing society?

This imagery calls to mind the colossus with feet of clay which is spoken about in the book of Daniel (ch. 2) – the statue king Nebuchadnezzar saw in his dream. Daniel explained the dream about the statue with its head of native gold, its chest and arms of silver, its belly and loins of copper, its feet partly made of iron, partly of clay. This statue was shattered by a small stone, which turned into a great mountain which filled the entire earth.

The message can be expressed in a complex way, but also very simply and clearly. In the Sermon on the Mount Jesus said to his disciples: 'No one can serve two masters ... You cannot serve God and Mammon' (Mt. 6:24). In the word Mammon lies the notion of *amana*, trust. Is it money or God in whom we invest our trust? Whom does Europe serve today?

Cannot the myths today serve as a vehicle for the evangelical message? The actual message is, to put it in the words of a Dutch poetess: 'The gentle forces will surely win in the end.'

PART FIVE

Final Thoughts

Chapter 13

Epilogue:
Approaching Christendom

KATE COOPER

Ammonius was a Christian brought up in Christian ways by his parents, but when he began to think philosophically he promptly changed to a law-abiding way of life. Origen, on the other hand, a Greek schooled in Greek thought, plunged headlong into un-Greek recklessness; immersed in this, he peddled himself and his skill in argument. In his way of life, he behaved like a Christian, defying the law; in his metaphysical and theological ideas he played the Greek, giving a Greek twist to foreign tales.[1]

Porphyry's view of Ammonius and Origen – to which Wolfgang Wischmeyer has called our attention – could serve as an emblem for what we have come to call the rise of Christianity. We can discern in early Christianity a complex and sometimes confused pattern of cultural opposition mingled with cultural borrowing. While Christian apologists such as Tertullian and Athenagoras insisted that Christians could and would serve as loyal citizens, what bothered the Pagans most about the Christians was their unwillingness to co-operate with the existing cultural hierarchy. Reserving an inferior but accepted place for 'traditional religions', Hellenism allowed for cultural diversity but withheld legitimacy from any movement which seemed disorderly or transgressive in nature. Christianity, by contrast, demanded allegiance to alternative – often highly articulate – social, religious and ethical codes, to which at least some Christians adhered even in the face of

---

[1] Eusebius, *HE*, 6.19.

reproval by their social betters, leaving the Roman governor Pliny to conclude that they were guilty of the crime of *contumacia*.

It is in part, then, a legacy of opposition which the early Christians bequeathed to the later churches. This legacy has, of course, been a two-edged sword: the history of mission teaches us that the Christian sense of self as cultural revolutionary can all too easily be taken as a licence for cultural imperialism. The advice which the historian of early Christianity can offer to the theologian or missologist is limited, and in some ways intrinsically negative. While history can sometimes indicate to us fairly clearly what the early church was not, it is often much less capable of telling us what – or how – it was.

History belies any attempt to define an essence of Christianity; although the early church historians themselves attempted to do so, arguing that the earliest communities were characterized by unity and consensus, while only later did division, dissension and heresy emerge. This model is most noticeable in Eusebius, but it has been thoroughly discredited since the days of Walter Bauer, who argued that what characterizes the earliest communities is in fact diversity, a pattern of difference which only subsequently crystallizes into an idea of heresy.[2] This is a point which has important consequences for the modern missiologist: the idea of a 'theological soul in a cultural body' can only be problematic to the historian. Close study of the evidence for the early Christian communities tells us that just as there was never any pristine moment of beginnings when the church knew a universal theological consensus – a point which leaps out at the attentive reader of our earliest Christian writings, the letters of Paul – so there was never, at least in terms which the historian can speak of, any such thing as the 'essence' of Christianity.

There may, however, be such a thing as 'the lessons of history': to watch the early Christian communities as they manoeuvre, learn and grow, is to learn something about the social bonds and social dangers which can be carried on the tide of Christian ideas. To the historian, the problem of Christianization – or Christendom – becomes fundamentally a question of the changing terms for the exercise of power in late Roman society. This, too, carries an

[2] Walter Bauer, *Orthodoxy and Heresy in Earliest Christianity* (Philadelphia: Fortress Press, 1971 / London: SCM Press, 1972).

important lesson: that the development and enactment of Christian community is always culturally specific, influenced by – and, in turn, influencing – the concrete and material conditions of the society around it.

There are a number of things which the historian can know about early Christianity. First, that to be a Christian was a matter of allegiance and belonging. Wolfgang Wischmeyer reminds us that this was often, and particularly after the time of Marcion, a question of commitment to the biblical text. If we understand this notion of textual loyalty in a late Roman way, however, we realize that the question of human allegiance figured very strongly as an overlay to the idea of textual allegiance. New Testament scholarship over the past two decades has repeatedly stressed the importance of understanding biblical communities through a Durkheimian lens: if we see the early Christians as participants in a Mediterranean society where the values of honour and shame are central, then interpersonal relationships – along with corresponding notions of performance and persona – become central to our way of seeing.

We also know that during the reign of Constantine, the meaning of belonging changed. Everett Ferguson and Paul Bradshaw see a shift from manner of life to correct doctrine as the criterion of belonging, as the church reinvents itself in a new state context, and reaches new audiences through ritual. Both David Wright and Eoin de Bhaldraithe have noticed a shift in the institutions of belonging, with the former noting the increasing importance of infant baptism, while the latter argues that the rise of interest in asceticism speaks to a need within the churches to find a place for the utopian impulse of earlier generations. A number of contributors have noted that the fourth-century church relies far more heavily on *coercitio* after the time of Constantine, but many see this as a trend which has deep roots in the pre-Constantinian period, reflecting changing patterns of social structure, and an increasing emphasis on the power and responsibility of élites within the Christian communities to impose order. Finally, to borrow a phrase from Wolfgang Wischmeyer, early Christian communities were able to put forward a claim of definite knowledge, an idea which would have exerted a powerful attraction on the late Roman imagination, with its emphasis on pluralism, fragmentation, and the provisional quality of human identity. This epistemological confidence can, however, be dangerous, as Anne Jensen suggests – especially in the context of a Christian empire.

What we do not know about the early Christians is perhaps more substantial. To begin with, we are uncertain of how the Romans understood *religio*, although it is clear that its meaning did not entirely overlap with its English cognate. This means that the distinction between sacred and secular which we moderns often find ourselves drawing has no secure basis in history: there is no reason to believe that the early Christians, or any other Romans, would have made such a distinction. Our notion of conversion, in turn, needs to be tailored to reflect this uncertainty. The shrill sectarianism of some of the post-Constantinian writers has led some writers to conclude that they were faced with a population which was broadly yet only superficially converted, but it is impossible to say what constituted a complete or satisfactory conversion, when we are uncertain whether or where a boundary was drawn between the sacred and the secular to begin with. On the other hand, as Anne Jensen argues, some Christian writers, such as the poetess Proba, were anything but sectarian, wishing to cultivate pluralism as a Christian value.

Similarly, it is difficult to understand the role of ideology and ideologues in early Christian communities. Prescriptive literature was not necessarily always taken as normative; rather than an indication of what went without saying, it was often, if anything, a sign that a given position did not enjoy consensus. Equally, as Rowan Williams has argued, what we might call the intrinsic content of a pronouncement was often far less important, to the early Christian, than the social dynamics of its production and reception.

Finally, there are a number of points on which the historian and missiologist can agree that we urgently need to know more. First, we need to understand the laity better. We know little about their role in communities, and even less about their point of view. Literacy levels among the early Christians may have been somewhat higher than in the surrounding society, but they are not likely to have been high – thus the experience of scripture, for example, would have been an oral, performative, community-based experience, rather than the individualistic experience that is often imagined by scholars of Protestant extraction. Similarly, we know very little about the dynamics of patronage in the early communities: money must have shaped pastoral dynamics, but our sources often try to occlude this fact. This is an issue which has enormous significance for the study of gender: the widespread evidence for the role of women as patrons within the early church communities may have far greater significance than has been generally allowed. Similarly, the increasing emphasis on the role of the clergy across the early centuries may well have been a reaction to the problem of money, and to a contest for control between established figures among the laity – many of them women – and a clergy who in many cases were less well-established than their lay counterparts.

We also need to know more about the early Christian legacy where violence is concerned. Martyrdom played a crucial role in the early Christian imaginative universe. The boldness of the martyrs, along with their ready acceptance of violence perpetrated against themselves and their disregard for physical suffering, exerted a powerful attraction on early Christian readers and writers, whatever the reaction of those who actually witnessed the spectacle of martyrdom. But to propose the church of the martyrs as a central Christian ideal could have – and still can have – bewildering social and theological consequences.

All of this leaves the dialogue between the historian and the missiologist in a delicate position. The missiologist poses important questions about the relationship between religion and culture in a society, and about the degree to which evangelical engagement can and should commit itself to cultural accommodation – questions to which the historian can give no firm answer. What the historian can offer is instead is a series of caveats.

First of all, the paradox that while the early Christian tradition was one which offered a claim of definite knowledge, there was never a consensus among the early churches as to what that knowledge actually entailed. This means that to distil the message of Christianity into human language always carries with it an existential leap, a leap which should be approached with perspicacity and a certain salutary dread. The historian can offer, too, a warning against the temptations of the Eusebian idea of a pristine early unity which devolved into dissent over time. To resist the temptations of the Eusebian model is to recognize that our earliest evidence for the Christian churches reflects a situation of dissent and diversity – to impose, that is, a discipline of forbearing against romanticizing the early churches. This forbearance can equally importantly be applied to the idea, or ideal, of early Christianity as a community of non-participation in the wider society. While under certain conditions this quality can be valid and even heroic, under others, it can have unnecessarily destructive consequences for an entire society.

If the fundamental question about Christendom, the question which lies behind many of the questions above, could be boiled down to its pith, it might be asked in the following way: 'Is this a movement that can be entrusted with absolute power?' To this question, both the historian and the missiologist would be likely to offer a negative answer, though for different specific and material reasons. It is on this last point that the missiologist may have the most to learn from the historian, but at the same time, the historian can also learn from the missiologist. As Antonie Wessels reminds us, missiology is a field which has in recent decades developed an increasing sophistication in the use of cultural and social anthropology, and increasing sensitivity to cultural context, to the socially and culturally grounded place of mythic language. And it is in this aspect that as much as learning from one another, missiologists and historians can perhaps most usefully take up the task of simply learning together.

Contributors

EOIN DE BHALDRAITHE, OCist., Abbot of Bolton Abbey, Moone, Co. Kildare, Ireland

PROF. PAUL F. BRADSHAW, Professor of Liturgical Studies, University of Notre Dame, Indiana; and Director of Notre Dame Arts & Letters London Program, England

DR KATE COOPER, Lecturer in Ecclesiastical History, University of Manchester, England

PROF. EVERETT FERGUSON, Professor of Biblical Studies Emeritus, Abilene Christian University, Abilene, Texas, USA

PROF. ANNE JENSEN, Professor of Church History, University of Graz, Austria

DR ALAN KREIDER, former Director of the Centre for the Study of Christianity and Culture, Regent's Park College, Oxford, England, and now Adjunct Faculty in Church History, Associated Mennonite Biblical Seminary, Elkhart, Indiana, USA

DR RITA LIZZI TESTA, Lecturer in Ancient History, University of Perugia, Italy

PROF. RAMSAY MACMULLEN, Dunham Professor Emeritus of History and Classics, Yale University, New Haven, Conn., USA

DR CHRISTINE TREVETT, Lecturer in Church History, University of Wales, Cardiff, Wales

PROF. ANTONIE WESSELS, Professor of Missiology and Religious Studies, Free University of Amsterdam, Netherlands

ARCHBISHOP ROWAN WILLIAMS, Newport, Gwent, Wales

PROF. WOLFGANG WISCHMEYER, Professor of Church History, University of Vienna, Austria

PROF. DAVID F. WRIGHT, Professor of Patristic and Reformed Christianity, New College, University of Edinburgh, Scotland

Index